Praise for *.NET—A Complete Development Cycle*

"Excellent step-by-step walkthrough of software development with .NET for architects and programmers. Great explanation of current software development methodologies, and a wealth of practical examples using current techniques."

—Phil Syme, Technical Lead, Watson Wyatt Worldwide
Washington, D.C.

"This book takes a unique approach to integrating real-world development examples to illustrate the phases and tasks of the software development lifecycle."

—Jackie Goldstein
Renaissance Computer Systems Ltd.
and MSDN Regional Director

"In this book the authors excel in presenting all aspects of the .NET development cycle in a format accessible to the beginner, and as a primer and reference for the experienced developer. It is exemplary in its encouragement of good software engineering technique from the outset by adhering to the Unified Process. This book is not only educational and informative, but working through it is fun!"

—Dr. Oliver Downs
Chief Scientist, Analytical Insights, Inc.
http://www.analyticalinsights.com

"As a software project manager, I found this book and accompanying CD to be a valuable aid to help sort out the practical application of .NET from all the hype."

—Daniel Paulish
Software engineering project manager with
more than 20 years' experience

.NET—A Complete Development Cycle

.NET—A Complete Development Cycle

Gunther Lenz

Thomas Moeller

✦Addison-Wesley

Boston • San Francisco • New York • Toronto • Montreal
London • Munich • Paris • Madrid
Capetown • Sydney • Tokyo • Singapore • Mexico City

The publisher offers discounts on this book when ordered in quantity for bulk purchases and special sales. For more information, please contact:

> U.S. Corporate and Government Sales
> (800) 382-3419
> corpsales@pearsontechgroup.com

For sales outside of the U.S., please contact:

> International Sales
> (317) 581-3793
> international@pearsontechgroup.com

Visit Addison-Wesley on the Web: www.awprofessional.com

Library of Congress Cataloging-in-Publication Data
Lenz, Gunther.
   .NET : a complete development cycle / Gunther Lenz and Thomas Moeller.
      p. cm.
   ISBN 0-321-16882-8 (alk. paper)
    1. Microsoft .NET. 2. Computer software—Development. I. Moeller,
Thomas. II. Title.
   QA76.76.M52L46 2003
   005.2'76—dc21   2003012210

ISBN: 0-321-1688-28
Text printed on recycled paper
1 2 3 4 5 6 7 8 9 10—CRS—0706050403
First printing, August 2003

The cover image perfectly reflects the intention of this book—to bring together the many different aspects of software engineering throughout the life cycle of a project. Like the two people in the image who are putting together two pieces of a puzzle, this book will show you software development from theory to practical application. You'll see the relationship between all aspects of software engineering: Microsoft .NET, project management, the project team, and the customer.

To Okson, because I love you,
and to my nieces Charlotte, Carina, and Maria.
Your smiles brighten my day.
—Gunther

For Claudia,
for always being there. With all my love.
—Thomas

Contents

Preface

The purpose of this book is to introduce and explain the practical application of software development with Microsoft .NET technologies (based on Visual Studio.NET 2003), state of the art tools, and good software engineering practices using the example of a real-world project. During the course of this book, you will experience the entire project life cycle of a project named Online Photo Shop.

As a reader of this book, you are integrated into the development team and are required to contribute to the success of the project with your own task assignments.

The project starts with a basic application, and then, as you move forward through new iterations of the project, the requirements gradually become more difficult. You begin by designing simple forms and advance to implementing a multithreaded application. You will support the capability of the software's users to upload pictures to order prints or customized merchandise from your customer's online business. You will learn the entire product development cycle—including wrap-up, maintenance strategies—and best practices, for the Online Photo Shop project.

Each chapter begins with an explanation of the pertinent theory, so you will see the connection between the theoretical knowledge of .NET software development and its practical application within a real-world project. This practical application of the theory is reiterated piecewise throughout the book. You can verify the successful completion of your own assigned tasks by checking your implementation against the sample solution for each chapter, which is provided on the accompanying CD.

In addition, you will find extensive reference sections at the end of each chapter to help you further explore topics of particular interest.

Who Should Read This Book?

Because of its unique combination of software engineering theory and practical application, *.NET—A Complete Development Cycle* is targeted toward readers in the following areas:

- Software engineers
- Students of computer science or related fields
- Team leads, project leads, and project managers
- Software quality and software process engineers

All readers in the target audience will profit from this book in many ways. The greatest benefits will be experienced by readers who are new to Microsoft .NET technology and those who are interested in the theory and practical application of the software engineering process within a realistic project, including the use of best practices.

You don't need knowledge of a particular programming language to work with this book, although a basic understanding of object-oriented programming as well as some programming experience will be helpful if you intend to follow the implementation sections.

How Is This Book Structured?

This book is structured like a real-world project, following the entire life cycle of Online Photo Shop step by step. Except for Chapters 1 and 2, which introduce the theory necessary to get the project started, each chapter corresponds to an iteration of the Unified Process, the software development process of choice for this project.

To differentiate the software engineering sections (which are more theoretical) from the programming sections, we use the following icons.

At the beginning of each software engineering section:

At the beginning of each programming section:

Other icons indicate at which point we are starting the various project workflows. In addition, each chapter is labeled with the current phase and iteration of the Unified Process. In this way, you can determine at any time exactly where you are during the course of the project.

What Is Covered in This Book?

Throughout the course of this book you face the challenges of a real software project. You will analyze these problems, develop solutions for them, and implement and test your solutions using the Unified Process, state of the art tools, and best practices. As you work through the development of the project, you will learn and apply a wide variety of .NET technologies, software engineering practices, and tools. The application you will develop involves image processing, so the results are immediately visible. The application is intended to be a starting point for further exploration of the possibilities of .NET application development.

Chapter 1, Introducing .NET, introduces the features of Microsoft Visual Studio.NET 2003. It has a short introduction to the main features of the .NET runtime and Framework Class Library.

Chapter 2, Introducing Software Engineering, serves as the starting point of the project. It outlines and explains popular software engineering approaches, focusing on the basics of good practices.

Chapter 3, A .NET Prototype, develops a simple application program to test the feasibility of building an application using .NET technology. It introduces the Visual Studio integrated development environment, its application wizard, the new programming language C#, and the use of Windows forms.

Chapter 4, Project Planning, focuses on capturing and analyzing requirements. You'll also learn about the methodologies and practices used during the project, including UML use case diagrams, coding standards, the test framework, configuration management, and the development cycle. We also examine XML document generation and the use of XSL stylesheets, which let us generate some of the project documentation automatically.

Like all the remaining chapters, Chapter 5, The Photo Editor Application, starts with the task of refining the project's requirements, continues with the analysis of the requirements, and then moves to the specification of the design. Before we start implementation, we discuss the detailed project schedule. Following that, we develop the implementation of a smart client Windows application, the first component of Online Photo Shop. In this chapter we implement the architectural baseline for this component, which covers loading, saving, and displaying digital pictures, basic imaging operations, and error handling.

In Chapter 6, GDI+ Graphics Extensions, we run into a real-world problem. After the requirements analysis and design are finished, one of the project's team members is leaving the project. It's up to us to invent strategies for how the project can recover. We then extend the photo editor by adding drawing and text features. The functionality is implemented using GDI+, which is part of the .NET Framework Class Library. We also demonstrate the handling of user inputs such as mouse events.

Chapter 7, Advanced GDI+ Operations, continues work on the requirements analysis and the design of the new features. You'll find out how to keep the project on track when the customer decides to change or add requirements during project development. In addition, this chapter explains advanced features of GDI+, including graded brushes, transparent bitmaps, and various fill styles to modify the images with sophisticated graphical overlays.

Chapter 8, Dynamic Loading of Components, deals with a common challenge in the software projects: how to increase the visibility of the project status to the team members. This is crucial because it helps everyone to stay focused and to identify potential problems as early as possible. In this iteration, we also implement an extensibility concept for the photo editor using plugins. We develop a set of plugins for various image-processing operations using different .NET programming languages (VB, C++, J#, and C#).

Chapter 9, Accessing System Resources, shows you how to exploit an important feature of .NET: integration of unmanaged code. The need for this exists when you must integrate legacy code into new products or when managed code does not achieve the required performance. Another example is the need to gain access to system resources and hardware not exposed through the Framework Class Library. This chapter demonstrates a solution for the latter case, when our project needs to access system resources (OpenGL) to allow the effective, hardware-accelerated implementation of 3D rendering capabilities.

Chapter 10, Performance Optimization, Multithreading, and Profiling, explains the basic dependency of the cost, quality, scope, and schedule of a project as we respond to our customer's request to move up the project deadline. On the technical side, in order to meet performance goals, we optimize certain imaging operations developed earlier in the book. This chapter introduces tools for profiling .NET applications and then shows how to improve execution time by using pointer arithmetic with "unsafe" code. Additionally, the basics of multithreading are explained and implemented. This chapter completes the development of the photo editor component of our project.

Chapter 11, Building the Web Application with ASP.NET, shifts the focus of the project from a smart client application to the development of the Web application, Online Photo Shop. This online shop allows customers to personalize products with their own digital pictures and photographs. The chapter introduces techniques for the development of dynamic Web applications using ASP.NET.

In Chapter 12, Security and Database Access, we add advanced features to Online Photo Shop, allowing users to log in for the checkout process and to store their personal profiles on the site for later visits. Security features and database access using ADO.NET are introduced and applied to implement these features.

Chapter 13, Product Release, concludes the project. We discuss product deployment strategies, conduct final integration testing, and trace all the requirement keys to ensure the full coverage of all project requirements. At last, the project is wrapped up, and we develop maintenance strategies. This chapter also assesses practices that worked well and areas that need improvement. As a result of this discussion, we identify a list of best practices.

How Should This Book Be Read?

This book guides you through a real-world project. Because we follow the nature of a real project, the later chapters depend on earlier chapters. Therefore, we recommend that you read through the book sequentially. You will have the best learning experience by following the step-by-step instructions. But if you want to skip the sections you are not interested in, you can use the section icons as landmarks.

When working through the book you have several options. You may want to follow all the implementation instructions step by step, or you may prefer to view the sample solution of each chapter as you work through the book. Both options are supported.

In addition, we recommend that you explore and implement additional features in your areas of interest. We encourage this further exploration by providing references to helpful material at the end of the chapters.

What Is Provided on the CD?

The CD contains the sample solution for each chapter of the book. The solution is found in a directory called `ChapterXX` (where `XX` is the chapter number).

In the `Chapters` directory, the source code is in the subdirectories of `src`. All projects and source code can be found in the Visual Studio.NET

Photo Editor solution that is part of the `src` directory. Within the source code, the sample solution for tasks that are assigned to you are identified by `#region Do It Yourself Chapter XX` (where XX stands for the chapter number). In addition, the `src` directory contains other projects and subfolders that include utilities and tools that are used and explained in the book.

The automatically generated documentation, such as comment Web pages, the defect tracking sheet, and requirements documentation, can be found in the `doc` subdirectory of each chapter's sample solution.

Assemblies of the project are provided in both release and debug versions. The debug version can be located in the `bind` subdirectory, and the release version of the assemblies is stored in the `bin` subdirectory of sample solution of each chapter.

Acknowledgments

Writing a book, we thought, would be fun and a lot of work. As it turns out, we were right, but it was even more work. From Gunther's original idea and proposal to the final book was a lot more work than we originally anticipated and took more than a year. But we enjoyed working together and exchanging ideas with many great people who contributed in one way or another to this book. Without their help, it would have been impossible to accomplish this task. We want to take this opportunity to thank these people.

First, we would like to thank Debby Lafferty for the initial encouragement in writing the proposal. Sondra Scott, the book's principal editor, who encouraged, guided, and supported us throughout the entire last year, Emily Frey, and the rest of the magnificent team at Addison-Wesley deserve our profound appreciation. Everybody did a great job and was wonderful to work with. Furthermore, we would like to thank Kathy Glidden from Stratford Publishing Services, Inc., for guiding us through the production process, and Betsy Hardinger, the book's copy editor, whose organizational and editing abilities got the material into its final form.

Our greatest gratitude must be expressed to our technical reviewers, Phil Syme and Jackie Goldstein, who helped us tremendously with their experience as authors of recently published books. Their tireless efforts and thorough reviews of every chapter were invaluable in assembling the final draft.

Furthermore, we would like to thank our friends and former colleagues: Oliver Downs, who took time out of his busy work schedule to review many of the book's chapters to provide us with valuable feedback, and Kallol Chaudhuri, who contributed many great ideas to the proposal and supported us in writing the first chapter.

In addition, we would like to express our thanks to our colleagues at Siemens Corporate Research for their support and for providing us with a wealth of good feedback: Thomas Murphy, Jean Hartmann, Monica McKenna, Daniel Paulish, Francois Bronsard, Michael Greenberg, Brian Berenbach, Gilberto Matos, Doris Germond, and Peter Spool.

We also would like to take this opportunity to thank the reviewers of our original book proposal, who provided us with many suggestions on the coverage of the book, which made writing this book possible in the first place: Chris Crane, Wendy Chun, Shaun Eagan, Joel Mueller, Kevin T. Price, and Scott Seely.

Personal Acknowledgments

Gunther Lenz

Most of all I would like to thank my parents, Elisabeth and Manfred Lenz, for their endless support in all my professional and private endeavors. Their support enabled me to gain all the valuable experiences that made this book possible.

In addition, I owe special thanks to my love, Okson Kim, who inspires me and is an incredible encouragement and support not only during the course of writing this book but also throughout our journey of life together.

Furthermore, I would like to thank Thomas Murphy, department head of the Software Engineering department, and Jean Hartmann, project manager of the Software Quality group, at Siemens Corporate Research for their managerial support in writing the book.

Last but not least, I would like to thank my sisters Martina and Christine and my friends, colleagues, former colleagues, and all the others who gave me encouragement and support during the very busy and sometimes hectic time I was writing the book.

Thanks to all of you :-)

Thomas Moeller

This is the first book I've co-authored, and the process of writing a book is very hard. I could not have done it without the generous, warm-hearted and never-ending love and encouragement of my fiancée, Claudia, and my wonderful family in Europe. Also my warmest appreciation to my oldest and closest friends from both sides of the Atlantic for their support during this and other difficult times and projects. Furthermore, I would like to take this opportunity to thank my colleagues at Siemens here in the United States and in Germany for supporting and believing in me throughout my professional career, especially Gianluca Paladini and James Williams, who gave me the opportunity to join a magnificent research group. Finally, I want to pay tribute to all those who taught, inspired, and mentored me. I owe you my success.

About the Authors

Gunther Lenz received a Masters degree in Electrical Engineering from the University of Munich, Germany, in 1997. He then spent four years working on the research and product development of a high-performance medical image-processing system, under FDA regulation. That project is part of a large-scale medical application programming platform called *syngo* (www.syngo.com). His role in the project changed over the course of time from software developer to team lead of subprojects involving software development as well as testing. His responsibilities varied from being an expert in design, implementation, and testing of optimized image-processing algorithms to acting as project manager of development and testing. During this time, working with Siemens Medical Solutions, he gained experience of the entire product life cycle under FDA regulation using state of the art software engineering practices.

In addition to his project experience, Gunther was a core member of the Software Engineering Process Group (SEPG). The task of the SEPG was to define, implement, and optimize the software development process that is followed by parts of Siemens Medical Solutions and Siemens Corporate Research.

Recently, Gunther joined the Software Engineering department of Siemens Corporate Research, where he is involved in the research and development of unique and innovative tools that help ensure software quality throughout the software development life cycle. His extensive experience in product development helps him identify problems, and research solutions to them, over a broad range of areas in the software engineering domain.

Gunther was an invited speaker at the SM (Software Management) 2003 conference, where he also acted as the track chair for the Methods and Techniques sessions.

He is an invited participant in the Strategic Design Review team of Microsoft Visual Studio.NET Enterprise, Whidbey version, and a member of the IEEE Computer Society.

Thomas Moeller (Möller in German) has 10 years of experience in the computer industry as a programmer, imaging software engineer, and researcher. He was a contributor to H.-J. Scheibl's textbook *Visual C++ 6.0 Für Einsteiger und Fortgeschrittene* (*Visual C++ 6.0 for Beginners and Professionals*), (Munich, Vienna: Hanser, 1999). He became a state-certified software technician at the Engineering School in Lutherstadt Eisleben, Germany. In 2000, he received the best in class honors awards with his Master of Computer Engineering degree from the University of Applied Sciences in Berlin. His research work included wavelet-based image compression under Dr. H. Cycon, and DNA capturing software development at the Institute of Biology at the Alexander-von-Humboldt University Berlin under Dr. Th. Börner.

Thomas is currently working in the Imaging and Visualization department at Siemens Corporate Research, Inc., Princeton, New Jersey, where he specializes in software architecture and algorithms for 3D medical imaging applications. He is the co-inventor of two U.S. patent-pending algorithms for volume segmentation and memory management for large volume visualization. His recent work also involves real-time 4D volume rendering for ultrasound images. Thomas is a member of the special interest group for computer graphics and interactive techniques of the Association of Computing Machinery.

CHAPTER 1

Introducing .NET

This chapter provides a brief introduction to Microsoft .NET. We use this technology throughout the book to explain and demonstrate good software engineering practices in a complete product development cycle.

1.1 The Need for .NET

.NET: Is it Microsoft's new silver bullet, or only another attempt to revive the software economy?

In fact there is a real need for a platform that can transfer information over a network without violating security restrictions. Let's take, for example, an online printing and embossing business where customers can order prints, posters, and memorabilia such as cups, T-shirts, mouse pads, and so on, containing images from the customers' digital photographs. The company needs a Web application that lets customers upload their digital files and place orders over the Internet in a secure fashion. Then the order information will be transferred to accounting and order processing.

This company also uses a great variety of raw materials such as photo paper, developer, print cartridges, and so on. One way of getting those materials at the best possible price is to purchase them on a business-to-business platform, where manufacturers and dealers are competing directly with each other. Furthermore, the company needs updates from the suppliers about availability, pricing, and delivery dates. Figure 1.1 visualizes such a scenario.

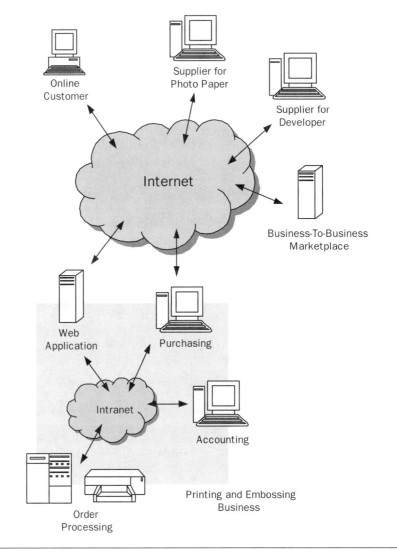

Figure 1.1 Connected Applications

The challenge is how to connect the various applications and services via the Internet or an internal company intranet. There needs to be a common language and, if possible, a common platform through which the information is exchanged. Microsoft's answer is based on Extensible Markup Language (XML), a universal language for data exchange. .NET provides the framework along with a rich class library that eases the task of creating small, independent applications that can be connected to build rich solutions.

It might seem that Microsoft's .NET initiative is basically a platform for Web services, but this is far from true. The printing company example overemphasizes the use of Web services. .NET brings many new features to the application developer that have little or nothing to do with Web services. Indeed this book addresses those other features while developing a more traditional Windows client and a Web application.

1.2 The .NET Framework

So far we've talked only about the Microsoft's .NET vision of distributed Web services connected via the Internet. For the application developer, however, the most important part to understand about .NET is the framework, which can be used to create a wide variety of applications. The .NET Framework consists of two parts (see Figure 1.2):

- The Common Language Runtime (CLR): the execution environment for .NET applications
- The Framework Class Library (FCL): the base classes of the .NET framework

1.2.1 The Common Language Runtime

The CLR, or .NET runtime, interfaces between the application and the operating system. When a .NET application is run, the CLR is responsible for loading the code and setting up the environment with the required resources. The CLR provides a number of other services to .NET applications, as described in the following paragraphs.

Managed Execution

Because the CLR manages resources and security restrictions for native .NET code, it is also referred to as *managed code*. The responsibilities of CLR management include verification of type safety, security checks, structured exception handling, memory allocation, and garbage collection.

Applications in .NET consist of one or more so-called assemblies. An *assembly* is a logical grouping of modules (code or resource files); it is also the smallest unit that can be shared, versioned, and have separate security

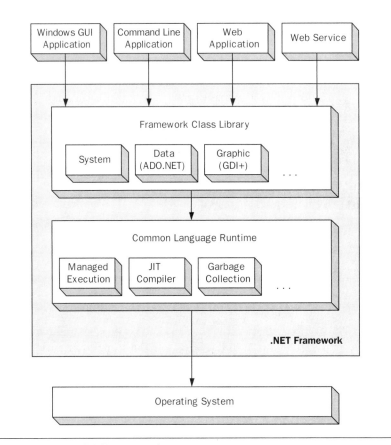

Figure 1.2 The .NET Framework

permissions applied to it. Furthermore, all modules within an assembly contain *metadata,* so the assemblies are self-describing. The CLR therefore knows about dependencies of an assembly without relying on external information such as registry settings. That also makes it easier to deploy assemblies than to deploy unmanaged code.

The managed code within assemblies is not native machine code but rather is an *intermediate language* (IL). IL is independent of the CPU on the target platform and, compared with native machine code, of a much higher level. When you compile .NET source code (such as Visual Basic or C#), the compiler generates managed program modules containing metadata and intermediate language, and these modules are then linked to assemblies. Any .NET application is typically deployed in this platform-independent form. Only after an assembly is loaded by the CLR on the tar-

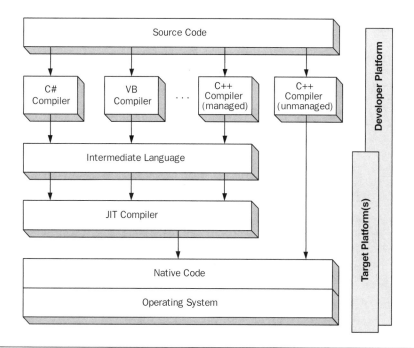

Figure 1.3 Compiling Source Code into Native Code

get platform is the IL compiled into machine code by the *Just-In-Time* (JIT) compiler. Figure 1.3 illustrates this procedure.

Deploying code in IL also allows the JIT compiler to optimize the code for the platform where it is run—for example, optimizing in terms of the amount of installed memory, the number of processors, and so on. The compiler can also take full advantage of the processor's instruction set. Remember that with natively compiled code you must decide which platform to optimize for before you distribute your application.

Language Independence

There are two reasons for the existence of different programming languages. One is evolution, and the other is the varying needs of programmers. For example, Basic and Pascal are casualties of evolution, whereas Visual Basic (VB) and Visual C++ (VC++) address different programming needs. Visual Basic and Visual C++ are aimed at divergent development segments. VB is excellent for rapid user interface (UI) development, and VC++ has great flexibility for specialized applications. Therefore, if you are developing large applications it would be very beneficial if you could exploit the strengths of various programming languages by using them together.

With the introduction of the Component Object Model (COM), it became possible to implement or call COM objects into any of the COM-enabled languages (including Visual Basic and Visual C++). But there were some limitations to this model. Interoperability with COM relied on the assumption that each language was able to work with a common set of data types. This, however, was far from reality.

The .NET Framework gives developers the flexibility to write programs in one of the many languages for which a .NET-compatible compiler is available. All .NET programming languages conform to a common object-oriented programming (OOP) model that supports single inheritance of classes, multiple inheritance of interfaces, and polymorphism. Classes can define methods, events, and properties. Because of this common model, classes can even inherit or catch exceptions from classes written in another language. Another important feature of the CLR is the Common Type System (CTS), which provides a common set of data types to all .NET languages. The ease with which a .NET application can be composed of modules written in different programming languages is a valuable benefit of the CLR.

Microsoft provides IL compilers for these programming languages:

- C++ with managed extensions
- C# (pronounced "C sharp")
- Visual Basic.NET
- JScript
- J# (a Java language compiler)
- IL assembler

The available language compilers from other companies include COBOL, Delphi, Component Pascal, Eiffel, Fortran, Oberon, Perl, Python, and Smalltalk, to mention only a few.

Platform Interoperability

One of the main reasons for Java's success is its platform independence. In Java it is possible to write code, compile it, and ship it. This code can be run on any machine or, for that matter, any operating system (OS) that has a Java Virtual Machine (JVM) running. As with Java, code compiled for

.NET can be run on any .NET-enabled platform. The advantage of .NET compared with Java is that you can use any .NET programming language with the .NET Framework, whereas the Java Virtual Machine supports only the Java language. However, at what point we will see real platform independence depends on when we see versions of the .NET Framework and its class library that have been ported to operating systems other than Windows.

In October 2000 Microsoft, along with Intel and Hewlett-Packard as cosponsors, proposed a large subset of the .NET Framework to the ECMA (European Computer Manufacturer's Association) for the purpose of standardization of JScript, C#, the Common Language Infrastructure (CLI), CLR, and IL. Furthermore, Microsoft has made available an implementation of the .NET Framework—an implementation that runs on Windows and FreeBSD computers and is commonly known as Rotor—under shared source. Another interesting development is the freeware project Mono (`www.go-mono.com`). The goal of Mono is to build a truly platform-independent implementation of .NET covering also ASP.NET, ADO.NET, and Windows Forms.

Garbage Collection

Every application uses *resources* such as memory buffers, network or database connections, and Graphics Device Interface (GDI) handles, to name a few. To access those resources a number of steps are necessary:

1. Allocate the memory for the object that represents a resource (for example, `new FileStream`).
2. Create the system resource (for example, `CreateFile`).
3. Use the resource (for example, `WriteFile`).
4. Close the resource (for example, `CloseHandle`).
5. Free the memory of the wrapper object.

The creation and closing of resources (usually referenced via handles) are still the responsibility of the programmer, but the CLR offers automatic memory management for steps 1 and 5. In fact many objects require memory only as a resource and don't deal directly with other system resources (for example, collections, arrays, strings, rectangles, and so on). These objects are managed entirely by the CLR. There is no need for the application programmer to free or delete objects after they have been created.

Automatic memory management might not be an issue to anyone familiar with Java, but most likely the average C++ developer will have some questions, if not reservations, toward it. This reaction is not surprising because memory leaks are one of the main reasons for unstable applications, and developers spend much time trying to reduce them.

Let's take a closer look at how the CLR manages memory, paying special attention to when and how memory can be reclaimed. The CLR requires all memory to be allocated from a *managed heap*. The main difference between a managed heap and a traditional heap is that with a managed heap the programmer never frees previously allocated memory.

You can picture a managed heap as a contiguous linear address space that is gradually filled over time. Each new memory request is served from the end of already committed memory. Figure 1.4 shows a managed heap after three objects have been created.

Allocating memory in this way is very efficient and fast. There are no lists to traverse in order to find an appropriate location for a given size memory block. Furthermore, the memory will be in a sequential order for objects that have been allocated in a sequence. This locality of memory that is allocated at about the same time also leads to better utilization of the CPU's cache. However, the size of the managed heap is not unlimited. So at some point the unused memory in the managed heap needs to be freed and compacted to allow new memory allocations. This task is performed by the Garbage Collector (GC).

The GC needs to know whether an object in the managed heap is still referenced and thus cannot be freed. When IL code is compiled into native machine code, the JIT compiler also creates an internal table that identifies which memory or which CPU registers contain object references. The GC uses these internal tables to determine whether an object is still used by the application. Those objects still in use are then compacted, starting at the beginning of the managed heap. Figure 1.5 shows a managed heap before and after garbage collection.

The GC must update all references to an object when shifting its memory within the managed heap. The rearranging and compacting step is obviously a very expensive task, and that is the major drawback of using a

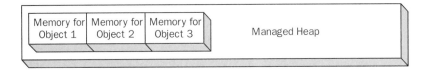

Figure 1.4 Managed Heap after Creation of Three Objects

Filled Managed Heap

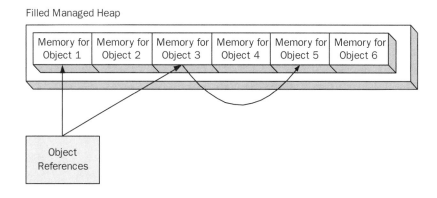

Managed Heap after Garbage Collection

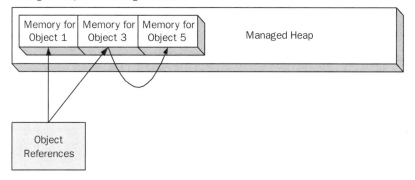

Figure 1.5 Managed Heap before (Top) and after Garbage Collection

managed heap. However, the programmer does not have to worry about the lifetime of objects and saves countless hours that otherwise would be spent trying to locate memory leaks.

Security

The CLR provides code access security for assemblies that are executed. Traditionally the user account that started an application decided whether to grant permissions to access certain system resources. That worked fine as long the source of the applications was known and trustworthy (for example, installed from a CD). However, with developments such as scripting capabilities for Web browsers and on-demand installation of plug-ins, it became necessary to set security permissions dynamically for different applications.

In .NET each assembly contains the information about the type of access it requires, and the CLR checks those against the permissions granted, which are inherited from a variety of rules:

- The system's security permissions
- Account under which the code is being run
- Other policies, such as "Assembly A from Web site `mysite.com` is allowed to access files only under directory X"

Versioning, or the End of DLL Hell

Dynamic link libraries (DLLs) were introduced to save disk space and memory. The common pieces of code used by various applications are deployed in the form of a DLL. The operating system then keeps track of the DLL dependencies and loads each DLL only once into memory.

However, there is also a problem in using common code across multiple applications. An update for an application often results in a DLL update, too. But overwriting a DLL may stop other applications from operating, a situation known as "DLL hell." In his January 2000 MSDN article "The End of DLL Hell" (`http://msdn.microsoft.com/library/default.asp?url=/library/en-us/dnsetup/html/dlldanger1.asp`) Rick Anderson pointed out three main causes for versioning conflicts with DLLs:

- Type I: The installer of an application overwrites an existing DLL with an older version of that DLL. Newer applications that depend on functionality provided by the later version of the DLL are now unable to load because of missing symbols.
- Type II: Applications often unknowingly rely on certain side effects of a current DLL. When a newer version of the DLL eliminates those side effects, the applications no longer work.
- Type III: Less commonly, a new version of a DLL introduces a new bug.

To address these problems the .NET Framework first distinguishes between private and shared assemblies. *Private* (or *isolated*) *assemblies* reside in the same directory as the program executable and are identified by the assembly's file name. No versioning is enforced because these assemblies are used only by one application and cannot be affected by changes made on the system or other applications. Indeed private assemblies are a general design guideline and the default in .NET applications.

But sharing assemblies between applications is often very useful. An obvious example is the Framework Class Library itself, which is explained later in this chapter. It would make little sense for each application to implement and maintain its own version of window and dialog classes. To share assemblies between applications in .NET, a programmer needs to take special steps. Specifically, *shared assemblies* require the use of globally unique names and should support *side-by-side execution*: the ability to install and execute multiple versions of a component on the same machine at the same time, even within the same process. The CLR ensures that, by default, the only version loaded of an assembly is the one that the application was built with. This default behavior, however, can be overridden via policy configuration, and Microsoft provides a graphical tool for that.

The .NET Framework Configuration utility, shown in Figure 1.6, can be found in the Control Panel under Administrative Tools. Using this tool, you can adjust configuration settings for the system as well as individual applications. For example, if you add an assembly to the Configured Assemblies folder, you can modify its binding policy so that applications requesting certain versions will instead be redirected to a different version of the assembly (see Figure 1.7).

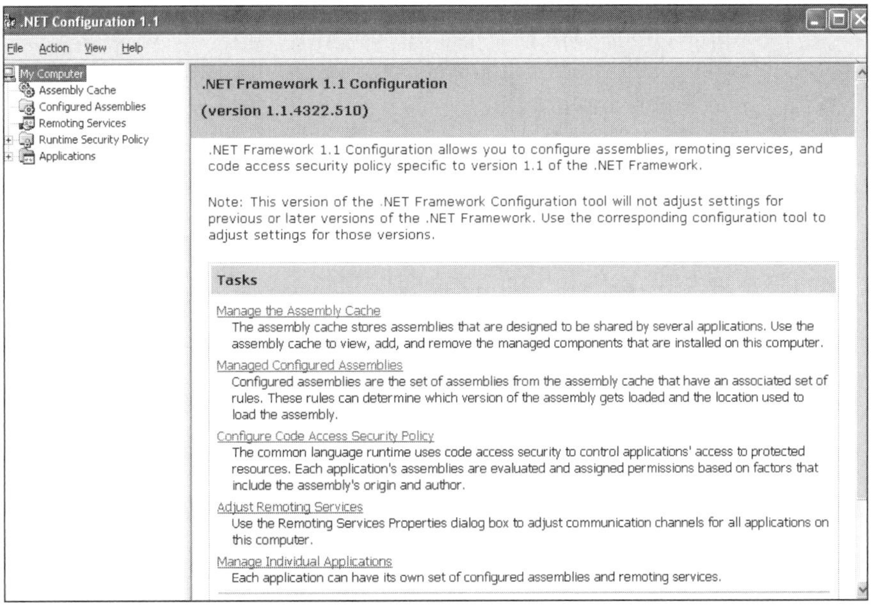

Figure 1.6 .NET Configuration Utility

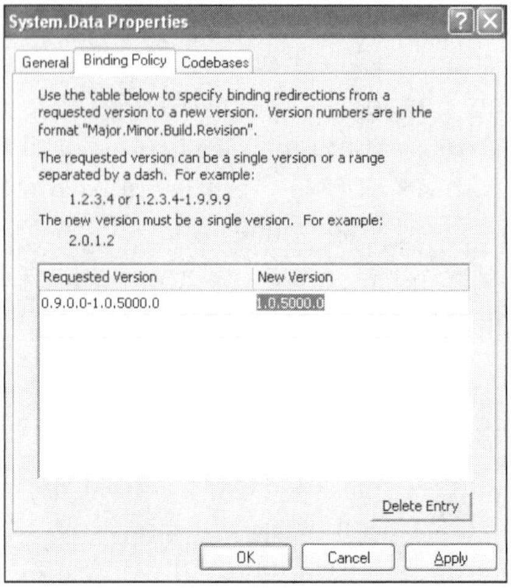

Figure 1.7 Assembly Binding Policy

Thus, you can redirect the binding to different versions as a general rule for all applications that request an assembly from the assembly cache; in addition, you can adjust these settings for an individual application only. To create rules that apply to a single application, you must add it to the Applications folder. The subfolders will show the assembly dependencies and will allow the configuration of assemblies and remoting services particular to this application.

Simplified Deployment and Upgrading

Deploying applications can be quite a hassle, especially if an application depends on COM objects that require updates in the system registry. As mentioned earlier with regard to versioning, .NET applications are by default isolated. This means that the required assemblies and the application's configuration file are located in the same directory as the program executable. Deploying a .NET application can be as easy as copying the application directory onto the target computer. Similarly, you can uninstall an application by simply deleting this directory. Of course, you can also create a Windows installer with the help of the Setup wizard included in Visual Studio.NET. This might be a better choice when additional configuration steps, such as database setup or the installation of shared components, are required.

A new form of deployment in .NET is the use of dynamic downloads. There are mainly two options for using this new feature:

- Controlling assembly download via a configuration file (using the `<codebase>` tag)
- Loading assemblies programmatically (using the `Assembly.Load From()` or `Assembly.Load()` method)

Dynamic downloads open a number of new deployment possibilities for .NET applications. You could certainly provide bug fixes as well as added-value features in this way.

Consistent Method Failure Paradigm

In Windows, the handling of API call failures is inconsistent. Most of the Software Development Kit (SDK) methods return status codes. ActiveX and COM functions return `HRESULT`, whereas Microsoft Foundation Classes (MFC) throw exceptions. In .NET all this is handled uniformly: All method call failures are reported via exceptions. In this way, developers can isolate error and recovery code from the main operating code. Moreover, the exceptions can be passed across modules. This is an advantage for applications that consist of modules written in different languages.

IL code that is generated by .NET compilers runs under the CLR. This means that the IL can generate managed exceptions that can be handled by any other managed code. These exception objects have (at least) a text description and a status code, but they can also contain other exception objects. Developers can use this feature to build a list of exceptions representing the effect of the exception as it is propagated through the call stack. If a remote object throws an exception, perhaps on another machine, the caller object can handle the exception.

In case of a successful method call, it is not necessary to have a return value for the status. Thus, the use of managed exceptions may result in a slight performance advantage without the need of frequently checking return values.

1.2.2 The Framework Class Library (FCL)

The .NET Framework provides a huge class library for all .NET programming languages; the FCL contains more than 5,000 classes. To make it easier to work with so many classes, these classes are organized in a hierarchy of more than 80 namespaces.

The root namespace is `System`, and every application will use at least some of the services it provides. For example, the namespace `System.Drawing` provides the programmer with classes that represent fonts, brushes, colors, and so on.

It would go beyond the scope of an FCL introduction to list all namespaces and the functionalities addressed by them. But despite its size the FCL is manageable, thanks to the logical grouping of the provided functionality. In fact, learning to use the FCL is rather simple compared with learning the Win32 application programming interface (API) because you can move gradually, exploring one new domain at a time. This section gives a high-level overview of FCL classes. Some of them are discussed in more detail throughout the remainder of the book.

The *System* Namespace

As we mentioned, the lowest-level namespace and root for all other namespaces in the FCL is System. It contains fundamental classes and types that define what is meant by "commonly used":

- Data types: These form the data types and arrays used by various programming languages (for example, int in C++).
- Events and event handlers: Events are handled by using delegates. Information is passed in the form of an EventArgs object to the EventHandler delegate.
- Interfaces: For example, IDisposable is used for classes that define a method to release allocated unmanaged resources.
- Attributes: *Attributes* allow custom information about a class or its members to be stored in the assembly's metadata (for example, an attribute that identifies a method as test code).
- Exceptions: When a fatal error occurs, the CLR provides this information to the Exception class of the FCL.

Diagnostics and Profiling

The FCL provides a number of diagnostic and profiling tools. They include classes for event logging (EventLog), high-resolution timers for performance evaluation (PerformanceCounter), tracing and assertions (Debug), and others in the System.Diagnostics namespace.

Configuration Management

Within the System.Configuration namespace you'll find a set of classes that give you programmatic access to .NET Framework configuration settings. `System.Configuration.Assemblies` and `System.Configuration.Install` provide classes to access assembly-specific settings and to write custom installers for your application.

String Manipulation

In the .NET Framework, strings are *immutable*, meaning that their values cannot be changed after they are created. That simplifies things such as ownership and threading issues but causes a performance penalty when you do even simple string manipulations such as deleting a single character (you must create a new string for this purpose). However, the FCL provides the `StringBuilder` class in the `System.Text` namespace to perform string manipulations efficiently. Furthermore, the `RegEx` and `Match` classes in `System.Text.RegularExpressions` allow the programmer to search strings using regular expressions.

Collections

A major factor in the popularity of the Standard Template Library (STL) in C++ has been a set of powerful classes that can be used to manage general-purpose collections. In the FCL, classes representing a number of collections—such as lists (sorted or unsorted), arrays, queues, and hash tables—are located in the `System.Collection` namespace. In the namespace `System.Collection.Specialized` you will find more specialized and strongly typed collections, such as the `StringCollection` class.

Input and Output

In the `System.IO` namespace the FCL provides numerous classes for reading and writing on data streams and files. The main distinction between files and streams is that *files* have persistent storage (a full path name), whereas *streams* are seen as reading and writing data to or from back-end storage, which can be one of many media such as files, networks, or even memory itself.

Remote Calls

The .NET FCL provides in its `System.Runtime.Remoting` namespace a set of classes that allow application developers to create distributed applications. You can use distributed computing to balance the work load of a given task across multiple computers in a network. The `RemotingServices` class provides methods that help you publish remote objects, whereas the `ObjRef` class holds the necessary information to work with a remote object.

Reflection

Occasionally an application needs to query information about an assembly and its data types or classes at run time. You might even want to create objects and invoke methods that have not been known at compile time. This approach, called *reflection,* is also referred to as *late-bound invocation.* For this, the FCL provides a set of classes contained mainly in the `System.Reflection` namespace.

Security

Another lower-level namespace is `System.Security`, which supports cryptography. *Cryptography* protects data from being viewed or modified and provides secure channels of communication over otherwise insecure channels.

Data Access with ADO.NET

ADO.NET is implemented in the `System.Data` namespace and provides classes to access various kinds of data sources such as Structured Query Language (SQL) or Open Database Connectivity (ODBC). ADO.NET, a rewrite of the earlier Active Data Objects (ADO), is an attempt to improve the way data is accessed specifically for Web-based applications. ADO.NET supports `DataSet`, a new, powerful, connectionless class that holds the result of a query independent of the data provider (it's like a memory cache for data). Furthermore, all classes in ASP.NET provide much better support for XML and are complemented by classes in the `System.XML` namespace, which also supports the use of Extensible Stylesheet Language (XSL) stylesheets.

Smart Client Applications

Forms and controls made Visual Basic the platform of choice for rapid user-interface-based Windows applications. Porting classes from VB, such as `Form`, `Button`, and `ListView`, gives the application developer full control over the rich features available on Windows platforms. All these controls are grouped in the `System.Windows.Forms` namespace. The FCL also provides a full set of graphics objects—such as the `Color` structure, the `Brush` class, the `Font` class, and so on—in the `System.Drawing` namespace.

Web Applications with ASP.NET

In the beginning stage of the Internet boom, the Internet was more or less a collection of static linked Web pages. However, with the growing popularity of the Internet, trying to manually keep all the sites up-to-date soon proved to be unmanageable. Microsoft addressed this need by introducing Active Server Pages (ASP). This simple but powerful scripting language for Microsoft's Internet Information Servers (IIS) allowed the creation of dynamic Web pages.

ASP.NET, which is implemented in the `System.Web` namespace, tries to overcome some of the shortcomings of the old ASP, such as poor performance and lack of reusability. For example, because the code was embedded into HTML documents, any reformatting often meant that developers had to rewrite the scripts that created the dynamic behavior. Also, the embedded scripts had to be interpreted by the IIS every time a browser requested the site, and that led to serious performance bottlenecks. ASP.NET addresses these problems and also introduces a number of new features:

- *Code behind*: This is the separation of code from the HTML documents and therefore from the look-and-feel HTML language.
- Compiled assemblies: The code is compiled by the JIT compiler into native machine code and does not need to be interpreted every time a page is requested.
- Choice of language: With ASP.NET, you can write programs in any supported .NET programming language.
- Event-driven: The old ASP scripting language was interpreted sequentially from the top to the bottom, whereas ASP.NET is event-driven, which means that small code blocks are written that respond to UI events. This allows the developer to focus more on what needs to be done rather than the when and how.
- Registry-free configuration and deployment: Each ASP.NET application stores its configuration settings in a private XML text file instead of the global IIS registry file. Also, unlike COM objects, the .NET assemblies do not have to be registered in the systems registry. Both of these features make deployment of ASP.NET applications as easy as a simple file transfer.

■ Web forms: The Framework Class Library includes the `System.Web.UI` namespace, which comes with a powerful set of prewritten functionality, such as calendar and time controls. And, unlike the old ASP, these new Web forms are browser-independent.

Web Services

As we mentioned earlier, there is more to the Internet than just Web pages. XML *Web services* are applications that you can call over the Internet and connect like building blocks to large solutions by using the Internet infrastructure. The applications can be written in different languages and run on different platforms. They communicate via XML or the Simple Object Access Protocol (SOAP), a lightweight XML-based protocol for the exchange of structured information. The `System.Web.Services` namespace consists of classes that let you create such Web services.

When a Web service is online, it can be registered in the Universal Discovery Description and Integration (UDDI), the yellow pages of all Web services. UDDI describes a business and the services it offers.

1.3 The C# Language

An introduction to .NET would be incomplete without a mention of the new programming language C#, which is also described as the native language for .NET. This is because much of the .NET Framework itself was written in C#.

The C# programming language seems to have its roots in C++ and Java. The basic syntax comes from C++, where the everything-declared-in-one-place structure is inherited from Java. C# programmers can enjoy an easier life with fewer worries because, just like the Virtual Machine for Java, the .NET CLR can provide many features, including automatic memory management and garbage collection. We will use C# as the preferred language throughout this book, and you will learn more about it starting in Chapter 3.

1.4 Debugging and the IDE

Visual Studio (VS) .NET is a development tool that developers can use to easily build powerful applications. As shown in Figure 1.8, .NET integrates many tools into a single environment. Here are some examples:

- Projects and workspaces provide a comprehensive view of all the files in a project. You can manage multiple projects in a single workspace.
- The IDE lets you use various programming languages—such as VB, C++, C#, J#, and others—to develop applications.
- The visual Form Designer enables the developer to create dialogs or Web forms without doing any programming.
- Visual Studio supports Internet applications development. It deploys the Web application to the IIS in a way that is transparent to the developer.
- The integrated debugger supports stepping through the source code even for remote Web applications.

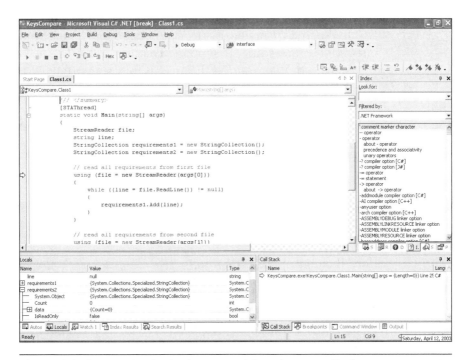

Figure 1.8 Debugging in the Integrated Development Environment

- .NET supports external tools such as the versioning control tools Visual Source Safe and Rational ClearCase and the performance analyzer Rational Quantify.

With the new Visual Studio.NET Version 2003, a number of improvements have been added. Those features include the following:

- Enhanced C++ floating point performance: Added support for Pentium 4 processors and the SSE/SSE2 instruction set enhances the performance of floating-point-intensive processing by as much as 20 percent.
- C++ Rapid Application Development wizards: New designers and wizards enable C++ developers to easily create forms-based .NET applications.
- Integrated smart device and wireless programmability: Support for the .NET Compact Framework has been added. This enables .NET developers to easily develop programs for Pocket PC or Windows CE. In addition, Visual Studio.NET supports more than 140 Internet-enabled mobile devices.
- Support for J# developers: To ease the transition of Java developers to the .NET Framework, J# is integrated into Visual Studio.NET.
- .NET Framework 1.1 support: The new .NET Framework 1.1 that ships with Windows .NET Server is fully supported in Visual Studio. NET 2003.

1.5 References for Further Reading

.NET Introduction

David Chappell, *Understanding .NET* (Boston: Addison-Wesley, 2002)

David S. Platt and Keith Ballinger, *Introducing Microsoft .NET* (Redmond, WA: Microsoft Press, 2003)

Jeffery Richter, *Applied Microsoft .NET Framework Programming* (Redmond, WA: Microsoft Press, 2002)

Application Development

Richard Grimes, *Developing Applications with Visual Studio.NET* (Boston: Addison-Wesley, 2002)

Microsoft Corporation, *Microsoft.NET Server Solutions for the Enterprise* (Redmond, WA: Microsoft Press, 2002)

Carsten Thomson and John Erik Hansan, *Enterprise Development with Visual Studio.NET* (Berkeley, CA: APress, 2003)

Security

Cyrus Peikari and Seth Fogie, *Windows .NET Security Handbook* (Upper Saddle River, NJ: Prentice Hall, 2002)

OOP and C#

Robin A. Reynolds-Haertle, *OOP with Microsoft Visual Basic and Microsoft C# .NET Step by Step* (Redmond, WA: Microsoft Press, 2002)

Simon Robinson et al., *Professional C#* (Birmingham, UK: Wrox Press, 2002)

ADO

Bob Beauchemin, *Essential ADO.NET* (Boston: Addison-Wesley, 2002)

Jeffrey P. McManus and Jackie Goldstein, *Database Access with Visual Basic .NET* (Boston: Addison-Wesley, 2003)

Rebecca M. Riordan, *Microsoft ADO.NET Step by Step* (Redmond, WA: Microsoft Press, 2002)

ASP and XML

Jeffrey P. McManus, *C# Developer's Guide to ASP.NET, XML and ADO. NET* (Boston: Addison-Wesley, 2002)

Eric Newcomer, *Understanding Web Services: XML, WSDL, SOAP and UUDDI* (Boston: Addison-Wesley, 2002)

Scott Short, *Building XML Web Services for the Microsoft .NET Platform* (Redmond, WA: Microsoft Press, 2002)

CHAPTER 2

Introducing Software Engineering

Before you start a software development project, it is important to decide on a suitable development strategy. This chapter discusses the possible software development strategies (also referred to as software development models or software development process) for the implementation of the Online Photo Shop, the photo-editing project that we use as an example throughout this book. For this discussion we assume that the development organization itself is already set up. This means that the number of team members, their skills, their responsibilities, and so on are already defined. (For information on how to set up a development organization, please refer to the book written by Dan Paulish, *Architecture-Centric Software Project Management: A Practical Guide,* Boston: Addison-Wesley, 2002).

We start by discussing why there is a need for a software development model, and then we review the most commonly used software development models. After that, we'll choose the model that best suits the Online Photo Shop project.

2.1 Introducing Software Engineering Practices

It is estimated that one-third of all software projects are canceled before the software is released. Of the remainder, two-thirds significantly overrun their budgets. Research also shows that more than 80 percent of all project errors are committed in the critical analysis and design phase before actual code is written (see also the CHAOS study of the Standish Group at `http://www.standishgroup.com/sample_research/chaos_1994_1.php`).

Even though these numbers may vary (depending on who publishes them), they show clearly that there is an essential problem with software development. What is the root cause of the problem? How can software development be made more predictable?

Looking at other engineering disciplines, such as civil engineering, we can see that a structured approach seems to be one of the keys for predictability and repeatability and therefore success. Let's take the example of building a house. To build a house, people typically follow a structured approach. First the budget is secured and then the land is acquired, followed by application for the necessary permits before a detailed plan of the house is developed. All these tasks are necessary to build a house within the constraints of time, cost, space required, and options chosen. It is very unlikely that someone would ask a contractor to build a house without agreeing on a plan that considers all the constraints. This approach seems to make sense. It has worked and will work for building many new houses.

Analyzing this kind of approach reveals some of the deficiencies in software development. Often, software developers write a program or code without having any plan in the form of a functional or design description (not to mention a refined, detailed plan). When that happens, the code often does not reflect constraints such as budget, functionality, modularity, reusability, maintainability, and available technologies. It is as if a building contractor were starting to build a house without knowing the location of the house and the architectural plan.

It is at this point that software engineering methodologies come into play. Software engineering methodologies try to structure software development in the same way other engineering practices are structured to make software development more predictable and repeatable, and therefore more successful.

Before introducing software engineering practices we have deliberately avoided the expression "software engineering." That's because if developers do not follow any methodology, there is no software engineering but only hacking. (See also Steve McConnell, *After the Gold Rush: Creating a True Profession of Software Engineering*, Microsoft Press 1999).

The next section describes how to find a suitable software development model for a project.

2.2 Choosing a Software Development Model

When you choose a software development model, it is important to choose one that fits the project and the environment it is intended for. As discussed in the next section, the traditional models work for more static projects. By "static" we mean projects whose requirements do not change very much during the project and where the technical uncertainty is very low. More dynamic models, such as Extreme Programming, Adaptive Software Development, and Scrum, try to take into account the dynamics of changing requirements, uncertainty in technologies, and changing project goals, and therefore these models are more successful in dynamic circumstances.

Based on the descriptions provided here, we will choose the most suitable model for the Online Photo Shop project. If you have a solid background in software engineering models, you may want to skip the following section and go directly to section 2.4.

2.3 Commonly Used Software Development Models

In the following paragraphs we introduce some commonly used software engineering methodologies and assess their advantages and disadvantages. We look first at the traditional models: Code and Fix, Waterfall, V, Spiral, Staged Delivery, and Evolutionary Prototyping. Then we look at the more dynamic models: Scrum, Adaptive Software Development, the Unified Process (UP), and Extreme Programming.

A software development model should not be dumped blindly onto the project but rather should be carefully chosen according to the project, the environment, and your goals. After a certain model is chosen, it must be adapted to fit the project and organizational culture. All the models discussed here are flexible enough that you can adjust them to the environment they are used in.

Before we get to the models, we want to say a few words about a new practice called *Agile software development*. This approach is not a lifecycle model, as many people believe it is. Instead, it is a methodology that is put on top of the lifecycle models. Agile software development was proposed by representatives of a number of software development methods, including Extreme Programming, Scrum, Adaptive Software Development, Crystal, Feature-Driven Development, Pragmatic Programming, and others sympathetic to the need for an alternative to documentation-driven, heavy-weight software development processes. The core values defined by Agile development are as follows:

- Individuals and interactions are more important than processes and tools.
- Working software is more important than comprehensive documentation.
- Customer collaboration is more important than contract negotiation.
- Responding to change is more important than following a plan.

These core values are used on top of a software development process to do Agile software development. For more information on Agile development see http://www.agilemanifesto.org.

2.3.1 The Code and Fix Software Development Model

Characteristics

This is not really a development model but nevertheless it is a very common practice in software development. Developers begin work without a set of good requirements or a vision, writing code as long as there is time and money. The release of a product depends on a miracle, as shown in Figure 2.1.

Definition

In the Code and Fix model, no real process is followed. The developers start hacking without a detailed idea of what the program should do and how the functionality should be implemented. If the project gets lucky and a little magic happens, the product will be released. Otherwise, the money or time runs out and the project becomes an entry in the statistics of canceled projects.

In many real-world projects, some sort of Code and Fix technique is used. Even when a process is in place or at least known, projects may resort to Code and Fix because of time pressure. It seems a waste of time to first plan the project properly in order to define requirements and design, and Code and Fix produces code fast. But that's an illusion. Even though Code and Fix might seem to produce a result faster than any other model, it is very unlikely that the result will satisfy the customers' wishes or needs. Nor

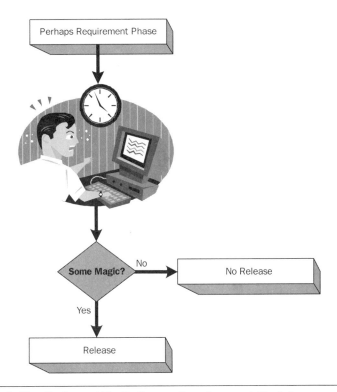

Figure 2.1 The Code and Fix Software Development Model

will it achieve extensibility or maintainability, attributes that require a well-defined design.

This model is pure hacking or coding, and it has nothing in common with a well-structured approach that promises success. From our experience, Code and Fix works only for rapid prototyping. Do not use this model for product development.

Pro

This approach has no planning phase and therefore yields early results.

Cons

It is not predictable and therefore depends highly on the individual. High maintenance and rework effort are the result of using the Code and Fix model.

2.3.2 The Waterfall Software Development Model

Characteristics

The Waterfall model is considered the grandmother of all the software engineering models and is the most well known of all software engineering methodologies. The Waterfall model works well in an environment of well-understood requirements. For the model to work well, you need to make sure that you eliminate the possibility of a lot of midstream requirements changes. This avoids a common source of problems when using this development model.

Definition

The Waterfall model is a sequential, document-driven methodology. To advance from the current phase to the next phase, the project team must review and release an artifact in the form of a document. The release of the corresponding document triggers the end of one phase and the beginning of the next (see Figure 2.2).

The Waterfall software development model uses sequential, non-overlapping phases and carries over documents from phase to phase. The project flow is as follows:

1. Concept phase: In this first step the business goals and constraints of the project are discussed, and the initial effort estimate is provided. The phase ends with the release of the concept document.
2. Requirements phase: After the concept document is reviewed and agreed upon, the requirements are engineered. The project team must completely understand the system, technologies, and constraints at this point in order to define a complete set of requirements for the system. The transition to the next phase occurs after the requirements document is approved.
3. High-level design phase: In this phase the system's overall architectural design is developed, and the functional modules are identified. At the end of this phase, the high-level design document is the milestone necessary to proceed to the detailed design phase.
4. Detailed design phase: After the functional modules are identified, the detailed design of these modules is worked out. At the end of this phase the detailed design document is released, providing the base for the implementation by the developers in the next phase.

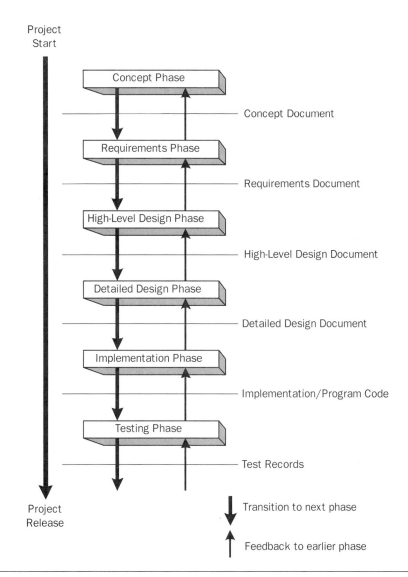

Figure 2.2 The Waterfall Software Development Model

   5. Code implementation phase: The system is implemented according
      to the system documents produced in earlier stages. In many proj-
      ects, unit testing is also part of this phase. At the end of the phase
      the code is implemented and is unit-tested as proof of the (correct)
      implementation.

6. Test phase: After implementation and unit testing of the code, the integration and acceptance testing takes place to verify that the system works as described and agreed upon. The test documentation and the passed test records are the final documents that are released before the product is shipped to the customer.

In the pure Waterfall model, the document of a given phase must be completed, reviewed, and released before the project can proceed to the next phase. It is easy to see that the process assumes that the problem, the domain, and the technologies are well understood. You must have this understanding in order to complete the planning before the implementation can start. If, during later phases, a problem is found that requires changes to previous phases, the project must roll back and correct all the affected documents before it can proceed.

Pros

The Waterfall model works well in projects that have stable requirements in a known technical domain, even with complex tasks. The Waterfall model enables planning and analysis of complex problems early in the project and therefore removes some of the risk from later phases, when it is much more expensive to fix problems. The model also works well with inexperienced or technically weak project teams because it adds a structured, well-planned approach to the project. Therefore, it minimizes unnecessary work due to inexperience or lack of technical knowledge.

Cons

On the downside the Waterfall model is sensitive to changes in phases that are already finished. It is often difficult to specify all the requirements before you do some of the design work. If it's necessary to make changes to requirements after the initial design work, the project must revisit the previous phase and adjust the work (or documentation) of that phase. These changes might trigger changes in the work that has been done in the earlier phase and consequently to its work artifact. Before the project can continue to the next phase, all the changes to all previous phases continue to be propagated upstream until they have been incorporated. It is easy to see that changes made midstream can cause massive rework.

Variations

The Sashimi model is named after the Japanese style of presenting fish in overlapping slices. This approach modifies the Waterfall by allowing for overlapping phases. The main advantage is that it reduces documentation and gives you the freedom to proceed with incomplete phases. The problem with this model is that the milestones are no longer obvious, and progress cannot be tracked as easily as with the pure Waterfall model.

Another variation, the Waterfall with Subprojects approach, allows for subprojects that can be executed independently. This lets you implement easily implemented features at an earlier stage, before the more complex and unknown features are completely planned. This approach is problematic if unforeseen dependencies are uncovered during later stages.

To reduce risk, you can modify the Waterfall model by adding a risk reduction spiral at the beginning. For example, you might define requirements and create the architectural design in a spiral development cycle and then use the Waterfall model for the remaining phases. You can extend this risk reduction to develop some high-risk subprojects in a complete Spiral model (see section 2.3.4) before committing to a full-scale project.

2.3.3 The V Software Development Model

Characteristics

The V model is a popular software development model for projects that have stable requirements within a known technical domain. It is an extended Waterfall model, adding more details on the validation and verification side. For each phase in development, there is an associated phase to verify and validate the result produced.

The V model is a sequential, document-driven software development model. At the end of each phase a document is produced that allows the project to proceed to the next phase.

Definition

Figure 2.3 shows the flow of the V model.

The project runs through the following phases:

1. Requirements phase: The customer, in cooperation with the project team, usually engineers the requirements. At the end of the phase an approved requirements specification is released with an initial effort estimate.

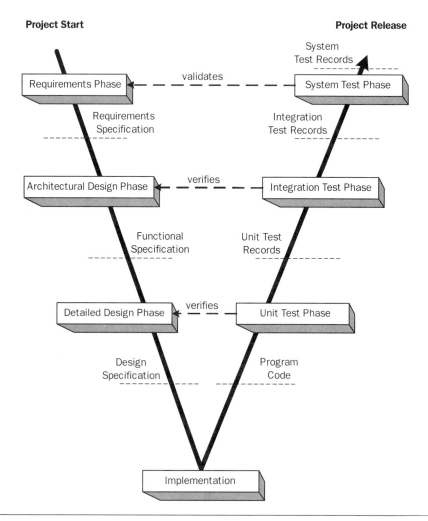

Figure 2.3 The V Software Development Model

2. Architectural design phase: The project team breaks the requirements down into functional pieces, defines how the different pieces of the system work together, and updates the effort estimate. The functional specification document is approved before the team moves on to the detailed design phase.

3. Detailed design phase: The team decides on the detailed design of the functional items. The end of this phase is marked by the release of the design specification.

4. Implementation: The code is implemented according to the specification.
5. Unit test phase: Unit tests are written and executed to verify that the design works as described in the design specification. For the project to move to integration test, the unit test records must show that all test cases passed.
6. Integration test phase: The integration tests verify that the software behaves as described in the functional specification. Integration records are produced for the test runs.
7. System test phase: The system tests validate that the system meets the requirements in the requirements specification. The passed system test records indicate that the system is ready for release.

The flow through the various phases shows that the V model is derived from the Waterfall model.

Pros

The V model works well in environments of stable requirements and well-known technical domains. The advantage of the V model is its focus on verification and validation. Each artifact on the left side of the V has a matching verification mechanism on the right side. The approach also works for larger teams.

Cons

If requirements change during the project, a lot of rework is necessary to update the relevant documents in order for the project to proceed. In many cases the documents on the left side of the V are ambiguous and therefore cannot be used directly for deriving tests. As in the Waterfall model, all the project planning must be done up front. This can be very difficult in a complex project or in unknown technical domains.

Variations

The W model adds a second V dedicated to testing, thereby adding even more focus on testing. The inserted V shows the collaboration between testing and development from the very early stages of development. So the model looks like \V/, or a W, as the name suggests. For more information please refer to `http://www.stickyminds.com` and search for the W model.

2.3.4 The Spiral Software Development Model

Characteristics

The Spiral model breaks the project down into risk-oriented subprojects. At the beginning of each phase or subproject, the risk is analyzed. Then the project team first addresses the subproject that implies the highest risk, followed by the one with the second-highest risk, and so on until all the risks are addressed. Risks can include unknown technology, possible performance problems, a poorly understood architecture, and others. The Spiral model then ends in a Waterfall lifecycle model.

Definition

Figure 2.4 shows the Spiral (or cinnamon roll) model with its iterative steps. Each iteration in the model forms one circle around the origin to form a spiral after all the iterations are performed.

The Spiral model consists of the following major activities to reduce the risk in a project:

1. Determine goals, alternatives, and constraints: In the first step of the iteration, you elaborate the goals for the product.
2. Evaluate alternatives: In this step you evaluate the alternatives collected in step 1. Typically you use a prototype implementation to determine the best possible solution or, in the worst case, to determine that the project is infeasible.
3. Identify and mitigate risks: After assessing the alternatives, you identify possible risks and mitigations. Identifying risks can turn out to be difficult in some cases. The risks to consider include technological risks, process risks, requirements changes, people risks (key people could leave), and safety issues (for example, in the medical domain patients could be at risk if images are displayed wrong and, because of that, the diagnosis is wrong). It is important to evaluate the input from all participating parties.
4. Develop the deliverables for the current iteration and verify that they are correct: This step is the implementation and verification of the artifacts for the current iteration.
5. Plan for the next iteration: After you have verified the currently implemented artifacts, you must plan the next iteration (if any). You should document possible improvements and evaluate known bugs (to fix them either in the current or in a later iteration).

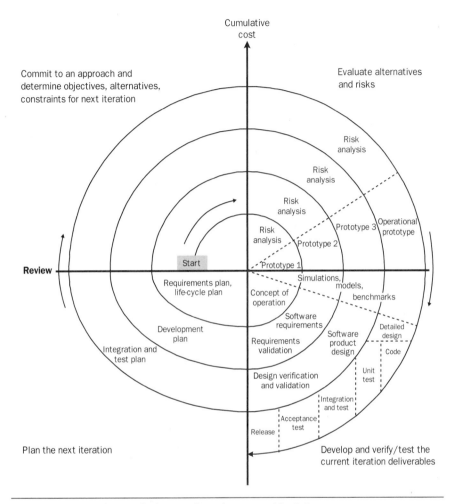

Figure 2.4 The Spiral Software Development Model

6. Decide and commit on the next iteration(s): The last step of the current iteration (or the first step of the next iteration) is to decide and commit on the next iteration. You determine which new features will be implemented and which bugs will be fixed in the next iteration. (The latter point assumes that software is never perfect and there are known bugs at this point. But even if there are no known bugs, there will surely be bug reports or requests for different behavior in implemented functionality). If another iteration is decided upon, the next iteration starts again at step 1.

The number of iterations and the order of the six steps are suggestions that work for most projects, but the model can be tailored to the needs of the project. In practice, the Spiral lifecycle model is often used in combination with other lifecycle models to effect risk reduction in early stages of the project. After the risks are addressed, another lifecycle model, such as the Waterfall model, is then used.

Pros

The advantage of this model is the breakdown of the development into small pieces so that the areas of risk can be tackled at the beginning of the project. It seems reasonable to deal with risks first. The more effort that is spent here, the less risk will be left in the project and the less likely it is that unpleasant surprises will be found toward the end of the project. The Spiral model can be used with other models, providing risk reduction in early stages of development. If no risk is involved, the risk analysis step can be skipped.

Cons

The Spiral model is quite complex. It requires management to be knowledgeable and thoughtful. It is sometimes difficult to define the milestones to decide whether the project is ready for the next iteration (especially if development is being done in parallel iterations or cycles).

Variations

As stated earlier, the Spiral model can be combined with any other lifecycle model for risk reduction in the beginning of the project

The WinWin Spiral software development model adds three extra activities to circumvent problems observed in the "basic" Spiral model. The activities added are as follows: identify the system's or subsystem's key stakeholder, identify the stakeholder's win condition, and negotiate a win-win reconciliation of the stakeholder's win condition. For more information on the WinWin Spiral software development model, see the references section.

2.3.5 The Staged Delivery Software Development Model

Characteristics

Staged Delivery is a lifecycle model that provides the software in staged releases; the most important features are developed in the early deliverables.

Staged Delivery shows incremental progress at each delivery to the client. This enables faster feedback from the customer on the currently implemented functionality. As a result, this model minimizes the risk of delivering a product that does not fulfill the customer's expectations. Furthermore, this model lets you incorporate changes as early as the feature is delivered to the customer. A working product can be shipped in short intervals.

Staged Delivery works well in areas of well-understood requirements, large projects, customers that want to use subsets of the features very early, and a project in which functionality can be split into subsets that can be developed independently (or at least with a sequential order).

Definition

The Staged Delivery lifecycle model is based on the Waterfall model (see Figure 2.5). It follows the Waterfall model throughout the concept, requirements, and high-level design phases. After completion of the high-level design, the Staged Delivery model proceeds through the detailed design, implementation, and testing phases in each stage. A releasable product is produced at the end of every stage.

The flow through the phases is as follows:

1. Concept phase: In this first step of the Waterfall model, the business goals and constraints of the project are discussed, and the initial effort estimate is provided. The phase ends with the release of the concept document.
2. Requirements phase: After the concept document is reviewed and agreed upon, the requirements are engineered. The project team must completely understand the system, technologies, and constraints at this point in order to define a complete set of requirements for the system. The transition to the next phase occurs after the requirements document is approved.
3. High-level design phase: In this phase the system's overall architectural design is developed, and the functional modules are identified. At the end of this phase, the high-level design document is released and the process moves to the low-level design phase.
4. Staged delivery phases: After the high-level design phase for the overall system is completed, n numbers of deliveries follow. Each delivery includes low-level design, implementation, debug, test, and delivery of a subset of functionality (see also the Waterfall model, steps 4 to 6). The number of staged delivery phases will

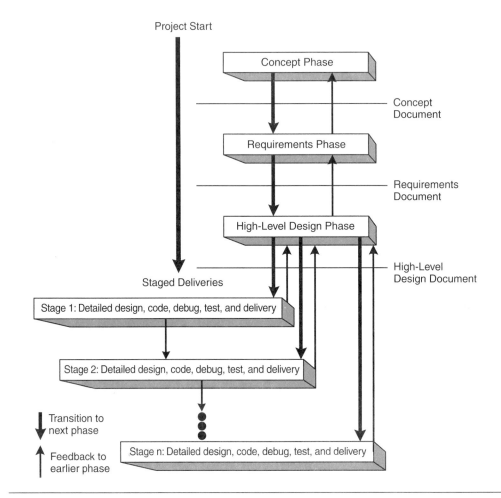

Figure 2.5 The Staged Delivery Software Development Model

depend on the point at which the customer is satisfied with the project and doesn't need any more improvements or the system is completed according to the specification.

Pros

The main benefit of the Staged Delivery model is the increased visibility it gives you of the project's progress and its support for frequent and predictable product releases. As a result, customer satisfaction increases. In addition, because the project team receives customer feedback quickly, it is easier to make customer-driven changes midstream.

Cons

If the software cannot be broken down into subsystems that can be delivered in stages, then staged delivery is not an option. Also, customers may change their minds after seeing the features implemented, and that may cause feature creep within a single stage because of changed requirements.

Variations

The Evolutionary Delivery approach is a mixture of the Evolutionary Prototyping model (discussed next) and the Staged Delivery model. Iterations are very short, and the project is released to the customer for feedback after each iteration. Depending on how many customer requests are taken into account, the development will look more like either Evolutionary Prototyping or Staged Delivery. If most of the customer feedback is implemented in the next iterations, the project cycle will look like Evolutionary Prototyping. If very few customer requests are honored, the project cycle will look like the Staged Delivery model.

2.3.6 The Evolutionary Prototyping Software Development Model

Characteristics

In the Evolutionary Prototyping model, you develop the system concept while moving through the project. In most projects that use Evolutionary Prototyping, the most visible aspects of the system are developed first and are shown to the customer. Based on customer feedback, the prototype is altered or extended, including requirements analysis, design, and maintenance. These incremental releases to the customer are repeated until the customer is satisfied with the solution and the project is released, or until the time and money for the project run out.

Definition

As its name suggests, in Evolutionary Prototyping (see Figure 2.6) the system starts with an initial idea or proposal, which is then prototyped and released to the customer in incremental releases based on feedback.

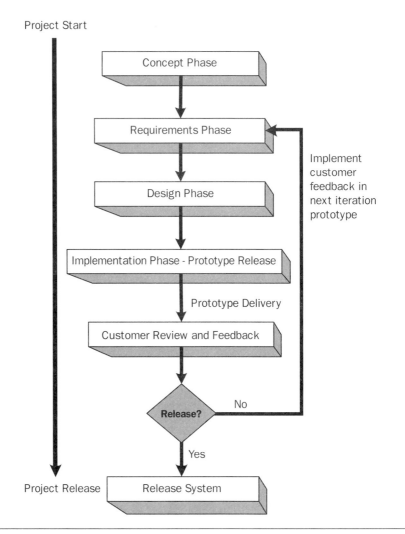

Figure 2.6 The Evolutionary Prototyping Software Development Model

The structured project flow looks like this:

1. Concept phase: The starting point is an initial concept or project proposal. This document may comprise the business goals for the project or the idea for an innovative new product.
2. Requirements phase: Based on the initial idea, the requirements are gathered for a prototype of the current iteration.

3. Design phase: The requirements are broken down into functional pieces, which drive the design of the system in the current iteration.
4. Implementation phase–prototype release: The system is implemented based on the specified design. The prototype is then released to the customer for review.
5. Customer review and feedback: The customer reviews the prototype and provides feedback on changes and new features to be built in the next iteration as requirements. Or the prototype is accepted and becomes the final released product.

Pros

In environments of fast-changing requirements, uncertain requirements, or lack of application knowledge by the customer and project team, or when the team is unsure of the best technical solution, Evolutionary Prototyping works very well. The obvious advantage is the visible signs of progress produced in each of the short iterations.

Cons

In the beginning of the project, it is not possible to know how many iterations it will take or how much time it will take to produce an acceptable product. With this approach, it is also possible to keep the project going until the product is released at the end of money or time.

Another drawback is that this approach is often used as an excuse for Code and Fix development. In contrast to Code and Fix, real Evolutionary Prototyping includes requirements analysis, design, and the production of maintainable code for every iteration.

Variations

Evolutionary Delivery is a mixture of Evolutionary Prototyping and Staged Delivery. It is discussed in section 2.3.5.

2.3.7 The Scrum Software Development Model

First used in 1987 by Ikujiro Nonaka and Hirotaka Takeuchi, Scrum is a highly productive software development model. Scrum is not an acronym but a term from rugby. It refers to a tight formation of forwards, who bind together in specific positions to get an out-of-play ball back into play (an action called a "scrumdown"). The Scrum software development model is an enhancement of the iterative and incremental approach of software development. Scrum implements a framework that empowers teams and strives for changes at any time in the development process. The two pillars on which Scrum is built are team empowerment and adaptability. To support the two pillars, Scrum defines a vocabulary and rules to reinforce common practices such as using small teams, enforcing a rule of not interrupting people who are working, and having a single source of work prioritization.

Definition

The goal of Scrum is to control the unpredictability and risk involved in software development. The result is the flexibility to change at any time in the process, leading to responsiveness and reliability.

The various phases defined in a Scrum project are shown in Figure 2.7.

The planning, architecture, and closure phases are linear in flow, whereas the *sprints* are iterative development cycles:

1. Planning phase: The new release definition is created based on the current known backlog of uncompleted tasks. In addition, a cost and schedule estimate is developed. If a new system is planned, then both conceptualization and analysis are done. For existing systems, this phase consists of limited analysis of the new functionality.

2. Architecture/high-level design phase: The architectural design, modifications, and high-level design of new or additional features are defined.

3. *Sprints*: These are the iterative cycles of software development. To proceed to the closure phase, management determines when the time, competition, quality, or functionality goals have been met and the iterations are complete. This approach is also known as *concurrent engineering*. A sprint is usually defined for one- to four-week periods of development; the interval time depends on complexity, risk, and the degree of oversight desired. The risk is assessed continuously, with risk controls and mitigations defined. One or more development teams work on one or more sprints at the same time. Each sprint consists of the following activities:

   Develop: For all changes to the system the following tasks are performed: A work packet is opened, and the team proceeds to the domain analysis, design, implementation, testing, and documentation of the changes.

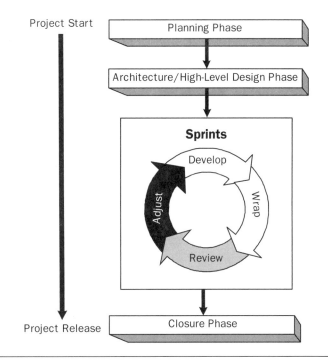

Figure 2.7 The Scrum Software Development Model

Wrap: The packets are closed, the executable version of the changes is created, and a description is provided of how backlog requirements have been implemented.

Review: The members of all teams meet to present their work and review work in progress, raising and resolving issues and problems and adding new items to the backlog. In addition, the risk is reviewed and appropriate mitigations are defined.

Adjust: All the information from the review meeting is gathered and implemented in packets.

4. Closure phase: If the management team feels that the variables of time, competition, requirements, cost, and quality support release of the product, the release is declared closed and the closure phase is entered. The main focus of this phase is to prepare the product for general release. This includes tasks such as integration, system test, user documentation, and preparation of training and marketing materials.

Pros

The Scrum model is designed to respond to the unpredictability of changes in external conditions and in the development environment throughout the cycle. In addition, the methodology frees the developers to focus on project development as learning occurs and the environment changes. Object-oriented technologies provide the basis for the Scrum technology. Objects, or product features, offer a discrete and manageable environment.

Cons

Procedural code development is inappropriate for the Scrum model because of its high number of intertwined interfaces. Also, in stable environments the traditional methodologies might be more efficient.

Variations

None.

2.3.8 The Adaptive Software Development Model

Unlike the traditional software development models, the Adaptive Software Development model takes into consideration that the system is not completely known at the start of the project and that the requirements can change rapidly. This is reflected in the three components of this model:

1. Speculate: This is the planning activity, when the goal or vision is defined (in traditional models this is the requirements engineering component). The word "planning" is avoided because the model anticipates that the goal will change during the course of development. This means that the product that was originally planned for might be different from the end solution. But the product that will be developed is what the customer really wants. This is in contrast to what often happens: The product meets the requirements but is not what the customer wants and needs.
2. Collaborate: This is defined as active communication between all parties involved. Open and active communication is identified as the base of success for the project.

3. Learn: This component involves evaluating the products of short iterations and learning from mistakes. Implementing ideas for improvement is a key practice in Adaptive Software Development.

The Adaptive Software Development model is an iterative, risk- and mission-driven, component-based, time-boxed, and change-tolerant process.

Definition

Figure 2.8 illustrates the Adaptive Software Development model.

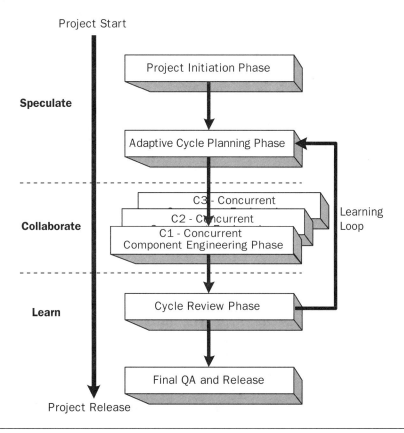

Figure 2.8 The Adaptive Software Development Model

The Adaptive Software Development model consists of the following activities:

1. The project initiation phase: The executive sponsor gathers information on the intent of the project, a firm idea of its scope, the intended schedule, and a projected resource utilization plan. For the customer, the project initiation phase constitutes a cost and benefit analysis and identification of the needed business functionality. The developer obtains information about the product to be developed as well as business information showing the intent behind the project.

2. The adaptive cycle planning phase: The first step in the cycle planning is to determine the project time-box. This is followed by the determination of the optimal number of cycles, including their time frames. For each cycle, a statement of objectives is written. In addition, the primary components, technologies, and support components are assigned to the cycles. The final step is to develop a project task list.

3. Concurrent component engineering phase: In this phase, the components are engineered and implemented. To speed development time and to produce more features in one cycle, more than one component can be developed in parallel.

4. Cycle review phase: The review at the end of a cycle should answer the following questions: Is the project on track (schedule, scope, defect level, resources)? Are the project artifacts still valid? Does each delivered component comply with the quality standards, technical specifications, and customer expectations? Has the work been done efficiently and effectively? All that information is used to make sure that the software delivered is actually the software the customer wants. The result of the review is fed into the learning loop to be used in improving and adapting the forthcoming cycles.

5. Final QA and release: After the final cycle is finished, a final quality audit is performed to make sure all the goals of the project have been achieved before the product is released to the customer.

The learning loop shown in Figure 2.8 is more than the kind of feedback loop found in other software development models. The learning loop in the Adaptive Software Development model answers the questions of step 4 and therefore gives vital information for the succeeding steps of the project. In addition, the released product is not necessarily the exact product that was originally speculated about but rather is the product that the customer wants or needs. This difference is crucial. Objectives, technologies, and requirements often change during the course of a project, but they are not considered because the process cannot react to changes midstream. The goal of the Adaptive Software Development model is to consider midstream changes as the natural flow of projects and to incorporate them into the development model.

Pros

The Adaptive Software Development model works very well for smaller teams (four to eight people) when the requirements technologies are uncertain or domain knowledge is missing. The model allows the team to speculate about the final product without providing a detailed plan up front. In this way, the team can continuously adjust the final product over the course of the project. The model also includes processes for tracking progress and identifying problem areas (scope, schedule, changing requirements) early on.

Cons

In areas of predictable requirements and technologies, the traditional methods will probably work more efficiently than the Adaptive model. In addition, managing an Adaptive project is very different from managing projects developed with the traditional models because the Adaptive approach is result-oriented rather than flow-oriented (like the Waterfall model).

Variations

None.

2.3.9 The Unified Process Software Development Model

The authors of the Unified Modeling Language (UML) defined a software engineering model called the Unified Process (UP). The Unified Process is a risk- and use-driven, architecture-centric, iterative and incremental software development model. This is a mature and open model. You may be familiar with the Rational Unified Process (RUP), which is a commercial extension of the Unified Process. The Rational Unified Process is entirely compatible with the Unified Process, but the RUP is more comprehensive and detailed.

Definition

The Unified Process is built on three basic principles:

- Use cases and risk identification plus mitigation
- Architectural design
- Iterative and incremental development

Figure 2.9 shows the Unified Process Software Development Model.

The Unified Process defines four phases. Each phase consists of one or more iterations, and each iteration is divided into five core workflow items: requirements, analysis, design, implementation, and test. The time spent in each part of the workflow depends on the phase the project is in. For example, in the inception phase most of the time is typically spent in the requirements part. In contrast, in the implementation phase most of the time is spent in the construction workflow.

Following is a breakdown of the phases, including their definitions and focuses:

1. Inception phase: The goal of the inception phase is to get the project started. Tasks include conducting a feasibility study, creating a business case, capturing requirements, and identifying risks. The focus in each of the five core workflow items is as follows:

   Requirements: Requirements are captured to help to scope the project.

   Analysis: A business analysis is done and the risk is analyzed.

   Design: The initial architectural document is developed.

   Implementation: A proof of concept or technology prototype might be developed.

   Test: Testing is usually not conducted because the prototypes typically are thrown away. But if the prototypes are evolved to a product, then testing might take place in this workflow.

2. Elaboration phase: In the elaboration phase the architectural baseline is created, the risk assessment is refined, quality attributes are defined, use cases are captured for 80 percent of the functional requirements, a detailed construction plan is defined, and a project plan (including cost, resources, time, equipment, and staff) is formulated. The tasks to be accomplished in the five core workflows for this phase are as follows:

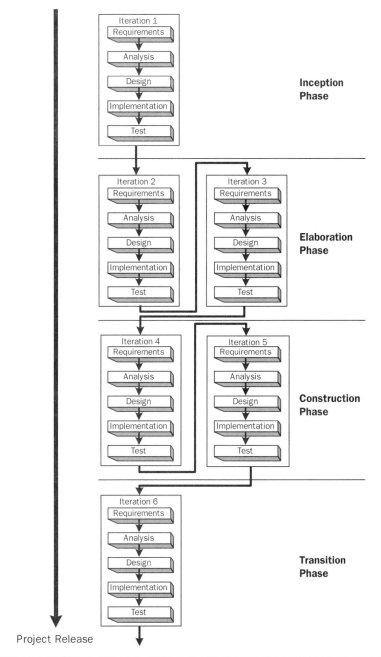

Figure 2.9 The Unified Process Software Development Model

Requirements: Requirements are refined.

Analysis: System goals are defined, and risk assessment is updated.

Design: A solid architecture is created.

Implementation: The baseline for the architecture is implemented.

Test: The new architectural baseline is reviewed and tested.

3. Construction phase: The construction phase focuses on the completion of the requirements, analysis, and design. In addition, the implementation is finished without compromising the design. The goal is to avoid "quick fixes" that often occur under time pressure and corrupt the design, resulting in low quality and high maintenance costs.

    Requirements: Requirements are completed, with special attention paid to ensuring that none were missed.

    Analysis: The system model is completely analyzed.

    Design: The design model is completed.

    Implementation: The initial product is implemented.

    Test: The initial product is tested.

4. Transition phase: The transition phase starts after the initial product testing has been performed and the system has been finally deployed. The goal is to release the product to the customer. All problems found in testing are fixed or deferred to the next version, and the product is prepared for rollout.

    Requirements: Usually not applicable in this phase. Requirements that are found to have problems may be deleted from the current release and deferred to a later release.

    Analysis: Usually not applicable in this phase. Problems that are found during testing may be analyzed for deferral to the next version.

    Implementation: Bugs found during testing may be corrected at this stage

    Design: The design may be adapted if problems are found in testing.

    Test: Integration testing, system testing, and acceptance testing are performed.

Pros

The Unified Process is a mature software engineering model. It is an iterative, requirements-driven, architecture-based approach to development. At the end of each phase, a go/no-go decision point provides visibility to managers on the status of the project.

Cons

The Unified Process does not cover the entire software life cycle. For example, maintenance and support are not covered. Therefore, it can be seen as strictly a development process.

Variations

The Rational Unified Process adds three core supporting workflows—configuration and change management, project management, and environment—to the model. It also adds more details and supporting tools. The Enterprise Unified Process (EUP) adds an infrastructure management workflow.

2.3.10 The Extreme Programming Software Development Model

Like the Adaptive Software Development model, the Extreme Programming (XP) model is a flexible, lightweight, people- and result-oriented development process that allows for requirements changes at any time during development. Extreme Programming defines 12 core practices that are essential to the success of an XP project:

- Test-driven development: Development depends heavily on tests. This can go as far as the test being written before the code to be tested is implemented.
- Planning game: Planning is done at the team level to ensure buy-in by the developers, as well as accurate estimates and simple, maintainable solutions.
- On-site customer: Requirements are written by the customer in the form of user stories. Thus, it is important to have a customer on site to quickly resolve questions that arise during development.
- Pair programming: Two people program together to ensure quality, code review, and mentoring.

- Continuous integration: Code modules are integrated into the project continuously to avoid a "big bang" at the end of the project.
- Refactoring: This practice keeps the code maintainable and the design as simple as possible.
- Small releases: Release cycles are usually two weeks.
- Simple design: The software is not overengineered; the simplest effective solution is implemented, and overhead is avoided.
- System metaphor: An explanation is developed of how the software will work.
- Collective code ownership: Everyone should know every part of the project.
- Coding conventions: Compliance with coding guidelines is important to keep the code easy to read and consistent.
- Sustainable pace: Developers work 40-hour weeks with overtime only if necessary. The project should not turn into a death march and burn people out.

Any project using XP will use all of these 12 core practices. The practices complement each other and make Extreme Programming work.

Definition

Figure 2.10 shows the Extreme Programming software development model.
For a team using all 12 core practices, the development process can be broken down into the following phases:

1. Customer input, architectural spike (a *spike* is an experiment that can be done by a single developer): In the beginning of the project, the requirements are established with so-called user stories. *User stories* are basically descriptions of the features the customer wants in the customer's language. In addition to the user stories, a *system metaphor* is defined to explain in plain language how the overall system works. Defining a metaphor can be seen as the vision statement for the project.
2. Release planning phase: The developers review the user stories and estimate the difficulty of implementing the features. The customer then prioritizes the requested features and lays out an initial project plan. The initial release plan will not be accurate, but it is good enough to get started. Later in the project the team will revise

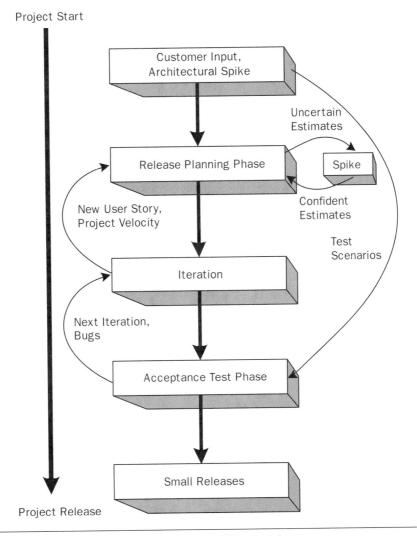

Project Start

Project Release

Figure 2.10 The Extreme Programming (XP) Model

the project plan using the knowledge gained through experience in several iterations.

3. Iteration: Each iteration starts with the planning of the current iteration. An iteration usually lasts no more than two weeks, and at the end useful, running software is delivered to the customer. The customer presents the features desired for the next iteration. The

programmers break the user stories down into tasks and estimate the work necessary to implement them based on the work accomplished in earlier iterations. The iteration plan then drives the development. If there are unfinished tasks at the end of the iteration, they are fed into the iteration planning for the next iteration. From development, new user stories may evolve, and information on the project velocity is extracted to feed into the iteration planning of later iterations.

4. Acceptance test phase: The customer tests the functionality of the current iteration. The functionality then is either approved for release or is rescheduled for changes or fixes in later iterations.

5. Small releases: The release cycle for small releases is about two weeks.

As you can see, communication and team effort are key focus points of Extreme Programming. An on-site customer implies a close relationship between the developers and the customer. Pair programming and the planning game help the team's internal communications.

Pros

For small project teams (up to about 12 programmers) in an environment of fast-changing or uncertain requirements, the Extreme Programming model works very well. It enables close customer interaction with short release cycles to show progress. It prioritizes tasks so that the customer's most important functionality is implemented first. The short iteration cycles enable adjustment of the release plan according to the actual progress made.

Cons

For large or distributed project teams, Extreme Programming is difficult because it depends heavily on the interaction among all participating parties. In addition, for projects with stable requirements, the traditional models work more efficiently. To achieve the best possible efficiency in Extreme Programming, even the office space should be set up to support close communication and pair programming.

Variations:

None.

2.4 Conclusion

Throughout the course of this book we use the Unified Process lifecycle model. This decision is based on the following reasoning.

Because the requirements for the project are more or less static, the Unified Process is a good choice. UP also enables us to explore the technological uncertainty at the beginning of the project by building a throw-away prototype. In addition, the traditional, well-structured approach with go/no-go decision points lets us track our progress and identify problems at the end of each iteration.

Within the iterations, we use the following icons to identify the core workflows:

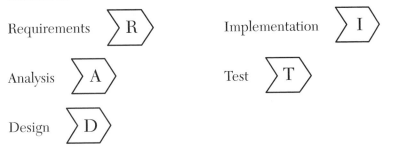

Requirements $\quad R$

Implementation $\quad I$

Analysis $\quad A$

Test $\quad T$

Design $\quad D$

The following icons are used to differentiate programming and software engineering sections throughout the rest of the book:

Programming Section

Software Engineering Section

2.5 References for Further Reading

General Project Management and Software Engineering Models

Jim Arlow and Ila Neustadt, *UML and the Unified Process* (Boston: Addison-Wesley, 2001)

Ken Auer, Ward Cunningham, and Roy Miller, *Extreme Programming Applied* (Boston: Addison-Wesley, 2001)

Kent Beck, *Extreme Programming Explained* (Reading, MA: Addison-Wesley, 1999)

Barry Boehm et al., *Developing Multimedia Applications with the WinWin Spiral Model* (http://sunset.usc.edu/publications/TECHRPTS/1998/usccse98-512/usccse98-512.pdf)

Barry Boehm et al., "Using the WinWin Spiral Model: A Case Study: (*IEEE Computer,* July 1998, 33–44)

Grady Booch et al., *UML Users' Guide* (Reading, MA: Addison-Wesley, 1998)

Dick Hamlet and Joe Maybee, *The Engineering of Software* (Boston: Addison-Wesley, 2001)

James A. Highsmith III, *Adaptive Software Development* (New York: Dorset House Publishing, 2000)

Graham Ian and Aan Graham, *Migration to Object Technology* (Reading, MA: Addison-Wesley, 1995)

Ivar Jacobson et al., *The Unified Software Development Process* (Reading, MA: Addison-Wesley, 1999)

Pankaj Jalote, *CMM in Practice* (Boston: Addison-Wesley, 2000)

Philippe Kruchten, *The Rational Unified Process* (Boston: Addison-Wesley, 2000)

Steve McConnell, *Rapid Development* (Redmond, WA: Microsoft Press, 1996)

Steve McConnell, *After the Gold Rush: Creating a True Profession of Software Engineering* (Redmond, WA: Microsoft Press, 1999)

Dan Paulish, *Architecture-Centric Software Project Management: A Practical Guide* (Boston: Addison-Wesley, 2002)

Hirotaka Takeuchi and Ikujiro Nonaka, "The New Product Development Game" (*Harvard Business Review,* January-February 1986, 137–146)

Hirotaka Takeuchi and Ikujiro Nonaka, *The Knowledge Creating Company: How Japanese Companies Create the Dynamics of Innovation* (New York: Oxford University Press, 1995)

http://www.stickyminds.com/sitewide.asp?Function=search&Kind=articlesandpapers&infotype=ART%2CCOL&freetext=*

www.extremeprogramming.org

www.xprogramming.com

CHAPTER 3

A .NET Prototype

 Unified Process:
Inception Phase and First Iteration

3.1 Getting Started

To get the project started we begin the inception phase of the Unified Process. In the first iteration, we must establish the feasibility of using .NET technology for the application development. As stipulated by the Unified Process, we will follow the five core workflows (Requirements, Analysis, Design, Implementation, and Test) in all iterations.

3.2 Evaluating .NET for Windows Client Applications

R Within this iteration we need to evaluate whether the use of Microsoft Developer Studio.NET is beneficial for the development of Windows applications. Also, we would like to see whether it is feasible to use C# instead of C++, something that might accelerate development time because, unlike C++, C# not only provides managed extensions but also is specifically developed for use in .NET.

A wide range of technologies can be used to develop Windows applications, including Visual Basic, C++, and Java. Because many Windows developers in our company are experienced C++ programmers and are familiar with Visual Studio 6.0, we need to explore the learning curve that team members have to go through when switching to the .NET technology. This effort must be weighed against the benefits that come with .NET, such as garbage collection for managed code, rich class libraries, and multiple language support.

3.3 Our First .NET Application

> A

It is important to stay focused on the requirements and not start developing an unnecessarily complex application. Therefore we choose a simple set of goals:

- Using the Microsoft Visual Studio.NET integrated development environment (IDE)
- Designing simple Windows forms
- Getting started with C# programming
- Using the .NET class library

To realize these goals we will implement a simple application, which we will call SmartNotes, that allows placing of electronic notes anywhere on the desktop. We will also integrate a "remind me later" function into this application. This should be sufficient for a first .NET technology evaluation.

3.4 Prototyping

> D

A common way to fulfill the goals of the inception phase is prototyping. Based on the experience gained from developing a prototype, project teams can make better technology decisions, create better designs, and build better implementations. Usually a prototype is a basic implementation of functionality to show whether a solution is feasible within given constraints. It is commonly used to evaluate the following:

- Unknown or new technologies
- Performance of hardware or software implementations
- Usage of system resources
- Alternative solutions

When the prototype is completed, two scenarios are possible: Either the prototype is thrown away and development starts over from scratch, or the prototype is evolved into the product. In the latter case the prototype undergoes a design and functional review, and adjustments are made where necessary to lead into a product.

The prototype developed throughout this chapter will be used only to evaluate feasibility and will not undergo further quality measurement to lead to product code in later iterations.

More about Prototypes The use and lifecycle models for prototypes are described in Steve McConnell's books *Rapid Development* (Redmond, WA: Microsoft Press, 1996) and *Code Complete* (Redmond, WA: Microsoft Press, 1993). Another good reference is *The Engineering of Software,* by Dick Hamlet and Joe Maybee (Boston, MA: Addison-Wesley, 2001). Readers interested in the definition of prototypes in terms of the Software Engineering Institute's Capability Maturity Model (CMM) will find Pankaj Jalote's book *CMM in Practice* (Reading, MA: Addison-Wesley, 1999) very helpful.

3.5 Implementing the SmartNotes Application

> I

Let's start with some practical exercises. It is assumed that you have successfully installed and started Microsoft Visual Studio.NET on your machine. Figure 3.1 shows the default startup screen.

Microsoft's development environment layout is by default tiled into three windows. The main window in the center is the document window,

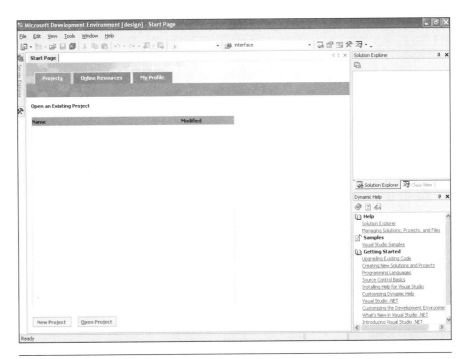

Figure 3.1 Microsoft Development Environment

which displays the Start Page tab. On the right side of the screen are two windows. The upper window contains Solution Explorer and Class View as well as Help Index and Help Search. The lower window displays either Dynamic Help (shown) or properties of selected objects. All the windows are tabbed, and you can switch between different contents using the tabs on the top or bottom of each window. You will learn more about these windows as we develop our first .NET application.

3.5.1 Creating a New Project

To create a new project for the SmartNotes application, click on the New Project button on the start page. In the New Project dialog, you can choose among various project types and templates. Click on Windows Application in the Visual C# Projects category. Then name the project SmartNotes, and choose a location to store the project files. The application wizard will then create a workspace containing a simple Windows application: an empty dialog box. Figure 3.2 shows the generated workspace.

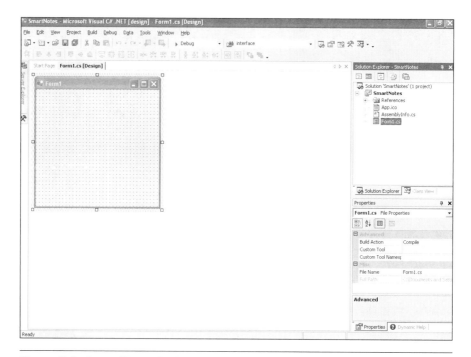

Figure 3.2 SmartNotes Project Workspace

Next, run the application generated by the application wizard. Compile and run it via the Build menu, or press F5 to do both. An empty window will be displayed.

3.5.2 Modifying Form Properties

Now we start modifying the appearance of the window to look something like a sticky note. To do so, close the window and choose the form in the design view (Form1.cs [Design]). Figure 3.3 shows the lower-right window on the screen, which now contains the properties of the form. You can modify a property value by selecting it in the Properties window and changing the value in the second column.

Let's try it out by changing the background color in the BackColor field to Info. We also want to give our form the look and feel of a window with a smaller frame. To achieve this, change the field FormBorderStyle to SizableToolWindow. Finally, we set the window title by changing the Text field to SmartNotes. Running the application again shows a small yellow window that is starting to look more like a little sticky note.

We encourage you to experiment further with the properties of a form. For example, you can prevent other applications from overlapping the notes window, or you can play with the opacity, a new feature introduced for Windows forms in .NET. In the remainder of this book we no longer

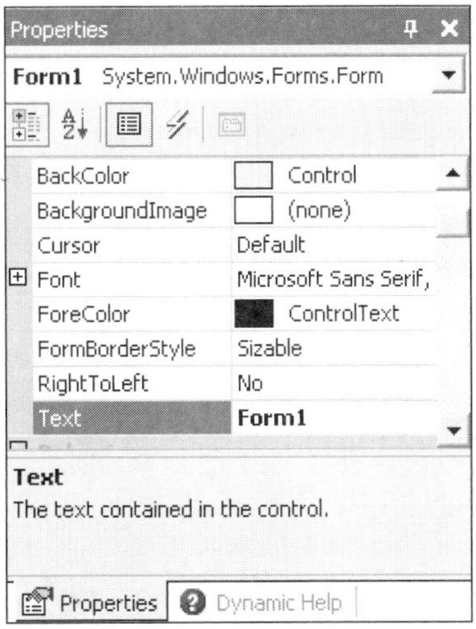

Figure 3.3 Properties Window

describe the procedure for changing object properties in detail but only give a table of properties and their new values.

Properties of Form1

BackColor	Info
FormBorderStyle	SizableToolWindow
Text	SmartNotes
TopMost	True
Opacity	85%

Some controls provide a large number of properties. Therefore, it might be easier to locate the properties given in the tables by pressing the alphabetic button in the Properties window.

3.5.3 Adding Controls to a Form

Next we will bring the notes window to life by adding a text field to the form. To do this, open the Toolbox (displayed in the far left of the screen) and drag a `TextBox` element into the design view of Form1. Alternatively, you can use a `RichTextBox` element, which offers additional features like colored text. If the Toolbox is not visible in your environment, select it from the View menu.

In the design view we can modify the location of the text field, but to resize it to the height of the form, we must set the Multiline property. Also, accept the property that lets users use the Return key to jump to the next line while editing text. After these modifications are finished, we can resize the text field to entirely fill the form window. Also change the background color, remove the border around the text box, and change the default text to something meaningful. If you wish, you also can change the font for the text field by expanding the `Font` property first and then adjusting the font face, style, size, or color.

Properties of textBox1

AcceptsReturn	True
Multiline	True
BackColor	Info
BorderStyle	None
Text	Enter your notes here . . .

When running the application now, you can enter multiple lines of text in the SmartNotes window. However, if you resize the window you will observe that the text field is not adjusted to the size of the window. To change this behavior, modify the Anchor setting in the Layout property. After you click on Anchor, a small window appears, as shown in Figure 3.4. Select all four boxes to bind all sides of the text box to the form size. Now the size of the text box will adjust to the size of the form window in which it is contained.

Without doing any "real" programming, we have created a simple notes application. What remains is to add the "smart" to it by implementing the "remind me later" functionality. This requires the user to pick a reminder date and time. For that, we add a link label that will open a new input form. Drag and drop a link label control from the Toolbox onto the form in the design view, and adjust its properties.

Properties of linkLabel1

(Name)	myReminderLabel
TextAlign	MiddleRight
Anchor	Bottom, Right
Text	Remind me later...

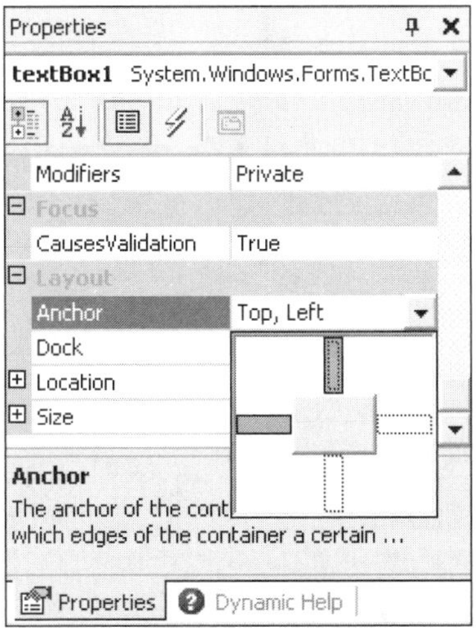

Figure 3.4 Anchor Settings

3.5.4 Adding a Form to the Project

A new input form is needed for the user to select the reminder date and time. To add a new form, go to Solution Explorer (upper-right window) and right-click on the SmartNotes project. This will display a context menu. There, first choose Add and then Add Windows Form, as shown in Figure 3.5.

Set the name of the new form to `Reminder.cs`, and click Open. This will automatically show the form's design view (`Reminder.cs` [Design]). As with creating a new Windows application project, the form is initially empty. First, we change the `TopMost` property to True to prevent the yellow notes window from overlapping this dialog, which also has the `TopMost` property set to True. This form does not need to be resizable. Change the `FormBorderStyle` to FixedDialog.

Properties of Reminder

TopMost	True
FormBorderStyle	FixedDialog

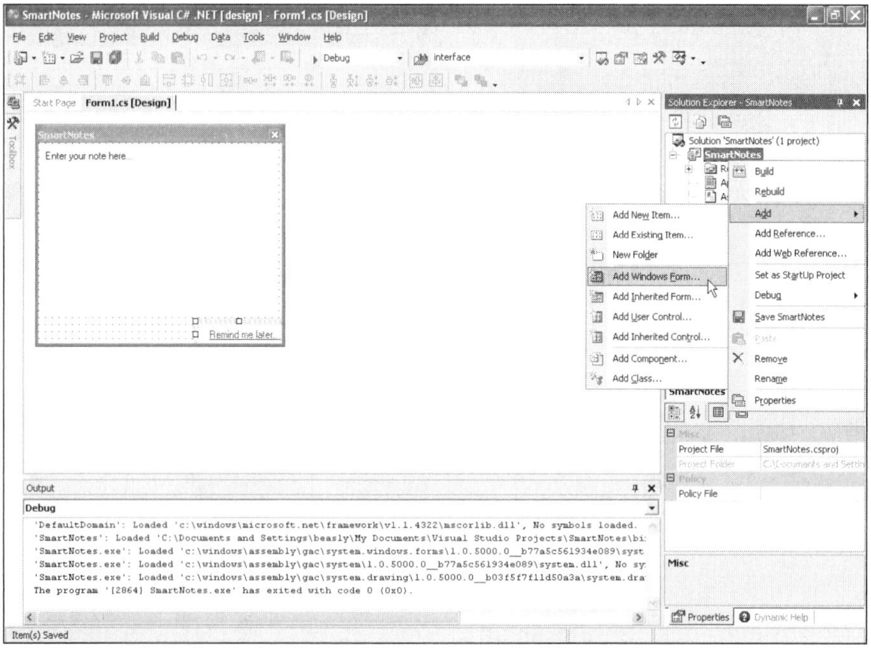

Figure 3.5 Adding a Windows Form

Next we will add the functionality that lets users suspend a note until a certain date and time. First let's add a control for picking the time. We drag and drop the `DateTimePicker` control from the Toolbox into the form's design view.

Properties of dateTimePicker1

(Name)	myTimePicker
Modifiers	Public
Format	Time
ShowUpDown	True

After adjusting the properties, drag and drop a `MonthCalendar` control from the Toolbox onto the form. Users will use this control to choose the date when the note will be activated again.

Properties of monthCalendar1

Name	myMonthCalendar
Modifiers	Public

Finally we place an OK button on the form, which completes the task of picking a reminder time and date. For this, add a `Button` control to the form and modify its properties to result in an OK command. Figure 3.6 shows the design view of the completed input form.

Properties of Button1

Text	OK
DialogResult	OK

3.5.5 Creating an Event Handler

Now that the design of our new input form is completed, it will be called when the user clicks on the link label in the yellow notes window. Generating an event handler for this link label is simple. You switch to the Form1.cs design view and double-click on the label. Visual Studio.NET automatically creates a stub for the event handler, so you simply fill in the blanks with customized code to react to the event.

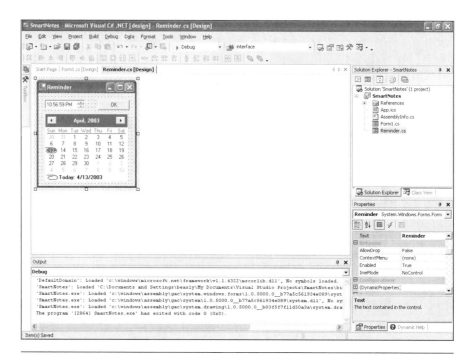

Figure 3.6 Completed Reminder Input Form

Listing 3.1 shows the generated method for the mouse click event. We fill this stub with code that first creates a new instance of the reminder form (class `Reminder`) and then calls the `ShowDialog()` member to display it. If the input form was closed with the OK button, a conditional block is entered in which the window will be temporarily hidden (we'll look at this code next). For now we check our progress by starting the application. Clicking on the link label now should show the input form for the reminder date and time.

Listing 3.1 Event Handler for Link Label

```
private void myReminderLabel_LinkClicked(object sender,
  System.Windows.Forms.LinkLabelLinkClickedEventArgs e)
{
  Reminder dlg = new Reminder();
  if (dlg.ShowDialog() == System.Windows.Forms.DialogResult.OK)
  {
    // retrieve user inputs and hide window
  }
}
```

3.5.6 Implementing a Timer

To complete the SmartNotes prototype we must go a bit deeper into C# programming. These are the three main steps that remain to be implemented:

1. Retrieve the reminder date and time from the input form, and store it in a member variable.
2. Hide the window.
3. Periodically check the reminder against the current time, and restore the notes window if the reminder date has expired.

We begin by adding a member variable to the `Form1` class that stores the reminder time and date. This task can be done easily with the help of the IDE. Switch from Solution Explorer to Class View in the upper-right window, and open the context menu of the class `Form1` by right-clicking on the class name. Then select the menu Add and then Add Field. A dialog will prompt you to add the access, type, and name of the field. Because this member is accessed only within the class itself, we change the field access to private. As shown in Figure 3.7, enter `DateTime` in the field type and set the field name to `myReminderTime`.

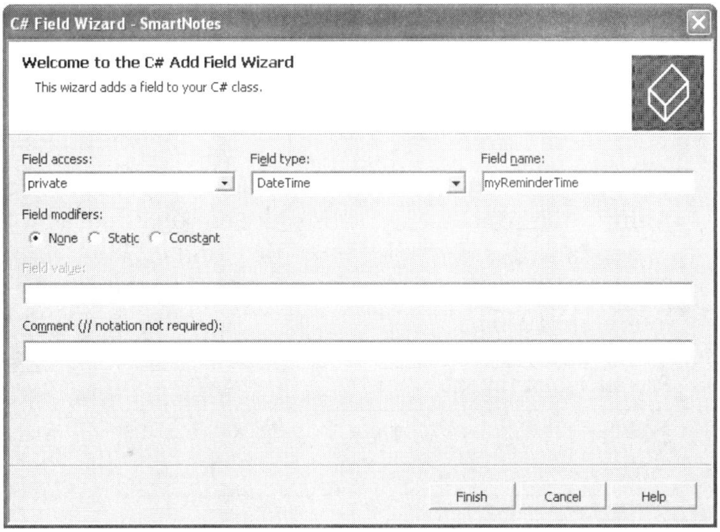

Figure 3.7 C# Field Wizard

The value of `myReminderTime` can easily be computed by adding the values of the selected date to the hours, minutes, and seconds of the selected time from the reminder dialog form. After we compute and store the time until the note should be suspended, the window is hidden from the desktop. Listing 3.2 shows the code for these two steps.

Listing 3.2 Added Member and Completed Event Handler for Link Label

```
// member field that stores the wakeup time
private System.DateTime myReminderTime;

private void myReminderLabel_LinkClicked(object sender,
  System.Windows.Forms.LinkLabelLinkClickedEventArgs e)
{
  Reminder dlg = new Reminder();
  if (dlg.ShowDialog() == System.Windows.Forms.DialogResult.OK)
  {
    // retrieve inputs and add date and time
    myReminderTime =
      dlg.myMonthCalendar.SelectionStart
      .AddHours(dlg.myTimePicker.Value.Hour)
      .AddMinutes(dlg.myTimePicker.Value.Minute)
      .AddSeconds(dlg.myTimePicker.Value.Second);

    // hide window
    this.Visible = false;
  }
}
```

Before we run the application again we also must add the code that restores the window after it is hidden. To periodically check the current time against the reminder time, drag and drop a `Timer` control from the Toolbox onto the `Form1.cs` design view. Then enable the timer, and set the interval to 1000 ms.

Properties of timer1

Enabled	True
Interval	1000

You associate an event handler with the timer by double-clicking on the control in the design view. Within the handler you must add a conditional statement that displays the window when the reminder time is up. The code for the timer is shown in Listing 3.3.

Listing 3.3 Event Handler for Timer

```
private void timer1_Tick(object sender, System.EventArgs e)
{
  if (myReminderTime.CompareTo(DateTime.Now) < 0)
  {
    // time is up, show window
    this.Visible = true;
  }
}
```

This concludes the implementation of the SmartNotes prototype. Figure 3.8 shows our first fully functional .NET application in action. Next we will assess what we have learned so far about using Microsoft Visual Studio.NET for developing smart Windows client applications.

Figure 3.8 SmartNotes Prototype Application

3.6 Visual Studio.NET: Platform of Choice

.NET comes with a powerful, rich class library that enables the creation of complex applications with a minimum of effort. The prototype application has shown that the IDE makes it easy to design user interfaces and implement the underlying logic. Complex canned user interface elements, such as the monthly calendar, reduce the programming effort. They are no longer an exclusive feature of Visual Basic but are available to all .NET programming languages.

Furthermore, programming in C# does not seem to introduce a high learning curve for developers who have C++ experience. In addition, C# gives us managed code and garbage collection, which make applications much more robust. They also reduce the implementation effort for almost any task because the developer can focus on logistics instead of resource management.

Developing the prototype has demonstrated that the .NET Framework, together with Microsoft Visual Studio and C#, makes a feasible platform for developing smart client applications for Windows.

3.7 References for Further Reading

Tom DeMarco and Timothy Lister, *Waltzing with Bears: Managing Risk on Software Projects* (New York: Dorset House, 2003)

Reinhold Ploesch, *Assertions, Scenarios and Prototypes: An Integrated Approach to High Quality Software* (Heidelberg, Germany: Springer Verlag, 2003)

CHAPTER 4

Project Planning

Unified Process:
Inception Phase and Second Iteration

This chapter continues the inception phase and describes the second iteration of the Online Photo Shop sample project. The goal is to define the project and to get it started. Therefore, the main focus in this iteration is on project planning.

In the inception and elaboration phase it is crucial to achieve agreement between the project team and the customer on the requirements and on the expectations for the functionality (expectations must be set to a realistic level) as well as to agree on the procedural approach that is to be taken to implement the project. A good practice is to plan the project in very close collaboration with the customer and transparently to all parties involved. This sets the groundwork for open communication and collaboration, which in the end is the base for success. Even though our customer may not be interested in the coding standards used by the development team or in how the reference documentation is created, these details should be discussed with, or at least communicated to, the customer.

Close collaboration and information exchange with the customer can help to build trust and additional confidence in the abilities of the project team, especially if a realistic, structured, and well-thought-through approach can be shown. In addition, transparent project planning lets the customer and each project team member know exactly what is expected, and we can immediately incorporate improvement suggestions from all involved parties. Usually, projects have major problems with communication between customer and project team only when there is too little communication, and never when there is too much (if indeed there can be too much communication).

As described in Chapter 2, the main focus in the inception phase is on the requirements and analysis workflows. Nevertheless all iterations must work through all five core workflows. More specifically, the following goals are set for the various workflows in the inception phase:

- Requirements: Requirements are captured to help to scope the project.
- Analysis: A business analysis is done, and the risk is analyzed.
- Design: The initial architectural design is developed.
- Implementation: A proof of concept or technology prototype may be developed.
- Test: Testing is usually not done because the prototypes are typically thrown away. In case the prototypes will be evolved to a product, the team may develop tests for the prototype.

We spend most of our time in this iteration on capturing and analyzing requirements. However, the design workflow defines and describes the architectural framework. The implementation workflow in this phase usually does not focus on actual coding but instead focuses on the implementation of procedures such as coding conventions and prototyping (as described in Chapter 3). Because there is no actual coding other than throw-away prototypes, the testing workflow does not really apply to the inception phase. Nevertheless, if the definition of test is stretched a little, it could be stated that software development artifacts (documents in this case) are usually "tested" by document reviews before they are released.

The inception phase defines the following go/no-go goals that are to be met:

- Prototype (if necessary)
- Project vision (considering main requirements and constraints)
- Business case
- Initial use case model (10 percent to 20 percent complete)
- Main requirements with unique identifier key
- Initial project plan (including iteration planning)
- Initial risk assessment
- Initial architecture

These goals define the to-do list for the project that we must complete to move to the next phase. This chapter addresses all the defined goals (except the prototype development for feasibility study) to finish the inception phase.

Unlike many real-life projects, the documentation for the project described in this book is not split into many different documents; instead, all the artifacts and information needed are collected in the software engineering sections of each chapter. For a small project team working on a small-scale project, this may be the most efficient way to produce the artifacts. Nevertheless, we should mention that, depending on the type and environment of the project, one or more documents may be produced. This means that each of the artifacts or groups of artifacts described in this chapter could be split into additional documents if needed (most likely this would be done for larger projects). On the other hand, in small projects (such as the Online Photo Shop project) all the information is collected in one document. It is the task of the project management to decide which approach will best fit the particular project.

As stated before, for this project all the information will be in one document: this book. Each chapter will define clear go/no-go criteria at the beginning of each iteration. At the end of each iteration or chapter (one chapter is equivalent to one iteration for most of the book), the go/no-go criteria are evaluated. Depending on the evaluation, either we enter the next phase or iteration, or we must do some rework before proceeding. Having these strict go/no-go criteria in short intervals enables accurate project tracking.

4.1 The Project Vision and Business Case

> R

The goal, or *vision*, for this project is to provide software components to a printing and embossing business that allows online ordering of prints and other items—such as cups, cards, T-shirts, mouse pads, and so on—that can be customized with digital photos. The new software will open the business to a new and larger customer base, allowing for future growth.

4.2 The Initial Use Case Model

Although the project vision gives us some idea about the business goal for the project, it does not yet address the scope. To achieve a detailed project agreement, we must create a high-level requirements specification that defines the scope of the project by listing functional and nonfunctional requirements. It should be emphasized that developing the high-level requirements specification often requires the involvement of many people

Table 4.1 UML-Defined Software Modeling Diagrams

Category	Diagrams
Structural diagrams	Class diagram, object diagram, component diagram, deployment diagram
Model management diagrams	Package diagram, subsystem diagram, model diagram
Behavior diagrams	Use case diagram, sequence diagram, activity diagram, collaboration diagram, state-chart diagram

with very different backgrounds, including business or customer representatives, managers, engineers, and salespersons.

During the course of this book the Unified Modeling Language (UML) is used for requirements gathering, requirements analysis, and software design. Altogether, UML defines 12 diagrams for modeling software systems. The diagrams are categorized in three groups, as shown in Table 4.1.

We will introduce several of the UML-defined diagrams, explaining them at the time they are first used. Class diagrams, package diagrams, sequence diagrams, and activity diagrams are introduced in this chapter and in Chapter 5. For more detailed information about UML, please see the references section.

A commonly used method to discover and break down high-level requirements in a well-understood language is the UML notion of *use case diagrams*. Figure 4.1 shows a high-level use case diagram for the Online Photo Shop project.

The symbols that look like people are *actors*. They represent outside persons or systems that interact with the system under development. For our project, there are two kinds of actors: the customer and the printing and embossing business. The use cases are visualized by ellipses and can be connected to other use cases to show their dependencies. The Online Photo Shop rectangle enclosing the use cases shows that these use cases are all part of the same system. It is also possible to create use case diagrams to visualize different systems by connecting two or more systems, showing their dependencies in the use case diagram.

The use case diagram in Figure 4.1 gives an overview of how the overall system will be used and of the external and internal interactions. Although this information is essential, it is not sufficient to capture all requirements. In our experience, use case diagrams are very useful to give a first overall

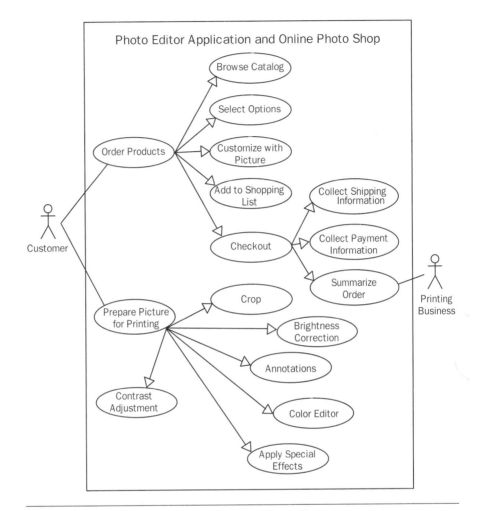

Figure 4.1 Use Case Diagram for Online Photo Shop

look at a system and to better illustrate how it fits into its environment. However, use case diagrams are not the most efficient method for adding details to requirements or for describing nonfunctional requirements (constraints, performance, and so on). To add this information, it is usually sufficient to develop a well-structured text document containing the initial use case diagram plus a description of all requirements. This doesn't mean that the use case diagram becomes obsolete after the inception phase; on the contrary, it will be well maintained throughout the entire project. It is a good practice to add new use cases whenever you see added value in extending the initial use case diagram.

4.2.1 Requirement Keys

To better identify the various requirements during all project phases, we assign a unique identifier, called a *key*, to each requirement. These keys let us trace each requirement throughout the core workflows and phases of the Unified Process. To ease the tracing process, we recommend avoiding the use of spaces and capitalized letters in the identifier name. Another good practice is to include a type specification in the keys because you may apply various procedures, such as code reviews, test, and so on, to various categories of requirements. In the field of medical devices, for example, life critical or hazardous functionalities require higher-quality measurements than do nonhazardous functionalities. For the Online Photo Shop project we distinguish between the categories shown in Table 4.2.

4.2.2 Using XML for Requirements Documents

Traditionally, you create a requirements specification document or table of requirements using a spreadsheet or word processor such as Excel or Word, or a text editor such as Framemaker, Tex, or Latex. The latter three

Table 4.2 Requirement Key Categories

Category	Description
F	This indicates a functional requirement describing a desired functionality or use case.
C	This requirement describes a general constraint of the system such as the targeted platforms.
P	Performance requirements are treated separately because they often change and need to be adapted to newly available hardware. In most cases performance requirements address the overall performance of a system and do not require unit testing.
R	Requirements that introduce a risk and therefore need special attention during implementation and test (for example, transmitting of credit card information online).

tools offer the big advantage of enforcing a structure on the document, letting the author focus on the content rather than the formatting. In addition, they create documents as simple text files, and that allows you to extract the requirement keys with little effort. However, these tools are not as easy to use and require training for the employees. Framemaker might be a good alternative for larger documents because the documents are edited using a WYSIWYG (what you see is what you get) view.

Framemaker also lets you save documents in plain XML format, which can be easily parsed. With the integration of the XML standard into new products such as C#, Visual Studio.NET, and Internet Explorer, we suggest the use of XML even for writing the requirements specification. For Microsoft Word, you must use a third-party tool (see, for example, www.logictran.com) to convert documents into XML format. This restriction will go away in Microsoft Word 2003.

We strongly encourage you to create the requirements document using a text editor and then export the document into XML format. Nevertheless, we show an example of how to create an XML requirements document without using any tool. In this way, you can learn the basics of XML and its use. The acquired knowledge will be useful when you try to trace the requirement keys through the stages of development in the transition phase.

Listing 4.1 shows a template requirements specification document defining one functional requirement key (F:image_crop) and a constraint (C:platform_os) for the target platform in the Online Photo Shop project. The requirement name consists of two parts in the XML file. The first part is the *prefix*, which identifies the category to which the requirement key belongs, as shown in Table 4.2. The second part is the actual name of the requirement. This approach lets us easily extract the category or requirement name when parsing the XML file with the help of a script, as shown later in the book.

Listing 4.1 RS.XML: XML Requirement Specification Template

```
<?xml version="1.0"?>
<doc>
    <assembly>
        <name>Online Photo Shop</name>
        <version>1.0</version>
    </assembly>
```

```
<requirements>

    <requirement name="F:image_crop">
        <summary>
        The editor should provide functionality to select a
        region of interest and crop an image to that region.
        </summary>
        <ref>img/crop_image.gif</ref>
    </requirement>

    <requirement name="C:platform_os">
        <summary>
        The target platform operating system is Windows XP
        Professional.
        </summary>
    </requirement>

</requirements>
</doc>
```

The structure of the document is fairly simple and easy to understand. XML requires each document to start with an `<?xml>` tag identifying the version of the XML standard used and to enclose the document with `<doc>` tags. Inside the `<doc>` tag we use the keyword `<assembly>` to begin a new system, and `<requirements>` to start a list of requirements for this system. The structure of the document can be defined according to the particular project needs. We choose to add a `<name>` and `<version>` tag to the assembly and to add a `<summary>` and optional `<ref>` tag for external references to each requirement.

The structure of XML is very clear, enabling easy addition of new requirements or even systems, but the readability of a plain XML document is not very good. This is where XSL stylesheets come into play. *XSL stylesheets* extract and format the requested data of an XML document in any desired way. Listing 4.2 shows an XSL stylesheet that transforms the XML requirement specification as shown in Listing 4.1 into an HTML file, which can be displayed using the Microsoft Internet Explorer Web browser. The XSL stylesheet shown in Listing 4.2 is provided with the sample solutions on the accompanying CD (RS.xsl). It can be customized and used as a template for other projects.

Listing 4.2 RS.XSL: XSL Requirement Specification Stylesheet

```xml
<?xml version="1.0" encoding="UTF-8" ?>
<xsl:stylesheet version="1.0"
  xmlns:xsl="http://www.w3.org/1999/XSL/Transform">
<xsl:template match="/">

<html>
<body>
  <h1>Requirement Specification</h1>
  <xsl:for-each select="/doc/assembly">
    <a>
      <xsl:attribute name="name">
        <xsl:value-of select="name" />
      </xsl:attribute>
      <h2>
        <xsl:value-of select="name" />
        V<xsl:value-of select="version" />
      </h2>
    </a>
    <table border="1" cellpadding="4" cellspacing="0">
      <tr bgcolor="#c0c0c0">
        <td><b>Requirement</b/td>
        <td><b>Type</b/td>
        <td><b>Summary</b/td>
      </tr>
      <xsl:for-each select="/doc/requirements/requirement">
        <tr>
          <td>
            <xsl:value-of select="substring-after(@name,':')" />
          </td>
          <td>
            <xsl:if test="starts with(@name,'C:')">
              Constraint</xsl:if>
            <xsl:if test="starts with(@name,'F:')">
              Functional</xsl:if>
            <xsl:if test="starts-with(@name,'R:')">
              <i>Risk</i></xsl:if>
            <xsl:if test="starts-with(@name,'P:')">
              Performance</xsl:if>
          </td>
          <td>
```

```
        <xsl:value-of select="summary" />
      </td>
    </tr>
  </xsl:for-each>
  </table>
  </xsl:for-each>
</body>
</html>
</xsl:template>
</xsl:stylesheet>
```

To associate the XML requirement specification document with this XSL stylesheet, we add the following line to the beginning of the XML document:

```
<?xml:stylesheet type="text/xsl" href="rs.xsl" ?>
```

Now we can open RS.XML with the Web browser, which is now linked to the stylesheet, and we can view a nicely formatted document. The HTML page lists the requirement keys, their category, and a summary, as shown in Figure 4.2.

Don't be discouraged if you don't yet fully understand the stylesheet file. You create the XSL file only once for a project, and you can use the provided XSL template as a starting point for other projects. It is also very likely that a stylesheet that meets the needs of a particular project already exists, or it can easily be developed by someone with XML knowledge in the project team.

It is not necessary for all the team members involved in defining the requirements to have knowledge about XSL or HTML. The advantage of having the requirements defined in an XML text file is that it not only lets us create nicely formatted HTML pages but also lets us extract information from it easily. For example, you can extract all requirement keys into a simple text file or even into a scripting job (to trace them to the actual implementation code or to determine test coverage).

Because of these advantages, we describe all requirements for Online Photo Shop using the XML and XSL files. To include the use case diagram in the requirements specification, we save the use case model in GIF format and add the following two lines to the stylesheet, right after the <h1> tag at the beginning of the file:

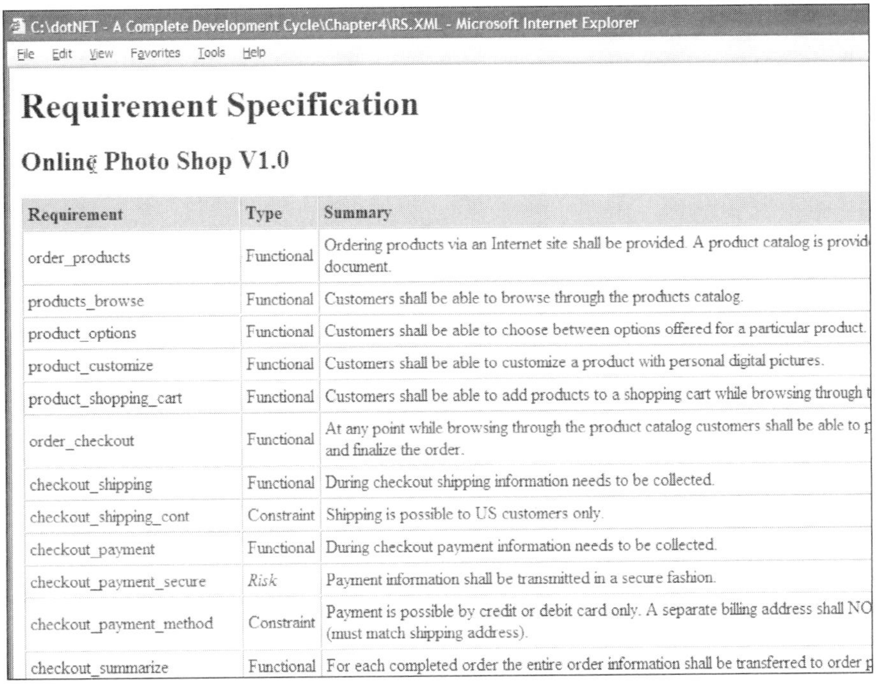

Figure 4.2 Requirement Specification Document in Internet Explorer

```
<h2>Use Case Diagram</h2>
<img src="use_case_diagram.gif" />
```

If you now open RS.XML in Internet Explorer, you can see the UML use case diagram in the first subchapter, and the list of requirements of Online Photo Shop in the second.

4.3 Project Requirements

Table 4.3 contains a list of all essential requirements for Online Photo Shop. This list was generated from an XML document, as described in section 4.2.2.

Table 4.3 Requirements Descriptions

Requirement	Type	Summary
F:order_products	Functional	Ordering products via an Internet site shall be provided. A product catalog is provided as an XML document.
F:products_browse	Functional	Customers shall be able to browse through the products catalog, which is provided in the form of formatted HTML documents.
F:product_options	Functional	Customers shall be able to choose between options offered for a particular product.
F:product_customize	Functional	Customers shall be able to customize a product with personal digital photos.
F:product_shopping_cart	Functional	Customers shall be able to add products to a shopping cart while browsing through the product catalog.
F:order_checkout	Functional	At any point while browsing through the product catalog, customers shall be able to proceed to checkout and finalize the order.
F:checkout_shipping	Functional	During checkout, shipping information needs to be collected.
C:checkout_shipping_cont	Constraint	Shipping is possible to U.S. customers only.
F:checkout_payment	Functional	During checkout, payment information needs to be collected.
C:checkout_payment_method	Constraint	Payment is possible by credit or debit card only. A separate billing address shall *not* be collected (must match shipping address).
R:checkout_payment_secure	Risk	Payment information shall be transmitted in a secure fashion.
F:checkout_summarize	Functional	For each completed order, the entire order information shall be transferred to order processing.
F:error_handling	Functional	Exception-handling mechanism needs extension to show error message in window on screen.
F:photo_editor	Functional	Customers shall be able to perform basic photo postprocessing on their digital photos.

Table 4.3 (*Cont.*)

Requirement	Type	Summary
F:image_crop	Functional	The photo editor shall provide functionality to select a region of interest and crop the image to that region.
F:image_brightness	Functional	The photo editor shall provide manual brightness correction.
F:image_contrast	Functional	The photo editor shall provide manual contrast correction.
F:image_color	Functional	The photo editor shall provide manual color adjustment for red/green/blue and hue/saturation/luminance.
F:image_graphics_annotations	Functional	The photo editor shall provide the possibility to attach customized graphical objects to the image.
F:image_graphics_special_effects	Functional	It shall be possible to use advanced graphical objects that use graded or opaque colors.
F:image_text_annotations	Functional	The photo editor shall provide a tool that allows adding text in different fonts and colors to an image.
F:image_3dtext	Functional	The photo editor shall allow the user to add three-dimensional text to an image.
P:editor_optimizations	Performance	The photo editor shall use optimization features such as multithreading to achieve better performance.
F:image_rotate	Functional	The photo editor shall be able to rotate an image by 90 degrees.
F:image_flip	Functional	The photo editor shall be able to flip an image vertically and horizontally.
F:image_special_effects	Functional	The photo editor shall provide special effects for image transformations.
F:editor_system_test	Functional	A test program shall show that the functionalities implemented fulfill the requirements.
F:image_format	Functional	The supported image formats are JPG and GIF. The supported image sizes range from 100 pixels to 2,048 pixels for both width and height.
C:online_shop_codebehind	Constraint	Web forms shall be created using the Visual Studio Web Form wizard and follow separation of code and design (code behind).

(continued)

Table 4.3 (*Cont.*)

Requirement	Type	Summary
C:online_shop_ stateservice	Constraint	To allow for future scalability, the ASP State service shall be used to implement session management.
C:imageprocessing_ library	Constraint	All implementations of image-processing algorithms that go beyond the provided functionality of the .NET Framework Class Library shall be encapsulated into a separate library.
C:platform_os	Constraint	The target platform operating system is Windows XP Professional.

4.4 Initial Project Planning

> A

The project planning for this project is divided into two sections: project management planning and project implementation planning. This structure provides an easy-to-use reference for both managers and developers. Project management planning deals mainly with higher-level managerial planning, whereas project implementation planning is focused on implementation-related details that the developers should follow during the course of the project.

4.4.1 Project Management Planning

Project management planning focuses on the procedures and tools imposed on the project to reduce risk, improve tracking, and improve quality. Even though commercial tools are available that provide process support for the whole life cycle, it was decided not to use these tools for the following reasons:

- None of the tools can be used without spending a considerable amount of time and effort in customizing it, setting it up, and training.
- For small teams, such as the three-person Online Photo Shop project, the tools would add unnecessary overhead.
- Not all of the automation the tools provide is needed for this project.
- The tools are expensive.

For completeness and for the interested reader, we'll mention that Rational provides a comprehensive tool collection that supports the Rational Unified Process (which is compatible with the Unified Process, as discussed in Chapter 2).

Software Configuration Management

Software configuration management (SCM) is a critical element for all development activities, not just coding. SCM facilitates change history and change control, and it enables parallel development. There are many strategies to SCM. In small projects with small teams, the strategy might be simply to compile the project, run the tests, zip the source files, and store them with a date and version indicator on a rewritable compact disc (CD/R).

A more advanced approach is to use tools such as Microsoft Visual Source Safe, WinCVS, or Rational ClearCase. All three tools provide advanced features for version control, including version history, branching, and merging. ClearCase also provides multisite support for distributed teams. In addition, you can find many other tools by searching the Internet for configuration management systems.

Recently a new approach to project code sharing over the Internet was introduced on the www.gotdotnet.com site. The Web site enables teams to share workspaces over the Internet by facilitating code sharing (for distributed teams even in different network domains), version control, and defect tracking.

The tool of choice for this project is Microsoft Visual Source Safe. It was chosen because of its rich set of features to support small team development in addition to its ease of setup and use. Visual Source Safe allows a developer to move files from the repository onto his or her local hard drive; this action is called *checkout*. When all the changes have been made (or a partial result has been achieved), the files are transferred back into the repository; this is called *checkin*. At checkin, new versions of the changed files are created, and all developers are able to see the changes. Configuration management enables you to roll back to previous versions if necessary, and it provides a change history that lets you backtrack changes. In addition, the configuration management systems enable parallel development and facilitate merging of the various changes. All versions are preserved and are easily accessible.

The only rule imposed on the developers is to provide meaningful summaries of the changes made as checkin comments. Good checkin comments enable the developers and management to find specific changes by browsing the version history without even looking at the differences in the source files.

Part of configuration management is to define a well-structured directory tree for the project source files and generated binaries. Figure 4.3 shows the directory structure of the Online Photo Shop as it is provided on the accompanying CD.

The name of the top-level directory usually is the same as that of the project (in our case, that would be Online Photo Shop). However, for easy navigability and because we are providing sample solutions for each chapter, we chose to name the top-level directory for each chapter's solution Chapter X, where X represents the chapter number.

The next level contains the doc, bin, bind, and src directories. The doc directory holds all documentation that is automatically generated from the source code. The bin directory holds the generated assemblies that were compiled in release mode, and the bind directory holds the generated assemblies that were compiled in debug mode.

The src directory contains one Visual Studio solution, which will hold all the subprojects and source files. The projects reside in the subdirectories of src. These subdirectories contain modules that can be built independently of each other (such as SomePlugIn, Photo Editor Application, and so on). Nevertheless, as mentioned before, for easier access and compilation these modules or projects (in terms of Visual Studio) are part of one *photo editor solution* that contains all subprojects.

The Test directory contains the source for all the developed unit test cases, and the PhotoEditor directory contains subdirectories for each project module, which in turn contain all necessary source files to build the

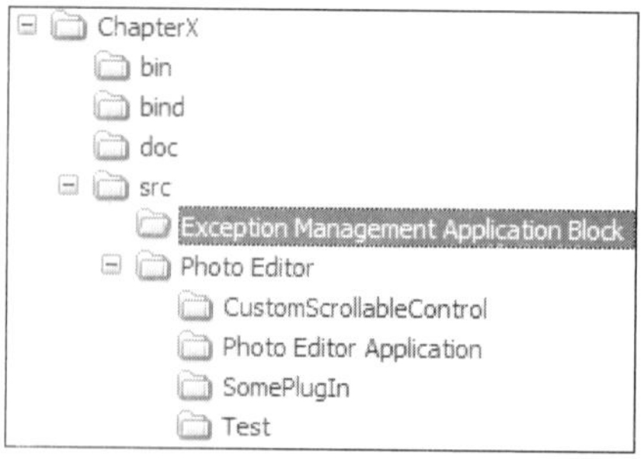

Figure 4.3 Directory Structure for the Online Photo Shop

independent modules. `Exception Management Application Block` is an example of an external source that is provided by Microsoft and is therefore not a subproject of the photo editor.

It is a good practice for the configuration management system administrator to create and set up the directory tree structure for a new project.

Requirements Tracing

In every project it is important to track the requirements throughout the development phases to make sure that none of the keys has been forgotten. This sounds trivial, but in practice it is not unusual to discover missing implementations of certain requirements just before or even after a product is released. For this reason we strongly encourage you to track requirements with unique keys from their introduction through design, implementation, and test.

Earlier in this chapter we introduced the requirement keys for Online Photo Shop using an XML document that allows easy extraction of the keys for tracing. The requirement keys also are added to each class or method header in the code that implements or tests certain functionality. To do that, we use an XML requirement tag. Listing 4.3 shows an example in which the functional requirement key `F:order_products` is added to the header of the class `WebForm1`.

Listing 4.3 Example for Class Header Containing a Requirement Key

```
/// <summary>
/// Summary description for WebForm1.
/// </summary>
/// <requirement>F:order_products</requirement>
public class WebForm1 : System.Web.UI.Page
{
    ...
}
```

In C# you can automatically generate documentation from the shown class headers using Visual Studio.NET (unfortunately, this feature is not yet available for VB). To automatically create the documentation from the source code, go to the project properties by right-clicking on the project in Solution Explorer and choosing `Properties`. The dialog shown in Figure 4.4 will open. Go to the Output section and type a file name (for example,

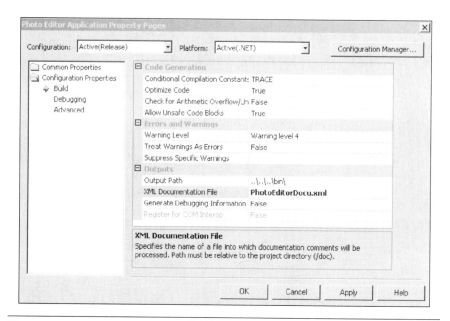

Figure 4.4 Creating XML Documentation from Code

`PhotoEditorDocu.XML`) into the XML Documentation File setting. After compiling the project, you will be able to find the XML documentation file in the output directory of the project.

The same scheme of adding the requirement tag also applies to analysis and design documents. Furthermore, it will be used within the test outputs (log files), a practice that allows us to estimate test coverage. Information on document extraction from XML documents is explained in more detail in the next iteration of the project (Chapter 5).

Effort Estimates and Resource Allocation

Based on the requirements, the team must estimate the effort for each requirement. It is important to emphasize that effort estimates should be a team effort and not just a management effort. Effort estimates are based on experience, the expertise of the developers, and the environment.

In this project the estimates are made by at least two people. One is the person most likely to implement the requirement, and the other one is a senior developer who is familiar with the project and the environment. The estimates are based on the ideal development time, not considering any destruction, breaks, customer support, or similar contingencies. If there is a big discrepancy between the two estimates, a discussion is initiated to resolve the differences and reach a conclusion with a reasonable estimate. If the two estimates are within a reasonable range, then we add 25 percent fudge time plus some risk buffer. The risk buffer depends on the complexity of the task. The more complex the task or the more uncertainty it involves, the more risk buffer we add. It should be mentioned here that vacation time and training should be accounted for in the schedule as nonworking time.

The initial effort estimate for Online Photo Shop is visualized in Visio and is shown in Figure 4.5.

As shown in the overview, the requirements have been grouped by the development team. This grouping is based on related functionalities and is a first guess that will be refined in the iteration planning. Even though it is not shown here, it should be mentioned that each requirement is estimated individually.

In later iterations, defects that have been found must be estimated and scheduled in the same way as we've described for new requirements. In fact, the defects can be seen as new requirements, and they will be scheduled according to their priority.

Iteration Planning

Iteration planning is the task of combining one or more requirements into iterations. Usually, you bundle related functionality into the same iteration. In discussions with the customer and based on the initial effort estimates, you decide and agree upon the features that will be worked on during each iteration. This ensures that requirements that are important to the customer will be provided as early as possible. Also, to identify possible problem areas as early as possible, you put requirements that have more risk into the earlier construction iterations (in addition to a developed prototype in the inception phase). Single iterations should not exceed much more than two weeks' effort. This improves the accuracy of your progress tracking and helps you uncover problem areas faster. Iterations can be worked on in parallel if there are limited and well-defined dependencies.

For the Online Photo Shop application, Table 4.4 shows the iterations that have been identified.

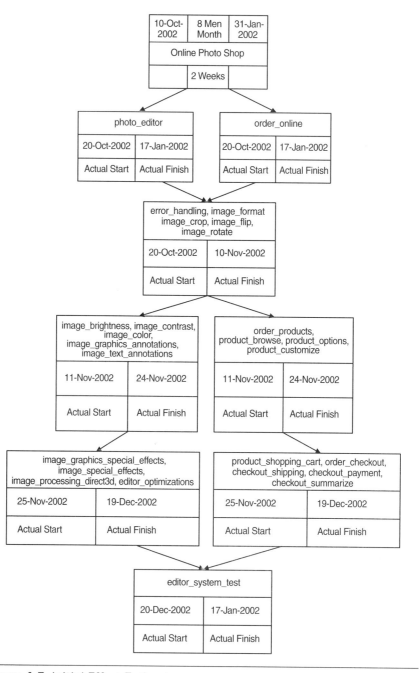

Figure 4.5 Initial Effort Estimate

Table 4.4 Iterations of the Online Photo Shop Project

Phase	Iteration	Type: Requirement Key
Inception phase	Iteration 1	N/A
	Iteration 2	N/A
Elaboration phase	Iteration 3	`F:photo_editor`
		`C:imageprocessing_library`
		`C:platform_os`
		`F:error_handling`
		`F:image_format`
		`F:image_crop`
		`F:image_flip`
		`F:image_rotate`
Construction phase	Iteration 4	`F:image_brightness`
		`F:image_contrast`
		`F:image_color`
		`F:image_graphics_annotations`
		`F:image_text_annotations`
	Iteration 5	`F:image_graphics_special_effects`
	Iteration 6	`F:image_special_effects`
	Iteration 7	`F:image_accessing_system_resources`
	Iteration 8	`P:editor_optimizations`
	Iteration 9	`F:order_products`
		`F:product_browse`
		`F:product_options`
		`F:product_customize`
		`F:product_shopping_cart`
		`F:order_checkout`
		`F:checkout_shipping`
		`C:checkout_shipping_cont`
		`F:checkout_payment`
		`C:checkout_payment_method`
	Iteration 10	`R:checkout_payment_secure`
		`F:checkout_summarize`
		`C:online_shop_codebehind`
		`C:online_shop_stateservice`
Transition phase	Iteration 11	`F:editor_system_test`

Even though the iterations are described sequentially in this book, some of the iterations (with few functional dependencies) can be worked on in parallel. The sequential presentation is chosen because the team is small and the book is sequential by itself.

As you can see, the iteration planning has refined the initial effort estimates by grouping functionalities to accommodate the customer's priorities and wishes.

Project Tracking

Initial effort estimates and resource allocations are the base for progress tracking. Because the iterations should not exceed two weeks and because each iteration defines clear go/no-go criteria, we can identify problem areas very early and take countermeasures. Project tracking is the basic control that proves that the plan as shown in Figure 4.5 corresponds with reality. We must make continuous adjustments to the plan to keep it current and to track the reality.

It is a common problem that the plan made in the beginning is not adjusted during the course of the project. This leads to wishful plans that soon have nothing to do with reality, and this means that no project tracking is possible and problems cannot be identified. For better visibility of the project status to all team members, we also encourage you to make the plan and current status visible to everybody on the project. In this way, all parties involved (even the customer) know exactly what the status of the project is and where problems have arisen.

Test Strategy

Testing must be planned with the same structured approach as development. This is essential if we are to deliver a high-quality product. In many real-life projects, testing is put off until the very end of the development cycle and is not included in the planning up front. As a result, if development finishes late, instead of adjusting the schedule the testing is cut by the amount of time development is late. For the Online Photo Shop project, testing is included in the planning stage of the project and is part of the go/no-go criteria. This practice ensures thorough testing throughout the project and for release.

The testing strategy is divided into two levels: low-level test, which will be referred to as *unit test*, and high-level test, which will be referred to as *system test*. Unit tests are typically developed and run by the developers in every iteration to ensure that the individual modules are working correctly in isolation. Unit tests usually are candidates for automation. If the unit tests are automated, they can be run after each build to ensure that the units are still working correctly and nothing has broken. On the other hand, system tests will be developed in the transition phase to ensure that the individual modules are working together as specified in the requirements. System tests can be used as acceptance tests to show the customer that the system is working as specified. For larger projects, you could organize a dedicated test team to develop the system tests in parallel with product development.

The tests in this project are defined as follows. Unit tests are derived from the design. Developers must log their result into a log file, indicating the requirement key tested and the result of the test cases, which is either passed or failed. At the end of each iteration, the unit tests for the implemented requirements are run. To proceed to the next iteration, all unit tests must pass, or else a defect report is filed and scheduled for a later iteration or version. For unit test automation, the unit tests will write the requirement key and the test result to an output file in XML format. Listing 4.4 shows a template for what the output should look like.

Listing 4.4 Example of Unit Test Documentation

```
<requirement>F:example_key</requirement>
<summary>
     Unit test summary description.
</summary>
<param testresult="result ">parameter description</param>
```

System tests are derived from the use cases and are run in the transition phase as proof that the system fulfills the requirements. The details of the system test development will be discussed in the workflows of the transition phase.

Defect Tracking

For accurate effort estimates and effective quality control, it is important to track defects from the very beginning of the project. The list of accumulated defects in the defect tracking system, called a *defect report list,* acts as a to-do list for the project. You use this to-do list to schedule time for fixing the defects found. A defect report should contain at least the following information:

- Unique ID: Every defect should be assigned a unique ID with which it can be identified and tracked.
- Submitted by: This is the name of the person who submitted the defect.
- Type: This specifies whether it is a software defect or a document defect.
- Category: This specifies whether this defect reflects an error or a wish for a change or addition.
- Summary: This short summary of the defect enables fast browsing through a list of defects.
- Current status: This indicates the work status of the defect. Typically, seven statuses are possible. *Submitted* means that a defect was found and entered into the system but has not yet been reviewed and scheduled for fixing. *In decision* reflects the situation in which the defect has been submitted and is being reviewed. The impact of the defect is analyzed, and it is scheduled for repair in this version or a later version, or it is terminated. If a defect is assigned to a developer, its status is set to *in work*. After the defect is solved, it is set to status *solved*. To make sure that the fix actually solves the problem, the defect is then sent to the responsible person to test the fix; if it is rejected, the status is set back to *in work*. Otherwise, the status is set to *validated*. Another option is to set a defect to status *not reproducible,* meaning that it cannot be reproduced but still should be tracked and kept in mind in case the defect appears again. There is one final option. At any time in the project, management can decide that a defect either has been solved through some other changes, was submitted in error, or is not a bug but rather a feature. In that case the defect report can be set to *terminated.*
- Priority: The priority indicates the importance of the defect to the customer. Depending on the importance, the fix is scheduled for solution. Typically the priority consists of three states: high, medium, or low priority.
- Assigned To (name): This is the name of the person who has responsibility for necessary action on the defect—for example, the developer who is assigned to fix the defect, or the test developer who is assigned to validate the implemented fix.

- Date submitted: This is the date the defect report was submitted.
- Version defect found: This is the version the defect was found in.
- Description: This is a description of how the defect can be reproduced. A good description is crucial in enabling the developers to reproduce and fix defects efficiently.
- Version scheduled for: This indicates the version in which the defect is expected to be fixed.

In addition, you can use a variety of custom fields for specific project needs. For metric support, the following fields could be added to the reports:

- Phase introduced: After the defect has been fixed, an analysis can be done to determine at which stage in development or which phase in the project the defect was introduced.
- Phase found: This field indicates in which phase the defect was uncovered. This information can give valuable data on the effectiveness of testing in each phase.
- Module: This is the module where the defect is located.
- Effort: This is the effort that was needed to fix the defect.

Many commercial tools support defect tracking, including Rational ClearQuest. Other tools can be found at the www.gotdotnet.com Web site. For larger projects, we strongly recommend using of one of the available defect tracking tools. Managing defects is a substantial task of project management, and in larger projects it can become very difficult to manage without the help of a good tool. However, for a small project like the one described in this book, a simple Excel spreadsheet checked into Configuration Management can be used for defect tracking (see Figure 4.6).

4.4.2 Project Implementation Planning

For the implementation of Online Photo Shop, the following rules are defined.

Code Documentation

In addition to the application itself, the reference documentation is part of the deliverable. For future enhancements and maintenance, it is important to provide meaningful and correct documentation. Good reference documentation provides the base for easy extension and maintenance.

UniqueID	Submitted by	Date Submitted	Summary	Type	Category	Current status	Priority	Assigned To (Name)	Version Defect Found	Description	Version Scheduled for
00001											
00002											
00003											
00004											
00005											
00006											
00007											
00008											
00009											
00010											
00011											
00012											
00013											
00014											
00015											
00016											
00017											
00018											
00019											
00020											
00021											
00022											
00023											
00024											
00025											
00026											
00027											
00028											
00029											
00030											
00031											
00032											
00033											
00034											
00035											
00036											
00037											
00038											
00039											
00040											
00041											
00042											
00043											
00044											
00045											
00046											
00047											
00048											
00049											
00050											
00051											
00052											
00053											
00054											
00055											
00056											

Figure 4.6 Defect Tracking Spreadsheet

There are several ways to generate documentation. One way is to produce documentation in parallel to the development of the code as another document. This approach has the advantage that the customer will receive an independent reference document. The big disadvantage of this approach is that the document must be kept in sync with all the changes that are made to the code due to bug fixes and implementation of new features. In reality, documentation created in this way is most likely to be out of sync with the code and therefore of only limited use.

It is better to generate the documentation from the code base. This means that the documentation is part of the source code. Whenever changes are made to the behavior of the code or new functionality is added, the descriptions, in the form of comments, are also updated. Certainly, this implies extra work for the developers, but this approach results in much less overhead. The developer is touching the source files anyway, and it takes very little effort to keep the documentation up-to-date by adapting the comments as changes are made.

In addition to the advantages we have mentioned, Visual Studio.NET now provides a tool to extract documentation from the code. To generate the documentation, go to Visual Studio's Tool menu and click on the option Build Comment Web Pages. This will automatically generate the HTML comment Web documentation. The tags to be used for the comment Web reports can be found in the example in Listing 4.5 or in the help menu of the Build Comment Web Pages tool.

To provide consistent documentation for Online Photo Shop, all comments for classes, methods, and parameters follow the guidelines as shown in the code example in Listing 4.5.

Listing 4.5 Example of Code Documentation

```
/// <summary>
/// Summary description for ExampleClass.
/// </summary>
/// <remarks> This is a remark for ExampleClass <\remarks>
/// <requirement>F:example_key</requirement>
public class ExampleClass
{
    /// <summary>
    /// Example private property description goes here
    /// </summary>
    private int classProperty;

    /// <summary>
    /// Example public method with one parameter
    /// <newpara> Starts a new paragraph in comments </newpara>
    /// </summary>
    /// <param name="param">parameter description</param>
    /// <returns>description of return Value</returns>
    public int InstanceMethod(int param)
    {
        // do something useful here
        return 0;
    }
}
```

Chapter 5 shows an example of the produced documentation in the next iteration of the project.

Note that Visual Studio ignores the `<requirement>` tag when generating the HTML Web comment documentation. This is convenient for this project because the requirement keys are used for internal requirement tracing purposes only and are not intended to add value to the HTML reference documentation.

Reviews

In many companies, the first line of defense in the quest to produce highly reliable and high-quality code is the use of code reviews or inspections. Commonly used methods are code walkthroughs, readings, and formal inspections.

Walkthroughs are informal processes in which two or more developers get together and review the code to identify potential problems. Often, they solve an identified problem during the walkthrough.

A more formal method is a *code reading*, when the author hands out a code listing to two or more reviewers. The reviewers then report errors back to the author. This approach was chosen by NASA in combination with testing to ensure high product quality.

A stricter approach than the reading is the *inspection*. For inspections, the participants should be trained beforehand. The training is important because during the review the participants fulfill specific roles, such as moderator, reviewer, and author. They often use a checklist and produce a written report with all the findings and resolutions that are to be incorporated into the reviewed work product.

All the review methods can be used for documents as well as code. During the review, it is important to keep the discussion focused on potential problems. Review time should not be used to debate style or coding techniques (as long as the implementation complies with the coding guidelines) but to find defects! In addition, developers should use the output of static code checkers to help them identify potential problems or even to check for compliance to coding guidelines.

For the three-person Online Photo Shop project, the reading method is used for all code and document reviews. The reviews take place before the work product to be reviewed is checked in to the configuration management system to be included for an official release.

Error and Exception Handling

An important implementation detail is how to handle errors. Typically, projects handle errors via either return values, exception handling, or a combination of both.

If return values are used for error checking, then each value returned by a function call needs to be checked for its status. If an error is flagged in the return status, the error must be handled before the program can continue.

In the Online Photo Shop project, the exception mechanism is used to propagate errors. This approach is chosen for several reasons. First, exceptions are thrown by the object in which the error occurred. This means that precise details of the error condition can be passed to the error-handling routine. Second, various exception types can be defined and the program can therefore react according to the causes of the error. Third, exception management code can be isolated from business logic code.

Another reason to use exception handling is that Microsoft provides an Exception Management Application Block for .NET that can be used as a framework for exception handling in any application (Chapter 5 explains the use of the Microsoft Exception Management Application Block). Several application blocks are part of the Microsoft Prescriptive Guidance Library, which can be downloaded from the MSDN Web page at `http://msdn.microsoft.com/downloads/list/bda.asp`. The solutions provided by Microsoft meet the following sets of requirements:

- Are based on field experience
- Contain the best advice available
- Are validated and tested
- Address real-world problems

To use the Exception Management Application Block, you do the following:

1. Build the `Microsoft.ApplicationBlocks.ExceptionManagement` project to build the `ExceptionManagement.dll` assembly.
2. Set a reference to the `ExceptionManagement.dll` assembly.
3. Add a `using` statement to reference the `ExceptionManagement` namespace.

You can then publish exceptions by using the code in Listing 4.6.

Listing 4.6 Example for Exception Handling

```
catch ( Exception ex )
{
    ExceptionManager.Publish( ex );
}
```

In this example the `DefaultPublisher` provided by the application block is used, and the exception is written to the Windows event log. For fatal errors (those that the application cannot recover from), this approach might be acceptable. But for less serious problems the user should be notified about the problem, some cleanup should be done to recover, and then the application should be able to continue in a stable state. This implies that the exception mechanism must be extended. The requirement with the key `F:error_handling` describes the use case for that. The extension is critical for the whole project and will be implemented in the code baseline produced in the next iteration. The details of the implementation of the custom exception handler, however, will be based on the Microsoft application block. For more detailed information on exception handling and the application block, please refer to the Web pages listed in the references section.

Project Coding Guidelines

To achieve better readability, maintainability, and understanding of the source code, we introduce coding guidelines for this project. As the name "coding guidelines" suggests, it is a guideline only. Nevertheless, it is important to adhere to these guidelines as much as possible. Usually the coding guidelines are outlined in an attachment to other project documents created in the inception phase. If you have a great many very rigid coding conventions, you may want to list them in a separate document. Table 4.5 shows the coding guidelines for the Online Photo Shop project.

The guidelines are recommendations and not strictly enforced (in contrast to the rules for code documentation described earlier in this chapter).

Table 4.5 Coding Guidelines: Naming Conventions

Identifier	Example	Guideline
Class	ApplicationDomain, FileStream, Button, String	The first character and the first letter of every concatenated word are capitalized.
		Use noun or noun phrase to name a class.
		Use abbreviations sparingly.
		Do not use a type prefix (such as C in CFileStream) for class names.
		Class names can start with an I even if they are not an interface if I is the first letter of an entire word that is part of the class name (such as IdentifyString).
		Compound words can be used for derived classes as appropriate (ApplicationException, which is derived from Exception).
Method	ToString, ClearAll, GetIntValue, Invoke	The first character and the first letter of every concatenated word are capitalized.
		Use verbs or verb phrases to name methods.
Interface	IDisposable, IServiceProvider, IFormattable	The first character and the first letter of every concatenated word are capitalized.
		Name interfaces with nouns or noun phrases, or adjectives that describe behavior.
		Avoid abbreviations.
		Use prefix I for interfaces.
		If a class is a standard implementation of an interface, then use similar names (the interface name should differ only by the prefix I).
		Do not use the underscore character.
Parameter	typeName, format, args	The first character of the identifier is lowercase, and the first letter of each concatenated word is capitalized.
		Use descriptive parameter names. The parameter names and type can be used to determine the meaning of the parameter in the context.

(continued)

Table 4.5 (*Cont.*)

Identifier	Example	Guideline
		Use names that describe the purpose of the parameter and not its type.
		Do not use reserved parameters.
		Do not prefix parameter names with Hungarian type notation.
Property	`BackColor`	The first character and the first letter of every concatenated word are capitalized.
		Use a noun or noun phrase to name properties.
		Do not use Hungarian notation.
		Try to include a property's type in its name. For example, use `TextColor`, `BackgroundColor`, etc. if the underlying type is `Color`.
Enum type	`ErrorLevel`	The first character and the first letter of every concatenated word are capitalized.
		Avoid abbreviations.
		Use the singular form of enum types (except for bit fields, which should be named in plural).
		Always add the `FlagsAttribute` to a bit field `Enum` type.
		Do not use the `Enum` suffix on `Enum` type names.
Enum values	`FatalError`	The first character and the first letter of every concatenated word are capitalized.
Event	`UserInput`	The first character and the first letter of every concatenated word are capitalized.
Read-only static field	`PixelValue`	The first character and the first letter of every concatenated word are capitalized.
Protected instance field	`pixelValue`	The first character of the identifier is lowercase, and the first letter of each concatenated word is capitalized.
Exception class	`ViewerException, WebException`	The first character and the first letter of every concatenated word are capitalized.
		Use the suffix `Exception`.

4.5 Initial Risk Analysis

Another essential part of project planning is analyzing and tracking the risks involved in developing the project. Even though software cannot directly harm people or equipment, it can cause harm and damage if it provides misleading or wrong information. In some cases these risks can include potential risks to human life or equipment damage. This is the case, for example, in regulated industries such as medicine, defense, and transportation systems.

Unlike these critical software products, the Online Photo Shop application does not impose any kind of risk to human life or equipment. Nevertheless, there are project risks that need to be analyzed and tracked.

Usually risk analysis is based on the project's requirements. Each requirement is analyzed for potential risks in case of malfunction. One approach is the so-called *fault tree analysis*, which identifies potential software functionality failures that could lead to risks. Another approach is the *failure mode analysis*, which is a bottom-up approach that analyzes how failures in low-level components alone or in combination can cause potential risks at the application level. In addition to these functionality-related risks, there are general project risks, which also need to be analyzed and tracked. The format shown in Figure 4.7 is used to analyze the risks for this project.

The initial risk analysis is based on the initial requirements. As with all project planning tasks, risk analysis must be worked on, updated, and extended throughout the development cycle. We need to incorporate all

Requirement Key:

Cause of risk	[The cause of the failure]
Impact of risk	[A description of the impact of failure]
Preventive action	[The action taken to mitigate the risk]
Remaining risk	[The remaining risk described and classified as follows: broadly acceptable, as low as reasonably possible (ALARP), and intolerable]

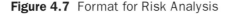

Figure 4.7 Format for Risk Analysis

newly identified risks as well as changes that are identified as impacting risk-related items.

For Online Photo Shop, the most critical part, and the only relevant safety requirement, is the online payment. Figure 4.8 shows the risk analysis for this risk. In addition, there are several project risks that are not related to any functional requirement but are still worth analyzing up front. Figure 4.9 shows two examples.

Requirement Key: `checkout_payment_secure`	
Cause of risk	Transactions are not handled in a secure fashion.
Impact of risk	Critical customer data such as personal information or credit card details are accessible to unauthorized users.
Preventive action	Reviews: The code that implements requirements identified as risk-related are subject to an inspection-type review.
	Design: The code implementing this requirement key shall be split into a separate file to clearly distinguish it from non-risk-related code. The design review of the risk implementation shall be subject of an inspection-like review.
	Test: The test for this requirement key shall also be split into a separate file to easily identify it. The test code shall be subject to an inspection-type review.
Remaining risk	The remaining risk is as low as reasonably possible (ALARP).

Figure 4.8 Analysis of Online Payment Risk

Requirement Key: N/A Feature creep

Cause of risk	Main requirements are changed and extended during the course of the project.
Impact of risk	Schedule slip.
Preventive action	Reviews: The requirements will be reviewed and agreed upon by all parties involved in the project.
	Intermediate deliverables: After each iteration that produces a working program, the progress is delivered to the customer for feedback on necessary changes.
	Impact analysis: New features or requirement changes during the course of development are analyzed in the same way new requirements were analyzed in the beginning of the project. If the schedule is impacted, it will be discussed with the customer, and after agreement the schedule will be adjusted.
Remaining risk	The remaining risk is as low as reasonably possible (ALARP).

Requirement Key: N/A Missing knowledge transfer

Cause of risk	Key people may leave or become unavailable during the course of the project.
Impact of risk	Schedule conflicts would arise.
Preventive action	Review: Through code and document reviews, knowledge is transferred to different people on the project → Cross training.
	Design: The code implementing the functionality shall be well documented.
Remaining risk	The remaining risk is as low as reasonably possible (ALARP).

Figure 4.9 Risk Analysis of Nonfunctional Requirements

4.6 Initial Requirements Analysis and Design

Having introduced the advantages and new features of .NET in Chapter 1 and successfully developed a prototype to evaluate this technology in Chapter 3, we now lay the groundwork for the implementation. To develop a good design, we must provide an important part that is still missing: the analysis of the requirements. This analysis describes "what" the system is supposed to do. When we have finished the initial analysis, we can derive the design—the "how" of implementing the system—from it.

For Online Photo Shop, we conduct a high-level analysis to show the various modules and packages of the project, their grouping, and a sequence diagram. In the elaboration phase (Chapter 5), we will show how to do a more detailed analysis and how to derive the architecture from the analysis.

The first step in analyzing the requirements and developing the high-level, overall system design is to identify the underlying structure of the product. From the requirements, we identify three distinct parts: the Online Shop part, a photo-editing part, and an image-processing part. Each of the parts has its own focus on functionality.

Analyzing the requirements further shows that there are very limited dependencies between the three parts, and therefore the system is divided into the three packages. Figure 4.10 shows a UML package diagram, which is fairly simple for the Online Photo Shop project because there are limited dependencies between the packages. Furthermore, the analysis shows that there are no anticipated dependencies between the Online Photo Shop and the image-processing library.

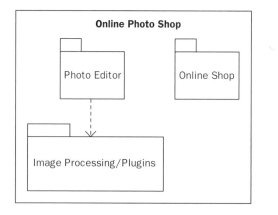

Figure 4.10 Package Diagram for the Online Photo Shop

4.6.1 The Photo Editor

Preparing a digital photo for printing can involve many, sometimes computationally expensive steps. Furthermore, users seldom accomplish the desired result on the first try, and when that happens they start over with a new image from scratch. Driven by the fact that photo postprocessing is typically an offline task, we implement the photo editor as a smart client application that can be downloaded from the business's Web site. The photo editor will provide the customer with a graphical user interface (GUI) to prepare an image for printing. Figure 4.11 shows a UML

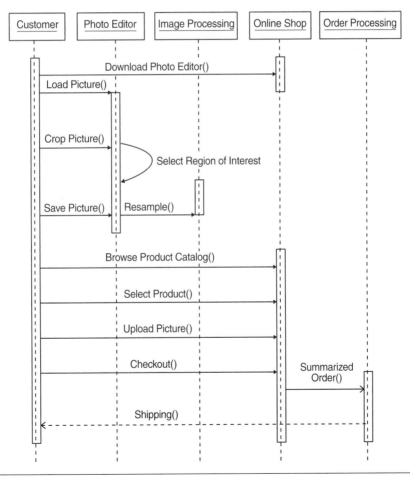

Figure 4.11 Sequence Diagram for Online Photo Shop

sequence diagram that illustrates a typical workflow for the Online Photo Shop system.

Sequence diagrams are used to visualize interactions among systems or objects, in this case the customer, the photo editor, the image-processing library, the online shop, and the business. These are shown as boxes at the top of a sequence diagram. The vertical lines are called *lifelines* and represent the life of the object or system that they are connected to during an interaction. Arrows can be connected between lifelines, showing messages or actions. The sequence of occurrence is always top-down.

4.6.2 The Image-Processing Library

All image-processing algorithms are encapsulated in a library. This allows their use in new projects or, if necessary, in the online shop Web application.

4.6.3 The Online Shop

Web Forms

The online shop allows customers to select products on the business's Web site and place them into a shopping cart. At any time a customer can proceed to checkout and complete the order by providing the business with payment and shipping information. Therefore, the main online shop implementation will be implemented in those two Web forms:

- Shopping cart form: This Web form enables customers to add products to a shopping cart. This form will use ASP.NET session management to implement a personal shopping cart for each visiting customer. The Web form accepts multiform encoded HTML-form postings from any calling Web page (`*.htm`) or Web form (`*.aspx`). Product identifiers, selected product options, a digital image for customization, and the caller's URL are passed as part of the multiform data posting.
- Checkout form: This Web form collects delivery and payment information from the customer. This module computes the total order cost, including shipping and taxes.

Code Behind

The implementation of Online Photo Shop uses ASP.NET's *code behind* technology, which means that the logic is separated from the presentation. If you don't separate the logic (code) from the presentation (design), it is very difficult to maintain the software. Each change in the design of a Web page can potentially break the code that is embedded in it. Creating Web forms using the Microsoft Visual Studio template separates code from design using code behind.

State Management

HTTP is a connectionless protocol and therefore is stateless. This means that a request to a Web server cannot rely on any previously made requests and must carry all necessary information to generate a response. To overcome this problem, ASP.NET introduces three methods of state management, which allow the Web server to store information for each client in a session object.

- In process: The session objects are stored within the Web server's process. That allows storing of references to any kind of objects without special handling. Also, the retrieval of those objects is very fast. However, this method does not work in a *Web farm* approach, in which a Web application is run on a cluster of servers, because the client requests can be directed to any of the Web servers. If a request is directed to a Web server that is different from the preceding one, the session, along with its objects, is lost.
- The State service: When you use the ASP.NET State service, all the session information is stored in a separate process, which can even reside on a different computer. To use ASP.NET, State service objects that need to be stored in a session must implement serialization methods. This entails some additional implementation effort but allows for future expansion and better maintenance. When the State service resides on a dedicated machine, the Web servers in a Web farm can be rebooted without causing downtime for the online shop. Figure 4.12 shows an example of such a configuration.
- SQL Server: State management using SQL Server is very similar to state management using the State service. In addition, SQL Server state management adds even more robustness to the system. The difference between the two methods is that the SQL Server state

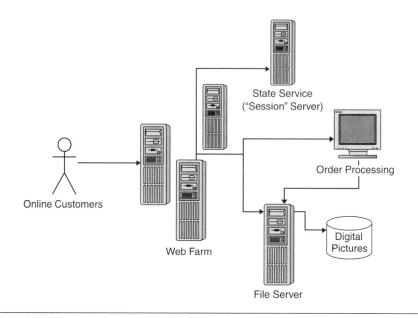

Figure 4.12 System Diagram for Online Shop

management method saves the state of a session in a SQL database instead of storing it in memory (as is done by the ASP.NET State service). This means that even if the designated computer that holds the session state goes down or is rebooted, the state is restored from the database after the computer is rebooted, and no state information is lost.

4.6.4 Defining Architectural Requirements

During the process of defining the initial architecture of the product, it is a good practice to describe architectural constraints in the form of new requirements that must be fulfilled in the implementation. The advantage of doing so is that the requirement key tracing takes care of making sure that the implementation was done according to the initial architecture document and that no new measurements must be implemented for this verification. Table 4.6 shows a list of requirements that apply to the online shop.

Table 4.6 Architectural Requirements for Online Shop

Requirement	Type	Summary
online_shop_codebehind	Constraint	Web forms shall be created using the Visual Studio Web Form wizard and follow separation of code and design (code behind).
online_shop_stateservice	Constraint	To allow for future scalability, the ASP State service shall be used to implement session management. "Scalability" refers to the ability of the Web service to handle parallel requests on multiple servers for load balancing and the possibility of adding more servers if necessary.
imageprocessing_library	Constraint	All implementations of image-processing algorithms that go beyond the provided functionality of the .NET Framework Class Library shall be encapsulated in a separate library.

4.7 Conclusion

At the end of the iteration (or phase, in this case) we need to check whether the project fulfills the goals set for this iteration.

The list of goals for this iteration was as follows:

- Project vision (considering main requirements and constraints)
- Business case
- Initial use case model (10 percent to 20 percent complete)
- Project glossary (main requirements with unique identifier key)
- Initial project plan (including iteration planning)
- Initial risk assessment
- Initial architecture

You can see that all the goals of this iteration have been met, and therefore the project is ready to proceed to the next iteration. Because this iteration was also the last iteration in the inception phase, the project is ready to move on to the elaboration phase. The elaboration phase, described in Chapter 5, focuses on analysis and design of the system. Based on the evolved design, an architectural baseline will be implemented. At the end of the elaboration phase, we will have built a running program that provides a limited set of features. That program, or architectural baseline, will be the base for all the development that continues throughout the project.

4.8 References for Further Reading

Unified Modeling Language (UML)

Grady Booch et al., *The Unified Modeling Language User Guide* (Reading, MA: Addison-Wesley, 1998)

Martin Fowler, *UML Distilled* (Reading, MA: Addison-Wesley, 1999)

http://www.omg.org/technology/documents/formal/uml.htm

Use Case Modeling

Jim Arlow and Ila Neustadt, *UML and the Unified Process* (Boston: Addison-Wesley, 2001)

Frank Armour and Granville Miller, *Advanced Use Case Modeling* (Boston: Addison-Wesley, 2000)

Kurt Bittner et al., *Use Case Modeling* (Boston: Addison-Wesley, 2002)

Alistair Cockburn, *Writing Effective Use Cases* (Boston: Addison-Wesley, 2000)

Configuration Management Tools

http://msdn.microsoft.com/ssafe/prodinfo/overview.asp

http://www.gotdotnet.com/community/workspaces/directory.aspx

http://www.rational.com/products/clearcase/index.jsp

http://www.wincvs.org

Code Review

Steve McConnell, *Rapid Development* (Redmond, WA: Microsoft Press, 1996)

http://www.sei.cmu.edu/ata/products_services/arid.html

http://www.scr.siemens.com

XML and XSL

Erik T. Ray and Christopher R. Maden, *Learning XML* (Sebastopol, CA: O'Reilly, 2001)

Aaron Skonnard and Martin Gudgin, *Essential XML Quick Reference* (Boston: Addison-Wesley, 2001)

```
http://www.w3C.org/xml
```

Exception Handling

```
http://msdn.microsoft.com/library/default.asp?url=/library/
  en-us/dnbda/html/emab-rm.asp
```

```
http://www.csharpfriends.com/Articles/getArticle.
  aspx?articleID=128
```

```
http://www.eastcoastgames.com/articles/cppexception.html
```

Coding Guidelines

```
http://msdn.microsoft.com/library/default.asp?url=/library/
  en-us/dnnetsec/html/seccodeguide.asp
```

```
www.microsoft.com/usa/presentations/ NET_Best_Practices.ppt
```

Risk Management

Steve McConnell, *Rapid Development* (Redmond, WA: Microsoft Press, 1996)

R. Max Wideman, *Project and Program Risk Management* (Newtown Square, PA: Project Management Institute, 1992)

```
http://www.sei.cmu.edu/programs/sepm/risk/
```

The Photo Editor Application

 Unified Process:
Elaboration Phase and Third Iteration

This chapter discusses the third iteration of the project, which corresponds to the elaboration phase of the Unified Process. In this phase the goals to be achieved are to provide an architectural baseline and to formulate a project agreement with the customer to further pursue the project.

The *architectural baseline* implements a working application with limited functionality. The implemented features in our example include exception handling, loading and saving images, and basic image operations. The project agreement that is signed at the end of this phase should include the time frame, equipment, staff, and cost. This leads to the goals that are set for this iteration:

- The vision and business case are updated.
- The requirements are refined and analyzed.
- The risk assessment is updated.
- A detailed project plan is developed.
- The executable program, implementing the architectural framework with UML documentation, is developed.
- The project agreement is signed by the stakeholders to continue the project.

Most of the milestones are based on the work products that were started in the inception phase. Based on those work products, the work breakdown into the five core workflows is as follows:

- Requirements: Refine the requirements and system scope.
- Analysis: Analyze the requirements by describing what the system does.

115

- Design: Develop a stable architecture using UML.
- Implementation: Implement the architectural baseline.
- Test: Test the implemented architectural baseline.

In the elaboration phase the main focus lies on the requirements and analysis workflows. But as explained in Chapter 2, all five core workflows are to be worked on in all phases. This means that in this iteration we spend a considerable amount of time in the design, implementation, and test workflows as well.

5.1 The Refined Project Vision and Business Case

The refined vision is based on the analysis discussed in Chapter 4 and adds new information.

The goal, or vision, for this project is to provide software components to a printing and embossing business that allows online ordering of prints and other items, such as cups, postcards, T-shirts, and mouse pads, that can be customized with digital images.

To accomplish this task, the user must download a photo editor application that is then installed on the customer's computer. After installation the user can alter images, adding graphics, text, and special effects. Users can then save the altered images on their local computers and later upload the images via the Online Photo Shop's Web site to order prints or customized products.

The new software will open the business to a new and larger customer base, allowing for future growth.

5.2 Refined Requirements for Online Photo Shop

5.2.1 Refined Use Case Diagram

The first task in refining the requirements is to reevaluate the use case diagram. Based on the initial requirements, analysis, and design decisions described in Chapter 4, we update the use case diagram as shown in Figure 5.1.

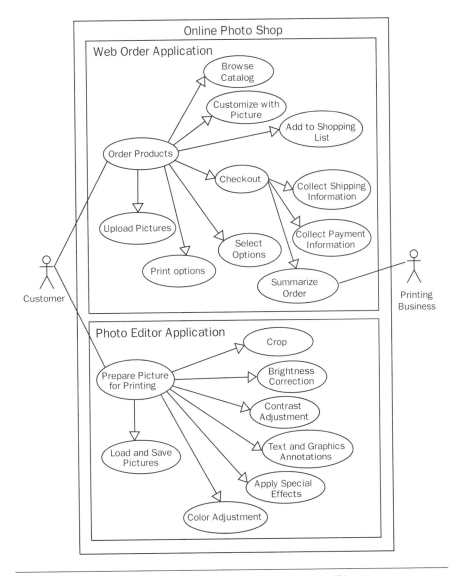

Figure 5.1 Refined Use Case Diagram for Online Photo Shop

The refined use case diagram clearly distinguishes the different parts of Online Photo Shop, as discussed in Chapter 4. Online Photo Shop provides a Web-based interface for ordering products, whereas the photo editor application is used to edit pictures on the local computer. Because of that, the photo editor and the Web order application are in different processes. This also means that they are two independent applications and have no anticipated dependencies. In addition, the new diagram shows additional use cases for loading and saving pictures in the photo editor, as well as a use case for uploading images to the Web application.

5.2.2 Refined Requirements List

The next task is to update the requirements. In addition to adding the new requirements, it is important to put more details into the requirements. These extra details include pre- and postconditions, functional descriptions, and constraints. Refinement of requirements will not be finished in this iteration, but the goal is to put all details of the use cases known at this point into the requirements to support the following activities:

- Negotiating the deliverable functionality with the customer, including the constraints
- Analyzing the requirements and developing a good design for the implementation
- Planning the project and providing reasonably accurate effort estimates (the effort estimates will be refined throughout development)
- Enabling project management to develop an accurate contract agreement with the customer

Table 5.1 shows the refined requirements for the current iteration.

For the remainder of the book, we show only the requirements that are to be implemented in the described iteration. The alternative would be to refine all the requirements in the first construction iteration, but we have not chosen that approach for several reasons. First, it is easier to focus on the functionality that needs to be implemented in the specified iteration. Second, if requirements must be changed because of design or implementation issues, the changes usually will affect only the current iteration's requirements, and the requirements in later iterations can take all these changes into account from the beginning. (If complete planning is done up front, it is like the Waterfall model. Changes in later phases could trigger many changes.) For reference, the complete list of refined requirements can be found in the Requirement Specification XML file of each chapter on the accompanying CD.

The refined requirements include more details on the actual use case functionality and consider known constraints. In every iteration, we refine

Table 5.1 Refined Base Requirement Description

Requirement	Type	Summary
F:photo_ editor	Functional	Customers shall be able to perform basic photo post-processing on their digital images. The GUI shall be similar to the GUI model provided in the file Photo EditorGUI.vsd. The GUI model shows the screen layout and the approximate position of the necessary buttons. The buttons to be used are not defined. The buttons should be chosen so that they can be used intuitively.
F:error_ handling	Functional	Errors shall be reported via exceptions. The exception-handling mechanism is based on the Microsoft Exception Management Application Block (described in detail later in this chapter) and needs to be extended to show error messages in a window on the screen. Every exception shall be displayed on the screen within a dialog window. A meaningful error message shall be displayed. For fatal errors, from which the application is not able to recover, the exception is written into the event log and the application is shut down.
F:picture_ load_and_save	Functional	It shall be possible to load pictures into the photo editor application, alter them, and save them either to the same or to a new file. An error message is displayed if the image format is not known (see also image_format).
F:image_crop	Functional	If an image is loaded, then the photo editor shall provide functionality to select a region of interest and crop the image to that region.
F:image_ rotate	Functional	If an image is loaded, the photo editor shall be able to rotate an image by 90 degrees in both directions.
F:image_flip	Functional	If an image is loaded, the photo editor shall be able to flip an image vertically and horizontally.
F:image_ format	Functional	The supported image formats are JPG and GIF. The supported image sizes range from 100 pixels to 2,048 pixels for both width and height. An error is reported if the image format is not known.
C:platform_os	Constraint	The target platform operating system is Windows XP Professional. No special hardware requirement is necessary.

the requirements that are to be implemented in that iteration. This allows us to choose the best possible design and therefore the best possible implementation for the system.

5.3 Analysis of the Photo Editor Requirements

> **A**

Next, we analyze the refined requirements. The goal in the analysis workflow is to describe what the system is supposed to do without defining how it does it (the time to define how the system is expected to be implemented is in the design workflow). For example, the `photo_editor` requirement key defines what the graphical user interface should look like without describing how it is implemented.

In this book, the analysis and design workflows are done *just in time*, meaning they are done within the iteration that implements the corresponding requirements. This approach is chosen because the team members are highly experienced programmers in the domain and technology we are using. Because of that, the effort estimates are based solely on the requirements and depend heavily on the experience of the team members. In addition, this approach provides a clearer structure for this book in describing the analysis, design, and implementation of the features within the chapter in which they are to be implemented. However, if a project has less-experienced team members or an unknown domain, it might be necessary to analyze all the requirements in more detail up front and to develop the complete design in the elaboration phase in order to provide a reasonable estimate. The estimates are the basis of the project agreement.

In the following subsections, we analyze, design, implement, and test the requirement keys implemented in this iteration and the requirement keys that define dependencies between the system's modules.

5.3.1 The `photo_editor` Requirement

The photo editor application will run in its own namespace. For this iteration, the photo editor application will provide basic functionality. The appearance of the GUI is defined in Figure 5.2 as a guideline.

The figure shows the screen layout and the controls used. It does not define the exact appearance or shapes of the resources that are used to implement the GUI. We're using a toolbar menu containing the items

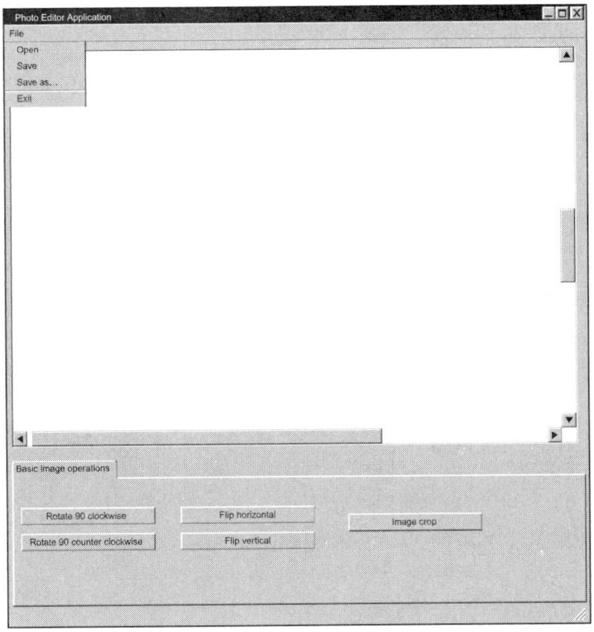

Figure 5.2 The Photo Editor GUI

Open, Save, Save As, and Exit. For the image-processing functionality, a
`TabControl` with buttons is provided. The idea is to group related functionality on one tab and to provide other tabs for other groups of functionality.

5.3.2 The `error_handling` Requirement

Errors are reported via the exception-handling mechanism. Various messages will be available to identify the error that led to the message. The
errors will be reported via message boxes and will contain meaningful error
messages.

5.3.3 The `picture_load_and_save` Requirement

Users will be able to load and save rectangular pictures. The load and save
option is part of the File menu, as shown in Figure 5.2. Users can browse
for files or specify a file manually, and we use the standard Windows Forms
Open/Save File dialog.

5.3.4 The `image_crop` Requirement

Image crop allows users to extract a rectangular part of the image. When the Crop button is pressed, a dialog window opens and the user is asked to type in the width and height of the cropped image. The image is cropped to the size specified by the user if the size specified is smaller than the actual image; otherwise, it is ignored. The cropping is done in a way that the midpoint of the original image is the midpoint of the cropping rectangle defined by the user. The area outside the cropping rectangle is deleted, and the new image in the new size is shown. If the defined cropping rectangle is larger than the image, no cropping is done.

5.3.5 The `image_rotate` Requirement

The image can be rotated in 90 degree steps clockwise and counterclockwise. The image will be shown in the same location and with the same midpoint as the original image.

5.3.6 The `image_flip` Requirement

By pressing the image flip buttons, users can *flip* the image either horizontally or vertically. By "flip," we mean mirroring the image. The position of the midpoint of the image stays the same. The image will be shown in the same location and with the same midpoint as the original image.

5.3.7 The `image_format` Requirement

The standard formats for pictures are supported. If an image with another format is selected, an error message will be shown.

5.3.8 The `platform_os` Requirement

All development and testing are done on Windows XP computers. Even though the application might be able to run on other versions of Windows operating systems, this will not be supported.

5.4 Design of the Photo Editor Application

We have analyzed the requirements and have defined what the system is supposed to do. The next step is to decide how the system will be implemented—in other words, to design the system.

A standard way to document software architectures is to use the Unified Modeling Language (UML). We mainly use UML class diagrams to define the structure of the photo editor software system. The design shows classes, attributes, operations, and the relationships among them. If you have a working knowledge of UML, you may want to skip the following brief introduction to UML class diagrams and go immediately to the provided class diagram of the photo editor in section 5.4.2.

If you're not familiar with UML, we offer a very short introduction to the class diagram in UML. This introduction is not intended as a tutorial on UML class modeling but rather aims to build a common vocabulary to help you understand the design of the system throughout the book. Therefore, the goal of this section is to give you just enough details to understand the class diagrams developed for the application. For more detailed information on UML and class diagrams, see the references section in Chapter 4.

5.4.1 Brief Introduction to UML Class Diagrams

The basic element of a class diagram is a class, which you model using a rectangular box. This box can contain the class name by itself and can also contain the class attributes and the operations defined by the class. Figure 5.3 shows sample class definitions.

Figure 5.3A shows a class that has sample attributes and an operation definition. The sampleOperation call returns a uint value, which is shown after the operation name and separated from it by a colon. In addition, the visibility of attributes and operations is shown in the class model by means of the provided prefix. Table 5.2 lists the supported visibility prefixes and their meanings. As you can see, in SampleClass the attributes are private and protected, whereas sampleOperation is defined as public.

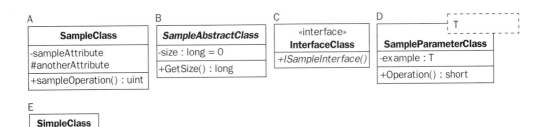

Figure 5.3 Sample Class Models

Table 5.2 Class Diagram Visibility Prefixes

Prefix	Visibility
– (hyphen)	`private`: Can be seen only within the class that defines it
#	`protected`: Visible within the class that defines it and by subclasses of the defining class
+	`public`: Visible to any class within the program

The sample class shown in Figure 5.3B is an *abstract* class. Abstract class names are shown in italics to distinguish them in the class diagram. Note, too, that the public operation `GetSize()` returns a `long` value, which actually is the `private` attribute size of `SampleAbstractClass`. The `private` attribute size is initialized to 0 (zero) and of type `long`.

An abstract class without any implementation in UML is called an *interface* class. Figure 5.3C shows a sample interface class identified by the stereotype `<<interface>>` above the class name. Interface classes provide no implementation, and this means that no section for attributes is needed in the class model. The operations in an interface class are shown in italics because they do not provide any implementation and must be implemented by the derived classes.

UML also lets you define parameterized classes. In C++ this feature is known as a *template* class (C# will provide support for parameterized or generalized classes in a coming version). Parameterized classes are identified by the parameter definition in the upper-right corner of the class model. Figure 5.3D shows a sample parameterized class.

The class shown in Figure 5.3D is a simple class showing only the class name. This type of model is usually used in overview diagrams of large systems.

To model the system, we must define relationships between the classes. The next section introduces the class relationship models in UML.

Class Relationships

Figure 5.4 shows the basic dependency principles among classes.

Figure 5.4A shows a *dependency* between `Class1` and `Class2`. The dependency indicates that changes to `Class2` could trigger changes in

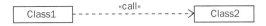

A Dependency

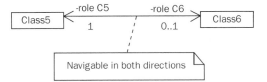

B Navigability

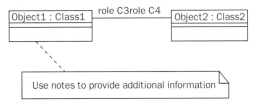

C Object Association

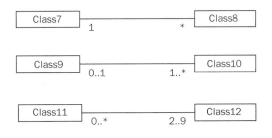

D Multiplicities

Figure 5.4 Class Dependency

Class1. Figure 5.4B shows navigability in both directions. *Navigability* shows the directions (unidirectional or bidirectional) in which the program can traverse the class tree. In the example, Class6 "knows" about Class5, and vice versa. The navigability diagram also shows how to use *notes* to add information to the class diagram if necessary. At both ends of the navigation relationship, you can show any multiplicity of the relation (see Figure 5.4D) for more detail).

Figure 5.4C shows an association relationship between two class instances (or objects) in addition to a note. The class instances are identified by the prefix object and the class name, which are separated by a colon and underlined. Both ends of an association can be labeled. The label is called a *role name*.

Another important part of class diagrams is the ability they give you to express *multiplicities*, as shown in Figure 5.4D. Multiplicity is expressed by a number on each side of the dependency connection. If no number is supplied, then the default, which is 1, is assumed. The meanings of the multiplicities numbers are as follows:

1	Exactly one
*	Many (zero or more)
0..1	Optional (zero or one)
1..*	One or more
0..*	Optional, one or many
2..9	Example of an m..n relationship; in this case, a two to nine dependency

Now let's look at the more advanced class dependencies, as shown in Figure 5.5.

Aggregation (shown in Figure 5.5A) is a *part-of* relationship. For example, a point is part of a circle. This sounds very simple, but then what is the difference between dependency and aggregation? Aggregation can be seen as a placeholder. In other words, you can use aggregation as an indication of a relationship without specifying the details of the relationship. This is possible because UML defines very little of the semantics of aggregation.

In addition to aggregation, UML offers a more defined variation called *composition*. Composition implies that the part-of object belongs only to one whole, and the part-of object's lifetime responsibility is with the object that contains it. Figure 5.5B shows that `Class2` is part of `Class1` and that `Class1` is responsible for creating and deleting objects of `Class2`.

Another dependency defined in UML is the generalization, shown in Figure 5.5C. *Generalization* can be seen as an *is-a* relationship. For example, a diesel engine is an engine, and a gasoline engine is an engine. This holds true if "engine" is defined as the commonalities of diesel and gasoline engines. Every diesel engine and every gasoline engine can then be defined by deriving from the general `engine` class and adding the specifics according to the engine type.

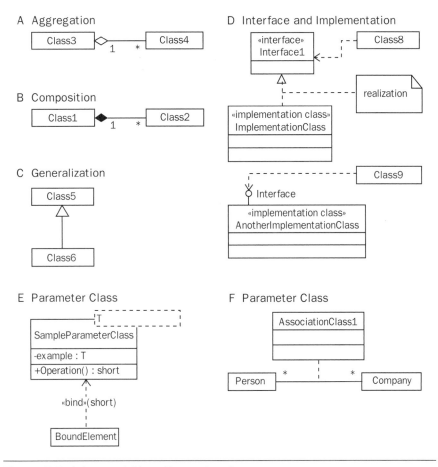

Figure 5.5 Advanced Class Dependencies

Interfaces and their implementation can be modeled within UML in two ways, as shown in Figure 5.5D. The first technique is to define an interface class that does not contain any implementation. This class is then connected to the implementation class via the *realization* dependency. In the example, Class8 calls on the Interface method, which is implemented in the ImplementationClass. The second way to show an interface in a UML diagram is by using an Implementation class that shows the provided interface with the lollipop representation. In the example, Class9 calls the Interface method of AnotherImplementationClass. In the first technique, you can explicitly show the interface definition and the implementation, whereas the second technique shows only the implementation class.

The use of parameterized classes is called *bound elements* and is known to C++ programmers as template classes. In Figure 5.5E, `BoundElement` is bound by a `short` parameter to `SampleParameterClass`. Parameterized classes cannot be extended by the bound class. `BoundElement` can use completely specified types from the parameter class. The only thing added to the parameter class is the restricting type information.

Association classes are used to add an extra constraint to a relation of two objects. This is shown in Figure 5.5F. Only one instance of the association class can be used between any two participating objects. In the example, a `Person` is working for at most one `Company` at a time (at least in theory). An association class is used to keep information about the date range over which each employee is working for each company. Because persons sometimes switch jobs, this information should not be kept within the person's class directly but rather in an association class.

In object-oriented programming, you usually try to limit dependencies to the absolute minimum. In this way, changes made to one class do not trigger endless changes to other classes. Necessary dependencies are usually kept on the interface level.

5.4.2 Design of the Photo Editor Application

The design of the photo editor application is done in Microsoft Visio. The decision to use Visio was made because in addition to providing tools to generate UML diagrams, Visio lets you generate code from class models. Also, Visio supports extracting class models from existing code, a capability that can be very useful when you're reengineering poorly documented software. Unfortunately, Visio has no support for the creation of XML documentation from the UML models. Therefore, during document review we must trace requirement keys manually through the design process.

The class diagram shows that the main application class, called `Photo EditorForm`, is derived from the `Windows.Forms` class. The `Windows.Forms` class provides Windows-related functionalities that are used by the photo editor. In addition, `PhotoEditorForm` creates an instance of `Exception Publisher`, which is derived from the `IExceptionPublisher` interface provided by the Microsoft application block. In addition, an instance of the `Picture` class is created. The `Picture` class instance holds the loaded image and provides the basic image-manipulating operations (such as rotating and flipping).

Figure 5.6 shows the class diagram for the photo editor application in this iteration.

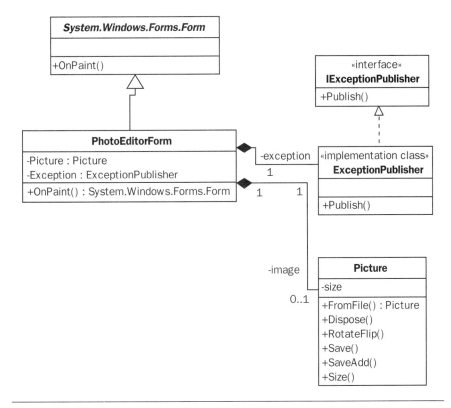

Figure 5.6 The Photo Editor Class Diagram

5.5 The Detailed Project Schedule

As mentioned earlier, it is important to track the project and update the plan constantly. In this iteration we develop a more refined project schedule, as shown in Figure 5.7. The project schedule is kept in Microsoft Visio as a Gantt chart, showing the various tasks, their dependencies, and the project milestones. Online Photo Shop is the overall project, and we indent all other tasks to show that they are defined as subtasks.

For easier readability, the requirements are grouped into blocks of related functionality. The name of the developer who is responsible for a block is shown in the resource column. Most of the blocks contain dependent or very small functionalities (or both). By combining these items into blocks, we make it easier to do tracking on a daily instead of an hourly basis.

Detailed Project Schedule: Online Photo Shop

ID	Task Name	Start	Finish	Duration	Resource Names
1	Milestone 1 (progress review)	11/11/2002	11/11/2002	0d	
2	Milestone 2 (progress review)	11/25/2002	11/25/2002	0d	
3	Milestone 3 (progress review)	12/19/2002	12/19/2002	0d	
4	**Online Photo Shop**	**10/10/2002**	**1/31/2003**	**82d**	
5	photo_editor	10/10/2002	1/7/2003	64d	GL, KC
6	order_online	10/10/2002	1/7/2003	64d	TM
7	error_handling, picture_load_and_save, image_format, image_crop, image_rotate	10/22/2002	11/8/2002	14d	GL
8	Image_flip	11/4/2002	11/8/2002	5d	Reader
9	image_brightness, image_contrast, image_color,	11/11/2002	11/20/2002	8d	GL
10	image_graphics_annotations, image_text_annotations	11/11/2002	11/20/2002	8d	KC, Reader
11	order_products, product_browse, product_options, product_customize	11/11/2002	11/20/2002	8d	TM, Reader
12	Risk Buffer	11/20/2002	11/22/2002	3d	
13	image_processing_direct_3d, editor _optimizations	11/25/2002	12/13/2002	14d	GL
14	image_graphics_special_effects, image_special_effects	11/25/2002	12/13/2002	14d	KC, Reader
15	product_shopping_cart, order_checkout, checkaout_shipping, checkout_payment, checkout_summerize	11/25/2002	12/13/2002	14d	TM, Reader
16	Risk Buffer	12/13/2002	12/18/2002	4d	
17	editor_system_test	12/19/2002	1/20/2003	22d	GL, TM, KC, Reader
18	Risk Buffer	1/20/2003	1/31/2003	10d	

Figure 5.7 Detailed Schedule

In addition to the tasks themselves, including their estimated duration, other milestones are defined and connected to the related tasks (as indicated by the lines that go from the milestones to the tasks). The milestones are review points at which the status of the project is reviewed and necessary adjustments are made. In the case shown in Figure 5.7, the milestones coincide with the end (or the beginning) of the iterations. This works well if the requirements are broken into small enough pieces (no longer than two weeks' worth of effort). If you cannot do this, you must either break the tasks into smaller pieces or define interim milestones.

From the detailed schedule, you can see that even though the iterations are described in a serialized fashion, iterations are actually worked on in parallel. This practice shortens the overall duration of the project. In our case, working on development tasks in parallel works very well because the photo editor application and the online shop have no anticipated dependency. The schedule shown is constantly refined and updated throughout the development cycle. Also, we have added risk buffers to the schedule. These buffers give the project additional time to react to unforeseen problems. Nevertheless, the risk buffers should not be used for adding new requirements or implementing new features.

Tracking is done in small meetings. We hold one weekly meeting to discuss problems, ideas, and management-related items; in addition, *stand-up meetings* (which last about 12 minutes) are held every other day for frequent status updates (no discussions are allowed at these meetings). Stand-up meetings often lead to the calling of a regular meeting at another time so that team members can quickly discuss problems found.

From the Gantt chart we developed in Visio, we can export a variety of diagrams, such as a timeline diagram. These exported diagrams are very useful for reports to the customer or upper management (assuming that the plan is kept up-to-date).

5.6 Implementation of the Photo Editor Application

After all the ground work is set, the implementation can start. To begin the implementation, a project workspace must be set up and added to configuration management. As mentioned in Chapter 4, the configuration management administrator is the person who should set up the directory structure. Based on the directory structure (see Figure 4.3), a solution is created that will contain all the subprojects of the software developed during the course of this book.

To create an empty Visual Studio solution, open Visual Studio.NET (see Figure 5.8). Then select Visual Studio Solutions and Blank Solution, and name the solution `Photo Editor`. The solution should be crated in the

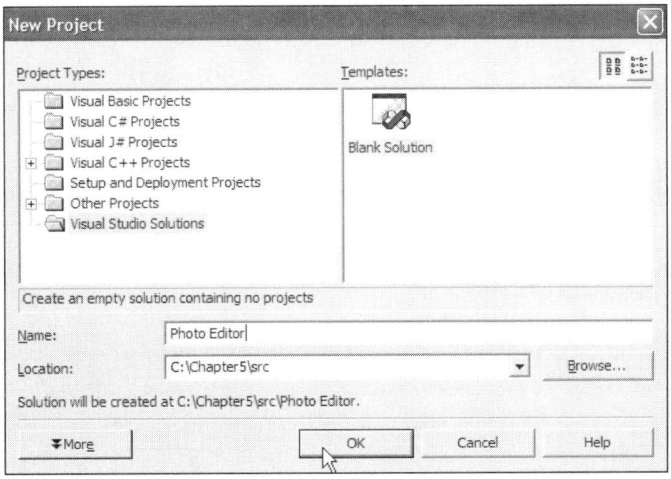

Figure 5.8 Creating an Empty Solution

`src` directory, so browse to `src` in your project directory tree and click on the OK button. The Visual Studio solution will be created.

5.6.1 The Basic Photo Editor Application

Now that we have an empty Visual Studio solution, we can add other projects to it.

Creating a Basic Application

We will develop the GUI and most of the functionality of the photo editor application in C# using Microsoft Visual Studio 2003. The first implementation step is to create a Windows application project; we will then extend it to provide exception handling and image loading, saving, and displaying. The application is created as a project within the Photo Editor solution.

Therefore, with the Photo Editor solution opened in Visual Studio, click on the File menu and then Add Project. Then choose New Project. In the dialog window that appears, choose Visual C# Projects and Windows Application. In the Name field, type `Photo Editor Application`. Click on OK, and Visual Studio.NET creates a new project within the Photo Editor solution.

The Microsoft wizard in the solution generates three files: `App.ico`, `AssemblyInfo.cs`, and `Form1.cs`. You can explore all three files by double-clicking on the file name in Solution Explorer. Obviously, `App.ico` is the icon associated with the photo editor application and can be customized. The `AssemblyInfo.cs` file contains assembly-related information such as version and binding. The version information is updated before all releases (including intermediate releases); binding will be discussed when the product is deployed to the customer in the final release. The more interesting file that was generated is `Form1.cs`. This file contains the form design and the code for the photo editor application. To see the generated code, go to the `Form1.cs [Design]` view, choose the form, right-click on the form, and choose View Code.

The top of the file shows various namespaces that are used in the application (similar to the kind of information you see in `#include` statements in C++). These `using` statements define shortcuts for the compiler to use in resolving externally defined namespaces. `Extern` in this case relates to objects that are not defined in the project's namespace. If a call to a method cannot be resolved, the compiler will try to resolve the call by checking the namespaces defined by the `using` statement.

Listing 5.1 shows the namespaces used by the code generated by Visual Studio.NET. The `System` namespace contains the basic .NET Framework types, classes, and second-level namespaces. In contrast, the second- and third-level namespaces contain types, classes, and methods to support various kinds of development, such as GUI, the runtime infrastructure, .NET security, component model, and Web services development, to name only a few categories.

In the photo editor application, you can see that several second-level namespaces are automatically included. The `System.Drawing` namespace, for example, provides rich two-dimensional graphics functionality and access to Microsoft's GDI+ functionalities. (GDI+ is explained in more detail in Chapter 6.) For the remainder of this chapter, we use GDI+ to provide a memory location where the image can be stored and then displayed; in addition, we use some GDI+ methods for image operations.

The `System.Collections` namespace holds collections of objects, such as lists, queues, arrays, hash tables, and dictionaries. In addition, `System.ComponentModel` implements components, including licensing and design-time adaptations. For a rich set of Windows-based user interface features, we also include the `System.Windows.Forms` namespace. Last but not least, the `System.Data` namespace lets us access and manage data and data sources. For more information on the namespaces provided by the .NET Framework, please refer to the MSDN help.

Listing 5.1 Using Externally Defined Namespaces

```
using System;
using System.Drawing;
using System.Collections;
using System.ComponentModel;
using System.Windows.Forms;
using System.Data;
```

The next section in the source file defines the namespace for the application, the basic application classes, and the methods. Listing 5.2 shows the source code that is created.

Listing 5.2 The Photo Editor Namespace

```
namespace Photo_Editor_Application
{
  /// <summary>
```

```
/// Summary description for Form1.
/// </summary>
public class Form1 : System.Windows.Forms.Form
{
  /// <summary>
  /// Required designer variable.
  /// </summary>
  private System.ComponentModel.Container components = null;

  public Form1()
  {
    //
    // Required for Windows Form Designer support
    //
    InitializeComponent();

    //
    // TODO: Add any constructor code after
    // InitializeComponent call
    //
  }

  /// <summary>
  /// Clean up any resources being used.
  /// </summary>
  protected override void Dispose( bool disposing )
  {
    if( disposing )
    {
      if (components != null)
      {
        components.Dispose();
      }
    }
    base.Dispose( disposing );
  }

  #region Windows Form Designer generated code
  /// <summary>
  /// Required method for Designer support - do not modify
  /// the contents of this method with the code editor.
  /// </summary>
  private void InitializeComponent()
```

```
    {
      this.components = new System.ComponentModel.Container();
      this.Size = new System.Drawing.Size(300,300);
      this.Text = "Form1";
    }
    #endregion

    /// <summary>
    /// The main entry point for the application.
    /// </summary>
    [STAThread]
    static void Main()
    {
      Application.Run(new Form1());
    }
  }
}
```

First, we define the namespace `Photo_Editor_Application`. This is the namespace that refers to all the classes, types, and methods defined by the photo editor application. Next, class `Form1` is defined as `public` and is derived from `System.Windows.Forms.Form`. This class implements the application window, which is called `Form1`, at least for now. The first property defined in the `Form1` class is declared `private`, named `components`, and defined to be of type `System.ComponentModel.Container`. The value is set to `null` to indicate that no initialization has yet been done.

Next, we define the public constructor of `Form1`. The implementation first calls the `InitializeComponent` method created by Visual Studio Designer. This method takes care of the necessary Windows Forms property initialization. You should not modify the Designer-generated part of the code directly, but you can do so through the properties window of `Form1.cs[Design]`.

After the constructor, the dispose method is defined. The `Dispose()` method is used to free system resources if they are no longer needed. Even though Visual Studio.NET provides garbage collection for allocated memory, we must explicitly delete other system resources at the time they are no longer used. Resources other than memory should be disposed of in order to keep the resource footprint (memory, disk space, handles, and so on) as small as possible. In the example, the components are disposed of if they were allocated (not `null`); to do this, we call the base class's dispose method.

Next comes a block specified with the `#region` and `#endregion` keywords. This block allows the developer to write code that can be expanded or collapsed within the Visual Studio.NET development environment. In the example, the `#region-#endregion` block encloses the initializing method of the Designer-generated form, as described earlier, and this code should not be altered. You can collapse the code by pressing the "-" symbol, or expand it by selecting the "+" symbol next to the keyword. Usually the IDE provides the expand-collapse feature automatically for multiline comments, class definitions, and method definitions, to name only a few. The developer can define additional collapsible and expandable regions. The region statements can be nested. In that case, the `#endregion` matches the last defined `#region` statement that has not yet been matched.

The final part of the code defines the `static main` entry point for the application. The application is defined to be running in a single-threaded apartment (STA), and the main entry point then creates and runs an instance of `Form1`.

The next step is to change the output directory of the compiler to the `bin` and `bind` directories. As mentioned in Chapter 4, the `bin` directory holds all assemblies necessary to run the photo editor application in release configuration, whereas the `bind` directory holds the same files but compiled in debug configuration. To change the output directory, choose the project in the Solution Explorer window and then choose Project | Properties | Configuration Properties | Build | Output Path; change the path to the `bin` directory (for release configuration) and `bind` (for debug configuration).

Before you check the source files into the configuration management system, you need to make some additional changes. For easier readability, maintainability, and understanding, it is worthwhile to rename some of the generated source files to more meaningful names. We do this before checkin because renaming files already under configuration management is not always easy.

Therefore, we change the name of the application source file from `Form1.cs` to `PhotoEditor.cs`. We do this by right-clicking on the file name `Form1.cs` in the Solution Explorer window and then going to the Properties window below Solution Explorer and changing the name in the File Name field. After the name is changed, we adjust other properties of `PhotoEditor.cs[Design]`. We select the corresponding tab and click on the form. We change the Text field to `Photo Editor Application`, and change the (Name) field to `PhotoEditorForm`.

To finish the cosmetics, click on the photo editor form and choose View Code (by right-clicking on the form and choosing the option). Change `Form1()` to `PhotoEditorForm()`, as shown in Listing 5.3.

Listing 5.3 `PhotoEditorForm` Creation

```
static void Main()
  {
    Application.Run(new PhotoEditorForm());
  }
```

Before you put the project into the source control system, make sure that it compiles. Go to the Build menu in Visual Studio, and choose Build Project (or use the shortcut by pressing Ctrl+Shift+B). If there are any errors during compilation, they will be shown in the output window below the main window. Double-clicking on the error message will open the correct source file to the approximate position of the error.

5.6.2 Using Version Control

The Visual Source Safe source control system integrates smoothly with the Visual Studio.NET IDE. There are several ways to communicate with it. The following assumes that Visual Source Safe is installed on the computer (even though working with other source control systems may be quite similar). The first possibility is to use the File | Source Control menu, which is shown in Figure 5.9.

Another method of communicating with the version control system is to configure a toolbar menu. Go to View | Toolbars | Source Control. You'll get a toolbar (shown in Figure 5.10) that can be added to the toolbar section of Visual Studio.

There is yet another way to check the project into the source control system. Right-click on the project in Solution Explorer and choose Add Solution to Source Control.

In our sample project, we add the project to the source control system by using the latter method. The system asks for the login credentials before the Visual Source Safe dialog appears, as shown in Figure 5.11.

Now we choose the name and location for storing the project in the source control system. For this project, we take the defaults suggested by Source Safe (location root and project name Photo Editor Application), so

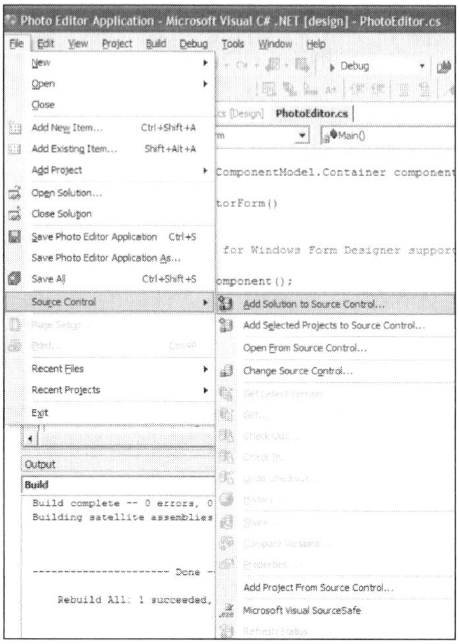

Figure 5.9 Visual Source Safe Menu

Figure 5.10 Visual Source Safe Toolbar

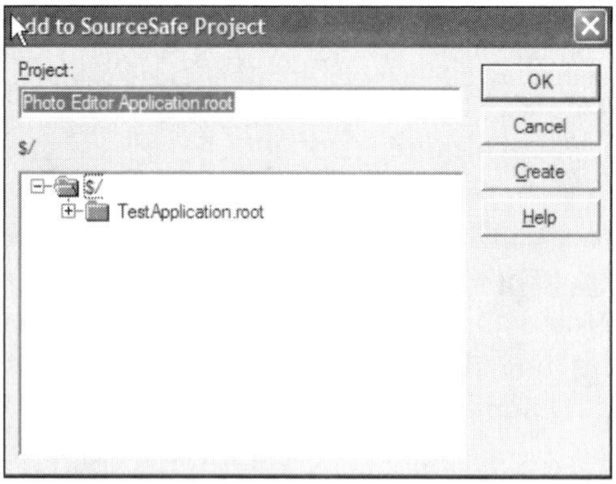

Figure 5.11 Source Safe Dialog

we just click OK. The system asks whether it should create the new project, and again we simply confirm by clicking OK. As you can see, all files in Visual Studio Explorer now have a little lock symbol next to them; this means that the files are read-only (checked in) under source control.

Before a developer can make any change to the files, he or she must check out the files to get write permissions to them. Checkout means that the developer will work on a private copy of the file. The developer works on the private copy, keeping it checked out, until the change is (partially) complete and compiled; then the file must be checked in. At checkin time the private file is added to the version control as the newest version of the file; the file becomes read-only again, and all developers on the project can see the the new file. Changes can be made only by the developer who currently has the file checked out. It is also possible to undo a checkout, thereby reverting to the original version of the file and discarding the changes made. (Nobody will ever know about the changes. Usually it is a good practice to save the changes under a different file name in a private file before undoing a checkout and losing the changes.)

Visual Source Safe provides many other useful tools, such as forcing the system to get the latest version of all files and comparing the changes in different file versions. Most of the functionality is self-explanatory. For more detailed information, you can consult the Visual Source Safe help files.

5.6.3 The Exception-Handling Application Block

The first "real" functionality that we will implement is exception management. As discussed earlier, exception handling in the photo editor application is based on the Microsoft Exception Management Application Block. You can download this application block from `http://msdn.microsoft.com/downloads/list/bda.asp`. You install the files by following the instructions on the screen. Alternatively, you can simply take the installed source files from the sample solutions provided on the CD under `Chapter5\src\Exception Management Application Block`.

Next, go to the installation directory of the application block and open the `Code` directory with a double-click in Windows Explorer. There are two versions of the exception management block installed. The first version is written in Visual Basic (`VB`), and the second version is implemented using C# (`CS`). We are interested in the C# version, so open the `CS` subdirectory and double-click on the Exception Management Application Block (CS) solution. This will open a solution with two projects: `Microsoft.`

`ApplicationBlocks.ExceptionManagement.Interfaces` and `Microsoft.`
`ApplicationBlocks.ExceptionManagement` in Visual Studio.NET.

To use the application blocks, we need to build both projects. *But*
before we actually build them, we first set the output path of both projects
to the `bin` and `bind` directories of the photo editor project. To set the output path of the compiler-generated assemblies, right-click on the project in
Solution Explorer. Choose Properties and go to Configuration Properties |
Build | Outputs | Output Path. Make sure that the configuration of the
selected project is set to Release. Choose the table entry for Output Path,
and navigate to the photo editor `bin` directory. Then choose Apply. If the
project is now being built in release mode, then the assemblies will be
saved in the `bin` directory of the photo editor project. Do the same for the
Debug configuration of both projects by specifying the `bind` directory as
the output path.

After that, build the solution by going to the Build menu and choosing
Build Solution (or by using one of the previously mentioned shortcuts).
Then change the build configuration in the Active Solution Configuration
list box and build this configuration as well. (Either use the menu bar or go
to the Build menu, choose Configuration Management, and choose Debug
or Release depending on the configuration you just built.) You can check
the success of the build by checking the `bin` and `bind` directories for the
created assemblies. You should be able to see `ExceptionManagement.dll`
and `ExceptionManagement.Interfaces.dll` in both directories.

After the assemblies are built, we add references to `Microsoft.`
`ApplicationBlock.ExceptionManagement.dll` and `Microsoft.Application`
`Block.ExceptionManagement.Interfaces.dll` to the photo editor appli-
cation project. To do this, you choose the menu item Project | Add Refer-
ence. Alternatively, you can right-click on the Photo Editor Application
project in Solution Explorer and choose Add Reference. A dialog box opens.
Choose Browse and navigate to the `bin` directory, where the assemblies for
the Microsoft Exception Management Application Block reside. (By referencing the assemblies in the `bin` directory we are referencing the assembly
that was built in release configuration. Alternatively, we could reference
the debug version. But we do not intend to debug the application block, so
we reference the release version.) Select the two assemblies and press OK.

Another Source Safe dialog box opens that lets you choose whether to
check out the project file for editing. Because we will add references to the
project, we need to update the file `Photo Editor Application.csproj` to
reflect these changes. Click OK to check out the file. You can add a com-

ment to the history of the file before checkout. The rule for the photo editor application is to add checkin comments that explain the changes made. In Solution Explorer, you can now see the newly added references in the Reference section. In addition to the references, we need to add a `using` statement to the photo editor application to indicate the use of the externally defined functionality. Again, the source control will ask whether the `PhotoEditor.cs` file should be checked out; we acknowledge this by choosing checkout. The added code can be seen in Listing 5.4.

Listing 5.4 Using the Microsoft Exception Management Application Block

```
using System;
using System.Drawing;
using System.Collections;
using System.ComponentModel;
using System.Windows.Forms;
using System.Data;


using Microsoft.ApplicationBlocks.ExceptionManagement;
```

Now that the photo editor application is aware of the exception management class, the classes and methods provided by it can be used. The provided default publisher logs the exceptions to the event log. This is not the behavior we intend for the photo editor application, so we must create a custom publisher. Before continuing, make sure that all changes are saved and the project compiles.

5.6.4 Customized Exception Handling

You create custom publishers by implementing the `IExceptionPublisher` `Interface`, which is defined in the `Microsoft.ApplicationBlocks.` `ExceptionManagement.Interfaces.dll` assembly. To keep the exception publisher code separate from the application code, add a new file to the photo editor application project. To add a file, right-click on Photo Editor Application in Solution Explorer and choose Add | New Item (see Figure 5.12).

Select Class in the dialog box and type the name `ExceptionPublisher.` `cs` for the file. Click on Open; this will open a new file with the added name selected. The file contains the `using system` statement and shows that it is

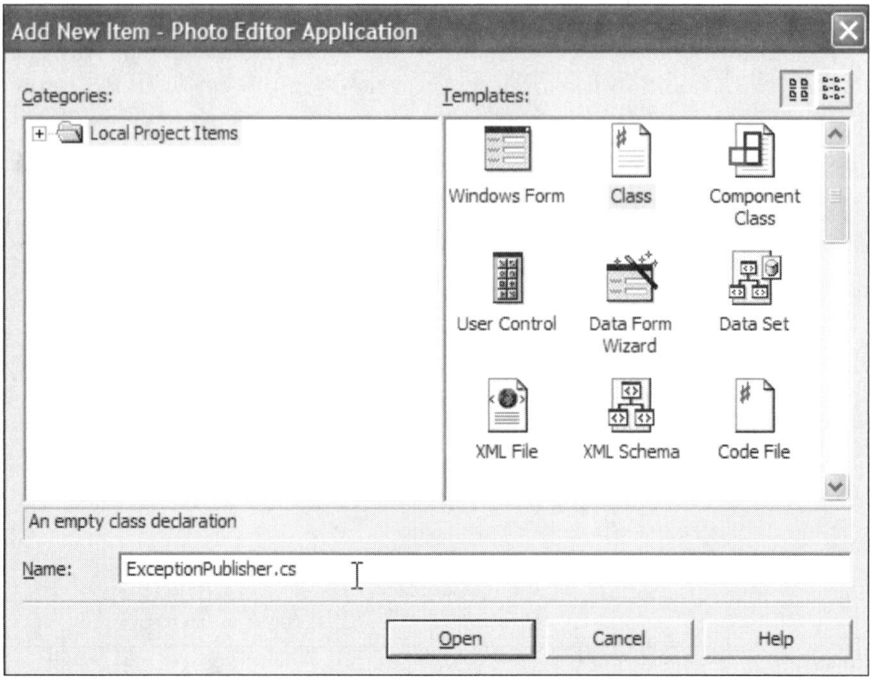

Figure 5.12 Adding the `ExceptionPublisher.cs` File

part of the `Photo_Editor_Application` namespace. In addition, a class definition for class `ExceptionPublisher` and its constructor are provided. The new file is automatically added to Visual Source Safe and is marked as checked out (marked with a red check mark next to the file name in Solution Explorer).

Next, we add the `using` statement for the Exception Management Application Block in the same way as was shown for the `PhotoEditor.cs` file. In addition, we add the `using System.Windows.Forms` statement for Windows Forms support. Then we must derive the `ExceptionPublisher` class from `IExceptionPublisher`. Therefore, we change the class definition to `public class ExceptionPublisher : IExceptionPublisher`. When we're finished typing, a stub for the `IExceptionPublisher` interface can be added automatically by pressing the Tab key (otherwise, we simply type it in as shown in Listing 5.5). The finished `Publish` method is shown in Listing 5.5. It also shows the three arguments the `Publish` method takes.

Listing 5.5 Publish Interface Implementation with XML Documentation

```
#region IExceptionPublisher Members
    /// <summary>
    /// Custom Publisher, displays error message on screen.
    /// </summary>
    /// <param name="exception">Exception, containing meaningful
    /// error message</param>
    /// <param name="additionalInfo">Provides additional info
    /// about the exception</param>
    /// <param name="configSettings">Describes the config
    /// settings defined in the app.config file</param>
    public void Publish(Exception exception,
      System.Collections.Specialized.NameValueCollection
      additionalInfo,
      System.Collections.Specialized.NameValueCollection
      configSettings)
    {
      // TODO:  Add ExceptionPublisher.Publish implementation
      string caption = "Photo Editor";
      DialogResult result;

      // Displays the MessageBox.

      result = MessageBox.Show( exception.Message, caption,
        MessageBoxButtons.OK,
        MessageBoxIcon.Error, MessageBoxDefaultButton.Button1,
        MessageBoxOptions.RightAlign);
    }
#endregion
```

To generate nicely formatted documentation from the source code, we add the XML description as specified in Chapter 4. You generate the documentation from the code by selecting the Tools menu in Visual Studio and choosing Build Comment Web Pages. Then select the radio button Build for the entire solution, and specify Save Web Pages in the doc directory of your project (in the sample solution this is Chapter5\doc) and click OK. The documentation is generated, and an Explorer window opens that shows the generated solution's comment Web pages. Click on the namespace to navigate down the program documentation tree and open the next lower level.

According to the requirements, exceptions are to be published via a message box displaying meaningful error messages. This leads us to the next implementation step, which is to implement the message box. The easiest way to display a message box is to use a Windows message box. The `System.Windows.Forms` namespace, which we have already added to the `using` statement section, provides the functionality to display a simple message box. Several overloaded types of message boxes are supported by the .NET Framework. The one that we use here is as follows:

```
MessageBox.Show( text, caption, buttons, icon, defaultButton, options);
```

The message box used in this example takes six parameters, which are explained in Table 5.3. For other variants of the message box, please refer to the MSDN help.

To use the customized exception publisher, the final step is to provide a configuration file. The configuration file makes the exception application block aware of the custom publisher that is to be used (this is similar to registration of the custom publisher). To add an application configuration file, right-click on Photo Editor Application in Solution Explorer and choose

Table 5.3 `MessageBox.Show` Parameters

Parameter Type	Name	Description
`string`	`text`	Text to be displayed in the dialog box, which is the error message in this case.
`string`	`caption`	Text displayed in message box title.
`MessageBoxButtons`	`buttons`	The buttons to be displayed in the dialog window. For the error message dialog window, this is just the OK button.
`MessageBoxIcon`	`icon`	This defines the icon displayed in the message box. For an error message the displayed icon is a red circle with a white x inside.
`MessageBoxDefaultButton`	`defaultButton`	The default button. In this case there is only one button displayed, so `button1` is the only and default button.
`MessageBoxOptions`	`options`	The text in the message box is right-aligned.

Add | New item. In the dialog window that opens, choose Application Configuration File and press Open. A configuration file is added to the solution. Change the configuration file to correspond with Listing 5.6.

Listing 5.6 `App.config`: The Application Configuration File

```
<?xml version="1.0" encoding="utf-8" ?>
<configuration>
  <configSections>
    <section name="exceptionManagement"
      type="Microsoft.ApplicationBlocks.ExceptionManagement.
      ExceptionManagerSectionHandler,
      Microsoft.ApplicationBlocks.ExceptionManagement" />
  </configSections>

  <exceptionManagement mode="on">
    <publisher assembly="Photo Editor
    Application"type=
     "Photo_Editor_Application.ExceptionPublisher"
      fileName="c:\PhotoEditorExceptionLog.xml"/>
  </exceptionManagement>
</configuration>
```

As you can see, the configuration file provides information regarding the customized publisher. The configuration entry `<publisher assembly=...` defines the name of the assembly in which the customized exception publisher is defined. The `type="..."` defines the namespace and the method name for the publisher, whereas the file name specifies the log file name to which exceptions are logged in case the defined publisher cannot be found. If an exception occurs, the Exception Manager Application Block will now know about the customized exception publisher and will call the specified exception publisher.

Make sure that the project compiles, and check in all the changes by choosing the Pending Checkins tab below the main window. When you check in a file, usually it is good practice to provide a meaningful comment. The comment for the checkin at this point might read, "Added custom exception handling using the Microsoft Exception Manager Application Block. Exceptions are published in a window on the screen." After typing the comment, choose Check In. A dialog opens if the files really should be checked in. Click on OK, and all the changes are available in the repository, visible to everybody on the team.

Now the exceptions can be used in the photo editor application. All code that could possibly throw an exception should be put in a `try-catch-finally` block:

```
try
{
  // Some code here
    *

    *

    *

  //in case a problem is found, an exception can be thrown
  throw(new Exception("Some information here"));
}
catch(Exception exception)
{
    ExceptionManager.Publish(exception);
}
finally
{
  // Code here will always be executed, whether
  //there was an exception thrown or not.
}
```

The example also shows how an exception is thrown within a method and how it provides additional information as a string. C# defines a `finally` block in addition to the `catch` block. The `finally` statement can be put after the `catch` block. The code in the block is always executed, either after the `catch` is finished or if the `try` block is finished.

An Important Note on Code Conventions From this point on, it is your task to provide the `try-catch` statements during the implementation of the code, even if it is not explicitly mentioned in the descriptions of the implementation. In addition, for the remainder of this book it is assumed that you will add the XML comments according to the coding guidelines while implementing the functionalities.

It's also up to you to save and check in files whenever you achieve an intermediate result. It is good practice to check in only code that is compiling and that has the added XML documentation.

The sample solutions that are provided on the accompanying CD contain comments and exception code.

5.6.5 Loading an Image

After the implementation of the custom exception publisher is completed, we start to implement the basic functionality of the photo editor application: loading an image. The .NET Framework provides standard file dialogs for loading and for saving files. The standard implementation of the Windows File dialog provides a window that enables the user to browse, select, name, and filter files. Because this functionality corresponds to what was specified in the requirements, the photo editor application uses the .NET-provided standard file dialogs. To start the implementation, we click on the `PhotoEditor.cs[Design]` tab and choose the Photo Editor Application form.

Next, we set the WindowState in the Layout section of the properties to Maximized. This sets the main window to maximized when the application is started. Compile and run the solution to see the described effect. After that, we add the File menu to the form. Go to the Toolbox, choose MainMenu, and drop the main menu on the form. (The Toolbox is usually shown on the left border of the screen. If the Toolbox is not visible, go to the View menu and select Toolbox, or simply press Ctrl+Alt+X.)

This action adds an empty menu bar to the form. Rename the menu to `MainMenu` in the properties window. To do that, first make sure that `main Menu1` is selected. Then go to the menu bar and type `&File` where the text Type Here is shown, and press Return. This will add a top-level menu item called File. The prefix `&` indicates that the shortcut to access the menu is the Alt+F key combination. After that, change the name of the menu in the properties section to `FileMenu`. Add a submenu item for the Open File menu item, as shown in Figure 5.13.

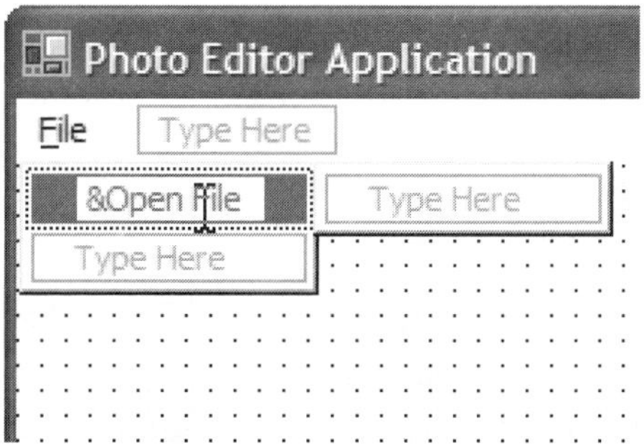

Figure 5.13 Creating the File Menu

Change the name in the property section of the submenu item to `Open File`. To add functionality to the menu, double-click on the OpenFile menu item. The `PhotoEditor.cs` source file will be opened, and the Designer adds a stub implementation of the `OpenFile_Click` event handler. The Designer also adds code to make the system aware of the function that handles the event of the specified type. Listing 5.7 shows the generated code that initializes some properties of the OpenFile menu item and registers the event handler method.

Listing 5.7 Adding an Event Handler Method

```
//
// OpenFile
//
this.OpenFile.Index = 0;
this.OpenFile.Text = "&Open File";
this.OpenFile.Click +=
    new System.EventHandler(this.OpenFile_Click);
```

To load an image, we must add a new field to the `PhotoEditorForm` class. To add new fields to a class using the Visual Studio class wizard, click on the Class View tab, right-click on the class, and select Add | Add Field. In the dialog window that opens, you specify the properties of the field. To create the field, specify `private` as the field access, `OpenFileDialog` as the field type, and `loadFileDialog` as the field name. Alternatively, simply add the field to the class manually by adding the following line to the class:

```
private OpenFileDialog loadFileDialog;
```

At initialization time the `loadFileDialog` object is created and memory is allocated for it. To do that, add the following line to the constructor `PhotoEditorForm()`:

```
//
// TODO: Add any constructor code after InitializeComponent call
//
loadFileDialog = new OpenFileDialog();
```

Finally, you implement the `loadFileDialog` in the `OpenFile_Click()` method, as shown in Listing 5.8.

Listing 5.8 The File Open Dialog

```
loadFileDialog.Filter = " jpg files (*.jpg)|*.jpg| gif files
(*.gif)|*.gif| bmp files (*.bmp)|*.bmp| All files (*.*)|*.*";
     loadFileDialog.ShowDialog();
     loadedImage = new Bitmap(loadFileDialog.FileName);
     this.Invalidate();
```

First, you define a file filter whose task it is to show only files of certain file types within the chosen directory. Files of other types (or file extensions) than the ones specified are not shown in the dialog window. This filter operation is provided by the `OpenFileDialog` class, which defines a `Filter` property that can be used to filter files by their types. In our example, the files that are of interest are image files of various types. The supported types are images with the extensions `.jpg`, `.gif`, and `.bmp`. In addition, we want to show all files in a directory when the file name is specified as "*.*".

After the file filter is defined, the standard Windows File Open dialog box is shown by calling its method `ShowDialog()`. A file dialog window appears that enables the user to browse directories and select a file. After the user has selected a file and clicked the Open button, the selected file name can be extracted from the file dialog object using the `FileName()` method. The .NET Framework provides converters to load and save the most commonly used image types. For all image types supported by the photo editor application, converters are provided by the .NET Framework. Thus, we need no customized functionality to work with the various image types. For supported formats and available conversion types, refer to the MSDN help pages.

To work with the loaded image, we must create a `Bitmap` object and allocate memory for it. We do this by calling the `Bitmap` constructor with the file name as a parameter and assigning the image to `loadedImage`. The loaded image field is not yet defined. Therefore, we add the following line to the `PhotoEditorForm` class:

```
private Bitmap loadedImage;
```

As you can see, the application uses a bitmap type image to work with rather than using the type under which the image was actually stored. It is at this point that Windows' automatic image type conversion saves a lot of work. To show the loaded image on the screen, we next force a refresh, invalidating the current Windows form. Invalidating the window (or parts of it) sends a paint message to the appropriate window: either the control or the child window. As a result, the part of the screen that has been invalidated is redrawn using the `Paint` event handler method.

Before an image is loaded by the user, a default image will be shown. The image provided is `Hawaii.jpg` and should be located in the `bin` and `bind` directories if the debug version is run. To initialize the bitmap, simply add a line to the `PhotoEditorForm` constructor:

```
loadedImage = new Bitmap(@"Hawaii.JPG");
```

The last step tells Windows that custom drawing is needed for this form. To do that, you overridee the `OnPaint` method. To implement that method, you can either add the event handler manually by typing or create a stub implementation using Visual Studio.NET. To automatically create a stub, click on PhotoEditorForm in the `PhotoEditor.cs [Design]` view, and go to the properties section. If you press the yellow lightning symbol underneath the Solution Explorer window, you will see a tab with all the events listed. Double-click on the `Paint` event. This will create a stub implementation. Then implement the code as shown in Listing 5.9. The implementation reveals that the `Graphics` class is used to save the image in memory, which is then displayed on the screen.

Listing 5.9 Overriding the `OnPaint` Method

```
/// <summary>
/// Custom paint method.
/// </summary>
protected override void OnPaint(PaintEventArgs e)
{
  try
  {
    Graphics deviceContext = e.Graphics;
    deviceContext.DrawImage(loadedImage, 0,0);
  }
  catch(Exception exception)
  {
   ExceptionManager.Publish(exception);
  }
}
```

Compile and run the project. The default image will be displayed as the background image when the application is first started. To display another image, go to File | Open File. The Open File dialog will be shown, and you can browse the file system. Select an image, and it will be displayed in the application window.

5.6.6 Scrolling and Basic Image Operations

Loading a large image or resizing the application window shows a drawback of the current implementation: If the image is larger than the application window, only part of the image is shown. A better behavior for a Windows application is to show scrollbars if the image is larger than the window. Because the photo editor should be a well-behaved application, we need to add scrolling.

Depending on the needs of an application, there are several ways to add scrolling capabilities. Table 5.4 gives a short overview of the various techniques, describing how they are implemented and when they should be used.

Table 5.4 Comparison of Scrolling Techniques

Scrolling Technique	Description	When to Use
Using a scrollable control	These are controls directly or indirectly derived from `System.Windows.Forms.Scrollable Control`. They support scrolling, provided by the .NET Framework. For example, `TextBox`, `ListBox`, and the `Form` class itself support scrolling.	Use this scrolling technique when there is no need to draw in the control with GDI+, the control is composed of this custom control and other controls, and the virtual space is limited.
Placing a non-scrollable control in the `Panel` control	An instance of the `Picture` control is created, and the `Picture` control is placed in a `Panel` control. You then create a new image in which you can draw (possibly using GDI+). Then the background image of the custom control is set to the new image (including the graphics you were drawing).	Use this technique if you want to be able to draw into the image with GDI+, the custom control is not composed of other custom controls, and the virtual space is limited.

(continued) |

Table 5.4 (*Cont.*)

Scrolling Technique	Description	When to Use
Using the `UserControl` class with child controls	Derive the control from the `UserControl` class, build an image, draw into the image, and set the `BackgroundImage` property of this control to the build image.	Use this technique if you need to draw into the limited virtual space (possibly using GDI+) and you're using child controls (constituent controls) of the custom controls.
Smooth scrolling	Create a custom control that derives from the `User` control, add vertical and horizontal scrollbars as child (constituent) controls, and write a `Paint` event handler that draws the image incrementally according to the scrollbar's position. In addition, the background color of the part of the control that is not covered by the image can be drawn in a defined background color.	This technique creates a polished and professional appearance. The image scrolls smoothly to the desired position rather than jumping to the new position, as it does when you use the build in scrolling.

For the photo editor application, we choose smooth scrolling to give the application a professional and polished appearance. This also lets us support graphics drawn with GDI+, something that is necessary for the supported graphics and text overlays described in the later chapters.

5.6.7 Refactoring of the Current Code

Before we begin implementing scrolling, we must do some refactoring of the existing project code. Even though the implemented code works and shows a quick result, we need to adapt it to meet the approved design and to give us the flexibility to accommodate the implementation of functional requirements to be added in later iterations.

According to the design specification, the `Picture` class should be split out as an independent class. This makes perfect sense, because the image and all its properties should be self-contained and separate from the GUI code. To add a new class, go to Solution Explorer, right-click on Photo Editor Application, and select Add | Add Class. Type `Picture` for the name of the class to be created, and press Open. After that, add a reference to the `System.Drawing` namespace to the new file by adding the following statement:

```
using System.Drawing;
```

The reference is needed to access the type `Bitmap`, which is used to store the image.

To implement the functionality to load an image, to the `Picture` class we add a `public` method named `LoadImage` with the return type `void` and no parameters. Switch to the class view and right-click on the `Picture` class and Add | Add Method. Or simply add the following line:

```
public void LoadImage() {...}
```

We also add a field for storing the image data. Add the following line to the `Picture` class:

```
private Bitmap loadedImage;
```

In C#, properties (also called *accessors*) are used to access `private` field data. To add the property, right-click on the `Picture` class (in the Class View tab of Solution Explorer) and select Add | Property. This will display a dialog box as shown in Figure 5.14.

Enter the data as it is shown in Figure 5.14, and press Finish. The property functionality with public accessor methods is generated automatically and is added to the class. To actually return the loaded image when the `get` method is called, change the return value from `null` to `loadedImage`. For now, the `set` part of the property is not used. In theory you could set the image by assigning the loaded image to the provided value:

```
loadedImage = value;
```

The next step is to add to the `PhotoEditorForm` class a `public` field that is of type `Picture` and is named `PictureObject`. This field will hold a reference to an instance of a `Picture` class object. The `PictureObject` then needs to be initialized with an allocated `Picture` class instance. This is done in the constructor of the `PhotoEditorForm`. Add the following line to the `PhotoEditorForm()` constructor:

```
PictureObject = new Picture();
```

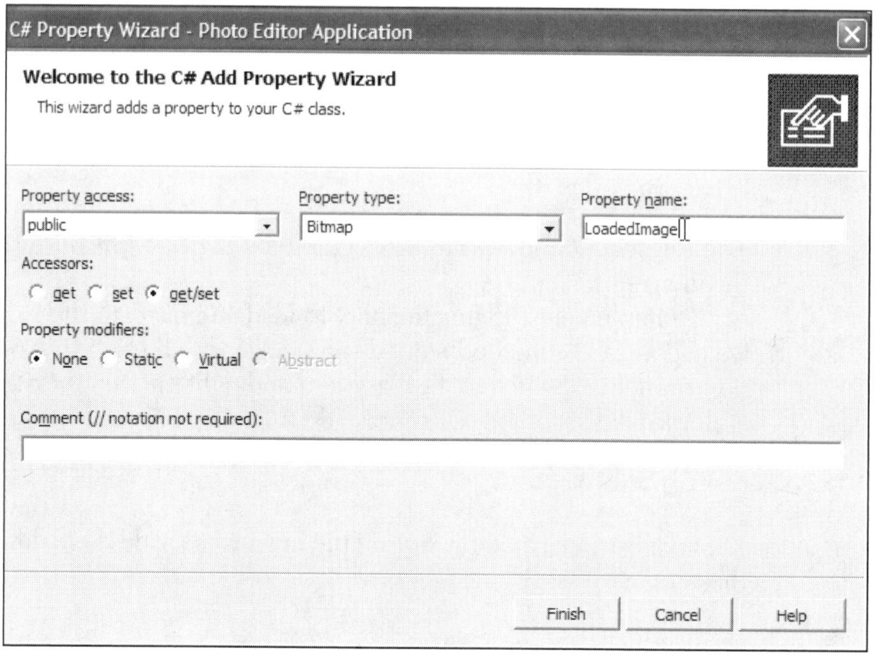

Figure 5.14 Adding the `loadedImage` Property

The previously added lines in the `PhototEditorForm` constructor need to be deleted because the `OpenFileDialog` and the `loadedImage` functionalities are now responsibilities of the `Picture` class. Therefore, we delete the following lines in the `PhotoEditorForm` constructor:

```
loadFileDialog = new OpenFileDialog();
loadedImage = new Bitmap(@"Hawaii.JPG");
```

Next, in the `OnPaint` event handler method, the `PictureObject.LoadedImage` should be painted instead of the default image. We implement this by changing the `DrawImage` call in the `OnPaint` event handler to look like this:

```
deviceContext.DrawImage(PictureObject.LoadedImage, 0,0);
```

To load an image via the `Picture` class, we change the `OpenFile_Click` event handler method to call the `LoadImage` method of the `Picture` class by adding this line:

```
PictureObject.LoadImage();
```

From the same method, we move the code for opening the file dialog window to the `LoadImage` method of the `Picture` class. Basically this is all the code except the following line:

```
this.Invalidate();
```

Now add the following statement to the `Picture.cs` file:

```
using System.Windows.Forms;
```

Then add a field for `OpenFileDialog` to the `Picture` class by adding this line:

```
private OpenFileDialog loadFileDialog;
```

Now it is time to load the default image at startup and to create an instance of `OpenFileDialog` in the `Picture` class constructor. Therefore, we add the following two lines to the `Picture` class constructor:

```
string defaultImage =
    PhotoEditorForm.GetApplicationDirectory + @"\Hawaii.jpg";
loadFileDialog = new OpenFileDialog();
```

You can see in this code that we have introduced an additional method to the `PhotoEditorForm` with the name `GetApplicationDirectory`. When you call this method, the path to the directory in which the photo editor application was started is returned. This is necessary in case a user starts the application from a different directory via the command line (in that case, if we would search the current directory for the default image we would search in the directory the command line shows and not the directory where the application was started). To make this work, add the following lines to the `PhotoEditorForm` class:

```
// Get the directory in which the application was started.
// Note: In C# you can initialize a member at definition time.
// The compiler will take care of initializing the member in the
// constructor of the corresponding class.
private static string applicationDirectory = Application.StartupPath;
```

```
/// <summary>
/// Accessor to the Application directory.
/// </summary>
public static string GetApplicationDirectory
{
  get
  {
    return applicationDirectory;
  }
}
```

To complete the refactoring, we delete the fields for `loadFileDialog` and `loadedImage` from the `PhotoEditorForm` class. Check the implementation by compiling and running the application.

Even though the changes made in this section are not very large, they show that refactoring can take a substantial amount of time. We think that this time is well invested if developers consistently try to improve the existing code. This does not mean that the implementation should necessarily become more complex by refactoring, but if developers identify possibilities to improve existing code with regard to maintainability and extensibility (if needed), the refactoring should be implemented (in fact, refactoring should simplify the code by making it easier for other developers to read and understand). We also strongly recommend that you do refactoring in very small steps. Refactoring can be a powerful tool if done consistently over the life cycle of a project. On the other hand, refactoring can become a nightmare if it is not done consistently throughout the whole life cycle of the project and if it is not done in small chunks with thorough testing in place.

5.6.8 Creating a Custom Control for Smooth Scrolling

Even though Visual Studio provides a wide variety of controls and wizards, sometimes it is necessary to develop controls with different, customized behavior. For the scrolling in this project, we want to provide smooth scrolling, something that the Visual Studio controls do not provide. Therefore, we'll develop a custom control. Before we start, it's a good idea to check whether a control that satisfies the needs of the project has already been developed and is available on the Internet.

As mentioned earlier, we want to implement the smooth scrolling control to give our application a professional feel when users scroll an image. The advantage of developing a custom control for this is that we can use the control in other applications if needed. Another advantage is certainly that implementation of a custom control is a common task in application development, and we want to show how to develop and use a custom control to extend the features provided by Visual Studio.

For the implementation details of `CustomScrollableControl`, please refer to the sample solution on the CD. The project can be found in the `Chapter5\src\Photo Editor` directory. Instead of showing all the implementation details here, we explain the functionalities implemented and the necessary properties without the implementation details. You can implement the custom control based on the description of the functionality, or simply read through the text while checking the source code for the implementation details. If you try to implement the functionality, the Web comment report, which is available in the `doc` directory, might be helpful. It shows all members of the `CustomScrollableControl` class along with comments explaining the functionality.

To create custom controls, add a new C# project to the photo editor solution. The type of the project is a Windows control library, and the name of the control is `CustomScrollableControl`. After the project and its files are generated, change the name of the generated file and the class name from `UserControl1` to `CustomScrollableControl` and change the output directories to `bin` and `bind`.

Do It Yourself Try to implement the `CustomScrollableControl` feature. Use the description here, the comment Web pages in the `doc` directory, and the sample solution to guide you through the implementation.

5.6.9 Implementation of `CustomScrollableControl`

All fields are defined as `private`, and accessor methods are provided for fields that need to be accessed by other classes.

The `Image scrollingImage` field is used to store the image that is displayed in the control. The `get` property for this field returns the image; the `set` method sets the scrollable image and calls a method to adjust the scrollbars.

Another field needed is a point that specifies the viewport coordinates. `Point viewportCoords` represents the coordinates of the image relative to the control. The *viewport* defines the coordinates of the image relative to the window. If the image is not scrolled, the pixel at position (0/0) of the picture is shown at position (0/0) of the control. If the image is scrolled by 100 pixels in y direction, the picture position (0/100) is shown at the (0/0) position of the custom control.

`Rectangle ScrollingImageArea` is a convenience accessor that returns a rectangle whose size is measured from the origin of the control to the x-coordinate of the vertical scrollbar and the y-coordinate of the horizontal scrollbar. This is equivalent to the area of the control that is available for drawing the image and is defined as the client area minus the area that is taken by the scrollbars.

The base functionality of this control is to scroll through an image smoothly. Therefore, we add vertical and horizontal scrollbars to the `Custom ScrollableControl` form. The scrollbars can be dragged from the toolbox onto the form. The scrollbars are positioned and docked in the form to the right and the bottom of the form, as in other Windows applications.

`private void drawImage` is a helper method that is used to calculate and draw the correct portion of the bitmap in the custom control. This method is called directly by the scrollbars whenever a change is detected. The method clips the region of the image to the area of the image that is visible in the control and draws the image. To clip the region, we use a `Rectangle` method that is defined in the `Windows.System.Drawing` namespace.

We customize the `Paint` event handler using `private void Custom ScrollableControl_Paint` so that we can repaint parts or the entire image (in case, for example, the image is restored after the control was minimized). The GDI+ drawing surface, provided as a parameter to `PaintEventArgs`, is stored in a local variable called `graphics`. Then a `solidBrush` is created to fill the client area with a solid color. Next, we check whether the `scrollingImage` exists. If it does not, then there is no image and the complete client area is filled by the solid brush.

After that, a local variable of type `Rectangle` is created. The rectangle to the right of the image and left of the scrollbar is calculated and stored in the local variable `rect`. If the calculated rectangle is not empty, this area will be filled with the solid brush. After that, we do the same thing for the area below the image and above the horizontal scrollbar. Then the small rectangle in the lower-right corner is calculated and filled with the solid brush.

The `private void adjustScrollBars` method dimensions and sets certain properties for the scrollbars. This method does not take any parameters. A constant field is defined that is used to calculate the number of incremental steps for each scroll request. Then we check whether an image exists. If it does, the minimum and maximum values of the scrollbars are set to 0 and the width or height of the image. In addition, we define the behavior of small and large changes to the scrollbars. The actual values of the scrollbars are set to the corresponding value of the viewport (meaning the coordinates of the upper-left corner in the actual image).

The `private void scroll` method is the heart of the custom scrolling functionality. This is the code that actually does the smooth scrolling. This method handles the scrolling from the given previous position to the current position of the scrollbars. To achieve a smooth scrolling effect, the viewport is incrementally changed until it is in the new end position. In between the incremental steps, the method is sleeping for a short time to simulate the effect of a sliding image. Therefore, two constants are defined. The first constant is used for the time period during which the control sleeps before displaying the next image position relative to the viewport, and the second is a divisor for the difference calculation of the previous and the current position of the scrollbar.

We also create a local variable that holds the drawing context; this variable is checked to see whether the previous value of the scrollbar is the same as the current value. If it is not, we must apply horizontal scrolling. A Boolean local variable indicates that the direction the scrollbar was moved, and the defined integer divides the absolute change that was made into the smaller, incremental steps. The incremental steps are then checked to see whether they are smaller than 1. If they are, then the value is set to 1 for scrolling up, or to –1 for scrolling down. Following that, the loop in which the incremental scrolling over the image is executed.

Then some checks are added to make sure that scrolling is stopped if the image is shown according to the scrollbar position and that the stepping did not go too far (if it did, the values are set to the final position). Before the image is drawn at its new position (with respect to the control), the control sleeps for a specified amount of time. Then the image is drawn, and the next image position is calculated and displayed. This continues until the image is shown in its final position, in which case a `break` statement is executed what makes the program jump out of the `while` loop.

`private void hScrollBar_Scroll` and `private void vScrollBar_Scroll` are the event handlers for the scrollbars. The `Scroll` event is triggered whenever the user clicks on the scrollbar and changes its position. The parameters that are passed to the event handler methods are references to the sender's `object` and `ScrollEventArgs`. The `ScrollEventArgs` object provides information on the scroll type. If the user clicks on the small arrows of the scrollbar, either a `ScrollEventType.SmallDecrement` or a `ScrollEventType.SmallIncrement` is provided. If the user clicks inside the scrollbar or drags the scrollbar, a `ScrollEventType.LargeDecrement` or `ScrollEventType.LargeIncrement` type is provided. The event handlers for the scrollbars usually contain a `switch` statement, depending on the scroll type. In the case of `customScrollableControl`, the event handler stores the previous position of the viewport in a local variable before it assigns the current position to the viewport. Then the scrolling method is called with the previous position and the new position.

   `private void CustomScrollableControl_Resize` implements the event handler for the `resize` event. The `resize` event is triggered whenever the control window is resized. In that case, the scrollbar position must be recalculated and the viewport may have to be updated. The implementation checks to see whether there is an image, and, if there is, the new `viewportCoords` are calculated. The `Math.Min` method is used to return the value of the smaller number that was provided. The `Math.Max` method is used to return the maximum value of the provided parameters.

   Build the custom control from the sample solution so that it can be used in Visual Studio.NET.

5.6.10 Configuring the Custom Control for Use in Visual Studio.NET

It's easy to configure Visual Studio.NET to use the custom control. Just go to the Tools menu. Choose Add/Remove Toolbox Items, and browse to the directory in which the control was built (navigate to the `bind` directory if the debug version is used; otherwise, go to the `bin` directory, assuming we set the output path correctly) and choose the control, as shown in Figure 5.15. The control is then shown in the Toolbox. Like any other control, it can be used by dragging it from the Toolbox onto the form.

   To implement the custom scrolling in the photo editor application, add the control to the form `PhotoEditorForm[Design]`. Position it as shown in the requirements and dock it to the top, left, and right of the form (by using the `Dock` property) and rename it `customScrollableControl`. Then double-click on the new control to create the `Load` event handler.

   The next step is to draw the image to the custom control instead of the Form. In order to do that, remove the following line from the `Paint` event handler:

```
deviceContext.DrawImage(PictureObject.LoadedImage, 0,0);
```

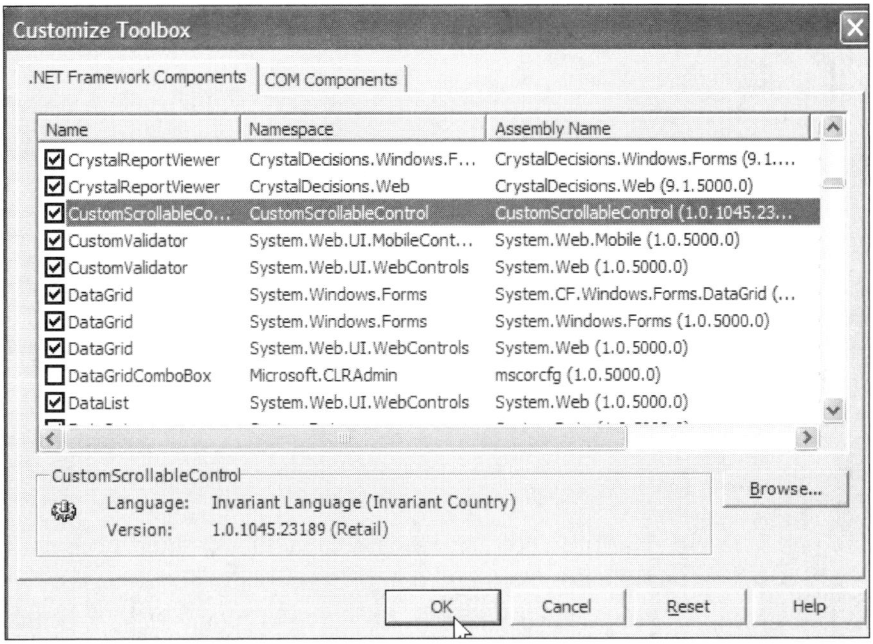

Figure 5.15 Adding a Custom Control to the Toolbox

Change the `OpenFile_Click` event handler method to display the image in the custom control, and invalidate the control to force a paint event. This will show the image within the new control. Listing 5.10 shows the new event handler.

Listing 5.10 The New `OpenFile_Click` Event Handler

```
/// <summary>
/// Opens a file dialog window so the user can select an
/// image to be loaded
/// </summary>
/// <param name="sender">A reference to the object calling
///    this method</param>
/// <param name="e">The event arguments provided by the
///    event handler</param>
/// <requirements>F:editor_load_and_save</requirements>
private void OpenFile_Click(object sender,
```

```
                    System.EventArgs e)
  {
    try
    {
      PictureObject.LoadImage();
      if(PictureObject.LoadedImage == null)
        throw(new Exception("Error, image could not be
              loaded"));
      DisplayImage();
    }
    catch(Exception exception)
    {
      ExceptionManager.Publish(exception);
    }
  }
```

In addition, a new `DisplayImage` method is introduced in this example. This method is implemented in the `PhotoEditorForm` class.

Its implementation sets the scrolling image of the custom control to the currently loaded image of the `Picture` class instance, and it invalidates the custom control. The implementation of the `DisplayImage` method is as follows:

```
public void DisplayImage();
customScrollableControl.ScrollingImage = PictureObject.LoadedImage;
customScrollableControl.Invalidate();
```

The application, in its first cut, shows the default image when first loaded. To get the same result with the custom control, we call the newly implemented `DisplayImage()` method from within the `customScrollable Control_Load` event handler (which was generated by Visual Studio.NET automatically by the double-click on `customScrollableControl` in the `PhotoEditor.cs[Design]` tab).

This completes the implementation of smooth scrolling. It is now time to test the implemented functionality. Running the application and loading an image shows that the scrolling works smoothly, but the image flickers when the scrollbar is moved. We can prevent this by setting a style property in the `CustomScrollableControl` constructor. As a result of the change, the background is not drawn in the background color before the image is drawn. The following line is used in the constructor to accomplish this:

```
this.SetStyle (ControlStyles.Opaque, true);
```

After this change, the control works without any noticeable flicker. The next step is to provide the tab control containing the buttons for the basic image operations.

5.6.11 Cropping an Image

Cropping an image means to cut a particular region out of the image, keep the cropped portion, and delete the rest. For the photo editor, users will crop their images to get them to a standard size and upload them to the online shop. In a later version, we might provide interactive graphics for this task, but for the first version we present a dialog box where users specify the new size of the image.

To implement the crop dialog box, choose `PhotoEditorForm` and go to the Toolbox to drag a `TabControl` onto the form. In the properties of the tab control, select the following properties:

Properties of TabControl

(Name)	tabControl
Dock	Bottom

A tab control is used to group related image-processing functionality. Later in the book we will add other tab controls. Now rename the tab control to `tabControl`. Add a tab to the control by selecting and then right-clicking on the `tabControl`. Then select `Add Tab` to add the actual tab. Set its properties as follows:

Properties of Tab

(Name)	basicImageOperations
Text	Basic Image Operations

When the photo editor application is now run, the screen layout should correspond to the GUI shown in the `photo_editor` requirements, except that the buttons are still missing. To add a button for the cropping functionality, drag a button to the tab. Change the displayed text on the button to `Crop Image`, and change the name of it to `cropImageButton`. Double-click on the button to add the event handler for the click event. We use a dialog box to collect the size information for the crop rectangle. To let users open a dialog box when the crop button is pressed, you must add a new form to the photo editor application. You do this by right-clicking the Photo Editor Application project in Solution Explorer and selecting Add | Add Windows Form. Name the new form `CropDialog`. Then drag two text boxes onto the form and change their properties as follows:

Properties of TextBox1 (Left) and TextBox2 (Right)

(Name)	imageWidth	imageHeight
AcceptsReturn	True	True
AcceptsTab	True	True
Text	Image Width	ImageHeight

In addition, add two buttons; change their names to `OKBtn` and `CancelBtn` (and change the text to be displayed on the button accordingly). Also add two labels next to the text boxes that explain what the text box input is—for example, "Enter new image height." The Form should now look approximately like Figure 5.16.

After adding all the design-related properties, we add the event handlers. A double-click on the image width text box will add an `imageWidth_TextChanged` event handler. Before implementing the event handler, add to the `CropDialog` class two `private integer` variables called `tempWidth` and `tempHeight` for the width and height. The event handlers are then implemented. To extract the new width from the text box entry, the `image Width` object provides a property, `Text`, that represents the text in the text box. This text is converted to an integer value and stored in the `tempWidth` variable. The functionality is shown in Listing 5.11.

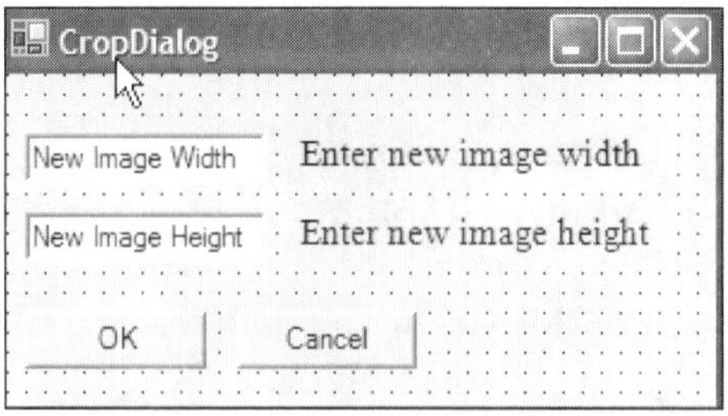

Figure 5.16 The Crop Dialog Box

Listing 5.11 The `TextChanged` Event Handler for the Width

```
private void imageWidth_TextChanged(object sender,
            System.EventArgs e)
  {
    tempWidth = Convert.ToInt32(imageWidth.Text);
  }
```

Do It Yourself Implement the height text box event handler method using Listing 5.11 as a template.

Next, we implement the OK and Cancel buttons. We start with the implementation of the Cancel button. To add the event handler for the button, double-click on the Cancel button in the `CropDialog.cs [Design]` view. If the Cancel button is selected, no cropping action is done and the `PhotoEditor` form should be invalidated (to force a repaint). In addition, the `CropDialog` box can be disposed of to indicate to the garbage collector that the memory is no longer being used. Therefore, we change the constructor of `CropDialog` to accept one argument of type `object` named `sender`. This object will be a reference to the calling `PhotoEditorForm` object. The `sender` object is then cast in the constructor to a `PhotoEditor Form` object and is stored in a local `private` variable of type `PhotoEditor Form` named `editorForm`. The code to be added to the constructor, after creating the `private` field, is as follows:

```
editorForm = (PhotoEditorForm)sender;
```

The `CancelBtn_Click` event handler is then implemented as shown in Listing 5.12.

Listing 5.12 The `CropDialog` Cancel Button

```
private void CancelBtn_Click(object sender, System.EventArgs e)
  {
    editorForm.Invalidate();
    this.Dispose();
  }
```

After that, we implement the OK button click event handler for the Crop dialog box. When the OK button is pressed, the stored values for width and height are sent to `PictureObject.CropImage`. The `Picture` object is then responsible for cropping the loaded image to the specified size. Therefore, we add the event handler by double-clicking on the OK button and adding the following lines to the event handler:

```
editorForm.PictureObject.CropImage(tempWidth, tempHeight);
editorForm.DisplayImage();
this.Dispose();
```

This will crop the image, assuming that a `CropImage` method is provided by the `Picture` class. Therefore, we must add the `CropImage` method to the `Picture` class in the next step.

Add a new `public void` method `CropImage` to the `Picture` class. This method takes two integer variables (the width and the height). Now that we have defined the signature, let's take care of the implementation. The `CropImage` method should check whether the provided parameters specify a region within the loaded image and whether the parameters are actually larger than zero. After that, the clip region needs to be calculated as a rectangle. We then clone the current image by applying the calculated cropping rectangle, and we store a copy of the cropped image in a temporary bitmap called `croppedImage`. The `loadedImage` is then set to the cropped image and is displayed. The complete implementation of the `CropImage` method is shown in Listing 5.13.

Listing 5.13 The `CropImage` Method

```
/// <summary>
/// Method called from CropDialog. The current
/// shown image is cropped to the size provided
/// in the parameters. The cropping is done
/// with a rectangle whose center is put on
/// the center of the image.
/// </summary>
/// <requirement>F:image_crop</requirement>
/// <param name="newHeight>height of the cropped
/// image</param>
/// <param name="newWidth">width of the cropped
/// image</param>
public void CropImage(int newWidth, int newHeight)
```

```
{
  // Check that cropping region is
  // actually within the image and that
  // the values provided are positive
  if((newWidth < loadedImage.Size.Width) &&
    (newHeight < loadedImage.Size.Height) &&
    (newHeight > 0) && (newWidth > 0))
  {
    int xmin = (loadedImage.Size.Width / 2) -
      (newWidth / 2);
    int xdim = newWidth;
    int ymin = (loadedImage.Size.Height / 2) -
      (newHeight / 2);
    int ydim =  newHeight;
    Rectangle rectangle = new Rectangle(xmin, ymin,
                  xdim, ydim);
    if(rectangle.IsEmpty)
    {
      throw(new Exception("Error, CropImage failed to
              allocate clipping rectangle"));
    }
    Bitmap croppedImage = loadedImage.Clone(rectangle,
          System.Drawing.Imaging.PixelFormat.DontCare);
    Bitmap oldImage = loadedImage;
    loadedImage = new Bitmap(croppedImage,
          rectangle.Size);
    if(loadedImage == null)
    {
      throw(new Exception("Error, Image memory allocation
              failed"));
    }
  }
}
```

The last step is to implement the `cropImage` button click event handler. First, create the event handler. Then in the event handler create a new `CropDialog` object and show the dialog on the screen by adding the following lines:

```
CropDialog openDialog = new CropDialog(this);
openDialog.Show();
```

This completes the implementation of the cropping functionality. Compile and run the project to see whether it works. If you added the XML code documentation while implementing the functionality, then you can also generate the comment Web pages and you will have a nice description of the newly added functionality.

5.6.12 Rotate and Flip an Image

Now we show how to implement the rotate and flip functionality. To support this, we add new buttons to the tab card of `PhotoEditor.cs[Design]`. Add the buttons to match the screen layout shown in Figure 5.17. Then rename them and change the text of the buttons.

To add the event handler method for horizontal flipping, double-click on the corresponding button. Before adding the event handler, though, you should consider that the flipping and rotating of an image are basic image operations and therefore they should be handled by the `Picture` class. Therefore, add to the `Picture` class a `public void` method called `Rotate FlipImage` that takes a parameter of type `RotateFlipType` that is named `rotateFlip`. (The `Bitmap` class actually supports rotating and flipping and provides an enumeration for various rotation and flip values.) Implement the event handlers for the button click events by passing the correct `RotateFlipType` to the `RotateFlipImage` method of the `Picture` class. (For information about `RotateFlipType`, see the MSDN documentation or the sample solution.) Then the `RotateFlipImage` method can be implemented as shown in Listing 5.14.

Listing 5.14 The `RotateFlipImage` Method

```
public void RotateFlipImage(RotateFlipType rotateFlip)
    {
      loadedImage.RotateFlip(rotateFlip);
    }
```

Figure 5.17 The Photo Editor Form Buttons

Do It Yourself Implement the functionality for vertical flipping, rotating clockwise, and rotating counterclockwise in the same way the horizontal flipping functionality was added. Use the enumeration members of RotateFlipType.

5.6.13 Save an Image

Before testing is started, we need to implement the last feature that is missing in the implementation. We have not implemented the functionality to save an image on disk. This task is very similar to the implementation of image loading. Instead of OpenFileDialog, we use SaveFialeDialog; and instead of loading the image, we save the image under the user-selected name.

Go to the [Design] view of PhotoEditor.cs and add a new menu item in the main menu, underneath the Open File entry. Name the menu item saveMenu, and change the text to &Save as .... Add the event handler for the click event. The save file functionality is also implemented in the Picture class. Therefore, add a public method called SaveFile() to the Picture class, and call it from the event handler of the Save button. To make SaveFileDialog work, add a private member variable to the Picture class of type SaveFileDialog, and in the constructor create the object for it. The SaveFile method then can be implemented as shown in Listing 5.15.

Listing 5.15 The SaveFile Method

```
public void SaveImage()
    {
      saveFileDialog.Filter = " jpg files (*.jpg)|*.jpg|
        gif files (*.gif)|*.gif| bmp files (*.bmp)|*.bmp|
        All files (*.*)|*.*";
      saveFileDialog.ShowDialog();
      loadedImage.Save(saveFileDialog.FileName);
      saveFileDialog.Dispose();
    }
```

After this change has been made, compile and run the application to see the result. The images can now be loaded, rotated, flipped, cropped, and saved. This is all the functionality that is needed for the project in the elaboration phase. The next task is to write unit tests to validate the implemented functionality.

Do It Yourself The buttons provided are not very nice-looking. You can make the program more appealing by adding bitmaps that show the user what the result of a requested image transformation will be. (Customize the rudimentary buttons provided, or develop custom bitmaps that can be loaded onto the buttons.) Also, we recommend that you change and play around with the implementation to see what improvements you can make.

Figure 5.18 shows the working application.

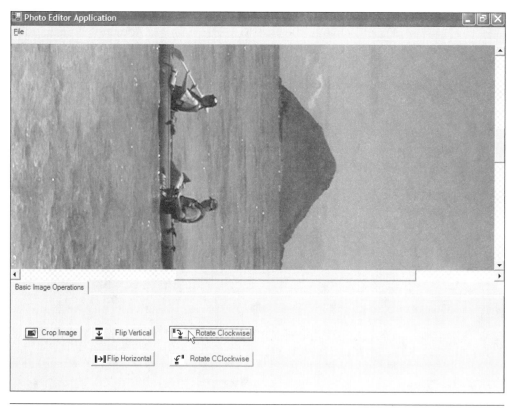

Figure 5.18 The Working Photo Editor Application

5.7 Unit Tests

The goal for the unit tests is to verify that all the required functionality is actually implemented and that the various modules are working in isolation. For the photo editor application, most of the required functionality is implemented in the `Picture` class. The only exception is the GUI. It is cumbersome to test the GUI automatically, and it is more an integration test rather then a unit test task. Therefore, the `F:photo_editor` key is not explicitly tested at the unit test level.

To test the load and save functionality, it would be an advantage to have overloaded methods where the test could specify the file name to be loaded or saved. With the current implementation of the `Picture` class, the file dialog would open every time the load functionality is called, making the automated tests very difficult. You can use a commercial capture replay tool to exercise these kinds of actions. Tools such as WinRunner do a good job on those things. But as mentioned, the easier solution (and probably the nicer solution as well) is to add two overloaded methods to the `Picture` class. The one overloaded method is the load method, which accepts a parameter of type `string`; the other is the save method, which also accepts a `string` parameter. The overloaded methods then load or save the picture under the provided file name. The implementation can be seen in Listing 5.16.

Listing 5.16 The Overloaded Save and Load Methods of the `Picture` class

```
/// <summary>
/// Opens the file with the provided name.
/// </summary>
/// <param name="fileName">name of the file to be opened</param>
/// <requirement>F:image_load_and_save</requirement>
public void LoadImage(string fileName)
{
  Bitmap oldImage;
  oldImage = loadedImage;
  loadedImage = new Bitmap(fileName);
  if(loadedImage == null)
  {
  throw(new Exception("Error, LoadImage with file name
    failed"));
```

```
    }
    oldImage.Dispose();

}
/// <summary>
/// Saves the current image
/// with the provided fileName.
/// </summary>
/// <param name="fileName">Name under which the image is
    saved</param>
public void SaveImage(string fileName)
{
    loadedImage.Save(fileName);
}
```

These two hooks can now be used by the test program to actually load and save an image without having to go through a file load and save dialog box. Very often, such hooks are implemented for testing. This is another reason to include the test team (if there is a separate test team available) in the project planning from the beginning. In this way, hooks for testing can be discussed in the planning phase of the project and implemented as features during development. In the photo editor project, this not as important because the development team also does the testing. Nevertheless, testing is incorporated in the project planning from the beginning.

5.7.1 The NUnit Test Framework

To test the `Picture` class functionality, an *automated test framework* would be very helpful. The framework we are looking for should be capable of running specified tests automatically, and it should show the result on the screen. Ideally it would have a GUI we could use to run selected tests, or it would run the tests from the command line (to let us run the tests every night using a script). It also should be easy to use so that we don't have to spend much time in training and setting up the test framework.

Luckily, such a test framework exists. Called NUnit, this framework is an automated test framework that is implemented for many programming languages in a similar form (for example, JUnit for Java, CppUnit for C++, and many more). The unit test framework was first developed for Smalltalk by the extreme programming group around Kent Beck. Later, the framework was ported to many languages and is now also available for Microsoft

.NET as NUnit. The framework can be downloaded from `http://www.nunit.org`. A quick-start guide and other documentation can be found at the site.

5.7.2 Unit Test Implementation

After downloading and installing the NUnit framework, we develop the tests (you will also find an installation of the NUnit test framework in the `src` directory). First, add a new class to the photo editor application project with the name `UnitTest`.

Add a reference to `NUnit.framework.dll` (which can be found in the `src\NUnit20\bin` directory), and add a `using` statement for `NUnit.Framework`. To use the classes provided by the `Picture` class, also add a `using` statement for the `System.Drawing` namespace that defines `Rotate FlipType`. To tell the framework that the class `UnitTest` contains unit test methods that are executable by NUnit, we add an attribute called `[Test Fixture]` before the class definition. Before implementing the actual test methods, we implement the setup and tear-down methods of the tests by inheriting two attributes from the unit test framework. The `SetUp` method is called before a test method is called, and the `TearDown` method is called after the test method is executed. The attributes used to indicate these methods are `[SetUp]` and `[TearDown]`.

For the unit tests of the `Picture` class, the `SetUp` method creates a new `Picture` object and writes to the standard output that a new test has started. In the `TearDown` method, the image is disposed of and an indication of the test result (passed or failed) is written to the standard output. Listing 5.17 shows the `SetUp` and `TearDown` implementation.

Listing 5.17 The Unit Test `SetUp` and `TearDown` Methods

```
namespace UnitTest
{
  [SetUp] public void Init()
    {
      Console.WriteLine("********* New Test-case: *******");
      Console.WriteLine("photo_editor");
      TestImage = new Photo_Editor_Application.Picture();
    }

    private Photo_Editor_Application.Picture TestImage;
    private bool amIPassed = false;
```

```
[TearDown] public void Destroy()
{
  TestImage.LoadedImage.Dispose();
  if(amIPassed)
  {
    Console.WriteLine("=> PASSED");
  }
  else
  {
    Console.WriteLine("%%%%%% Failed");
  }
}
}
```

For the file load test, we load the default image and check whether the loaded image has the correct dimensions. The save file test crops the image and saves it under a new file name. Then the regular default image is loaded again (to make sure the Picture object has been changed and has the original dimensions again) before the saved image is loaded. The saved image is checked to see whether its dimensions are the same as the cropping image information that was provided before the image was saved. The XML tag <requirement> </requirement> identifies which requirement key is tested in this test. To indicate that a method is a test method, the attribute [Test] is used before the method definition. The implementation can be seen in Listing 5.18.

Listing 5.18 Image Load and Save Test

```
/// <summary>
/// Test for F:image_load_and_save.
/// Windows standard dialogs are used, so really
/// this tests only whether the default image loaded has the
/// dimensions
/// that are expected!
/// </summary>
/// <requirement>F:image_load_and_save</requirement>
[Test] public void LoadandSaveImageTest()
{
  const string fileName = "Test.jpg";

  Console.WriteLine("image_load_and_save");
```

```
Assertion.AssertEquals("Load Image, width",
   TestImage.LoadedImage.Width, 2048);
Assertion.AssertEquals("Load Image, height",
   TestImage.LoadedImage.Height, 1536);

TestImage.CropImage(200, 400);
TestImage.SaveImage(fileName);

TestImage.LoadImage("Hawaii.jpg");

TestImage.LoadImage(fileName);

Assertion.AssertEquals("Load Image, width",
   TestImage.LoadedImage.Width, 200);
Assertion.AssertEquals("Load Image, height",
   TestImage.LoadedImage.Height, 400);
amIPassed = true;
}
```

We perform the actual test case by calling an `Assertion` method with the pass/fail criteria. If the test case fails, then the test is failed and the rest of the tests within this method are not executed even if there are more test cases defined. That is why the flag `amIPassed` can be set to `true` in case the end of the method is actually reached.

Do It Yourself Implement test cases for image cropping, rotating, and flipping in the same way it was done for loading and saving. Check the unit test project into Source Safe. A sample solution is provided with the source code on the accompanying CD.

Now that the test cases have been implemented it is time to run them to see whether the developed program actually does what it is expected to do. We can run the test either from the command line or via the NUnit GUI. In this chapter only the GUI is shown.

To start the tests, go to the Start menu; then go to Programs | NUnitV2.0 | NUnit-GUI. The NUnit GUI will open. Choose File | Open and navigate to the directory where the unit tests were built. The test tree will be shown, and the tests can be run by pressing the Run button. The result will look like Figure 5.19.

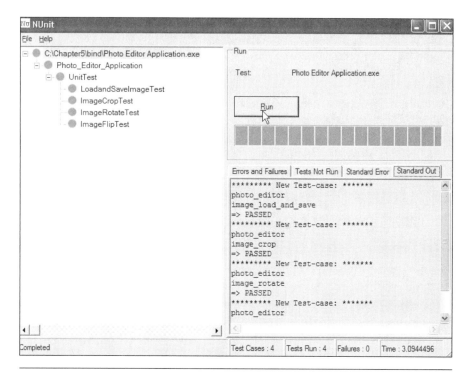

Figure 5.19 The NUnit GUI

The GUI gives a nice overview of the test result. If the progress bar is green, it means that all test cases passed. Otherwise, the bar will be red.

The Standard Out tab shows the results that were logged during the test run. If there are errors, information about the failed cases can be found in the Errors and Failures tab.

5.8 Conclusion

During the elaboration phase of our sample project, we design, develop, and implement a functional architectural baseline. We run the implementation and perform initial unit tests. We also update the project planning.

What remains is to produce the documentation from the source code. To provide a user's manual in the form of HTML pages, we produce the comment Web pages by going to the Tools menu and selecting the option

Build Comment Web Pages. In the displayed message box, we specify the destination where the files will be saved to (in our case, the documentation is stored in the `doc` folder of the project). Sample comment Web pages can be found in the `doc` folder in the sample solution. In addition, we produce the XML documentation, which is used for tracking (because it shows the requirement keys that have been implemented).

To produce the XML files, go to Solution Explorer, right-click on Photo Editor Application, and choose Properties. In the Configuration Properties dialog, specify the file name to be used as the XML documentation file. The XML file will be generated with every build, and the file will be saved in the build directory (`bin` or `bind` in the case of the photo editor project). The compiler will now create warnings if public members of a class do not specify an XML-style comment.

In addition to the documentation, we apply a label to the software and the documents (at least it should be done for the manually generated documents such as the project plan, the requirements document, and so on). To add a label in Visual Source Safe, open the Source Safe application and select the project. In the File menu choose Label. A window opens where you can specify the label. The label will be something like "Version 0.1.0." This complies with the Microsoft .NET standard, which uses three numbers to identify a specific version. Because the version produced is the first intermediate result, it is labeled with 0 (zero) for the main release, 1 for the intermediate release, and 0 for the minor releases. In addition, the `AssemblyInfo.cs` file of the Photo Editor Application should be adjusted to correspond to the version in the label before checkin.

5.8.1 Review

We must review the status of the project to decide whether the project will be continued. If the project is continued and an agreement with the customer is signed, then we check whether the project is ready to proceed to the construction phase. To decide whether the project is ready, we assess whether we have met the goals for the five core workflows:

- Requirements: Refine the requirements and system scope.
- Analysis: Analyze the requirements by describing what the system does.
- Design: Develop a stable architecture using UML.
- Implementation: Implement the architectural baseline.
- Test: Test the implemented architectural baseline.

It can be seen that the project meets all goals that were set for this phase and iteration. Therefore, the project is ready to move on to the next phase.

To get customer feedback early on, we deliver the project to the customer as intermediate V 0.1.0. It is crucial to deliver intermediate results that are functional but not yet the final product. In this way, the customer has a better understanding of the progress, and any changes that might be requested by the customer can be discussed and implemented as early as the intermediate project is delivered instead of at the end of the project. Especially with GUI development, this is very important. Another advantage of intermediate deliveries is that errors may be found by the customer and communicated to the development team while the product is still in development.

5.9 References for Further Reading

UML

Jim Arlow and Ila Neustadt, *UML and the Unified Process* (London, England: Addison-Wesley, 2002)

Martin Fowler, *UML Distilled* (Reading, MA: Addison-Wesley, 1999)

.NET Programming

www.dotnetexperts.com/resources/

www.gotdotnet.com

www.msdn.microsoft.com

The NUnit Test Framework

http://sourceforge.net/projects/nunit/

http:www.nunit.org

http:/www.xprogramming.com/software.htm

CHAPTER 6

GDI+ Graphics Extensions

 Unified Process:
Construction Phase and Fourth Iteration

Now that we have developed the architectural baseline in the elaboration phase, we can start the construction phase. This chapter describes the fourth iteration, which is part of the construction phase. The deliverables for the construction phase can be summarized as follows:

- The software product
- The UML model with supporting documents (if necessary) and the test suite
- The user manuals
- The project plan

Based on this list of deliverables, we can specify the tasks for the core workflows:

- Requirements: Uncover any requirement that has been missed, and refine the requirements that are implemented in this iteration.
- Analysis: Finish the analysis of the requirements implemented in this iteration.
- Design: Finish the UML design model for functionality implemented in this iteration.
- Implementation: Implement the functionalities as described in the requirements, analysis, and design documents for this iteration.
- Test: Unit-test the implemented functionality.

As mentioned in Chapter 5, in each iteration described in this book we will refine the requirements, analysis, design, implementation, and test of the functionality that is to be implemented in the current iteration. At the end of all iterations in the construction phase, the product is released. The go/no-go criteria for each chapter are therefore related to the functionality

179

discussed in that chapter. This strategy enables us to work on independent features in parallel (assuming that the overall design is known and the anticipated dependencies are defined).

6.1 Requirements for the GDI+ Extensions

> R

To draw simple shapes and text, we have already defined two requirements: `image_graphics_annotations` and `image_text_annotations`. In this chapter these two keys are refined, analyzed, designed, and implemented.

When we refine requirements, good domain knowledge is essential. Ideally the system is described in terms of a requirement that does not leave any room for interpretation. However, for complex solutions such as an image-processing application that would be very difficult. For this reason, we try to describe the requirements in a way that leaves little room for interpretation by covering the most obvious ambiguities; but we are aware that there might be changes to the requirements during development. Because the software developers are very familiar with the domain and because the customer is encouraged to provide feedback after each of the short iterations, this approach seems to be sufficient. However, we recommend that when you develop requirements descriptions for projects such as database systems or interfaces (especially interfaces between systems developed by different teams in parallel), ambiguity is to be avoided at all costs.

The refined requirements shown in Table 6.1 provide more detailed information on the functionality that needs to be implemented.

An alternative to having only two requirement keys would be to split the keys into multiple subkeys. For example, we could introduce a key for each graphical primitive type. There are reasons to split a key, and reasons not to split it. It basically depends on the granularity we need for planning, reporting, and tracking. In this project, all the graphical-overlay-related keys are implemented by the same developer, who is familiar with GDI+ and image processing. Therefore, the task is small enough to keep them in only two keys. If the developer were not familiar with GDI+ or if the requirements were implemented by different developers in parallel, it would make sense to split them up.

Nothing else has to be done in this iteration regarding the requirements workflow. Therefore, the next step is to proceed to the analysis workflow to analyze the requirements.

Table 6.1 Refined Requirements Descriptions for GDI+ Extensions

Requirement	Type	Summary
F:image_graphics_ annotations	Functional	The photo editor shall provide the possibility to attach customized graphical objects to the image. The graphics primitives types provided are lines, circles, and rectangles. The primitives are drawn at a user-defined position within the image by selecting a shape type, which can then be drawn interactively using the mouse. The graphic is stored in a list and can be removed by selecting the area of the start or endpoint with a mouse click. To permanently add the graphics to the image, it is possible to burn the graphics onto the bitmap by selecting the Apply button. It shall also be possible to reset the image shown to the original image by selecting the Reset button.
F:image_text_ annotations	Functional	The photo editor shall provide a tool that allows adding text in different fonts and colors to an image. After selecting the graphics, overlay-type text can be written at a user-selected position within the image. Different fonts are not supported in this iteration. The text otherwise shall behave like a graphic.

6.2 Analysis of the GDI+ Extensions Requirements

>A> The analysis of the requirements for this chapter also includes the F:photo_editor requirement key. The reason is that to access the functionality described in the two keys just described, the selection must be made from within the photo editor application. Therefore, the GUI must be adapted to reflect these additional buttons.

As with all the requirements gathering and analysis, this update of the GUI should be done in close collaboration with the customer. Defining the GUI is probably the most important task because the GUI is what the customer and users will experience first. In addition, developing a solid GUI definition will eliminate a lot of possible ambiguity regarding the functionality of the business logic (or, in our case, the image-processing part). This is because the GUI defines the possible ways a user can access the business logic. For example, consider the rotation feature implemented in Chapter 5. The buttons allow the user to rotate the image only in 90 degree steps clockwise or counterclockwise. This in turn enables the developer to use the system-provided `RotateFlipType` instead of implementing a customized rotate feature that would allow for arbitrary rotation angles.

6.2.1 The `photo_editor` Requirement

Figure 6.1 shows the changes to the GUI. To access the new functionality, we add a new tab to the existing tab control. The layout of the new tab is shown in the lower part of the figure.

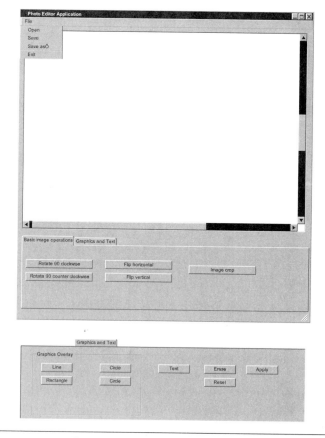

Figure 6.1 The Photo Editor GUI

6.2.2 The `image_graphics_annotations` Requirement

Users can add a graphics overlay element to the image by selecting one of the buttons for the shapes. If a shape is selected, a left mouse click within the image will put the *start point* of the shape at the selected position. The start point for a line is simply the first point of the line, whereas the start point for a rectangle is the upper-left corner, and for a circle it is the upper-left point of the enclosing rectangle. By moving the mouse while pressing down on the left mouse button, users can resize the shape. The new mouse location relative to the start point will define the new size of the shape. When the mouse button is released, the shape is drawn on top of the image.

The shapes are drawn in black, with a default line thickness of 2. The application will be able to call one draw method to draw all the primitives without having to distinguish between them. Users can erase any drawn primitive by using the erase tool and clicking the mouse button within a ±5-pixel area of the start or end point. To make the changes to the bitmap permanent, users use the Apply button to "burn" the graphics onto the bitmap. In addition, a Reset button is provided to enable the user to revert to the originally loaded image.

6.2.3 The `image_text_annotations` Requirement

Users will add text overlays to the image by selecting the Text button. After selecting the text overlay, users add text to the image by clicking within the image to open a dialog box. The dialog box displays a field where the user can enter text, which is drawn after the OK button is applied. The position selected with the mouse corresponds to the upper-left corner of the first letter of the text to be inserted. The text uses the default font and size, and its color is black.

6.3 Design of the GDI+ Extensions

D〉 Based on the analyzed requirements, we specify the design. The functionalities to be implemented are text and graphics primitives. It would be convenient for the application to be able to treat all graphical overlays, such as circle, line, and rectangle, generically and not have to know which object it is actually dealing with. For example, if the application would like to draw a graphical overlay object it would simply call a draw method without knowing whether the object to be drawn is a rectangle, a line, or a circle.

We can achieve this behavior if we arrange the graphical objects in a tree structure with a general graphical object as parent. So one goal of the design is to specify the design in a tree structure that allows the application to treat all the primitives and compositions of them uniformly.

6.3.1 Using Design Patterns

The foregoing problem description sounds like a problem that has been solved by other programmers many times before. Therefore, it might be worthwhile to see whether an abstract solution to the stated design problem is available. If it is, we can adapt it to fit the needs of the photo editor application.

An abstract solution to a particular software design problem is called a *design pattern*. It is a solution to a problem that occurs in the same form over and over again. A design pattern is formulated so that it can be applied whenever the problem occurs. Design patterns are usually described in UML, because it is a common language for software design. One of the advantages of describing a design in UML is that it is independent of the programming language or the domain.

Many programmers have used design patterns, perhaps even without knowing it. Design patterns are not new inventions but rather are collections of reusable solutions for common software design problems. For the programmer they are a reference to solutions that can be adapted to concrete problems. For inexperienced programmers, design patterns can teach them how to avoid common problems by using the solutions that are provided by experienced colleagues. The first published collection of design patterns was the book *Design Patterns: Elements of Reusable Object-Oriented Software,* by Erich Gamma, Richard Helm, Ralph Johnson, and John Vlissides (for more information, see the references section). These authors are also known as GoF, which stands for Gang of Four. This book contains 23 design patterns for object-oriented software design and is the reference used in this book.

The patterns in the design patterns book are divided into three categories: creational, structural, and behavioral. Each described design pattern is structured via four essential elements:

- The pattern name: This element is the descriptive name of the pattern. The name is a handle that identifies the pattern. Usually, the name reflects the pattern's structure.

- The problem: This element explains the problem and the context the design pattern corresponds to.
- The solution: This element provides an abstract description of a design problem by explaining the elements, relationships, responsibilities, and collaborations that make up the design pattern.
- The consequences: This element describes trade-offs in the design that are critical for the evaluation of design alternatives.

The patterns in *Design Patterns* are descriptions of communicating objects and classes that are customized to solve a general design problem in a particular context.

To identify the applicable design pattern (if it exists) that suits the needs of the GDI+ extension of the photo editor, we review the design problem: The image and graphical objects are to be represented by a tree structure. The `PhotoEditorForm` class needs to treat all objects in the tree uniformly.

With this problem statement in mind, we search the 23 published design patterns for an applicable design pattern.

Using the Composite and Iterator Design Patterns

The type of problem we have described should be located in the section of the book devoted to structural patterns. Therefore, we review only the seven published design patterns in that category for applicability. We find that the description of the Composite design pattern fits the design problem of the photo editor application very well.

In fact, the Composite pattern states exactly the problem that needs to be solved in this chapter. Therefore, we identify the Composite pattern as a possible abstract solution and analyze it in more detail. Figure 6.2 shows the static structure of the Composite design pattern.

Based on the class diagram, the participants and their responsibilities are described in Table 6.2.

The client uses the interfaces defined by the component. If a leaf is called directly, the operation will be executed, whereas if a composite is called then the composite might do some preprocessing and then forward the call to the operation on the leaf nodes.

Based on the abstract solution, we adapt the solution to solve our specific design problem. Therefore, the client that is defined corresponds to the application that calls operations on either the leaf or the composite.

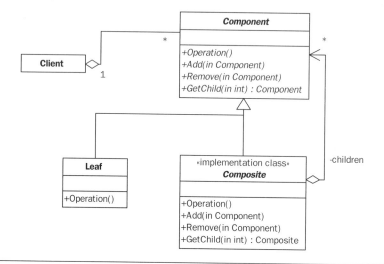

Figure 6.2 The Composite Design Pattern

Table 6.2 Participants in the Composite Design Pattern

Participant	Responsibility
Client	Calls the interfaces provided by the component to manipulate leaf and composite objects.
Component	Declares the interface for the objects in the composition and implements default behavior for the common interfaces if appropriate. In addition, declares the interfaces to access and manage child components. Optionally the component can also define interfaces to access the parent of an object.
Leaf	Represents a leaf object of the composition (leaves do not have children) and implements the manipulators for the primitive objects in the composition.
Composite	Defines the behavior for components that can have children and stores the child components. In addition, it implements child-related operations in the component interface.

The composite is equivalent to the class Picture. The Picture class can contain a list of graphical components. The components themselves are leaf nodes and cannot have any children. The component class will be an abstract class that provides the common functionality. Figure 6.3 shows the class diagram for the photo editor, including the adapted Composite design pattern.

In addition, the Picture class must provide a list that stores the components created. The list must provide the functionality to add, remove, and clear the list. In C++ this is very often done by using a pattern called Iterator. The Iterator design pattern provides sequential access to elements of an aggregate object, such as a list, without exposing the underlying repre-

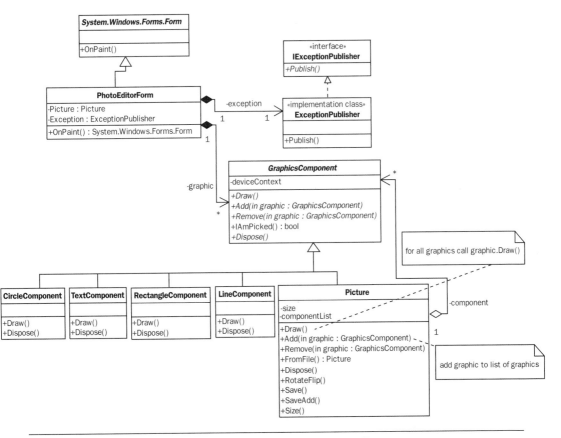

Figure 6.3 The Photo Editor Using the Composite Design Pattern

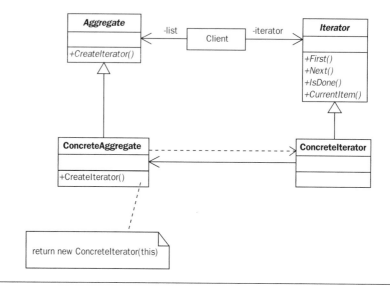

Figure 6.4 The Iterator Design Pattern

sentation. In addition, the Iterator pattern lets us traverse the list in various ways without having to define many iterator interfaces.

To accomplish this, the Iterator pattern separates the iterator from the list (see Figure 6.4). An abstract iterator and an abstract list are defined. The abstract class defines the common interfaces for the iterator and list. The derived, concrete iterator and list then implement the functionality.

Table 6.3 shows the participants of this design pattern and their responsibilities.

Table 6.3 Participants of the Iterator Design Pattern

Participant	Responsibility
Aggregate	Provides an interface for creating an Iterator object.
ConcreteAggregate	Implements the creation of the Iterator and returns an instance of the correct ConcreteIterator.
Client	The client that uses the list and iterates through it.
Iterator	Provides the interfaces for accessing and traversing elements.
ConcreteIterator	Implements the Iterator functionality and keeps track of the current position in the traversal of the aggregate.

The shown concept of asking the aggregate object to create the corresponding Iterator is also known as the Factory method design pattern. The Factory method uses two class hierarchies: one for the aggregate and one for the Iterator. The `CreateIterator` method sets the connection between the two.

This example shows that design patterns are often used together with other design patterns to solve complex design problems. For the photo editor application it is not necessary, though, to go overboard with any more design patterns. The only other thing we need is a list, which enables us to retrieve, add, remove, and clear components.

Figure 6.5 shows the complete static class diagram for the implementation of this iteration. The next step is the analysis workflow.

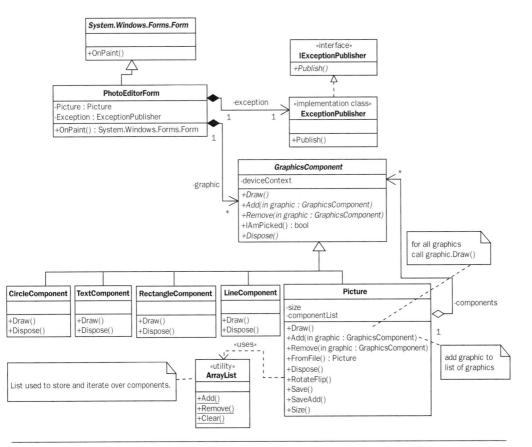

Figure 6.5 The Added List Component

6.4 Project Management Issues

This section summarizes the project management issues for this iteration. First, we need to check the schedule against reality, and then we update the list of defects before we implement the new features.

6.4.1 Schedule Issues

Unfortunately, one of the developers has decided to leave the project to take on a new assignment. This is certainly bad news, and the project schedule is in serious danger. We discuss the possible options for reacting to this change. Table 6.4 lists some possible options along with some of their advantages and disadvantages.

Table 6.4 Recovery Options

Option	Advantage	Disadvantage
Hire an additional, new developer.	The work load for each developer on the project stays the same. The schedule might not need to change.	Mentoring a new developer takes away valuable time from the senior developers. Especially in complex projects, the mentoring can take a lot of time. Therefore, the schedule might still slip.
Let the schedule slip.	If the project is not time-critical, this option allows us to deliver all the functionality without losing time to interview, hire, and mentor a new developer. In addition, the defined risk buffers can be used to make up for some of the time.	The product will be released late.
Reduce the scope of the project.	Features that are not highly important to the customer can be rescheduled for a future release, and the product is delivered on time.	Not all features are delivered. Therefore, the schedule of the final release might slip or some functionality might not be delivered.

The following key points are identified to help us decide on a recovery plan:

- The project is already in the construction phase.
- Domain knowledge is very important.
- Risk buffers were defined to help recover in situations like this.
- The project is time-critical to the customer in order to open the new online market.

Based on this information and discussions with the project team and the customer, the decision is made to proceed with the current project team; the schedule will slip at most by one week if it becomes necessary to use all the risk buffers. In addition, project management agrees to compensate the developers for any overtime that might be necessary to deliver the product on time. Figure 6.6 shows the resulting new project schedule.

So far, we haven't had to cut any of the features to finish the project on time. The way we resolved the schedule problems due to this unforeseen circumstance—in close collaboration between the project team and the customer—is usually a successful recovery method. This approach depends heavily on the trust and open communication of all involved parties.

Chapter 6, Detailed Project Schedule: Online Photo Shop

ID	Task Name	Start	Finish	Duration	Resource Names
1	Milestone 1 (progress review)	11/11/2002	11/11/2002	0d	
2	Milestone 2 (progress review)	11/25/2002	11/25/2002	0d	
3	Milestone 3 (progress review)	12/23/2002	12/23/2002	0d	
4	**Online Photo Shop**	**10/10/2002**	**2/5/2003**	**85d**	
5	photo_editor	10/10/2002	1/7/2003	64d	GL
6	order_online	10/10/2002	1/7/2003	64d	TM
7	error_handling, picture_load_and_save, image_format, image_crop, image_rotate	10/22/2002	11/8/2002	14d	GL
8	image_flip	11/4/2002	11/8/2002	5d	Reader
9	image_brightness, image_contrast, image_color,	11/11/2002	11/20/2002	8d	GL
10	image_graphics_annotations, image_text_annotations	11/11/2002	11/22/2002	10d	GL, Reader
11	order_products, product_browse, product_options, product_customize	11/11/2002	11/20/2002	8d	TM, Reader
12	Risk Buffer	11/20/2002	11/22/2002	3d	
13	image_processing_direct_3d, editor_optimizations	12/4/2002	12/23/2002	14d	GL
14	image_graphics_special_effects, image_special_effects	11/25/2002	12/19/2002	18d	GL, Reader
15	product_shopping_cart, order_checkout, checkaout_shipping, checkout_payment, checkout_summerize.	11/25/2002	12/23/2002	20.5d	TM, Reader
16	Risk Buffer	12/26/2002	12/30/2002	3d	
17	editor_system_test	12/30/2002	1/31/2003	24.5d	GL, TM, Reader
18	Risk Buffer	1/31/2003	2/5/2003	4d	

Figure 6.6 New Project Schedule

The project team must commit to the new schedule, management must honor the need for the developers to work overtime to achieve the tough deadlines, and the customer must be assured that the new schedule is realistic and achievable.

Only if this trusting relationship has been built will a successful recovery be possible. In many projects this does not happen, and the resulting risks are not discussed with the customer early enough. Instead, at the very end of the project the delay becomes obvious, and the only recovery methods at that point are to slip the schedule or cut features and quality (reduce testing). Resorting to less or no testing is often taken as a resolution for schedule problems. In this project, though, quality is of high importance, and we did not consider it an option to take away time from testing to make the deadlines. (In the long run it is generally not a good policy to cut quality in order to make the schedule, even though it happens very often in projects and seems to help in the short term.)

6.4.2 Reported Defects

After the first, unofficial release of the project was delivered to the customer, some defects were reported. The defects were reviewed, assigned to developers, and scheduled for fixing in a specific release. None of the defects requires major rework. Therefore, this work is not reflected in the schedule.

For defects that require rework of more than half a day, the time it takes to fix them should be reflected in the schedule. Smaller rework packages, such as the ones described in this chapter, were already calculated in the original development time as part of the added judge time. Therefore, no extra schedule update is necessary for them. Figure 6.7 shows the new defect tracking sheet.

Now that the planning is complete, it is time to implement the required features.

UniqueID	Submitted by	Date Submitted	Summary	Type	Category	Current status	Priority	Assigned To (Name)	Version Defect Found	Description	Version Scheduled for
00001	Customer	10-Nov-02	Menu item missing	Software	Error	In Work	2	Reader	V0.1.0	In the main menu some options are missing in the drop down menu(see requirements for specification).	V0.2.0
00002	Customer	10-Nov-02	Meaningfull error message if default image can not be found missing	Software	Error	In Work	2	LG	V0.1.0	If Photo editor is started and default image is not found application does not show a meaningful error message.	V0.2.0
00003	Customer	10-Nov-02	Application crashes when window is minimized	Software	Error	In Work	1	LG	V0.1.0	Minimize window	V0.2.0
00004											
00005											
00006											
00007											

Figure 6.7 New Defect Tracking Sheet

6.5 GDI+ Programming

Before we dive any deeper into the application programming, let's look at some basic concepts of the GDI+ library.

6.5.1 What Is GDI+?

GDI+ is an object-oriented library for application programmers to support the task of graphics programming. The origin of the GDI+ library can be found in the GDI (Graphical Device Interface), which is part of the Windows operating system. More specifically, GDI+ is a wrapper around the system's GDI calls. The goal of the GDI library is to shield the application developer from some of the system details by providing an additional layer of abstraction. For example, developers program the functionality of "drawing" on the screen in the same way they program "drawing" on a printer. It does not matter whether the memory in which the graphic is defined is printed or is shown on the screen. GDI takes care of the differences.

One of the major advantages of GDI+ compared with GDI is that GDI+ is fully integrated into the .NET Framework as an object-oriented library.

6.5.2 GDI+ Namespaces

To support the application programmer, GDI+ defines six namespaces in `System.Drawing.dll`:

- `System.Drawing`: This namespace provides the basic graphics functionality. It defines drawing surfaces, images, fonts, colors, brushes, and pens.
- `System.Drawing.Text`: Additional functionality for advanced font usage is defined in this namespace.
- `System.Drawing.Imaging`: This namespace provides additional functionality for advanced imaging operations.
- `System.Drawing.Drawing2D`: This namespace defines advanced vector graphics and raster functionality.
- `System.Drawing.Printing`: Print and print-preview functionalities are provided in this namespace.
- `System.Drawing.Design`: This namespace defines functionality for design-time support of custom controls.

The various namespaces will be explained in more detail at the time they are used.

The main features of the GDI+ library can be summarized as follows:

- It supports three drawing surfaces (memory, screen, and printer).
- It supports text drawing.
- It contains image and bitmap functionality.
- It lets you execute two-dimensional graphics primitives and transformations on any drawing surface.
- It provides object-oriented interfaces.
- It extends the capabilities of GDI by supporting more image formats, additional transformations, alpha blending, and gradients.
- It is interoperable with any .NET application.

6.5.3 The Basics of GDI+

This section defines a basic vocabulary that is needed for the implementation of GDI+ functionality. It is not supposed to be a tutorial on GDI+ but rather gives you a brief introduction to help you understand the GDI+ functionality used in the sample project and to help you build a common vocabulary.

The Drawing Surface

GDI+ defines three *drawing surfaces*: memory, screen, and printer. Each is characterized by the following elements:

- Size: The size of the drawing surface is measured in pixels, where a pixel is a square entity and the smallest possible drawing unit. After you create a drawing surface, you can query the size and in some cases change it.
- Resolution: The resolution of a drawing surface is usually measured in dots per inch (DPI) or in pixels per inch (PPI). A given value describes a square area, with the value of the number of pixels in the horizontal and vertical directions per inch.
- Color: The color depth describes the capability of displaying various colors. GDI+ internally represents each color with three values. The red, green, and blue (RGB) components describe the color of each pixel. Each color component in GDI+ can have a value between 0 and 255. This results in the capability of displaying a maximum of

16,777,216 colors, which corresponds to a color depth of 24 bits. In case of incompatibility of the drawing surface with the currently used color scheme, GDI+ tries to adapt the colors through a process called *dithering*. Dithering uses alternating colors for two adjacent pixels to create the illusion of a color that cannot be drawn because the color depth is not supported by the drawing surface. In some cases, this behavior is visually jarring. You can avoid dithering by asking the system for the nearest color that is supported. In addition, GDI+ provides an *alpha* component for each pixel, which can be used to define the transparency or opacity of a color, something that can be used for special effects.

Table 6.5 shows the three drawing surfaces along with their characteristics.

Table 6.5 Drawing Surfaces and Their Characteristics

Drawing Surface	Resolution	Size	Color Depth
Memory	The default resolution for images allocated in memory is 96 DPI. If an image is loaded from a file, the resolution is also read from the file. The resolution can be changed at any time.	The size is specified when the surface is created. If an image is loaded from a file, its size is also read from the file.	Monochrome, grayscale, color map, 16- to 64-bit, and alpha values are the possible parameters for images allocated in memory.
Screen	96 DPI	Size depends on the client area of the window that is displayed on the screen.	Usually 24 bits. If necessary, dithering is used for drawing the image on the screen.
Printer	Resolution depends on the printer and therefore depends on the printer driver. Can be changed if the printer driver allows changing resolution.	Size depends on the page size that is supported by the printer driver.	Typically 24 bits, but GDI+ and the printer driver are responsible for drawing the image on a printer surface.

The drawing surfaces are encapsulated in the GDI+ `Graphics` class. If you have some exposure to GDI programming, you will realize that the `Graphics` class is associated with a specific device context.

The `Graphics` class lets you query for details of the instantiated drawing surface, such as its size and resolution. In addition, the `Graphics` class provides operations to *transform* images (for example, to rotate, flip, and clip) and to draw basic graphics primitives onto the drawing surface (for example, lines, ellipses, rectangles, text, and images); these primitives are then displayed on the screen, printed, or written into memory. For a comprehensive list of methods provided by the `Graphics` class, please refer to the MSDN help pages.

The Coordinate System

To work with images, graphics, and other operations related to image processing, it is very important to understand the basic coordinate system on which all the GDI+ operations are based. The GDI+ *coordinate system* is raster-based. In this case, *raster-based* means that the image is stored as a two-dimensional grid. Within this grid, the upper-left corner is defined as the origin of the coordinate system.

Graphics primitives such as lines, rectangles, and circles are defined by two points within the coordinate system. For lines, these points are the start and end points, and for rectangles and circles they are the coordinates of the upper-left and lower-right corners of the bounding rectangle (in the case of the rectangle, this is the actual rectangle).

What happens if the graphics primitive that is drawn does not exactly fit into the raster grid? This is shown in Figure 6.8. In that case, when you're drawing a diagonal line, a stair-step effect might become visible because of the limited resolution. This stair-step effect is called *aliasing*. To make this effect less visible, you can use a smoothing technique called *antialiasing*. This is also shown in the example in Figure 6.8.

Antialiasing is also used by GDI+ if the application provides coordinates in floating point numbers instead of integers.

GDI+ Pens and Brushes

To draw the graphics, GDI+ defines various pens and brushes. *Pens* are used to draw points, lines, and the outlines of shapes, whereas *brushes* are used to fill shapes with patterns and colors. The most important properties of pens and brushes are listed in Table 6.6.

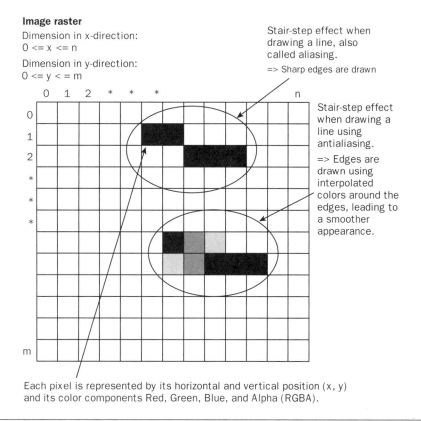

Image raster

Dimension in x-direction:
0 <= x <= n

Dimension in y-direction:
0 <= y < = m

Stair-step effect when drawing a line, also called aliasing.
=> Sharp edges are drawn

Stair-step effect when drawing a line using antialiasing.
=> Edges are drawn using interpolated colors around the edges, leading to a smoother appearance.

Each pixel is represented by its horizontal and vertical position (x, y) and its color components Red, Green, Blue, and Alpha (RGBA).

Figure 6.8 GDI+ Basics

The various properties will be explained at their first use in the upcoming chapters. Definitions are also available in the MSDN documentation.

Table 6.6 Properties of Pens and Brushes

Drawing Object	Properties
Pen	Width, patterns or styles, end styles (arrows and other shapes), join styles
Brush	Textures, gradient brushes, hatch (to fill a region with a pattern)

6.6 Drawing GDI+ Primitives

The list of features to be implemented in this iteration is quite comprehensive. Therefore, we present here a rough outline of the various tasks. This list will also enable you to navigate more easily through this iteration if you're using the book as a reference for your own applications.

The following list shows the high-level tasks that need to be done in order to draw graphics primitives and text on the screen. It also shows the tasks that have to be done to fulfill the requirements of this chapter:

- The `Graphics` reference to the `customScrollableControl` must be passed to the graphics primitives in order for the primitives to draw themselves on the screen.
- A `GraphicsComponent` class must be defined. All graphics, text, and picture classes will derive from it.
- We must define the line, circle, rectangle, and text classes. All these classes derive from the common graphics `Component` class (see the design specification in section 6.3).
- The picture component needs to implement a list that contains all the graphical objects that are to be drawn on the screen. We must implement functionality to add and remove graphical objects.
- The `Draw` method of the `Picture` class must iterate through all the components to call the corresponding `Draw` method (so that the primitives can draw themselves on the provided graphics drawing surface).
- We must define a new tab control within the photo editor GUI and add buttons for the new functionalities.
- To let users select the desired graphical tool (such as the line or circle), we must define an enumeration in the `PhotoEditorForm` class.
- We must implement mouse event handlers.
- We need to add other functionality (such as picking an object or removing components), some cosmetics, and some bug fixes.

Now that the high-level tasks are presented, the implementation (fun) can begin.

6.6.1 The Infrastructure Implementation

The first task is to create the graphics component class. The component class acts as the base class for all the graphics primitive classes (components) and the `Picture` class. Therefore, we add a new class file to the Photo Editor Application project and give it the name `GraphicsComponent.cs`. The new class, if generated with the class wizard, is defined within the namespace `Photo_Editor_Application`. Also, make sure you have included the `using` statements for the `System` and the `System.Drawing` namespaces at the beginning of the class file.

Defining the Abstract `GraphicsComponent` *Class*

The `GraphicsComponent` class itself is defined as follows:

```
public abstract class GraphicsComponent
```

The `abstract` keyword indicates that this class cannot be instantiated (as with C++ classes that contain pure virtual methods). Therefore, abstract classes can be used only as base classes. In addition, abstract classes can (but are not required to) contain abstract methods. If an abstract class defines abstract methods, then the methods define the signature but do not provide any implementation. All classes that derive from an abstract class are required to provide implementations for all inherited abstract methods. To make the point even clearer, abstract methods and properties can be defined only in abstract classes. In addition to classes and methods, property access methods can be declared as abstract. The `abstract` property method does not provide any implementation for the `get` or `set` property, but it defines the `get` and/or `set` stubs without implementation.

Based on these qualities of abstract classes, it is obvious that abstract classes cannot be defined as `sealed` (where the keyword `sealed` indicates that no other class can derive from it).

Listing 6.1 shows the very basic implementation for the `Graphics Component` class.

Listing 6.1 Abstract `GraphicsComponent` Class

```
using System;
using System.Drawing;

namespace Photo_Editor_Application
{
  /// <summary>
  /// Abstract Component class.
```

```csharp
/// Every graphic primitive and picture has to derive from
/// this class. It provides the common interfaces the
/// application can use.
/// </summary>
public abstract class GraphicsComponent
{
  /// <summary>
  /// Constructor.
  /// </summary>
  public GraphicsComponent()
  {

  }

/// <summary>
/// Abstract method to be implemented by the derived
/// classes to draw the corresponding primitive into
/// the drawing surface.
/// </summary>
public abstract void Draw();

/// <summary>
/// Method to add a component to the list of components.
/// Default behavior is to do nothing.
/// </summary>
public virtual void Add(GraphicsComponent comp){}

/// <summary>
/// Method to remove a component from the list of components.
/// Default behavior is to do nothing.
/// </summary>
public virtual void Remove(GraphicsComponent comp){}

/// <summary>
/// Accessor method for the static deviceContext
/// field that holds the graphics reference to
/// the drawing surface.
/// </summary>
public static Graphics DeviceContext
{
  get
  {
```

```
      return deviceContext;
    }
    set
    {
      deviceContext = value;
    }
  }

  /// <summary>
  /// Holds the drawing surface.
  /// </summary>
  private static Graphics deviceContext;
  }
}
```

First, the constructor is provided. The constructor does not implement any functionality. After that you can see the declaration of the abstract method `Draw`, which is declared but does not provide any implementation. That is, the implementation is left to the derived classes. In addition, two `virtual` methods for adding and removing components from the list of components are defined.

Virtual methods, unlike `abstract` methods, provide a default behavior for the functionality defined. However, virtual methods allow the derived classes to provide their own specialized implementation. The default implementation for both accessor methods is to do nothing at all. Virtual methods do not have to be implemented by the derived classes (in which case, the default behavior is used).

Next, the `private static` field `deviceContext` and its property accessor method are defined. The `deviceContext` field holds the reference to the `Graphics` object in order to draw the components on the drawing surface. The keyword `static` indicates to the compiler that only a single instance of the field exists for all objects created. A static field is used here because all the components will share one drawing surface.

In addition to this implementation, some helper functionality and properties must be provided by the `GraphicsComponent` class to support the drawing of the components. We implement two `private` fields of type `Point` that represent the `start` (upper-left) and the `end` (lower-right) points of the graphics components. These fields define the components completely as long as we draw with only one default color and line width. (Remember that a line is defined by two points, and the rectangle and circle are defined by the start point and their width and height, where the width and height can be calculated from the two upper-left and lower-right points.)

Another functionality that we need to provide for all the components is a method that transforms coordinates from screen coordinates into image coordinates. This feature is used in case the image is larger than the custom scrollable control and the user has scrolled the image. If the graphics primitive is then drawn, it will be at the same position with respect to the control, but not relative to the image. This means that the graphics will not scroll and will not be bound to the position in the image but rather will stay at the same position within the control. This is because the coordinates provided by the mouse event always correspond to the position of the mouse within the control, and not to the position relative to the image (as shown in Figure 6.9). In fact, the system doesn't really know which position in the image is shown. The management of which part of the image is shown in the control is the responsibility of the custom control that displays the

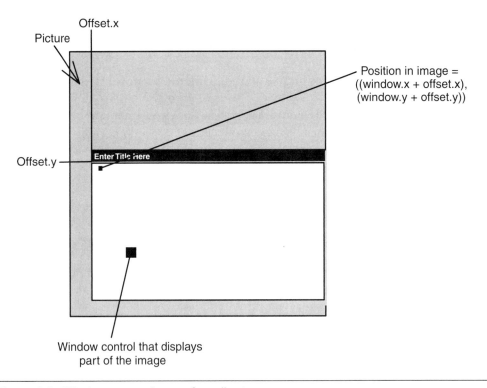

Figure 6.9 Window versus Image Coordinates

image. All the system knows is the control and the position of the mouse pointer within the control. Therefore, we must convert and store the coordinates provided by the mouse event handlers into coordinates relative to the image. The GraphicsComponent class provides this functionality. The transformation method is also used when the graphical components are drawn to convert the image coordinates back to viewport coordinates.

The GraphicsComponent class implements a property and a set accessor method to store the location of the viewport coordinates. This property, called viewportCoords, is declared static because all graphical components draw in the same window with the same viewport coordinates. Then we provide a method that converts the coordinates of a point relative to the image into coordinates relative to the window. Listing 6.2 shows these additional functionalities of the Component class.

Listing 6.2 The Component Class Helper Functions

```
public abstract class GraphicsComponent
{
  /// <summary>
  /// Constructor initializes the start and end point
  /// of each primitive to be the origin.
  /// </summary>
  public GraphicsComponent()
  {
    startPoint.X = startPoint.Y = 0;
    endPoint.X = endPoint.Y = 0;
  }

          *


          *


          *


  /// <summary>
  /// Accessor method for the coordinates of
  /// the upper-left corner of the primitive, or
  /// the start point of a line.
  /// </summary>
  public Point StartPoint
  {
```

```csharp
    get
    {
      return startPoint;
    }
    set
    {
      startPoint = value;
    }
  }


  /// <summary>
  /// Accessor method for the coordinates of
  /// the lower-right corner of the primitive, or
  /// the end point of a line.
  /// </summary>
  public Point EndPoint
  {
    get
    {
      return endPoint;
    }
    set
    {
      endPoint = value;
    }
  }


  /// <summary>
  /// Calculates the coordinates within the display
  /// window from a
  /// point relative to the image.
  /// </summary>
  /// <param name="imagePoint">Point in image
  /// coordinates</param>
  public Point CalcViewportCoords(Point imagePoint)
  {
    Point viewportPoint = new Point(imagePoint.X -
        viewportCoords.X,
      imagePoint.Y - viewportCoords.Y);
    return viewportPoint;
  }
```

```
/// <summary>
/// Set method for the coordinates of
/// the image within the display window.
/// </summary>
public static Point ViewportCoords
{
  set
  {
    viewportCoords = value;
  }
}

private Point endPoint;
private Point startPoint;
private static Point viewportCoords;
}
```

After the `Component` class is implemented, we must change the existing `Picture` class to be derived from the `GraphicsComponent` base class. In addition, we must implement in the base class (`GraphicsComponent`) the methods defined as `abstract`. Furthermore, we must create and manage a list of components. Luckily, the .NET Framework provides a class called `ArrayList`.

The `ArrayList` class provides several convenience functions for list management, and these functions are useful for our implementation of the component list. The add, remove, clear, and dynamic size allocation features are used for this implementation. Please see the MSDN files for a complete description of the functionalities provided by `ArrayList`. Because the `ArrayList` class is defined in the `System.Collections` namespace, this namespace must be included in the `Picture.cs` file.

Listing 6.3 shows the features we have added to the `Picture` class. You can see that the `Draw` method is marked with the keyword `override` to indicate that it overrides, or in this case implements, the `Draw` method declared by the base class `GraphicsComponent`. The `Draw` method loops through all the components in `ArrayList` and calls the `Draw` method of each component. The `foreach` loop is used to loop through the list and to draw all the components. In general, `foreach` loops are used to iterate over arrays and collections without changing them.

The rest of the shown implementation is self-explanatory. It basically deals with `ArrayList` management. In addition to the shown implementation, we add the following line to the constructor of the `Picture` class to create an `ArrayList` at initialization time. Initially, an array of 20 components is created. This seems to be a good value, and the `ArrayList` class will expand the list if necessary.

```
compList = new ArrayList(20);
```

Listing 6.3 The `Picture` Class

```
using System;
using System.Drawing;
using System.Windows.Forms;
using System.Collections;

namespace Photo_Editor_Application
{
  /// <summary>
  /// Image class stores all image-related data.
  /// It also provides the basic functionality and
  /// is derived from the Component class.
  /// </summary>
  public class Picture : GraphicsComponent
  {

            *

            *

            *


    /// <summary>
    /// The Draw method walks through the list
    /// of created components and calls the Draw
    /// method for each of the components.
    /// </summary>
    public override void Draw()
    {
      foreach(GraphicsComponent obj in compList)
      {
        GraphicsComponent theComp = (GraphicsComponent)obj;
        theComp.Draw();
      }
    }
```

```
/// <summary>
/// Method adds a new component to the list of
/// components.
/// </summary>
public override void Add(GraphicsComponent comp)
{
  compList.Add(comp);
}

/// <summary>
/// Removes a component from the list of components.
/// </summary>
public override void Remove(GraphicsComponent comp)
{
  compList.Remove(comp);
}

/// <summary>
/// Clears the list of components.
/// </summary>
public void ClearComponentList()
{
  compList.Clear();
}

private ArrayList compList;
private Bitmap backUpImage;
  }
}
```

Now that the groundwork is finished, it is time to start implementing the first graphical component. As an example, we'll show the `Rectangle` primitive. We leave the implementation of the `Line` and `Circle` primitives to you.

6.6.2 Drawing GDI+ Graphics Primitives: Lines, Rectangles, and Ellipses

The implementation of the graphics primitives is fairly easy. The implementation of all the graphical components can be broken down into five steps:

1. Create the component and implement the inherited abstract methods. Implement a `Draw` method that draws the graphical component.

2. Add a button to the graphical user interface.
3. Add the graphics tool to the enumeration of selection tools.
4. Create an event handler for the button click event. In the event handler, reset all buttons and the selected tool if another tool has already been selected. If no tool has been selected, then set the selected tool enumeration to the corresponding value.
5. Implement the action that needs to be taken for the mouse down, mouse up, and mouse move events if the corresponding tool was selected. For example, on mouse down, a new graphics component is created and the position of the mouse is stored as the start and end points. A flag is set to indicate drawing, and the component is added to the list of components to be drawn in the `Picture` class. Then on mouse move, if a tool was selected and the drawing flag is set, then the corresponding graphics component is drawn by using the current mouse position as the new end point. If the mouse up event handler is called, indicate that no more drawing will occur.

According to our to-do list, we first add another class named `Rectangle Component`. For the implementation, only the constructors and the implementation of the abstract `Draw` method have to be provided by the class. The constructor does not implement any functionality. The `Draw` method has the responsibility to draw the specific graphics primitive on the drawing surface. The drawing surface is provided by the `static` base class property.

Drawing a rectangle on the provided drawing surface is straightforward. The `Graphics` object, in this case stored under the name `deviceContext`, provides a number of draw methods. One of the supported draw methods is the `DrawRectangle` method, which is what we use to draw the rectangle. It defines multiple overloaded methods to draw a rectangle. The overloaded method used in this example expects as parameters a pen (which in this iteration will be a black pen), the x- and y-coordinates of the upper-left corner, and the width and height of the rectangle to be drawn. Before sending the coordinates to the drawing method, we convert them from image coordinates to display window coordinates (as mentioned earlier, all the coordinates that we store in a component are relative to the image and must be converted at drawing time).

One additional consideration is worth mentioning. To draw the graphics object, GDI+ expects the width and height to be positive. Therefore, we check whether the end point stored in the object is indeed below and to the right of the start point. If it is not, the coordinates of the points must be switched so that we can draw the rectangle with positive width and height.

Therefore, we first check whether the calculated width and height are negative numbers. If that is the case, the start and end points must be exchanged, and the width and height must be provided as absolute numbers (the other option would be to recalculate the coordinates).

The Math namespace provides the ABS method, which returns the absolute value of a provided number (meaning it always returns a positive number; for example, –45 returns 45). We then check whether the width is negative. If the width is negative, only the x values of the start and end points are swapped, and the width is converted to a positive number so that we can draw the rectangle. After that, the height is checked, and the appropriate action is taken to ensure proper drawing. If everything is in order, the rectangle is drawn without doing any calculation.

Listing 6.4 shows the implementation of the rectangle component.

Listing 6.4 The Rectangle Implementation

```
using System;
using System.Drawing;

namespace Photo_Editor_Application
{
    /// <summary>
    /// The RectangleComponent class implements the
    /// functionality to draw a rectangle in the picture.
    /// </summary>
    /// <requirement>F:image_graphics_annotations</requirement>
    public class RectangleComponent : GraphicsComponent
    {
        /// <summary>
        /// Constructs a Rectangle object.
        /// </summary>
        public RectangleComponent()
        {

        }

        /// <summary>
        /// Method that draws the rectangle component into the
        /// graphics
        /// object. The DrawRectangle method provided by GDI+ is
        /// used to
```

```
/// actually draw the graphic primitive. Depending on
/// the mouse
/// movement, the width, height, and position are
/// adjusted.
/// </summary>
public override void Draw()
{
    int width =
        CalcViewportCoords(EndPoint).X -
        CalcViewportCoords(StartPoint).X;
    int height =
        CalcViewportCoords(EndPoint).Y -
        CalcViewportCoords(StartPoint).Y;

    // if width and height are less than zero, then
    //exchange start and end point.
    if(width < 0 && height < 0)
        DeviceContext.DrawRectangle(Pens.Black,
            CalcViewportCoords(EndPoint).X,
            CalcViewportCoords(EndPoint).Y,
            Math.Abs(width), Math.Abs(height));
    else if (width < 0)
        // if only width < 0 then x coordinate of start
        // and end point have to be
        // swapped in order to draw the rectangle with
        // positive width and height.
        DeviceContext.DrawRectangle(Pens.Black,
            CalcViewportCoords(EndPoint).X,
            CalcViewportCoords(StartPoint).Y,
            Math.Abs(width), height);
    else if (height < 0)
        // if only height < 0 then y coordinate of start
        // and end point have to be
        // swapped in order to draw the rectangle with
        // positive width and height.
        DeviceContext.DrawRectangle(Pens.Black,
            CalcViewportCoords(StartPoint).X,
            CalcViewportCoords(EndPoint).Y,
            width, Math.Abs(height));
    else
        // if everything is OK then just draw the
        // rectangle using the provided coordinates.
        DeviceContext.DrawRectangle(Pens.Black,
```

```
                          CalcViewportCoords(StartPoint).X,
                          CalcViewportCoords(StartPoint).Y,
                          width, height);
              }
        }
}
```

The rectangle component is now ready to use. The next step is to extend the photo editor application to let users select a drawing tool by using a button from the GUI. Therefore, a new tab needs to be added to the tab control of the `PhotoEditor.cs[Design]` page. This is done by right-clicking on the existing tab control and selecting Add Tab. After the tab is created, change the properties as follows:

Properties of the Overlay Tab

(Name)	Overlays
Text	Graphics and Text

Then add a button to the new tab and change its properties as follows:

Properties of the Rectangle Button

(Name)	RectangleButton
Text	Rectangle

After that, create an event handler for the button click event. To let users distinguish various tools, we define an enumeration `toolSelection`, whose elements are the tools that are defined or `None`. The enumeration members defined until now are the rectangle tool or none. Then the button style is changed if it was selected. If any tool (except `None`) was already selected, then the tool is deselected and the button style is changed back to the standard appearance. We also implement a helper method that resets all the buttons and the selected tool, as shown in Listing 6.5.

Listing 6.5 The `RectangleTool_Click` Event Handler

```
/// <summary>
/// Convenience method to reset all buttons to
/// default appearance and to reset toolSelected.
```

```csharp
/// </summary>
private void resetButtons()
{
  // Resets all the implemented graphics tool buttons
  RectangleButton.FlatStyle = FlatStyle.Standard;

  // Resets the tool currently used to none.
  toolSelected = 0;
}

// All possible tools that can be selected
private enum toolSelection { None = 0, RectangleTool}

// Tool currently selected
private toolSelection toolSelected;

/// <summary>
/// Sets the selected tool to RectangleTool if no tool
/// was selected before. If a tool was selected before
/// then the tool selection is reset to no tool.
/// </summary>
/// <param name="sender">Object that sent the event.</param>
/// <param name="e">Parameters provided by the event.</param>
private void RectangleButton_Click(object sender,
            System.EventArgs e)
{
   if(toolSelected == toolSelection.None)
   {
     // Calls the convenience method to
     // reset the buttons to no tool selected.
     resetButtons();
     toolSelected = toolSelection.RectangleTool;
     // Changes the appearance of the button to show it
     // is actually selected
     RectangleButton.FlatStyle = FlatStyle.Flat;
   }
   else
   {
     // Calls the convenience method to
     // reset the buttons to no tool selected.
     resetButtons();
   }
}
```

Now that the button can be selected, we proceed to implement the mouse event handlers for interactive drawing of the graphical component.

6.6.3 Handling Mouse Events and Interactive Drawing

Before we start to implement the mouse event handler, it is important to explain the principles of event handlers in .NET and explore how they differ from the C/C++ event handlers of previous Visual Studio implementations.

Even though automatically generated event handlers were used earlier in the book (the button click events were generated by the class wizard), it is worthwhile to look behind the scenes to see how event handlers work. The knowledge you gain about event handlers in this section will help you to understand and implement the mouse event handlers used for interactive drawing in this chapter.

Delegates and Events

Events are raised in response to actions such as mouse moves, clicks, or other program logic. Two parties are involved in event handling. One is the object that raises the event, also called the *sender object*. The other participant is the object responding to the event, also referred to as the *event receiver*. The sender object does not know which object or method will respond to or handle the event it raises. For that reason the .NET Framework provides a type called a *delegate*, which is similar to a function pointer in C/C++. Delegates use the Observer design pattern. Unlike function pointers, though, the delegate class has a signature, and it can hold references that match this signature. This is why delegates offer the big advantage (compared with function pointers) of being type-safe. In addition, a delegate can hold more than one reference.

To use a delegate, it must be declared, assigned, and invoked. The following example shows these principles:

```
// declaration of a delegate
delegate int DelegateExample();

// assigning a delegate method to be called is
// MyClass.InstanceMethod
DelegateExample delegateType = new
  DelegateExample(MyClass.InstanceMethod);

//Call the event handling Instance Method
delegateType();
```

Later in this chapter you will learn how to implement a delegate.

What is the connection between delegates and events? The answer is fairly easy: Events are declared using delegates. An event allows clients to define methods that are called if a certain event occurs. In .NET, an event is declared as taking two parameters: One is the *object source,* which indicates the source of the event. The other one is an additional parameter, `e`, which encapsulates additional information regarding the event. The type of `e` should derive from the `EventArgs` class. If no more information is supplied to the delegate, then the .NET-defined delegate type `EventHandler` can be used. This is all you need to know to understand events in .NET.

To see how these concepts work, take the Visual Studio Designer as an example. If you add a new button and need to add its click event, all you have to do is to double-click the new button in the Designer. The Designer automatically generates code for the click event by linking the event handler method to the event, assigning the delegate method, and supplying the body for the event handler method (using the signature provided by the event source). All you have to do is to fill in the functionality.

Implementing Event Handlers for Interactive Drawing

This section describes the steps to implement interactive drawing of the rectangle component. First, we let the components know in what window they will be drawn: We set the static `GraphicsComponent` field `deviceContext` to a reference to the `Graphics` object of `customScrollableControl` in the `PhotoEditorForm` constructor. In addition, we set the `isDrawing` flag to `false` in the constructor.

After that, we implement the mouse event handlers. To add the event handler for the mouse, select the `customScrollableControl` in `Photo Editor.cs[Design]`, go to the properties, and select the event symbol (the lightning symbol). Double-click on the event that needs to be added (the events needed are `MouseUp`, `-Down`, `-Move`, `-Enter`, and `-Leave`). If a mouse event handler is called (such as down, move, or up), some action must be taken to draw the selected component, if any was selected.

If the `customScrollableControl_MouseDown` event was encountered, the corresponding component object is created. In addition, the start and end points of the component are initialized to the current coordinates (where the current mouse coordinates are provided in the event arguments). In addition, the component is added to the component list of the `Picture` object. If an invalid tool was selected, an exception is thrown.

Then the `isDrawing` property is set to `true` to indicate that the component was created and needs to be drawn if the mouse is moved or the mouse button is released.

When the `customScrollableControl_MouseMove` event handler is called, we first check whether a tool was selected. If a tool was selected, then the mouse pointer is changed to a cross shape. Then we check whether a component was created and needs drawing. If the `isDrawing` flag is set to `true`, then the coordinates must be updated and the object must be redrawn with its new lower-right-corner position.

Next, the `customScrollableControl_MouseUp` event handler is implemented. If the mouse button is released, then the component's end position is updated to the current mouse position and the `isDrawing` flag is set to `false` before the screen is redrawn.

In addition, we add the `customScrollableControl_MouseEnter` event handler to change the cursor shape to a cross shape if a tool is selected and the mouse pointer enters the control.

Listing 6.6 shows the changed parts of the code.

Listing 6.6 Interactive Drawing

```
namespace Photo_Editor_Application
{
  /// <summary>
  /// The GUI class for the photo editor application.
  /// </summary>
  /// <requirements>F:photo_editor</requirements>
  public class PhotoEditorForm : System.Windows.Forms.Form
  {
      *


      *


      *

  /// <summary>
  /// Constructor of the application class.
  /// PhotoEditorForm provides the GUI for the photo
  /// editor project.
  /// </summary>
  public PhotoEditorForm()
  {
```

```
                    *
                    *
                    *

    //sets the private property to not drawing
    isDrawing = false;

    // Sets the static property of the component to the
    // Graphics object of the window it is drawn in
    Component.DeviceContext =
      customScrollableControl.CreateGraphics();
      // Display the Image at startup
}

// Indicates that if a tool was selected, the mouse button
// was selected
// and is not released yet => currently drawing the selected
// component
private bool isDrawing;

// All possible tools that can be selected
private enum toolSelection { None = 0, RectangleTool}
// Currently selected tool
private toolSelection toolSelected;

// The selected component that is currently drawing
private Component compObject;

// If tool was selected and mouse is clicked in the window
// then
// create the component, initialize the variables, and draw
// everything.
private void customScrollableControl_MouseDown(
  object sender,
  System.Windows.Forms.MouseEventArgs e)
{

  // Check whether a drawing tool is selected and
  // whether we need to draw.
  if(!isDrawing && (toolSelected != toolSelection.None))
  {
    switch(toolSelected)
    {
    //create component according to tool selected
```

```
    case toolSelection.RectangleTool:
        compObject = new RectangleComponent();
      break;
    default:
        toolSelected = toolSelection.None;
        throw(new Exception("Error, Tool selected not
      implemented")) ;
  }
  // Set the Graphics referenced in
  // the component to the window object.
  GraphicsComponent.DeviceContext =
      customScrollableControl.CreateGraphics();
  // Add the component to the
  // list that needs to be drawn.
  PictureObject.Add(compObject);
  // Get the coordinates and
  // transform them to coordinates
  // relative to the image
  Point tempPoint =
      new Point(e.X +
      customScrollableControl.ViewportCoords().X,
    e.Y +
      customScrollableControl.ViewportCoords().Y);
  // Set the points
  compObject.StartPoint = tempPoint;
  compObject.EndPoint = tempPoint;

  // Now we started drawing a component
  isDrawing = true;

  // Display the image plus the components.
  DisplayImage();
  PictureObject.Draw();
  }
}

// Event Handler for mouse move,
// draws component when in draw mode.
private void customScrollableControl_MouseMove(object
      sender, System.Windows.Forms.MouseEventArgs e)
{
  // Check whether there was a tool selected.
  if(toolSelected != toolSelection.None)
```

```
    {
      // Change cursor to cross shape.
      Cursor.Current = Cursors.Cross;
    }
    // Check whether in drawing mode.
    if(isDrawing)
    {
      // Set new coordinate of end point for component
      // in
      // coordinates relative to the image.
      Point tempPoint = new Point(e.X +
            customScrollableControl.ViewportCoords().X, e.Y +
            customScrollableControl.ViewportCoords().Y);
      compObject.EndPoint = tempPoint;
      // Draw everything
      DisplayImage();
      PictureObject.Draw();
    }
  }

  // If mouse button is released and drawing mode then
  // add object to list and redraw everything
  private void customScrollableControl_MouseUp(object
      sender, System.Windows.Forms.MouseEventArgs e)
  {
    if(isDrawing)
    {
      // Update end point to final position relative to image
      tempPoint = new Point(e.X +
        customScrollableControl.ViewportCoords().X, e.Y +
        customScrollableControl.ViewportCoords().Y);
      compObject.EndPoint = tempPoint;

      // Reset mode to not drawing
      isDrawing = false;

      // Display all
      DisplayImage();
      PictureObject.Draw();
    }
  }

  private Point tempPoint;
  // If mouse enters control and a tool is selected
```

```
// then change the cursor to cross
private void customScrollableControl_MouseEnter(object
              sender, System.EventArgs e)
{
  if(toolSelected != 0)
  {
    Cursor.Current = Cursors.Cross;
  }
}

// If mouse leaves control make sure
// mouse pointer is standard
private void customScrollableControl_MouseLeave(
              object sender, System.EventArgs e)
{
  Cursor.Current = Cursors.Default;
}
  }
}
```

This completes the implementation of the Rectangle tool. If the Graphics and Text tab is selected, then the Rectangle tool can be chosen. When the mouse button is clicked and the mouse is moved, the application starts drawing the component. The drawing continues until the mouse button is released.

If you test your application now, you will notice that the graphic flickers while it is being drawn and that the graphic disappears when the mouse is not moved or the mouse button is released. What happened is that custom ScrollableControl is repainted and the components are not. This means that the image has been painted over the graphics, and that makes them disappear. You can avoid this by adding a paint event handler for custom ScrollableControl to the PhotoEditorForm class. In the event handler, we simply call Draw() on the graphics components. Here is the implementation:

```
private void customScrollableControl_Paint(object sender,
                    System.Windows.Forms.PaintEventArgs e)
{
  // First update the viewport Coordinates.
  GraphicsComponent.ViewportCoords =
      customScrollableControl.ViewportCoords();
```

```
// Draw all graphic components.
PictureObject.Draw();
}
```

This fixes the problem. You can also see that before the components are redrawn, we first update the viewport position to make sure that the graphics are painted at the correct position if scrolling was done.

Do It Yourself   The implementation of the line and the circle is very similar to the implementation of the rectangle. For the line component, the line can be drawn from start to end point without any adjustment, no matter where the end point is positioned relative to the start point. To implement the drawing of the circle, you use the `DrawEllipse` method, which actually takes the same parameters as the rectangle call because in the case of the ellipse, the bounding rectangle is provided in order to draw. Here are some hints:

1. Create the respective component class (derived from the `Graphics Component` base class).
2. Add a new enumeration value for the component to the `tool Selection` enumeration.
3. Add a button to the GUI, and implement the click event handler.
4. To create the component, implement the cases for the mouse down event.
5. Create a group box around all the added buttons according to the GUI requirement.

6.6.4 Drawing Text in GDI+

The strategy for displaying text is essentially the same as that for drawing graphical components. But some additional work must be done to make this work. To hold the text that is to be displayed when drawing the text component, we define a member `textInput` of type `string` and an accessor. In addition to the position and the text, we need to know in what font and with which brush the text is drawn. The font defines the type of the letters used, and the brush defines the color of the characters. Therefore, we create a member that holds an instance of a font; for the brush, we use the system-defined brush in the color black.

Now the text can be drawn using the `DrawString` command of GDI+. Listing 6.7 shows the implementation of the text component.

Listing 6.7 Text Drawing Component

```
/// <summary>
/// The text component is responsible for drawing
/// text to the drawing surface.
/// </summary>
/// <requirement>F:image_text_annotations</requirement>
public class TextComponent : GraphicsComponent
{
  /// <summary>
  /// Constructor for text component.
  /// </summary>
  public TextComponent()
  {

  }
  /// <summary>
  /// Accessor for textInput, which represents the
  /// text to be drawn.
  /// </summary>
  public string TextInput
  {
    get
    {
      return textInput;
    }
    set
    {
      textInput = value;
    }
  }

  /// <summary>
  /// Draws the text into the Graphics object provided.
  /// </summary>
  public override void Draw()
  {
    Font ff = new Font("Arial",18);
    Point tempPoint = new Point(StartPoint.X, StartPoint.Y);
    tempPoint = CalcViewportCoords(tempPoint);
    DeviceContext.DrawString(textInput, ff, Brushes.Black,
                  tempPoint.X, tempPoint.Y);
```

```
// Dispose of the font created
    ff.Dispose();
  }

  private string textInput;
}
```

After the `TextComponent` is implemented, we need to add the support for the new functionality in the `PhotoEditorForm` class.

The first step is to add `TextTool` to the `toolSelection` enumeration in the `PhotoEditorForm` class. After that, we add to the GUI a button with the name `TextButton` (we also change the text of the button to `Text`); we create the button click event handler by double-clicking on the button. In the button click event handler, we set `toolSelected` to the `TextTool` enumeration member, if no tool was selected before.

Next, we change `customScrollableControl_MouseDown` to support text drawing. If the mouse button is pressed within the control and the text tool is selected, then a text box is shown on the screen that allows the user to enter some text. After the OK button is pressed, a callback method is called and the text is displayed with its upper-left point at the position where the mouse was clicked. Therefore, we add a private member variable of type `TextBox` to the `PhotoEditorForm` class:

```
private TextBoxInput inputTextBox;
```

Then we add following lines to the constructor of the `PhotoEditor Form` in order to create a text box:

```
// Create TextBoxInput to get the input text
inputTextBox = new TextBoxInput();
```

Now we can implement the `customScrollableControl_MouseDown` event handler. First, we check whether the selected tool is *not* the `Text Tool`. If the selected tool is not the text tool, then we continue as usual. If the text tool was selected, then we create a `TextComponent` object. Then we set the viewport coordinates and set the current mouse position to the upper-left point of the text box. Then we show a dialog box for text input and register the event handler, as described earlier in this chapter.

`MyEventHandler` is the event handler called by the text box after OK is clicked. Within the handler we extract the text that was entered, and then we add the component to the list so that it gets drawn with the other components. After that, the image is displayed and the graphics are drawn on the screen.

Listing 6.8 shows the implementation of the text box creation and callback function definition using a delegate.

Listing 6.8 Using a Delegate to Display Text Input

```
// If tool was selected and mouse is clicked in the window then
// create the component, initialize the variables, and draw
// everything.
private void customScrollableControl_MouseDown(object sender,
              System.Windows.Forms.MouseEventArgs e)
{
  // Go here only if tool is not textTool
  if(toolSelected != toolSelection.TextTool)
  {
    // Check whether tool is selected and drawing and it is not
    // the select tool.
    if(!isDrawing && toolSelected != ToolSelection.None)
    {
      switch(toolSelected)
      {
        //create component according to tool selected
        case toolSelection.LineTool:
          compObject = new LineComponent();
          break;
          *
          *
          *
      }
      // Display the components.
      PictureObject.Draw();
    }
  }
  else
  {
    // Create component
    compObject = new TextComponent();

    // Set Graphics object to the customScrollableControl
    GraphicsComponent.DeviceContext =
```

```
        customScrollableControl.CreateGraphics();
      tempPoint = new Point(e.X +
        customScrollableControl.ViewportCoords().X, e.Y +
        customScrollableControl.ViewportCoords().Y);
      compObject.StartPoint = tempPoint;
      compObject.EndPoint = tempPoint;
      // Show the text input box
      inputTextBox.Show();
      // Register the callback function
      inputTextBox.CallMethod(new
          TextBoxInput.Feedback(MyEventHandler));
  }
}


// Delegate example for callback function.
void MyEventHandler(string text)
{
  TextComponent texC = (TextComponent) compObject;
  texC.TextInput = inputTextBox.TextInput;

  //Add component to list
  PictureObject.Add(compObject);

  //Display everything
  DisplayImage();
  PictureObject.Draw();
}
```

Obviously, the TextBoxInput implementation is still missing. This class allows the user to enter text that is displayed via a dialog window. The TextBoxInput class provides the declaration for the delegate method and its signature. To implement this feature, add a new form to the solution with the name TextBoxInput. After creation, modify the user interface to look similar to Figure 6.10.

Don't forget to enable multiline text and enable return characters.

After the GUI is created, we add the event handler for the OK button click. To implement the functionality, we first declare some fields and helper methods in the TextBoxInput class. A private field of type string is added to hold the text that was entered by the user. Then the delegate method and its signature are declared. In addition, we define a private field

Figure 6.10 Text Input Window

of type `delegate`, which holds the callback method provided by the client. Then we implement a `CallMethod` that is instantiated by the client in order to register the `callback` method. Within the `call method`, the `callback` method is stored in the private field that was created earlier, and the client method is called to display the current text.

Last but not least, we provide the button click event handler. If the OK button was pressed, then the text entered is stored in the `textInput` field, the text box is hidden (disappears from the screen), and the callback method is called. Listing 6.9 shows the implementation of `TextBoxInput`.

Listing 6.9 Text Box Implementation, Including Delegate Declaration

```
/// <summary>
/// Summary description for Form1.
/// </summary>
public class TextBoxInput : System.Windows.Forms.Form
  {
        *

        *

        *

    // Holds the text to be displayed.
    private string textInput;
    /// <summary>
    /// Accessor to the text input.
    /// </summary>
    public string TextInput
```

```
    {
        get
        {
            return textInput;
         }
    }

    /// <summary>
    /// Declaration of the client delegate that
    /// is called when the
    /// Text Box OK button was pressed!
    /// </summary>
    public delegate void Feedback(string text);

    Feedback tempMethod;
    /// <summary>
    /// CallMethod used to register the callback function.
    /// </summary>
    /// <param name="feedback">Function Pointer</param>
    public void CallMethod(Feedback feedback)
    {
      tempMethod = feedback;
      feedback(textInput);
    }

    /// <summary>
    /// Event handler called when the text box
    /// has done its duty.
    /// It's time to call the registered callback method.
    /// </summary>
    /// <param name="sender">sender object</param>
    /// <param name="e">additional info</param>
    private void textOKButton_Click(object sender,
                    System.EventArgs e)
    {
      textInput = this.textBox1.Text;
      this.Hide();

      CallMethod(tempMethod);
    }
}
```

After implementing the interactive drawing capabilities, we implement a selection handler, a region of interest, an Apply button to "burn" the graphics into the image, and a Reset button that provides the capabilities to restore the originally loaded image.

6.6.5 The Region of Interest, Erase, Reset, and Apply Functionality

Of the remaining components, let's first discuss the region of interest (ROI) tool. If the ROI tool is selected and the mouse button is clicked inside the control, then a rectangle will be drawn in a gray color. To store a reference to the ROI component in the `PhotoEditorForm` object, we use a `get` accessor that can be called from other modules of the program. If the mouse up event is encountered, then the ROI component is removed from the list of components that need to be drawn. The implementation of the ROI component is essentially the same as the rectangle and can be found in the sample solution of this chapter on the accompanying CD.

Do It Yourself Implement the ROI tool. This implementation is essentially the same as that of the rectangle, with three differences: the color in which it is drawn, the property field that holds a reference to the component, and the removal of the component from the list of objects that need to be redrawn after the mouse up event is published.

Another feature that needs to be implemented is the erase tool. If the erase tool is selected and the mouse is moved over the start or end point of a nonpermanent component, then users can delete the component from the screen by clicking the mouse button within the displayed marker. To implement this, first create a button called Erase and create the event handler for the `EraseButton` click event. Implement the event handler by resetting the buttons and setting the tool to `SelectTool`. Add `SelectTool` to the enumeration of `toolSelection`. Next, check whether the erase tool is selected if the current mouse position is in the range of a component. If it is, draw a marker in the form of a red rectangle around the start and end points.

But be careful: The coordinates must be converted to compensate for scrolling. Another helper method is included. It is called `PositionIs Component`.

This method is provided by the `PictureComponent` class. You can find the implementation in the sample solution for this chapter on the accompanying CD. The `PositionIsComponent` method walks through the component list and checks whether the mouse pointer is within the picking area of a graphics component (where the *picking area* is the area around the start and end points of a component). When walking through the component list, the `Picture` class calls each component and calls the new method `isPicked`, which is implemented by `GraphicsComponent`. The `isPicked` call to a component returns `true` if the mouse pointer is within the picking area. If a component returns `true` from the `isPicked` method, then the `PositionIsComponent` call returns a generic reference to that object. The generic reference is of type `Object`. We therefore must cast the returned value to a `GraphicsComponent` object in order to use it. The implementation can be seen in Listing 6.10.

Listing 6.10 Erase Tool Implementation Using Picking

```
// Event handler for mouse move,
// draws component when in draw mode.
private void customScrollableControl_MouseMove(object sender,
      System.Windows.Forms.MouseEventArgs e)
{
        *
        *
        *

  if(toolSelected == toolSelection.SelectTool)
  {
    const int delta = 10;
    compObject = null;
    // check whether mouse is moved over a component
    // start or end point by providing image coordinates
    compObject =
    (GraphicsComponent)PictureObject.PositionIsComponent(
      e.X +
        customScrollableControl.ViewportCoords().X,
      e.Y +customScrollableControl.ViewportCoords().Y);

    if(compObject != null)
    {
      Graphics myDC =
```

```
            customScrollableControl.CreateGraphics();
        // convert coordinates to viewport coordinates.
        Point tempPoint = new Point(compObject.StartPoint.X
            - 5,
            compObject.StartPoint.Y - 5);
        tempPoint =
            compObject.CalcViewportCoords(tempPoint);
        myDC.DrawRectangle(Pens.Red, tempPoint.X,
            tempPoint.Y, delta, delta);
        tempPoint.X = compObject.EndPoint.X - 5;
        tempPoint.Y = compObject.EndPoint.Y - 5;
        tempPoint =
            compObject.CalcViewportCoords(tempPoint);
        myDC.DrawRectangle(Pens.Red, tempPoint.X,
            tempPoint.Y, delta, delta);

    }
  else
  {
    // Draw everything
    DisplayImage();
    PictureObject.Draw();
  }
}
```

The method `PositionIsComponent` of the `Picture` class walks through the list of components. On each component in the list, it calls the `IsPicked` method with the mouse position coordinates as arguments. The `IsPicked` method checks whether the component's start or end point is within a range of 5 pixels of the current mouse position. If it is, then `true` is returned to the `Picture` class; otherwise, `false` is returned. If the return value is `true`, then the `PositionIsComponent` method returns a reference to that component to the `PhotoEditor` form; otherwise, `null` is returned. If a reference to a component is returned to the mouse move event handler, then a red rectangle is drawn around the start and end points of the component.

If the mouse button is clicked, the same check must be done in order to verify whether a component is picked. If a component is picked and the Erase tool is selected, then the returned component is removed from the list of components by a call to the `Remove` method with the component as an argument. This will make the component disappear from the screen.

The last two features that are still missing are the `apply functionality` (to permanently add the drawn graphics to the bitmap) and the `reset` method, which reloads the original image. The implementation of both functionalities is easy.

To apply the graphics to the bitmap, the components must be drawn into the `Graphics` object of the bitmap instead of the `customScrollable Control`. You do this by simply exchanging the `Graphics` object of the `custom ScrollableControl` temporarily with the `Graphics` object of the bitmap and calling `Draw` on the `Picture` component. After the list of components is drawn, the image is invalidated and the list of graphics component objects is deleted.

You can implement the reset functionality by storing a copy of the loaded image in a member field of the `Picture` class. At the time of reset, the backup image can simply be copied into the loaded image.

Do It Yourself Implement the `PositionIsComponent`, `IsPicked`, and event handlers as described here. Also add the reset and apply features. A solution can be found in the sample solution of this chapter on the accompanying CD.

6.6.6 Debugging and Defect Resolution

Before the project can proceed to the testing workflow, we must resolve the defects that were reported and scheduled for this iteration. The defects are scheduled for resolution according to their priority. Defects with the highest priority are scheduled first.

To debug more efficiently, it seems to be a good idea to set the debugger to break on any exception, even if it is handled. In .NET Studio, you do this by choosing the Debug menu and then choosing Exceptions. A window opens, as shown in Figure 6.11.

Choose the option to break for handled exceptions. This will help you locate the defect in case a handled exception occurs at the time of the error. Next, run the application in Debug mode (go to the Debug menu and choose Start) and minimize the application. An exception is caught (see Figure 6.12).

The exception that occurred during execution was thrown in the `custom ScrollableControl`'s `adjustScrollBars()` method. In the debugger you can watch the values of the local variables by browsing through the window

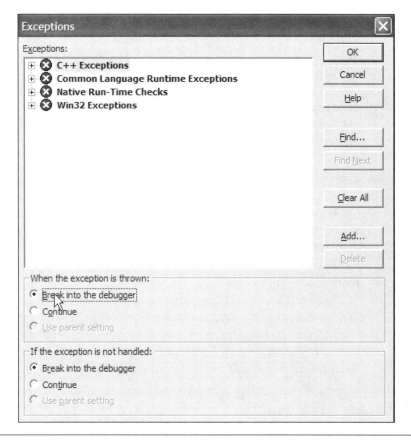

Figure 6.11 Debug Exceptions

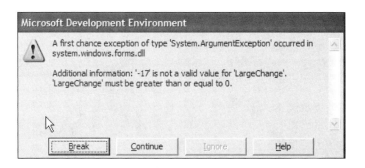

Figure 6.12 `CustomScrollableControlException`

in the lower-left part of the Visual Studio window. You can see a suspicious value that most likely is the source of the exception in the `ScrollingImage Area.Width` value. It seems that this value is out of bounds (it is actually negative).

To fix this problem, we must check the width and the height of `ScrollingImageArea` for valid values before doing any calculation. Therefore, add the following line to perform the calculation only if these values are within the range:

```
if(ScrollingImageArea.Width >= 0 && ScrollingImageArea.Height >= 0) {***}
```

Compile the solution, including `customScrollableControl` and `Photo EditorApplication`, and run the same scenario again. The bug is fixed— easy, wasn't it? Now the status of the defect can be changed to "solved" in the Excel spreadsheet, and the changes should be checked in with a comment indicating that the bug was fixed.

The next reported defect that needs some rework is the error message in case the default image cannot be found in the current directory. This fix is also fairly trivial. All that needs to be done is to put the `LoadImage` call within a `try-catch` block, and an exception with the meaningful message must be thrown if the load operation failed. The solution could look like Listing 6.11.

Listing 6.11 Load Image Bug Fix

```
// Load default image and throw exception if not found
string defaultImage =
    PhotoEditorForm.GetApplicationDirectory + @"\Hawaii.jpg";
try
{
  LoadImage(defaultImage);
}
catch(Exception e)
{
  Exception b = e;
  throw(new Exception("Check if default image Hawaii.jpg is in the
path!"));
}
```

Double-check that the fix works, rename the image, and run the scenario that produced the error condition. As you can see, a meaningful error message is produced that the user can use to resolve the problem of the missing image.

Do It Yourself Fix the last open defect from the defect spreadsheet. A solution is given in the sample application provided on the accompanying CD.

6.7 Unit Tests

> T

The unit tests for this iteration are added to the unit tests developed in Chapter 5. The strategy is to test the units and, in particular, to test units that are used often and that are used by many components. For that reason, in addition to the tests of the line, circle, rectangle, and text components we develop tests for the coordinate transformation and picking functionalities.

The tests for the graphics components basically check whether the coordinates of the start and end points are stored and retrieved correctly. In addition, we test the picking of the components, the coordinate transformation, and the list that holds the components.

As a starting point, Listing 6.12 shows the rectangle unit test, which sets the start and end points. The points are set, and a check is implemented to verify that the coordinates correspond to the original coordinates after they are retrieved. In addition, we check whether picking works correctly on the component.

Next, the component list test is shown. The test creates several components, puts them into a list, and checks whether they are still the same. To support the testing, we put a hook into the Picture component. This hook is an accessor method called GraphicsComponentList, and it enables us to retrieve a reference to the component list of the PictureComponent class (obviously, the hook is implemented in the PictureComponent class). The test also removes entries from the list and checks whether the correct entries were removed by checking the removed components against the original list and by comparing the count of the list members with an expected value. In addition, the list is emptied and we check whether the list does not contain any objects after it was cleared.

The final test case checks whether the calculated viewport coordinates are correct. This is done by setting artificial viewport coordinates that are used to calculate expected values when the viewport is not set to the origin (meaning that the image has been scrolled).

Listing 6.12 Unit Tests for GDI+ Components

```
/// <summary>
/// Test for F:image_graphics_annotations.
/// Sets the start and end points and
/// checks whether they were set correctly.
/// Also checks whether picking is done
/// correctly.
/// </summary>
/// <test>F:image_graphics_annotations</test>
[Test] public void RectangleTest()
{
   Console.WriteLine("image_graphics_annotations");
   RectangleComponent myRect = new RectangleComponent();
   myRect.StartPoint = new Point(0, 0);
   myRect.EndPoint = new Point(100, 200);
   Assertion.AssertEquals("Rectangle (0, 0) (100, 200)",
     myRect.StartPoint.X, 0);
   Assertion.AssertEquals("Rectangle (0, 0) (100, 200)",
     myRect.StartPoint.Y, 0);
   Assertion.AssertEquals("Rectangle (0, 0) (100, 200)",
     myRect.EndPoint.X, 100);
   Assertion.AssertEquals("Rectangle (0, 0) (100, 200)",
     myRect.EndPoint.Y, 200);
   Assertion.AssertEquals("Pick rectangle test",
     myRect.IsPicked(0, 0), true);
   Assertion.AssertEquals("Pick rectangle test",
     myRect.IsPicked(97, 198), true);
   Assertion.AssertEquals("Pick rectangle test",
     myRect.IsPicked(95, 200), false);

   myRect.StartPoint = new Point(200, 10);
   myRect.EndPoint = new Point(10, 5);
   Assertion.AssertEquals("Rectangle (200, 10) (10, 5)",
     myRect.StartPoint.X, 200);
   Assertion.AssertEquals("Rectangle (200, 10) (10, 5)",
```

```
      myRect.StartPoint.Y, 10);
   Assertion.AssertEquals("Rectangle (200, 10) (10, 5)",
      myRect.EndPoint.X, 10);
   Assertion.AssertEquals("Rectangle (200, 10) (10, 5)",
      myRect.EndPoint.Y, 5);
   Assertion.AssertEquals("Pick rectangle test",
      myRect.IsPicked(197, 12), true);
   Assertion.AssertEquals("Pick rectangle test",
      myRect.IsPicked(13, 7), true);
   Assertion.AssertEquals("Pick rectangle test",
      myRect.IsPicked(0, 10), false);
   amIPassed = true;
}


   /// <summary>
   /// Test for F:image_graphics_annotations.
   /// Creates components, puts them in the list, and
   /// removes them to check whether the list is handled
   /// correctly.
   /// </summary>
   /// <test>F:image_graphics_annotations</test>
   /// <test>F:image_text_annotations</test>
   [Test] public void PictureListTest()
   {
      Console.WriteLine("image_graphics_annotations");
      int i;
      ArrayList lineList = new ArrayList(10);

      for(i = 0; i < 10; ++i)
      {
         lineList.Add(new LineComponent());
         TestImage.Add((LineComponent)lineList[i]);
      }
      ArrayList cList = TestImage.ComponentList;
      for(i = 0; i < 10; ++i)
      {
         Assertion.AssertEquals("Line list test ",
               lineList[i], cList[i]);
         Assertion.AssertEquals("Line list test ",
               lineList.Count, 10);
      }
```

```
        TestImage.Remove((Component)lineList[3]);
        lineList.Remove(lineList[3]);
        for(i = 0; i < 9; ++i)
        {
            Assertion.AssertEquals("Line list test ",
                lineList[i], cList[i]);
          Assertion.AssertEquals("Line list test ",
                lineList.Count, 9);
        }

        TestImage.Remove((Component)lineList[1]);
        lineList.Remove(lineList[1]);
        for(i = 0; i < 8; ++i)
        {
          Assertion.AssertEquals("Line list test ",
                lineList[i], cList[i]);
          Assertion.AssertEquals("Line list test ",
                lineList.Count, 8);
        }

        Assertion.AssertEquals("Line list test ", lineList.Count,
                cList.Count);

        lineList.Clear();
        cList.Clear();
        Assertion.AssertEquals("Line list test ", lineList.Count,
                cList.Count);

        amIPassed = true;
    }

    /// <summary>
    /// Test for F:image_graphics_annotations.
    /// Sets the start point and
    /// checks the coordinate
    /// transformation.
    /// </summary>
    /// <test>F:image_graphics_annotations</test>
    [Test] public void CoordTrafoTest()
    {
      Console.WriteLine("image_graphics_annotations");
```

```
RectangleComponent myRect = new RectangleComponent();
myRect.StartPoint = new Point(0, 0);

myRect.ViewportCoords =  new Point(10, 500);

Assertion.AssertEquals("Rectangle Viewport Coords (0, 0)
  => (10, 500)",
  myRect.CalcViewportCoords(myRect.StartPoint).X, -10);
  Assertion.AssertEquals("Rectangle
    Viewport Coords (0,0)
    => (10, 500)",
    myRect.CalcViewportCoords(myRect.StartPoint).Y, -
    500);

myRect.StartPoint = new Point(200, 651);

Assertion.AssertEquals("Rectangle Viewport Coords (200,
    651) => (10, 500)",
    myRect.CalcViewportCoords(myRect.StartPoint).X,
    190);
Assertion.AssertEquals("Rectangle Viewport Coords (200,
    651) => (10, 500)",
    myRect.CalcViewportCoords(myRect.StartPoint).Y,
    151);

amIPassed = true;
}
```

Do It Yourself Add similar tests for the line, circle, and text components. A sample solution is provided on the CD. Also think of more and better unit test cases. The provided cases can be seen as a very minimal set of tests. You are encouraged to cook up more tests to find hidden problems in the software.

Figure 6.13 shows the output of the sample unit test.

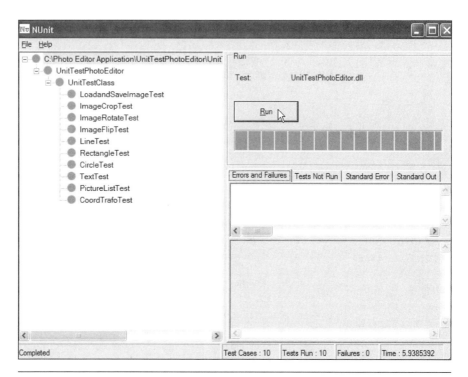

Figure 6.13 Unit Test Output

6.8 Conclusion

 This chapter describes the fourth iteration of the Unified Process and is part of the construction phase. All required functionality that was scheduled for this iteration has gone through the core workflows: requirements, analysis, design, implementation, and test. The implementation was run, and initial unit tests were performed. In addition, the project planning documents were updated. The code documentation was generated as described in Chapter 5.

6.8.1 Review

We must review the status of the project to decide whether the project can proceed to the next iteration. To decide whether the project is ready, the goals for the five core workflows must be met:

- Requirements: Refine the requirements and system scope.
- Analysis: Analyze the requirements by describing what the system does.
- Design: Develop the design of the required functionality for this iteration using UML.
- Implementation: Implement the required functionality.
- Test: Test the implemented features.

The project meets all goals that were set for this iteration and is therefore ready to proceed to the next phase.

6.9 References for Further Reading

Erich Gamma, Richard Helm, Ralph Johnson, and John Vlissides, *Design Patterns: Elements of Reusable Object-Oriented Software* (Reading, MA: Addison-Wesley, 1995)

```
http://thecodeproject.com/vcpp/gdiplus
```

```
http://www.c-sharpcorner.com/Graphics.asp
```

```
http://www.microsoft.com/whdc/hwdev/archive/video/GDInext.mspx
```

CHAPTER 7

Advanced GDI+ Operations

 Unified Process:
Construction Phase and Fifth Iteration

The fifth iteration of the construction phase is an extension of the existing GDI+ features that were implemented in the preceding iteration. For that reason, the deliverables are similar to the ones described in Chapter 6.

The go/no-go criteria for this iteration are essentially the same as the ones described in Chapter 6. The only difference is that the deliverables reflect the features that need to be implemented in this iteration. Here is the list of deliverables:

- Requirements: Uncover any requirements that have been missed and refine the requirements that are implemented in this iteration.
- Analysis: Analyze the requirements that are to be implemented in this iteration.
- Design: Update the UML design model.
- Implementation: Implement the functionalities as described in the requirements, analysis, and design documents for this iteration.
- Test: Unit-test the implemented functionality.

Even though this iteration is a continuation of the implementation in Chapter 6, the project must go through all workflows of the Unified Process. Therefore, we start with the requirements refinement.

7.1 Advanced GDI+ Extensions

> R The overall goal of the implementation in this iteration is to provide functionality that enables the user to draw graphical elements into the displayed image. The graphical elements can be drawn in various colors and with

various line thicknesses. In addition, users can choose to draw a frame of rectangular or ellipsoidal shape in a user-defined color. The frame is drawn with a solid opaque color on the outside border. Toward the center of the shape, the fill color becomes transparent. The refined requirements are listed in Table 7.1.

The two requirement keys shown in Table 7.1 are implemented in this iteration.

Table 7.1 Refined Requirement Description for GDI+ Extensions

Requirement	Type	Summary
F:image_graphics_annotations	Functional	In addition to the already specified requirement it shall be possible to draw the implemented graphical elements in a user-chosen color and line width. Users can adjust the color and width of the elements drawn by changing the color and line width controls that are provided. The drawn elements are automatically updated. The graphical elements are permanently added to the image (or burned into the image) by pressing the Apply button, after which the color and width cannot be changed. The Reset button provides the possibility to roll back to the originally loaded image.
F:image_graphics_special_effects	Functional	It shall be possible to use advanced graphical objects that use graded or opaque colors. The special effects are used to frame the image and fade in toward the image to show a foglike effect in the border area. The frame effect is applied with a rectangular or ellipsoidal interactive shape. The user can apply various colors, and the size of the border shall be adjustable by using a line width that can be set by the user. The Apply and Reset buttons work similar to the functionality described in the F:image_graphics_annotations key.

7.2 Analysis of the Advanced GDI+ Extensions Requirements

> A

After we refine the requirements, we need to analyze them. We start by updating the GUI to add the controls that allow the user to use the newly implemented functionality. The first requirement key we analyze is the `photo_editor` key, which needs to reflect the GUI changes.

7.2.1 The `photo_editor` Requirement

To provide the new functionality, we update the GUI to enable the user to access the new features. This update is based on the GUI introduced in Chapter 6. In close collaboration with the customer, we decide on the new GUI elements to use for the new functionality.

Usually, this process takes several rounds of discussions and evaluations before a decision is made. The decision process depends on many factors, such as industry standards, the capability and limitations of the provided functionality, and the targeted user group. For example, using radio buttons for the frame feature is a good choice because only one of the frames can be selected at any time. Radio buttons are often used in Windows applications to let users choose from a list of mutually exclusive functionalities. It could be argued that the graphical component functionalities implemented in Chapter 6 should also have used radio buttons. That would have been a good choice, but regular buttons were used because the customer preferred them for esthetic reasons.

For choosing the line thickness, we use a *spin* button, also called a *numeric up/down* button. The spin button enables the user to increment and decrement the line thickness by using only the mouse, without the need to type anything. Therefore, it is perfect for choosing the line thickness.

In addition, we introduce a button for the color functionality. The button opens a dialog box in which the user can choose a drawing color. Figure 7.1 shows the part of the GUI that is changed.

By default, both radio buttons for the frame feature are unselected. Furthermore, only one or none of the radio buttons can be selected at any time. If another graphics tool is selected, then the two frame tool radio buttons are set to not selected. The need for this is obvious if we consider the fact that only one drawing tool can be used to draw on the screen at a given time.

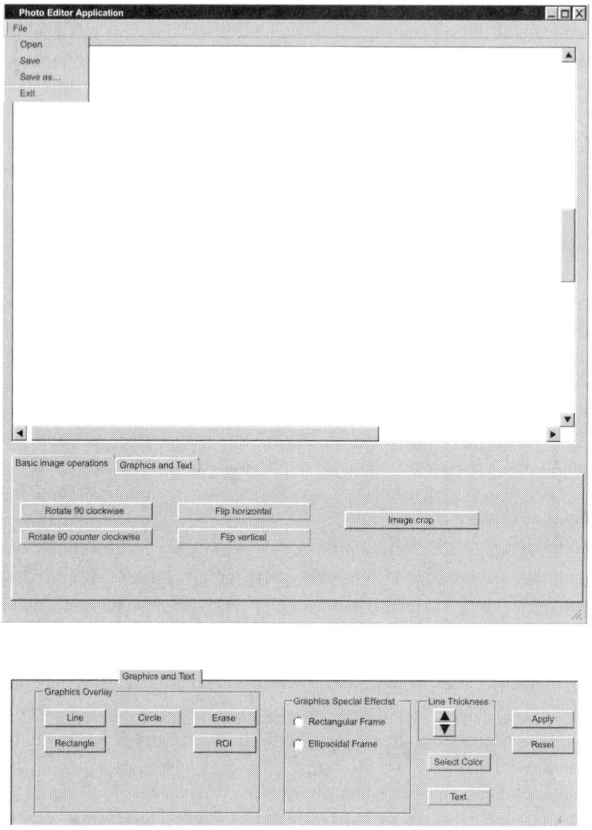

Figure 7.1 The Photo Editor GUI

As discussed next, users can set the line thickness between 1 and 20. The Select Color button opens a .NET Framework-provided standard color dialog that enables the user to choose a color.

7.2.2 The `image_graphics_annotations` Requirement

Users can draw a line, rectangle, or ellipse in various colors and line widths. They choose the line width by using a numeric up/down button, which increments or decrements through the range of possible line widths of 1 to 20.

Users choose the color by selecting the corresponding button of the GUI. If the button is selected, then a standard color dialog box is shown from which the user can select a drawing color. If a new line width or color is chosen, then all graphics primitives that are not yet permanently added to the image (by using the Apply button) are updated and drawn using the new color and line thickness.

7.2.3 The `image_graphics_special_effects` Requirement

A tool is provided that enables the user to draw an interactive frame object. The supported object shapes are a rectangle and an ellipsis. The thickness of the frame is adjustable from 1/40th of the shape's size up to the entire size.

In addition, the user can select a fill color to fill the shape. The fill color is solid on the borders of the shape and becomes transparent toward the center of the shape. If the frame width is the size of the rectangle, then the center is completely transparent, and this means that no color is visible except that of the original image. If the frame is smaller than the rectangle, the behavior is the same in that the center point is transparent even if that point is not within the frame to be drawn. Users can adjust the size of the border by using the line thickness spin button. If the value of the spin button is 20, then the complete rectangle is assumed to be the frame. The functionalities of the Apply and Reset buttons work according to the description in Chapter 6.

7.3 Design of the Advanced GDI+ Extensions

$\rangle$ D $\rangle$ To accommodate the new features, we extend the design by adding two new components: the rectangular frame and the ellipsoidal frame. In addition, we declare new member variables to hold additional information that is needed to draw the graphics primitives with the specified color and line width. Figure 7.2 shows the updated class diagram of the photo editor.

Now that the design is specified, we have some project management issues to take care of before we start the implementation of the new features.

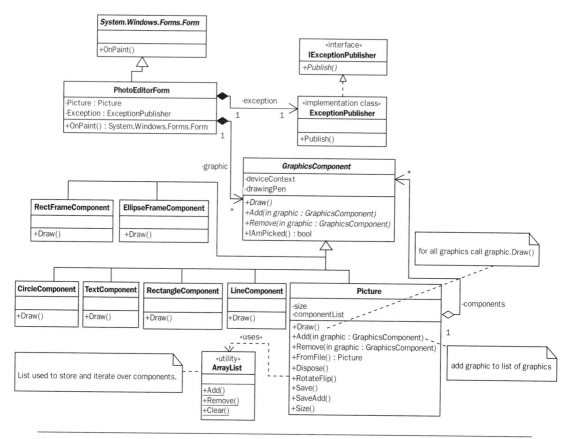

Figure 7.2 The Class Diagram

7.4 Project Management Issues

At the beginning of this iteration, the customer has requested additional features that are outside the scope of the agreed project.

7.4.1 Request for Additional Features

The customer has asked us to implement an additional feature that will enable the user to apply certain image filter operations such as edge detection and noise reduction. The requested features are quite advanced, and it will take a substantial amount of time to analyze the requirements and design and implement these features. The requirements are as follows:

- `image_noise_reduction`: The photo editor application shall enable users to reduce noise in an image by using a Gaussian noise reduction algorithm.
- `image_edge_enhancement`: It shall be possible to enhance edges in an image. A Sobel filter shall be available for the user to highlight edges (vertical and horizontal lines) within the image.

Without explaining the requested functionality in detail, it is clear that these features are additional effort that was not planned for. Therefore, in the discussion with the customer, project management provides three proposals on how to proceed with the request.

Feature Trading (Resolution Proposal 1)

The newly requested features will be provided within the released project, but certain other features will not be included. The only way to provide the new functionalities within the project timeframe is to "trade" them for features that were planned for (and that would need the same effort to implement). For example, the optimization of image-processing features or the three-dimensional text displays could be traded for the new features.

Deadline Extension (Resolution Proposal 2)

The deadline for the project is extended. The effort for the new features is estimated, and the project deadline will slip by that amount that time. By extending the deadline, we can deliver the additional features with this version of the product.

Rescheduling (Resolution Proposal 3)

Rescheduling is the preferred solution by the project team. The features will be added to the defect tracking list as wishes. The features will then be considered for a later release of the project. Adding them to the defect tracking list as a wish adds them to the project so that they will not get lost. The project team can plan for the new features in one of the next releases, combined with eventual bug fixes.

It is important to mention which proposed solution is the recommended one by the project team. Very often, the customer will choose the recommended option if good reasons are provided for it. In our case, we argue that the requested functionalities are very advanced features that will be used by only a few users. It seems reasonable to provide these advanced features in the second release of the photo editor application.

7.4.2 Resolution of the Request

The customer decided to follow our recommendation to schedule the functionality for a future release. Therefore, the two new requirement keys are added to the defect tracking Excel sheet that can be found in the `doc` directory of the sample solution on the accompanying CD.

The described scenario is very common. The customer tries to squeeze in more functionality without considering the impact on the project team and the schedule. Because our requirements were described in sufficient detail, the customer could not increase the scope of the project without providing new requirement keys. Therefore, it was obvious that the newly requested functionality was not in the scope of the project that was agreed upon.

Difficulties can arise if the requirements are not described in enough detail. Imagine a requirement key with this description:

> `image_graphics_special_effects`: Some advanced image-processing functionality shall be provided by the application. The functionality provided is, for example, a rectangular frame with fading colors toward the center of the rectangle.

If the requirements key had been described in such little detail, the customer could easily have argued that the requested functionality was within the scope of that requirement key. After all, the one example given was only one example—one of several features that should be provided.

Even though this argument sounds trivial, it has happened in more than one project we have worked on. Projects are often under tight time pressure in the planning phase, and project management is tempted to neglect planning, requirements analysis, and even design. The implementation starts as early as possible without much planning. But jumping into implementation without a planning phase makes the project basically unmanageable. If a customer can squeeze additional features into the project's scope without having to introduce new requirement keys—a process often termed *feature creep*—how can you estimate the project's effort in advance? Furthermore, how can you measure the progress of the project? How do you know which functionality to implement? How do you know what to test? How will you really know that the project is finished?

I am sure we could find many more reasons that vague requirements can cause a project to fail. But the sheer unmanageability of the project is enough to show why requirements should contain enough detail to describe the functionality to be implemented.

We cannot emphasize enough that the planning phase is crucial for the project's success. If the planning of the project is cut short, then the project is most likely doomed to fail.

7.5 Using Pens and Brushes in GDI+

To understand the features implemented in this iteration requires more knowledge about GDI+. Users will draw lines in different colors and use transparent brushes, so let's look at color and transparency.

7.5.1 Color in GDI+: Using the RGB and ARGB Formats

Until this point we have used the predefined system colors, such as `Pens.Black`, to draw the graphics primitives. These predefined colors are internally converted into RGB values via a lookup table. For more advanced image processing, which will be used in this iteration, it is necessary to understand how color components are handled internally. Therefore, this section describes the theory of color components.

As mentioned earlier, image data is stored internally in a two-dimensional raster. Each position in the raster, or each pixel, is stored using four color components. Three components of the pixel storage are used to define the color of the pixel. The fourth component is used to describe the transparency or opacity of a given pixel. The transparency or opacity value is also referred to as the *alpha component*.

The Alpha Component

Figure 7.3 shows the breakdown of each stored pixel into its components. As mentioned before, the alpha value describes the transparency or opacity of a pixel. The alpha component is specified as an integer in the range of 0 to 255, where 0 means the pixel is completely transparent (the background color is displayed) and 255 means that the pixel is completely opaque. In many cases the alpha value can be omitted, resulting in the GDI+ default alpha value, which makes the pixel look opaque by setting the value to 255.

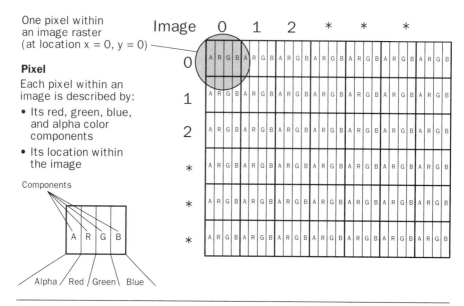

Figure 7.3 Pixel Components

The effect of an alpha value less than 255 can be observed in the Smart-Notes prototype application (developed in Chapter 3) or in the frame feature, which we implement in this chapter.

The RGB Components

The combination of the red, green, and blue (RGB) components describes the color for each pixel in the image. Typically, each component is stored as an 8-bit value, and this means that each color component can hold a value between 0 and 255. Thus, the color value can have one of $2^{(8*3)} = 16,777,216$ different values. Even though 8 bits per color component is typical, different sizes can be used. When you work with image data, it is essential to know, or to find out, what data size is used for the color components in the image.

Pixel Size as a Measure of Bits Per Pixel

Often in image processing, the term *bits per pixel* (bpp) is used to describe the memory size needed to store one pixel of the image. For an image stored in alpha RGB (ARGB) format with each component of 8 bits in size, the bits per pixel value would be 4*8 = 32 bpp. Omitting the alpha value would result in 24 bpp RGB image data. Knowing the bits per pixel, together with the image *raster size* (width and height), is essential for working with image data. It enables us to calculate the memory size that needs to be allocated for an image. We calculate the memory size by multiplying the width by the height and the bpp of the image. An example of this is shown in Chapter 8.

7.5.2 More on Pens and Brushes

Chapter 6 explains how to use a pen to draw the graphics objects. But pens and brushes offer a much wider variety of features than just drawing a simple line or filling a shape with a color. In the course of this book we use more advanced features of pens and brushes. For a complete reference on features provided for pens and brushes, please consult the MSDN documentation. We recommend that you explore additional features of GDI+ by adding new features to the application based on the sample solution provided with this chapter.

Brushes

GDI+ provides five brush types, each of which is defined by a class. Table 7.2 gives you a quick overview of these five classes. All the brush classes are declared sealed, and therefore they cannot be inherited by any other class.

Table 7.2 The Five Brush Classes in GDI+

Brush	Description
SolidBrush	Defines a brush of a single color. Brushes are used to fill graphics shapes, such as rectangles, ellipses, pies, polygons, and paths.
HatchBrush	Defines a rectangular brush with a hatch style, a foreground color, and a background color. There are six hatch styles provided.
	This class encapsulates both two-color gradients and custom multicolor gradients.
	(continued)

Table 7.2 (*Cont.*)

Brush	Description
LinearGradientBrush	All linear gradients are defined along a line specified either by the width of a rectangle or by two points.
	By default, a two-color linear gradient is an even horizontal linear blend from the starting color to the ending color along the specified line.
	Encapsulates a Brush object that fills the interior of a GraphicsPath object with a gradient.
PathGradientBrush	The color gradient is a smooth shading of colors from the center point of the path to the outside boundary edge of the path. Blend factors, positions, and style affect where the gradient starts and ends, and how fast it changes shade.
TextureBrush	Each property of the TextureBrush class is a Brush object that uses an image to fill the interior of a shape.

Brushes provide the developer with a wide variety of tools to fill shapes using different effects. It is outside the scope of this book to cover all the possible functionalities. Instead, we provide the basics you need to start working with brushes and pens and give enough details to enable you to explore more of the provided features.

Pens

To draw the geometric shapes introduced in Chapter 6, we use a pen with a solid color. GDI+ provides a single class for pens to be used for drawing. However, pens are slightly more complex than brushes because pens allow more properties to be specified to customize them. Table 7.3 lists some of the public properties of the Pen class.

Table 7.3 shows that using a pen can be quite powerful. We'll show you how to use a pen and how to set various properties on a limited number of examples. We recommend that you extend the application further in order to learn about the capabilities of the Pen class.

Table 7.3 The Public `Pen` Properties

Pen Property	Description
Alignment	Gets or sets the alignment of the pen in relation to the border of the object drawn.
Brush	Gets or sets a brush object that can be used to fill a drawn line.
Color	Gets or sets the color of this pen object.
CompoundArray	Gets or sets an array of values that specify a compound pen. A *compound pen* draws a compound line made up of parallel lines and spaces.
XXXXCap	Gets or sets different options of how the line start or end is drawn (e.g., whether the ends are drawn round, as arrowheads, and so on).
DashYYYY	Gets or sets different properties of a line that is drawn with a dash pattern.
LineJoin	Gets or sets the join style for the ends of two consecutive lines drawn with this `Pen` object.
Transform	Gets or sets the geometric transformation for this `Pen` object.
Width	Gets or sets this pen width.

7.5.3 The `GraphicsPath` Class

The GDI+-provided `GraphicsPath` class is used by applications to draw a series of lines and curves in order to describe an outline of shapes. In addition, `GraphicsPath` enables developers to access other functionality related to the outlined shape:

■ Drawing open and closed shapes using a pen
■ Filling the interior of shapes using a brush
■ Creating clipping regions

As you can see, `GraphicsPath` provides the application developer with lots of functionalities related to drawing and working with concatenated lines. In the case of the photo editor, `GraphicsPath` could be used to draw user-defined open or closed shapes. For more information on `Graphics Path`, search the help documentation provided with Visual Studio.NET.

7.5.4 The `Region` Class

A `Region` object describes a region that is zero or more areas of real estate on the drawing surface. In addition, by using two or more `GraphicsPath` objects, you can create a region as the result of mathematical operations such as algebraic set operations (see Figure 7.4).

Furthermore, the `Region` class provides many additional methods to manipulate and query regions. It is outside the scope of this book to explain all the functionality provided. For a complete list of functionalities, please consult the MSDN help documentation of the `Region` class.

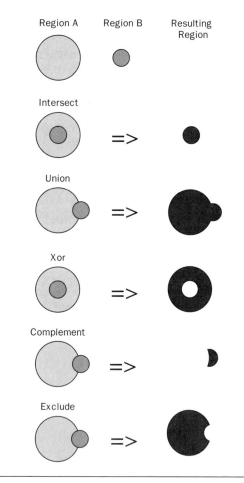

Figure 7.4 `Region` Object Algebraic Set Methods

7.6 Implementation of Regions, Pens, and Brushes

The implementation of this chapter is based on the application that was developed in Chapter 6. Therefore, we take the sample solution of Chapter 6 as a starting point.

Let's start the implementation by updating the GUI as it was defined in the requirements analysis. First, we use a numeric up/down or spin control to enable the user to choose a line width. In addition, we will add a button that opens a color dialog, which in turn enables the user to select a drawing color.

Drag a `NumericUpDown` control and a `GroupBox` from the Toolbox onto the Graphics and Text tab control. Place the `GroupBox` around the `Numeric UpDown` control as shown in the requirements. After that, drag a new button from the Toolbox to the tab control. Change the properties of the new elements to the values shown in Table 7.4.

Then add event handlers for the button click event of the button and the value changed event of the `NumericUpDown` control by double-clicking on the corresponding GUI element.

In the next step, we add a private property to the `GraphicsComponent` class. The property is used to hold the values of the user-selected color and line width. We have multiple options for how we can implement this. The first option is to simply add two properties and have each property hold one of the values. This means that we would add a `selectedColor` and a `selectedLineWidth` property.

This seems reasonable at first, but let's consider what we will use the properties for. Both values define how the graphics are drawn on the screen

Table 7.4 GUI Element Properties

GUI Element	Property	Value
NumericUpDown	(Name)	penNumericUpDown
	Minimum	1
	Maximum	20
GroupBox	(Name)	lineThickness
	Text	Line Thickness
Button	(Name)	selectColorButton
	Text	Select Color

(with which color and line width). The actual drawing will be done using a pen. Therefore, another option is to use a `Pen` object to store the user-selected values. Using a pen to store the selected values gives us the flexibility to add other pen properties (which might be required in the next release) without having to add any new properties. To support new pen properties, we simply add a user interface control and store the selected value in the existing `Pen` object. The `Pen` object defaults to the drawing color black and the line width of 1. If the user selects different values, they will be stored in the `Pen` object.

To draw the components with the specified line width and color, we must change the `GraphicsComponent` class and the `Draw` method of the graphics components. Because the requirement states that all graphics in the list of graphics are to be drawn using the same color and line width, one `Pen` object can be shared among all the components. Therefore, the pen is provided by the `GraphicsComponent` class. Simply add a `private static Pen` property named `drawingPen` to the abstract `GraphicsComponent` class:

```
private static Pen drawingPen = new Pen(Color.Black, 1);
```

In addition, we implement the public accessor methods for the `Pen` property so that we can access the pen from the `PhotoEditorForm` class. We also change the various components. Right now they use `Pens.Black` in the draw methods, but in the new version they need to use the static `drawing Pen` of the `GraphicsComponent` class. With these changes made, the graphics components are drawn with a `Pen` object instead of a black pen.

The graphical objects are then drawn with these properties as long as the user does not select any other color or line width.

In the next step, we add the event handlers for `penNumericUpDown_ValueChanged` and `Button_Click`. The implementation of `penNumericUp Down_ValueChanged` is fairly simple. The new value selected in the control is stored as the new width of the `Pen` object. In the case of the `selectColor Button_Click` event, we create an instance of the system-provided `Color Dialog` and show it on the screen. The dialog, provided by the .NET Framework, allows the user to select the color. When the user selects the color and closes the color dialog by clicking on the OK button, the selected color value is stored as the new pen color and the color dialog is disposed of.

Listing 7.1 shows the implementation of this functionality.

Listing 7.1 Event Handler Implementation

```
/// <summary>
/// Event handler for the NumericUpDown control, which
/// enables the user to select the line width of the pen.
/// </summary>
private void penNumericUpDown_ValueChanged(object sender, System.
EventArgs e)
{
  try
  {
    GraphicsComponent.DrawingPen.Width =
          (float)penNumericUpDown.Value;
    DisplayImage();
  }
  catch(Exception exception)
  {
    ExceptionManager.Publish(exception);
  }
}

/// <summary>
/// Opens a color dialog box to enable the user
/// to select a color for the pen.
/// </summary>
private void selectColorButton_Click(object sender, System.EventArgs e)
{
  try
  {
    // Opens and shows a color dialog box.
    ColorDialog myDialog = new ColorDialog();
    myDialog.ShowDialog();
    // Sets the pen color to the selected color.
    GraphicsComponent.DrawingPen.Color = myDialog.Color;
    // Delete the color dialog.
    // Not really necessary because garbage collection
    // will take care of it anyway.
    myDialog.Dispose();
    DisplayImage();
  }
  catch(Exception exception)
  {
```

```
     ExceptionManager.Publish(exception);
  }
}
```

With that change in place, the graphics components are drawn with the user-selected color and line width if specified.

7.6.1 Using Regions for the Frame Implementation

In addition to the capability of drawing the graphical objects with different line widths and colors, we implement a frame tool to support rectangular and ellipsoidal frames. The first step is, as always, to update the GUI with the new controls to access the functionality. Therefore, we add the elements listed in Table 7.5 to the GUI and arrange them as shown in the requirements. Also, we change the properties of the new controls to the values shown in the table.

Make sure that the radio buttons are placed on top of the group box. This is important because the .NET Framework provides radio buttons placed on a group box or a panel with exclusive selection properties. This means that at most one of the radio buttons that are placed on a specific panel or group box can be selected at any time. See the MSDN help pages for more details on this feature.

After the GUI is updated, we need to implement the event handlers for the `CheckedChanged` event of the two added radio buttons. We add the event handlers by double-clicking on the controls in the design view. The `CheckedChange` event is called every time the selection of radio buttons changes. Note that the radio buttons in the group box are already exclusive. This means that only one or none of the buttons can be selected at any time without us having to do anything.

Table 7.5 Added GUI Elements and Their Properties

GUI Element	Property	Value
RadioButton	Text (Name)	Rectangular Frame RectFrameRadioButton
RadioButton	Text (Name)	Ellipsoidal Frame EllipseFrameRadioButton
GroupBox	Text	Graphics Special Effects

Within the event handler the selected tool needs to be changed to the corresponding frame tool. Therefore, we add two new values to the `tool Selection` enumeration. One is called `RectFrameTool`, and the other is `EllipseFrameTool`. In addition, the radio buttons are unset if a reset on the buttons is called. Therefore, change the `resetButtons()` method to also unset the radio buttons by setting the `Checked` property of the radio buttons to `false`. After all that, we implement the `CheckedChanged` event handlers, as shown in Listing 7.2.

Listing 7.2 Event Handler Implementation

```
/// <summary>
/// Sets the currently selected tool to
/// the RectangleFrameTool.
/// </summary>
///<requirements>F:image_graphics_special_effects</requirements>
private void RectFrameRadioButton_CheckedChanged(object sender,
System.EventArgs e)
{
  try
  {
    toolSelected = toolSelection.RectFrameTool;
  }
  catch(Exception exception)
  {
    ExceptionManager.Publish(exception);
  }
}

/// <summary>
/// Sets the currently selected tool to
/// the EllipseFrameTool.
/// </summary>
///<requirements>F:image_graphics_special_effects
/// </requirements>
private void EllipseFrameRadioButton_CheckedChanged(object sender,
System.EventArgs e)
{
  try
  {
    toolSelected = toolSelection.EllipseFrameTool;
  }
```

```
catch(Exception exception)
{
  ExceptionManager.Publish(exception);
}
}
```

Now that the new tools can be selected, the corresponding components must be implemented as children of the `GraphicsComponent` class.

The Ellipsoidal Frame Implementation

In this section we show the implementation of `EllipseFrameComponent`. The implementation uses advanced GDI+ features such as `GraphicsPath`, `PathGradientBrush`, and `Region`.

We create the new component as we did the other components. First, we add a new class to the photo editor application project that is named `EllipseFrameComponent`. Like all the components, this class is derived from the `GraphicsComponent` class. The responsibility of this class is to draw an ellipsoidal frame with the user-defined color and line width. As stated in the requirements, the frame width is assumed to be the entire area of the ellipse if the line width is set to 20. The region area is filled with a brush that is set to transparent color in the center of the shape and to opaque color at the border areas. Because the new class is derived from a class with abstract methods, we must implement the `Draw` method that overrides the `GraphicsComponent`-defined `Draw` method.

The ellipse frame component is more complex than the components we implemented in Chapter 6. Here, we want to draw a region with an ellipsoidal shape using a user-defined border width and a graded brush in a user-defined color. Last but not least, we must make some calculations before we can do the actual drawing. Therefore, we first need to define the region of the border we want to draw. This region consists of an inner and an outer border, where each border is defined by an ellipse.

We define two rectangle properties in the `EllipseFrameComponent` class. One rectangle is used to store the enclosing rectangle of the outer ellipse, which serves as the outer border of the frame. The second rectangle is used to describe the enclosing rectangle of the ellipse that describes the inner border of the frame. To draw the frame, we create a `GraphicsPath` instance from which the region of the border will be derived. Then we calculate the outer enclosing rectangle. This is similar to the calculation of the circle component shown in Chapter 6, but instead of drawing the circle, the calculated size is assigned to the `outerRectangle` property.

Now that the outer ellipse is defined we need to calculate the border width. Recall that a pen size of 20 means that the entire shape is handled as border area. Also consider the fact that the border appears on two sides of the image. These considerations result in a formula to calculate the border width and height:

$$\text{border} = (\text{shape size} * \text{pen width}) / (2 * 20)$$

Now that the border width and height are calculated, we can define the upper-left corner coordinates of the enclosing rectangle for the inner ellipse:

$$x \text{ inner} = x \text{ outer rectangle} + \text{border width}$$

$$y \text{ inner} = y \text{ outer rectangle} + \text{border height}$$

This gives us all the information we need to calculate the inner ellipse or, better, its enclosing rectangle. In the next step, we calculate the inner rectangle width and height:

```
width inner = width outer – 2 * border width
height inner = height outer – 2 * border width
```

This defines both of the enclosing rectangles for the inner and outer ellipse.

With the inner and outer ellipse known, we can calculate the resulting region of the border. The border is defined as the area of the outer ellipse excluding the area of the inner ellipse. We can calculate this region by using an xor operation on the outer and inner ellipse. After the border region is defined, it can be filled with a color using a `PathGradientBrush`.

So much for the theory. For the implementation, we add an ellipse to the graphics path with the outer enclosing rectangle as an argument. Then we create `PathGradientBrush` with the graphics path as the size argument. With the brush defined, the center color is set to transparent and the surround color is set to the user-selected color (which is black if none was selected). Add the inner ellipse to the graphics path, and use the new graphics path for the xor algebra operation on the region of the outer ellipse. This will create the region of the outer ellipse excluding the inner ellipse, which essentially is the border we want to draw. After that, call the `FillRegion` method on the `Graphics` object and provide the region and brush as arguments.

The complete implementation is shown in Listing 7.3.

Listing 7.3 The Ellipse Frame Component Implementation

```
using System;
using System.Drawing;
using System.Drawing.Drawing2D;

namespace Photo_Editor_Application
{
  /// <summary>
  /// The EllipseFrameComponent class implements the
  /// functionality to draw an ellipse-shaped frame.
  /// </summary>

  ///<requirement>F:image_graphics_special_effects</requirement>
  public class EllipseFrameComponent : GraphicsComponent
  {
    /// <summary>
    /// Constructor for circle component.
    /// </summary>
    public EllipseFrameComponent()
    {
    }

    /// <summary>
    /// Draws the circle in the provided Graphics object.
    /// Calculates the bounding box so that width and height are
    /// always > 0.
    /// </summary>
    public override void Draw()
    {
      // Properties needed to draw the border.
      Region region;
      Rectangle outerRectangle;
      Rectangle innerRectangle = new Rectangle();
      // Create a graphics path object
      GraphicsPath gp = new GraphicsPath();
      int width =  CalcViewportCoords(EndPoint).X -
```

```
   CalcViewportCoords(StartPoint).X;
int height = CalcViewportCoords(EndPoint).Y -
   CalcViewportCoords(StartPoint).Y;
// Check whether width and height are zero.
// If so set them to 1.
if (width == 0) width = 1;
if (height == 0) height = 1;
if(width < 0 && height < 0)
   outerRectangle = new
      Rectangle(CalcViewportCoords(EndPoint).X,
      CalcViewportCoords(EndPoint).Y,
      Math.Abs(width),
      Math.Abs(height));
else if (width < 0)
   outerRectangle = new
      Rectangle(CalcViewportCoords(EndPoint).X,
      CalcViewportCoords(StartPoint).Y,
      Math.Abs(width),
      height);
else if (height < 0)
   outerRectangle = new
      Rectangle(CalcViewportCoords(StartPoint).X,
      CalcViewportCoords(EndPoint).Y,
      width,
      Math.Abs(height));
else
   outerRectangle = new
      Rectangle(CalcViewportCoords(StartPoint).X,
      CalcViewportCoords(StartPoint).Y,
      width,
      height);

// Calculate the border width and height.
// If the Line Thickness is set to the maximum value
// of 20 then the whole rectangle is assumed to be border.
int borderWidth =
   (int)(Math.Abs(width)*DrawingPen.Width)/40 ;
int borderHeight =
   (int)(Math.Abs(height)*DrawingPen.Width)/40 ;
// Set enclosing rectangle for inner ellipse,
// taking into account the border width.
innerRectangle.X = outerRectangle.X + borderWidth;
```

```
      innerRectangle.Y = outerRectangle.Y + borderHeight;
      // Border is on both sides. Adjust width and height of
      // inner ellipse accordingly.
      innerRectangle.Width =
        outerRectangle.Width - borderWidth*2;
      innerRectangle.Height = outerRectangle.Height -
        borderHeight*2;

      // Add the enclosing Rectangle to the
      // GraphicsPath.
      gp.AddEllipse(outerRectangle);
      // Use a PathGradientBrush to fill the region.
      PathGradientBrush pgb = new PathGradientBrush(gp);
      // Set the center color to Transparent = Alpha equals 0.
      pgb.CenterColor = Color.Transparent;
      // More than one surround color can be defined.
      // In this example the colors are set to the
      // value the user selected or black as default.
      pgb.SurroundColors = new Color[]
      {
        DrawingPen.Color
      };
      // Create a region the size of the outline rectangle
      region = new Region(gp);
      // reset the graphics path.
      gp.Reset();
      // add the inner ellipse to the path
      gp.AddEllipse(innerRectangle);
      // subtract the inner ellipse from
      // the region by doing Xor.
      // The result is just the border with the specified size.
      region.Xor(gp);
      // Fill the region using the PathGradientBrush
      DeviceContext.FillRegion(pgb, region);
      // Dispose of the brush, graphics path, and the region.
      region.Dispose();
      gp.Dispose();
      pgb.Dispose();
    }
  }
}
```

Do It Yourself Implement `RectFrameComponent` in the same way as shown for `EllipseFrameComponent`. The implementation is straight-forward and very similar to the one shown.

A sample solution is provided with the solutions for this chapter on the accompanying CD.

Wiring the GUI Event Handlers and the New Components Together

Our final task is to create an instance of the component. The instance is created when the mouse down button event is encountered and one of the newly implemented tools is selected at the time of the mouse event. Therefore, simply add two `case` statements to the mouse down event handler of the `customScrollableControl`, as shown in Listing 7.4.

Listing 7.4 The Updated Mouse Down Event Handler

```
case toolSelection.RectFrameTool:
  compObject = new RectFrameComponent();
  break;
case toolSelection.EllipseFrameTool:
  compObject = new EllipseFrameComponent();
  break;
```

The new components can now be used.

This implementation shows how easy it is to support new components. We extended the application by using of the Components design pattern, which enables the application to treat all components in the same way without having to know what type of component it is dealing with. Figure 7.5 shows the application with the newly added features.

Do It Yourself Here are some suggested extensions you can implement to learn more about the usage of GDI+ not discussed in this book.

Extend the text component so that users can draw the text in user-defined fonts and colors. Hint: The Toolbox provides a control that enables font selection.

Extend the graphics components so that users can draw each line in a different color.

Add selection, dragging, and resize capabilities to the application.

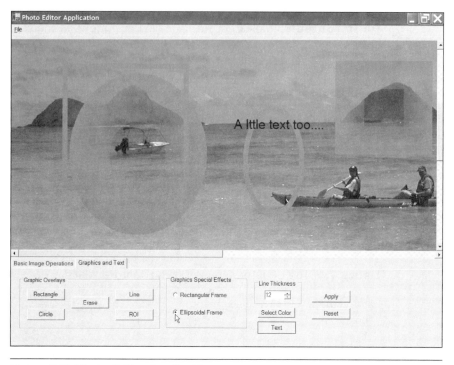

Figure 7.5 Photo Editor Application

Try to optimize the screen updates by using partial screen updates, which update only the region of the screen that changed (instead of updating the whole screen at every update).

7.7 Unit Tests

As in the previous iterations, the implementation must be tested before the project can move on to the next iteration. The tests should verify that the new objects are working OK. In addition, the added `Pen` object must be tested.

Based on the unit tests that were developed in Chapter 6, we implement new test cases to verify the correct behavior of the units implemented in this iteration. The unit tests will look very much like the unit tests for the rectangle and circle components in Chapter 6 because the functionality is very similar.

This section shows the unit test implementation for the ellipse frame (see Listing 7.5). The EllipseFrameTest first writes to the console to output the requirement key it is testing. In this case it is the image_graphics_special_effects requirements key. Then we create a Pen object with Color.WhiteSmoke as the pen color, and we choose a line width of 7. Then the static Pen property of GraphicsComponent is assigned to a reference to the pen we created.

After that, we create test cases for the ellipse frame that are very similar to the tests we implemented for the circle component. We create the EllipseFrameComponent and assign start and end points of the enclosing rectangle. We then check whether the component was set to the correct coordinates. Then we check a couple of points for correct picking. We then set the start and end points to different values and repeat essentially the same checks with different parameter values. After that we add one more check to see whether the pen of GraphicsComponent is still using the defined color and width. If all checks succeed, then the test case passes.

Listing 7.5 The EllipseFrameComponent Unit Test

```
/// <summary>
/// Test for F:image_graphics_special_effects.
/// Sets the start and end points and
/// checks whether the coordinates were set correctly.
/// Also checks whether picking is done
/// correctly.
/// </summary>
/// <test>F:image_graphics_special_effects</test>
[Test] public void EllipseFrameTest()
{
  Console.WriteLine("image_graphics_special_effects");
  Pen testPen = new Pen(Color.WhiteSmoke, 2);
  GraphicsComponent.DrawingPen = testPen;
  EllipseFrameComponent myC = new EllipseFrameComponent();
  myC.StartPoint = new Point(0, 0);
  myC.EndPoint = new Point(100, 200);

  Assertion.AssertEquals("Circle (0, 0) (100, 200)",
    myC.StartPoint.X, 0);
  Assertion.AssertEquals("Circle (0, 0) (100, 200)",
    myC.StartPoint.Y, 0);
  Assertion.AssertEquals("Circle (0, 0) (100, 200)",
```

```
      myC.EndPoint.X, 100);
   Assertion.AssertEquals("Circle (0, 0) (100, 200)",
      myC.EndPoint.Y, 200);
   Assertion.AssertEquals("Pick circle test",
      myC.IsPicked(0, 0), true);
   Assertion.AssertEquals("Pick circle test",
      myC.IsPicked(97, 198), true);
   Assertion.AssertEquals("Pick circle test",
      myC.IsPicked(95, 200), false);

   myC.StartPoint = new Point(205, 10);
   myC.EndPoint = new Point(10, 5);
   Assertion.AssertEquals("Rectangle (205, 10) (10, 5)",
      myC.StartPoint.X, 205);
   Assertion.AssertEquals("Rectangle (205, 10) (10, 5)",
      myC.StartPoint.Y, 10);
   Assertion.AssertEquals("Rectangle (205, 10) (10, 5)",
      myC.EndPoint.X, 10);
   Assertion.AssertEquals("Rectangle (205, 10) (10, 5)",
      myC.EndPoint.Y, 5);
   Assertion.AssertEquals("Pick circle test",
      myC.IsPicked(12, 2), true);
   Assertion.AssertEquals("Pick circle test",
      myC.IsPicked(97, 198), false);
   Assertion.AssertEquals("Pick circle test",
      myC.IsPicked(201, 7), true);

   Assertion.AssertEquals("Pen Rectangle Frame test",
      GraphicsComponent.DrawingPen.Color, Color.WhiteSmoke);
   Assertion.AssertEquals("Pen Rectangle Frame width test",
      GraphicsComponent.DrawingPen.Width, 2);
   testPen.Dispose();
   amIPassed = true;
}
```

The test case shown in Listing 7.5 is a very short example of what we possibly could test to make sure the component works correctly. We leave it to you to extend the tests to make them more sophisticated. For example, you could provide some test hooks in the application that enable you to check the calculation of the inner ellipse or even the application-side calculated region of the border. There is no limit, and we encourage you to take some time to enhance the very simple unit tests provided here.

Do It Yourself Add a test case that ensures that `RectFrameComponent` is implemented correctly and that the unit works as specified in the requirements description. Keep in mind that the integration tests will have to test the behavior of the units working together in the system function as described.

In addition, think of more test cases that can be used to test the new components.

7.8 Conclusion

 After the functionalities are implemented and the unit tests are passed, we review the project to decide whether the go/no-go criteria set for this iteration have been met. If the criteria are fulfilled, then the project team will move on to the next iteration in the construction phase.

7.8.1 Review

The following goals must be met in order for the project to proceed to the next iteration:

- Requirements: Refine the requirements and system scope.
- Analysis: Analyze the requirements by describing what the system does.
- Design: Develop the design of the required functionality for this iteration using UML.
- Implementation: Implement the required functionality.
- Test: Test the implemented features.

The listed goals of the iteration have been achieved. The required functionality was refined and analyzed, and the detailed design was specified. Furthermore, the requirements were implemented, and initial unit testing was performed to make sure the implementation is working as specified.

Therefore, the project is ready to move on to the next iteration (the sixth) of the construction phase.

7.9 References for Further Reading

http://msdn.microsoft.com/library/default.asp?url=/library/
   en-us/cpguide/html/cpcondrawingeditingimages.asp

http://thecodeproject.com/vcpp/gdiplus

http://www.c-sharpcorner.com/Graphics.asp

http://www.microsoft.com/whdc/hwdev/archive/video/GDInext.mspx

CHAPTER 8

Dynamic Loading of Components

Unified Process:
Construction Phase and Sixth Iteration

This chapter introduces image-processing algorithms that are used to transform an image. The described functionalities are written as independent components (also referred to as *plugins*). The plugins are implemented in various .NET languages and are loaded at run time.

The deliverable artifacts for this iteration are the same as described in Chapters 6 and 7. The major difference lies in the functionality that is delivered. Therefore, the first task in this iteration is to refine the requirements to be implemented.

8.1 Requirements for Image Postprocessing Components

R

The functionality to be implemented in this iteration is split between three requirement keys. In agreement with the customer, all the functionality described in this chapter will be provided as *dynamically loadable* components. This means that the application loads the components at run time if they are available.

As mentioned earlier, sometimes dynamically loadable components are also referred to as plugins. The name is drawn from the fact that the components are interchangeable as long as they conform to the defined interface specification. If a component complies with the definition, it can simply be plugged in and the application can use it. Providing dynamically loadable components enables the customer to exchange components without having to recompile the application. This in turn allows us to provide optimized or changed components by simply swapping assemblies. In addition, using plugins allows us to support new components very easily.

The first requirement key, `image_contrast`, deals with the functionality that enables the user to change the contrast of an image. In discussions with the customer, it turns out that we also need to support the capability to change the color distribution of the pixels in the image. The color and contrast requirements are merged into one requirement key. Therefore, the `image_contrast` requirement is renamed `image_contrast_and_color`. We merge the keys because from our experience, the implementation of the two functionalities is very similar and not very time-consuming.

The second requirement key that needs to be implemented is the functionality to change the brightness of an image. This requirement is specified in the `image_brightness` key.

The final requirement that is implemented in this iteration is a tool that enables the user to remove the "red eye" effect in a small, defined area of the loaded image. The requirement key used to describe this functionality is `image_special_effects`.

As mentioned earlier, all three requirements are implemented as dynamically loadable plugins. This means that the developed components are bound to the application, not at compile time but rather at run time. This *run time binding*, also referred to as *late binding*, enables us to change the behavior of the application by simply exchanging a component assembly. No recompilation of the application is needed at all. This technique makes the application more flexible by enabling the customer to provide optimized or enhanced plugins without having to change the application code.

Table 8.1 shows the refined requirements.

Table 8.1 Refined Requirements Descriptions for the Image Postprocessing Components

Requirement	Type	Summary
F:image_contrast_and_color	Functional	It shall be possible to change the contrast and the color of an image using track bar controls. The functionality shall be provided via plugins that are loaded at run time.

Table 8.1 (*Cont.*)

Requirement	Type	Summary
F:image_brightness	Functional	The brightness of the image can be changed by using a track bar control. The functionality shall be provided via plugins that are loaded at run time.
F:image_special_ effects	Functional	It shall be possible for the user to remove red eyes in a square area within the image by selecting the tool. A red square will be shown on the screen to identify the areas where the red eye removal can be applied with a left mouse click. The functionality shall be provided via plugins that are loaded at run time.

The task for this iteration is to provide these requirements by following the process steps defined in the Unified Process. Therefore, the next step is to further analyze the requirements to get a clear picture of what the system is supposed to do.

8.2 Analysis of the Image Postprocessing Requirements

To access the new features, we need to first define some new GUI elements. For this reason the analysis starts with the `photo_editor` requirement key.

8.2.1 The `photo_editor` Requirement

Figure 8.1 shows the changes to the photo editor GUI. The functionalities implemented in this chapter are advanced image-processing operations and are not related to the already implemented features. Therefore, a new tab is added to the existing tab control. This new tab will hold the new controls used for the functionalities implemented in this iteration. The layout is shown in the lower part of Figure 8.1. The contrast, brightness, and color functionalities are implemented using `TrackBar` controls. Because of their appearance, the `TrackBar` controls are sometimes referred to as *sliders*.

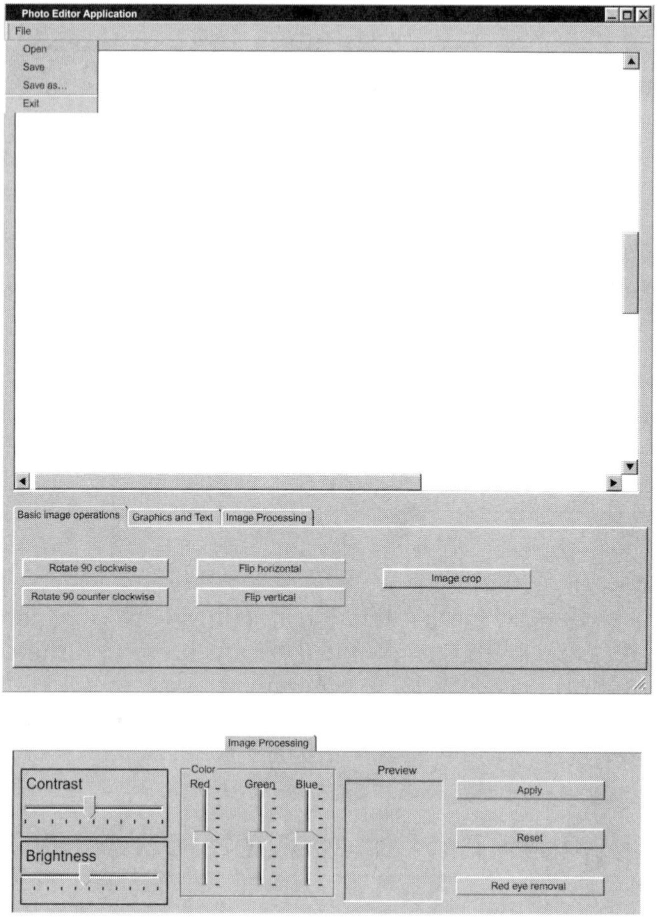

Figure 8.1 The Photo Editor GUI

Some image-processing algorithms that are applied to the whole image can take a long time. By "long," we mean not at interactive speed; the user must wait for the result of the calculation for multiple seconds. Therefore, we will provide an image preview pane. This preview pane shows a thumb-nail image of the loaded picture. If the user changes a control setting, the preview image will immediately show the result. In this way, the user can interactively check and adjust the requested image operations before applying these changes to the image, something that will take some time.

If the user decides that the image operation shown in the preview is as expected, then the operation can be applied to the whole image by using the provided Apply button.

If the applied changes turn out to be not as expected or if the Apply button was pressed by mistake, the user can revert to the originally loaded image by selecting the Reset button.

In addition, we will provide a button for the red eye removal tool. If the red eye removal tool is selected and the mouse is moved within the image area, then a red rectangle with a width and height of 10 pixels is shown at the current mouse position. If the user then clicks on the image, the area within the shown rectangle will be taken to apply the red eye removal functionality. The rest of the image, outside the shown rectangle, stays untouched.

The plugins (or components) can be written in any language supported by Visual Studio.NET.

8.2.2 The `image_brightness` Requirement

The brightness of the image can be adjusted according to the selected value of the contrast track bar. The brightness of the image is calculated by taking the color values of the pixels and adding the value of the brightness control. The colors are distributed according to the following formula:

$$\text{value}*0.299 = \text{red}, \text{value}*0.587 = \text{green}, \text{value}*0.114 = \text{blue}$$

The range of the slider is -300 to 300. To make the application more responsive, all changes are shown in the preview window first. If the user wants to make the changes permanent, then the Apply button must be pressed. This results in recalculating the whole image. If the changes are not satisfactory, users can press the Reset button, which resets the image to the originally loaded image. If the plugin component cannot be found in the application directory, an exception is thrown.

8.2.3 The `image_contrast_and_color` Requirement

The contrast is adjusted using histogram calculation and an equalization technique. The formula for histogram equalization is provided by the customer. The user can provide a correction factor using a `TrackBar` control. The range of the control is -100 to 100, and the color values are distributed according to the following formula:

$$\text{value}*0.299 = \text{red}, \text{value}*0.587 = \text{green}, \text{value}*0.114 = \text{blue}$$

In addition to the contrast adjustments, users can change the color values of all pixels in the image by using `TrackBar` controls. Each of the RGB color components is adjustable via its own control in the range of –100 to 100. The value of the slider is added to the corresponding color component of each pixel in the image.

To make the application more responsive, all changes are shown in the preview window. If the user wants to make the changes permanent, the Apply button must be pressed. This will result in recalculation of the entire image. If the changes were not to the satisfaction of the user, a Reset button is provided that resets the image to the originally loaded image.

If the dynamically loadable component cannot be found in the application directory, an exception is thrown.

8.2.4 The `image_special_effects` Requirement

The special effect provided is a red eye removal tool. The tool can be selected by clicking the provided button on the GUI. If the tool is selected and the mouse is within the area of the image, then a red rectangle is shown to indicate the area where the red eye removal will take effect. The rectangle will be 10 pixels wide and 10 pixels high. The rectangle is drawn in red, and its origin is the current position of the mouse. On a mouse click, the calculation is applied to the part of the image that is enclosed in the square. The red eye reduction is calculated by reducing the red component of the pixels in the selected area to 80 percent of its original value; the other color values are untouched.

If the dynamically loadable component cannot be found in the application directory, an exception is thrown.

8.3 Design of the Image-Processing Components Using Late Binding

$\left\rangle D \right\rangle$ The time spent in design in this iteration is less than in the previous chapters. This is in accordance with the definition of the Unified Process. Recall that in the beginning of the construction phase the design workflow is one of the main tasks, but as we progress through the construction phase, the focus shifts to spending more time in the implementation and test workflows.

Because the architectural baseline is only extended by the late binding functionality, we will spend less time in the design workflow compared with earlier iterations. The major design requirement for this iteration is to provide the ability to load components at run time. Furthermore, the plugin components can be written in any of the languages that Microsoft Visual Studio.NET supports (VC++, C#, VB, and J#).

8.3.1 Design of the Language Extension Components

Up to this point, we have used compile time, or *early*, binding to access information in other assemblies (such as `customScrollableControl`). In this chapter the application's design is extended to allow for run time, or *late*, binding of certain components.

This means that a type of the component that is loaded at run time must be defined so that it can be invoked by the application at run time. Therefore, we first define a common method signature for the loadable component's interface. The following is the method signature used for the dynamically loadable components described in this chapter:

```
void ProcessImage(Bitmap source, int param1, int param2, int param3);
```

The parameter `source` of type `Bitmap` is used to provide a reference to the image on which the image-processing operation is to be performed. The three integer type parameters will hold additional information that might be needed for the requested image-processing calculation. The additional information can be the corresponding `TrackBar` position or any other information needed by the component to perform the requested operation.

The updated class diagram reflects these changes and can be seen in Figure 8.2.

The class diagram shows that the components are invoked at run time by the application. The component assemblies are provided as dynamic link libraries. The application will search for the plugins in the default location. To invoke the functionality at run time, all components must be located in the application's installation directory. For development this means that the release version of the components can be found in the `bin` directory, whereas the debug versions are stored in the `bind` directory. Figure 8.3 shows a package diagram to visualize the assembly structure.

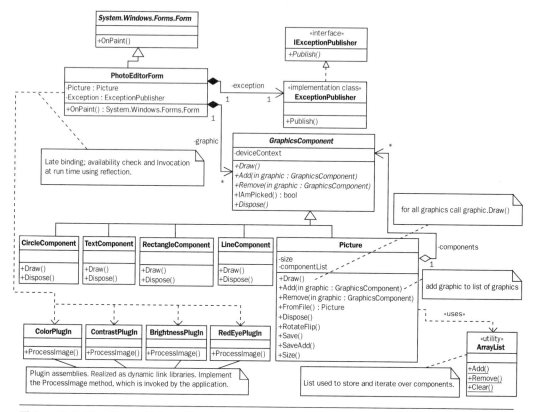

Figure 8.2 The Photo Editor Class Diagram

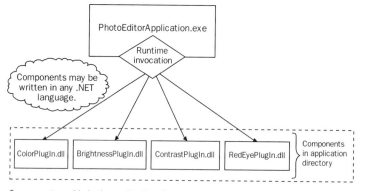

Components reside in the application directory. For development the release-compiled components reside in the bin directory, whereas the debug-compiled components reside in the bind directory.

Figure 8.3 The Photo Editor Package Diagram

This concludes the design changes that we analyze in order to implement the required functionality. Now it's time to move on to the implementation workflow.

8.4 Project Management Issues

During the development of the preceding iteration, members of the project team brought up a new project management issue. During discussions in the regularly scheduled project meetings, some team members said that they did not really know the actual status of the project. In addition, most of the project team members thought that not enough focus was given to monitoring the identified risk items and their mitigations.

Both issues are valid complaints and need to be addressed. Even though both items were monitored by project management, it seems that their tracking is not visible enough to the project team. Therefore, a special meeting is scheduled to discuss the issue and to find an efficient solution that resolves these shortcomings.

It is crucial for the project management to listen to the project team if a lack of communication has been identified. If the project team members do not know what the status of the project is at any given time, how can they be held responsible for finishing the project on time? In addition, for the motivation of the individuals it is important to communicate the overall tasks of the project, its current status, and upcoming work packages. If the project team is not kept in this loop, sooner or later the team will suffer. It is also important to assign tasks for which the developers are held responsible. In addition, it should be clear to all the team members how their individual contributions will help the project to succeed.

It is also important for the team members to have the perspective of knowing about upcoming tasks or projects. In many projects, the communication does not include updating the project team on tasks that might or will come up. In many of these projects, we have found motivational problems simply because team members did not know what their next task would be (or whether there would be one at all) and how their contribution fit into the overall project.

For all these reasons, we think that open and honest professional communication must flow from the top down, and the feedback must flow bottom-up, for a project to succeed. If we look at a concrete project, the truth of this observation becomes obvious. The project management has the information about new or existing projects, customer problems, and so on. This information must be communicated to the developers (perhaps the information can be filtered to take some of the pressure off the project team) so that they can do their tasks and stay motivated. By the same token, to keep the project on track or to improve the process, project management is dependent on feedback from the project team in order to make adjustments if roadblocks are identified.

8.4.1 Improving Project Visibility

The two issues that were brought up by the development team deal with visibility. Even though the project plan is available to everyone on the team, the developers still feel that they do not really know what the current status of the project is. In addition, the status of the project regarding the identified risks is not clear to the team members. At the special meeting called to resolve these issues, they are discussed and ideas are collected on how to improve the situation. After a lively discussion, an agreement is achieved on ways to make the project and risk management more visible.

All requirement keys are written on 3×5 index cards. The cards are divided into sections listing the requirement key, the responsible developer's name, the due date, and the completion date. An example is shown in Figure 8.4.

These index cards are then posted on a wall that everyone passes by many times a day.

In addition, the wall holds a project plan with the iteration and project deadlines clearly visible. The requirements index cards are pinned to the plan. A developer who has finished a task updates the card by adding the completion date. At the end of an iteration, all index cards that are posted within the timeframe of the iteration are finished and show a completion

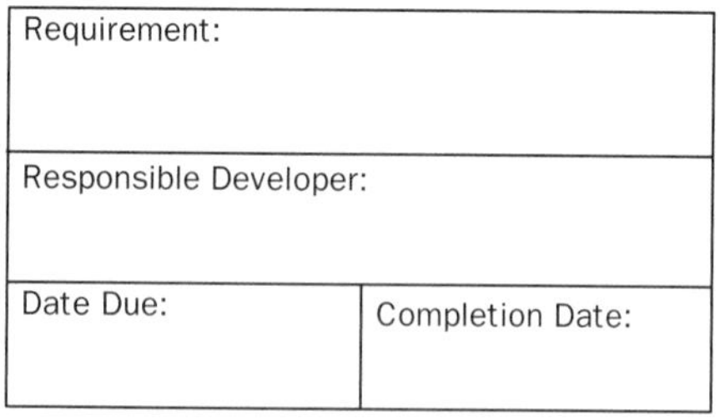

Figure 8.4 Requirements Index Card

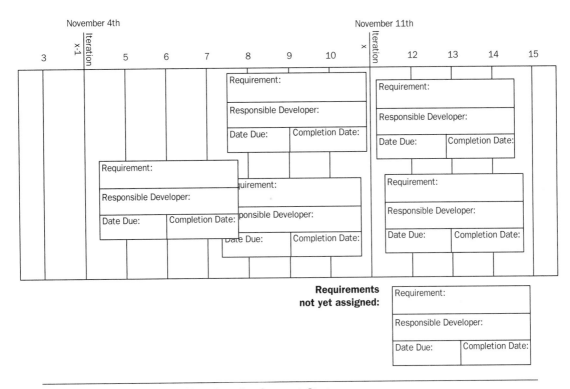

Figure 8.5 Project Plan Showing the Current Status

date. For every iteration that is completed on time, project management rewards the team with a catered lunch. Figure 8.5 shows an example of the posted project plan.

Posting the project plan makes the project's current status easily visible to the developers, and it also communicates the upcoming requirements. The cards listing the requirements not yet assigned show the team the tasks that remain.

Now we turn our attention to making risk management more visible to the developers. To solve this problem, the development team and project management decided to post a risk management table next to the project plan. This table uses index cards to show each risk, along with its status and mitigation. The green section is used to post risk items that have been monitored. Any risk items that are likely to occur are moved to the yellow state, indicating the need for close monitoring and special attention. If an event identified as a risk is actually coming true, the item is moved to the red

Risk Table

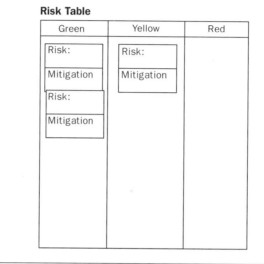

Green	Yellow	Red
Risk:	Risk:	
Mitigation	Mitigation	
Risk:		
Mitigation		

Figure 8.6 Risk Table

status section, which means that immediate action is necessary. Most likely, one of the mitigations is executed, and the risk item will revert to yellow or green status. Figure 8.6 shows a sample risk table.

The project team feels that these changes provide enough visibility of the deadlines and the assigned and upcoming tasks. In addition, this solution provides a clear picture of the responsibilities for each task. It also gives the developers an incentive to complete a task: signing it off on the project plan. Furthermore, this approach encourages developers to help each other if it becomes obvious that a task will otherwise be delayed.

8.5 Implementing Dynamically Loadable Image Postprocessing Plugins

The .NET Framework lets programmers search an assembly to identify the types and methods it provides. The functionality to do so is encapsulated in the `System.Reflection` namespace. Reflection can be used to query metadata about an assembly, to use types from an assembly, and to emit program code at run time. In the example of the photo editor, we use this functionality to search the metadata of files in a predefined directory to find image-processing plugins.

The plugins will be provided in various programming languages to show how language interoperability works in a .NET application.

8.5.1 Late Binding and Reflection

The .NET Framework provides the concept of reflection to query for information on types and metadata from an assembly's *manifest,* which contains information that describes the assembly completely. For a complete description of the assembly manifest, refer to the MSDN help files.

The capability of querying data from the manifest is built into the System.Reflection namespace, which defines many classes to provide the developer with a wide range of functionality. The functionality ranges from querying information about assemblies to emitting code to create types at run time.

The feature we are looking for is runtime invocation, also referred to as late binding. Late binding enables the photo editor application to query type information and to invoke methods, defined in other assemblies, at run time. The photo editor application uses reflection and late binding to load the plugin assembly functionalities at run time. The advantage of this feature is that it allows customers to write their own implementations, which can simply be exchanged with the existing assemblies in the application directory without the need to recompile the application. As a result, customers can change the behavior of the application or provide optimized versions of the plugins without any application changes or compilation.

Loading an Assembly at Run Time

In this section, we develop the base functionality to dynamically load various components in the photo editor. In the first step of the implementation we introduce a new class named PlugInInterface to the Photo Editor Application project. This new class keeps the interface definition of the dynamically loadable components separate from the application code.

First, we add some namespaces to the file. The dynamic loading uses the System.Reflection namespace to receive information on the methods defined in an assembly. Therefore, we add this namespace to the file. In addition, we use the System.Drawing namespace, which includes the Bitmap definition. To search a directory for files, we also include the System.IO namespace, and, last but not least, we use the exception management block. Therefore, we also add the `Microsoft.ApplicationBlocks.Exception Management` to our list of namespaces.

In addition, we define some private class properties. For example, we define a private string property that holds the postfix "`PlugIn.dll`" of the components that we are looking for. To store the prefix of the component, we also define a string property. In addition, we define three integer values that correspond to the parameters that are needed by the image-processing calculation within the components. The resulting code can be seen in Listing 8.1.

Listing 8.1 `PlugInInterface`, Part 1

```
using System;
using System.Reflection;
using System.Drawing;
using System.IO;
using Microsoft.ApplicationBlocks.ExceptionManagement;

namespace Photo_Editor_Application
{
  /// <summary>
  /// Interface used to load the provided plugins
  /// dynamically.
  /// </summary>
  public class PlugInInterface
  {
    // postfix for all dynamically loadable components
    private static string searchPlugInString = "PlugIn.dll";
    Assembly assembly;
    private Bitmap tmpBitmap;
    // values of the parameters
    private int param3;
    private int param2;
    private int param1;
    // name of the operation and prefix of the component
    private string sliderName;

    /// <summary>
    /// Constructor
    /// </summary>
```

```
public PlugInInterface()
{
  //
  // TODO: Add constructor logic here
  //

}
```

Now that the properties are defined, we start to implement the actual interface that is responsible for loading a component at run time in order to execute a requested image-processing operation. We define the actual interface method, `ApplyImageProcessing`, as `public` so that it can be called by the application. It does not accept any parameters. In this method the first action we implement is to create the name of the component that we want to load. The name is a concatenation of `sliderName` and `search PlugInString`, and the result is a string of the form "`xxxxPlugIn.dll`", where `xxxx` is the name of the requested operation.

Now that we have the complete name of the component, we search the current directory for all files with the same name. The matches are stored in a string array named `filenames`. To search files in a given directory, the .NET Framework class `Directory` is used. This class is defined in the `System.IO` namespace and defines a method called `GetFiles(...)`, which returns an array of strings in which each string represents a file in the directory searched. The components of the photo editor are stored in the application directory. This means that the application always uses the assembly found the same directory as the application.

Then we check whether a file with the requested name actually was found. If no file was found, an exception is thrown. After that, we also check whether more than one match was found; if it was, we also throw an exception to indicate an error (this is very unlikely because two files in the same directory cannot have the same name). Listing 8.2 shows the implementation of the functionality.

Listing 8.2 `PlugInInterface`, Part 2

```
      *
      *
      *
/// <summary>
/// Searches the PlugIns directory for a DLL with the
```

```
/// specified name. If none is found then an exception
/// is thrown.
/// Otherwise it tries to invoke the method ProcessImage
/// with the specified
/// parameters.
/// </summary>
public void ApplyImageProcessing()
{
  try
  {
    #region ApplyImageProcessing Code from Chapter 8
    // Concatenates the operation name with
    // the suffix "PlugIn.dll"
    string operation;
    operation = sliderName + searchPlugInString;

    string[] filenames =
      Directory.GetFiles(PhotoEditorForm.GetApplicationDirectory,
        operation);

    // If no PlugIn is found indicate an error by
    // throwing an exception.
    if(filenames.Length == 0)
    {
      throw(new Exception("Error, PlugIn could not be found in
        the specified location"));
    }

    // This should never ever happen! Two files cannot have
    // the same name
    // and reside in the same directory!
    // But anyway the check does not hurt either. Better safe
    // than sorry ;-)
    if(filenames.Length > 1)
       throw(new Exception("Error, More than one PlugIn could
         be found in the specified location"));
```

Now that the component's DLL file has been found, we are ready to load the component and to invoke the method so we can apply the image-processing operation requested by the application. To query the types defined in the located assembly, we must first load the assembly. To load the assembly we use the System.Assembly namespace, which defines vari-

ous `Load` methods and overloads. The following example uses `Assembly.`
`LoadFrom(filename)`. The return value is of type `Assembly` and is stored in
the private member variable `assembly`. Then we load all the defined types
in the assembly. As mentioned earlier, the manifest of an assembly describes the assembly. We use the `GetTypes` method to extract the types
defined in the loaded assembly. The call to that method returns an array
that contains all such types.

Member Invocation at Run Time

Parameters that need to be passed to the method to be invoked are passed
with an array of type `object`. This array holds the parameters that are
required by the `ProcessImage` method. To match the signature of the
`ProcessImage` method, we create an `object` array of size 4. Remember, the
design specification says that the `ProcessImage` method is defined to take
four parameters. The parameters are a `Bitmap` (to hold a bitmap reference
to the image) and three `Integer` parameters to hold additional information
as needed.

   After setting the parameters, we search the loaded assembly for the
methods it defines. .NET provides the `GetMethods()` method, which is
used to discover methods defined in the loaded assembly. The array that is
returned is of type `MethodInfo`. The application then iterates through this
array to find a method that matches the name `ProcessImage`.

   For error-handling purposes, we also define some helper properties.
First, we create a local variable of type `bool` with the name `methodNot`
`Found` and initialize it to `true`. This variable is used to check whether a
method with the specified name was found in the list of methods. After
that, we define a `const` string that holds the name of the method that is
invoked. According to the design specification, the name is "`ProcessImage`".

   The final step is to create a local variable of type `object`. This variable
is used to hold the invoked method.

   Now that the setup is complete, we use a `foreach` loop to iterate over
the methods defined in the assembly. The loop iterates over the array of
methods returned by the call to `GetMethods()`, as described earlier. If a
method with the name "`ProcessImage`" is found, then an instance of the
type is created using `Activator.CreateInstance(theType[0])`. In addition, the `methodNotFound` flag is set to `false`, indicating that a method with
the provided name was found in the assembly. Next, we call `theType[0].`
`InvokeMember(***)` to actually invoke the method of the plugin assembly.
The following parameters are passed to the invoked method:

- The name of the member to be invoked.
- A flag indicating that a method has been invoked.
- A `System.Reflection.Binder` object, which in this case is `null` and therefore default binding is used.
- The object that defines the member that is invoked.
- An array of `int` parameters.

After the method is called, some error handling is done if the invocation failed. Depending on the type of error that occurred, different error messages are provided.

The resulting code can be seen in Listing 8.3.

Listing 8.3 `PlugInInterface`, Part 3

```
        *

        *

        *

// Load the plugin assembly that was found.
assembly = Assembly.LoadFrom(filenames[0]);
// Query the loaded assembly for types defined.
Type[] theType = assembly.GetTypes();
// Create an object array that holds the parameters for
// the method to be called.
object[] param = new Object[4];
param[0] = tmpBitmap;
param[1] = param1;
param[2] = param2;
param[3] = param3;
// Get all the methods defined in the plugin assembly
MethodInfo[] methods = theType[0].GetMethods();
// used to remember whether a method with name
// methodName was found. If not an error will
// be signaled.
bool methodNotFound = true;
// Defines the name of the method
// that needs to be defined in each plugin
// in order to invoke it.
const string methodName = "ProcessImage";

object assemblyObject;
// Iterate through the methods defined
```

```
          // in the assembly that was found and
          // check whether a method with the specified
          // name is defined in the assembly.
          // If so, invoke the method.
          foreach(MethodInfo NextMethod in methods)
          {
#endregion
            if(NextMethod.Name == methodName)
            {
              // Create an instance of the type found in the plugin
              // assembly
              assemblyObject = Activator.CreateInstance(theType[0]);
              try
              {
                methodNotFound = false;
                // Invoke the member whose signature matches
               // void ProcessImage(Bitmap, int, int, int);
                theType[0].InvokeMember(methodName,
                   BindingFlags.InvokeMethod,
                   null,
                   assemblyObject,
                   param);
              }
              // Exception at this point most likely means that
              // none of the methods with the correct name
              // had the correct signature!
              catch(Exception e)
              {
                 throw(new Exception(e.Message + " \n\n Method with
                   the specified signature could NOT be found in
                   PlugIn DLL. Or an exception was thrown within the
                   invoked method!"));
              }
            }
          }
          if(methodNotFound)
          // If no method with the correct name was defined by the
          // assembly
          // then indicate the error to the user!
            throw( new Exception("Error PlugIn does NOT define a
              method with the name ProcessImage!"));
```

```
      }
      catch(Exception exception)
      {
        // If the invocation has failed, an
        // error message is displayed.
        ExceptionManager.Publish(exception);
      }
    }
}
```

In addition to the code shown in Listing 8.3, we implement an accessor for the private properties we defined. The complete solution can be found on the accompanying CD in the sample solution of Chapter 8.

To support the `PlugInInterface` we also make changes to the `Photo EditorForm` class. All we need to do is to create an instance of the class in the constructor of `PhotoEditorForm` by adding the following lines:

```
// Create an instance of the plugin interface class
// in order to be able to use dynamic loading.
plugInInterface = new PlugInInterface();
```

In addition, we define a method that in turn calls the `ApplyImage Processing` method defined in `PlugInInterface`. Simply add the method as shown here:

```
/// <summary>
/// This method is called when a new thumbnail is
/// calculated for previewing a transformation.
/// </summary>
private void applyImageProcessing()
{
  // Call the PlugInInterface method to do the magic.
  plugInInterface.ApplyImageProcessing();
}

private PlugInInterface plugInInterface;
```

This completes the framework implementation of the dynamically loadable plugin component. In the next step, we extend the application to show a thumbnail image that serves as a preview pane to show the result of a requested operation.

8.5.2 Adding a `PictureBox` for Previewing Image Operations

This section describes the implementation of a `PictureBox` that is used to provide the user with a preview of an image operation before it is applied to the whole image. The first step is to add a new tab to the photo editor application GUI. Change the name of the new tab to Image Processing. After that, drag a `PictureBox` from the Toolbox onto it. Position and resize the `PictureBox` according to the GUI requirements shown earlier in this chapter. In addition, specify the following properties of the picture box:

Properties of the PictureBox

Name	picturePreView
BorderStyle	Fixed3D

Then select the text tool and type the text `Preview` on top of the `PictureBox`. To show an image within the preview box, we must create a thumbnail image of the loaded image. The thumbnail image will then be displayed in the `PictureBox`. To implement this feature, add a `private` member variable of type `Image` called `thumbImage` to the `PhotoEditorForm` class. With the `private` member variable created, it is now possible to store a thumbnail image of the loaded image. To create a thumbnail, we use the `GetThumbnail(...)` method in the `PhotoEditorForm` constructor, as shown in Listing 8.4. The parameters provided to the `GetThumbnail` call are as follows:

- The width and height of the `PictureBox`
- `null` (for the delegate `Image.GetThumbnailImageAbort` of GDI+, which actually is not used but must be provided)
- `IntrPtrZero` (which is defined as the callback data)

`PicturePreView.Image` is set to `thumbImage` in order to display the thumbnail.

Listing 8.4 Creating and Displaying a Thumbnail Image

```
// Create a thumbnail image from the loaded image.
// The image will be displayed in the preview of the
```

```
// image-processing tab.
thumbImage = PictureObject.LoadedImage.GetThumbnailImage(
        picturePreView.Width,
        picturePreView.Height,
      null,
        IntPtr.Zero);

picturePreView.Image = thumbImage;
```

If a new image is loaded, we must update and display an updated
`thumbImage`. Therefore, add the same functionality to the `OpenFile_Click`
event handler of the `PhotoEditorForm` class. With these changes in place,
the preview image is shown in the newly added picture box. Compile and
run the application to see the new feature working.

The next step is to implement the image-processing components that
can be loaded at run time and the GUI controls needed to provide the
parameters for the requested image-processing operation.

8.5.3 Implementation of a `TrackBar` Control

The GUI elements used to control the image-processing functionalities
are, as specified in the requirements, `TrackBar` controls. As an example of
the implementation of such a control, we'll look at the implementation of
the contrast track bar.

We start by dragging a `TrackBar` control from the Toolbox onto the
Image Processing tab. Do the same with a `groupBox`. Position and adjust
the `groupBox` so that it encloses the track bar. Update the text of the group
box to `Contrast`, and change the properties of the `TrackBar` as shown here:

Properties of TrackBar

TickFrequency	10
TickStyle	BottomRight
Maximum	100
Minimum	−100
LargeChange	10
Cursor	Hand
Name	trackBarContrast

After the changes to the properties have been made, double-click on the `TrackBar` to generate an event handler for the corresponding scroll event. The scroll event is called every time the track bar is moved.

This puts everything into place for us to start implementing the scroll event handler of the track bar. For the contrast calculation, only one parameter value is needed, so we set the unneeded parameters of the `plugInInterface` instance to 0. In addition, we set the `sliderName` to `"Contrast"`, which is the name of the calculation that is requested:

```
plugInInterface.Param2 = 0;
plugInInterface.Param3 = 0;
plugInInterface.SliderName = "Contrast";
```

Then set `Param1` of `plugInInterface` to the current value of the track bar control:

```
plugInInterface.Param1 = trackBarContrast.Value
```

Next, we create a copy of the current thumbnail image. We do this so that we can revert to the original thumbnail if users move the track bar to a different position without first applying the operation to the whole image (because all operations are based on the loaded image and not on the previously calculated image shown in the preview pane). The `Image` class provides the `Clone` method, which is used to get an exact copy of the thumbnail. Create the thumbnail image clone. Then call the `applyImage` method, which will dynamically load `ContrastPlugIn.dll`. A reference to the thumbnail image is provided to the interface object as the image on which the operation is performed. The complete implementation of the scroll event handler can be seen in Listing 8.5.

Listing 8.5 The Scroll Event Handler of the Contrast Functionality

```
/// <summary>
/// Event handler for the scroll event of
/// the contrast control. Calls
/// applyImageProcessing(...)
/// </summary>
/// <param name="sender">Sender object.</param>
/// <param name="e">Event arguments.</param>
/// <requirements>F:image_contrast_and_color</requirements>
private void trackBarContrast_Scroll(object sender,
```

```
  System.EventArgs e)
{
  try
  {
    // Reset the values of parameters 2 and 3
    plugInInterface.Param2 = 0;
    plugInInterface.Param3 = 0;
    // Set the name of the operation to be applied
    plugInInterface.SliderName = "Contrast";
  plugInInterface.Param1 = trackBarContrast.Value;
// Creates a copy of the thumbnail image to be displayed in
    // the preview pane, showing the applied changes.
    picturePreView.Image = (Image)thumbImage.Clone();
    plugInInterface.TmpBitmap = (Bitmap)picturePreView.Image;

    // Call to apply the requested operation to
    // the thumbnail image.
    applyImageProcessing();
  }
  catch(Exception exception)
  {
    ExceptionManager.Publish(exception);
  }
}
```

8.5.4 The Language-Independent Plugin Implementation

After we implement the required GUI controls, the preview pane, and the dynamic loading capability, the last missing piece is the plugin component itself. The way the loader is written enables us to provide the plugin components in any .NET language. The only restriction is that the assembly defines a public method called `ProcessImage`, which takes a reference to a bitmap and three integer values as parameters. The components must have the suffix and type "`PlugIn.dll`", and they must be stored in the application directory so that the application can locate the component at load time.

In the following subsections we show how to implement dynamically loadable components in different .NET languages. The functionalities are described as they are implemented.

For some of the image-processing calculations, it is necessary first to translate the color image into a representative grayscale image. The next section shows how this is done.

Using Luminance to Translate an RGB Color into a Grayscale Image

The contrast and brightness calculations that are to be provided as plugin components are very well defined on images in grayscale formats but not on color images. Therefore, it is necessary to translate the color image into its corresponding grayscale image. This means that the three RGB color components are transformed into their corresponding gray values.

One way to do that would be to take the average of the three color values, but that would result in a grayscale image that looks distorted. The reason is that the human eye is not equally sensitive to different colors. To compensate for this difference in sensitivity, we use a formula that considers this fact when translating the image. A commonly used method for this compensation is recommendation 601 of the CCIR (Comite Consultatif International des Radio-communications), which is defined as follows:

$$Luminance = R*0.299 + G*0.587 + B*0.114$$

Luminance is the gray value corresponding to the color values of a pixel defined in RGB mode. In the remainder of this chapter this formula is used to translate a given RGB image into a grayscale image if necessary.

The C++ Contrast Plugin

The first dynamically loadable component that is implemented is the contrast plugin. We implement this component using C++. To start, we add a new project to the Photo Editor solution of type `Class Library (.NET)` and name it `ContrastPlugIn`. This creates the necessary header and `.cpp` files.

Before starting to implement the functionality, we change some project settings in order to save the created DLL in either the `bin` or the `bind` directory, depending on the build configuration. Select the project in Solution Explorer, and right-click on it. Select Properties. Under Configuration Properties | General | Output Directory, change the entry to `..\..\..\bind` for the debug build configuration, and to `..\..\..\bin` for the release build configuration.

After that, we are ready to add the necessary methods to the header file and rename the created class `Contrast`.

Two methods are used for the contrast functionality. One is the public `ProcessImage` method, which is invoked by the application. The second is a private helper method with the name `calcNewValue`. Listing 8.6 shows the header file with the added methods. Note that the class uses .NET-provided garbage collection, which is defined by using the `__gc` flag. If no garbage collection is to be used, the flag `__nogc` is used instead. The rest of the file contains the definition of the methods.

Listing 8.6 The `ContrastPlugIn` Header File

```
// ContrastPlugIn.h
#pragma once
using namespace System;

namespace ContrastPlugIn
{
  /// <summary>
  /// Class used for contrast calculation.
  /// Dynamically bound by the application
  /// at run time.
  /// </summary>
  ///<requirements>F:image_contrast_and_color
  ///</requirements>
public __gc class Contrast
  {
  public:
    // Method invoked by the application
    void ProcessImage(Drawing::Bitmap& image, int param,
        int unused1, int unused2);

  private:
    // Helper method
    unsigned int calcNewValue(unsigned int colorValue,
        double colorFactor, unsigned int pixValue,
        double factor, unsigned int maxPixValue, double lookUpValue);
  };
}
```

To make this change compile, we add a reference to the `System.Drawing.dll` namespace.

The next task is to implement the actual functionality for the contrast calculation. First, let's examine some theory about the contrast calculation.

Using the Histogram Calculation in the Contrast Functionality

The customer provides the following explanation for the contrast functionality: The photo editor application will use a technique called histogram equalization to perform the contrast calculation. *Histogram equalization* means that, based on a calculated histogram, the pixel values are redistributed so that each pixel value has an equal opportunity to occur within the image.

The first step is to calculate the grayscale histogram of the image. To do that, we walk through each pixel of the image. Each RGB value is transformed into the corresponding luminance value. The histogram then counts how often each luminance value is represented in the image. Thus, the histogram is an array whose size corresponds to the number of possible gray values in an image. Each pixel with a certain luminance value adds 1 to that array element. The histogram calculation can be seen in Figure 8.7.

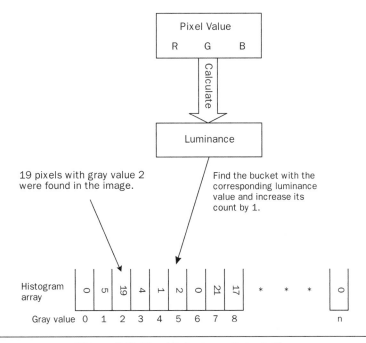

Figure 8.7 The Histogram Calculation

The sum of all the values in the histogram array will be equal to the number of pixels in the image. For example, imagine a binary image with two possible gray values (0 and 1) that is 10 pixels by 10 pixels, with each value (0 and 1) occurring 50 times. This would result in a histogram of an array of two fields. Each field would contain the value 50 for the number of times each value (0 or 1) was represented in the image.

After the histogram of the image is calculated, we compute a lookup table for the equalized image. A *lookup table* specifies an array having the same size as the histogram and is used to transform any given gray value into a new (in this case equalized) value. Each pixel value is exchanged with the value provided by the lookup table, as shown in Figure 8.8.

The computation of the lookup table values is based on the previously calculated histogram. The values are calculated by accumulating the pixels of the histogram having the same or lower values. This number is then multiplied by the number of possible gray values and divided by the total number of pixels in the image.

Each pixel value is then exchanged with the corresponding value in the lookup table. The result is a new image in which the color values are evenly distributed (equalized). The implementation can be seen in Listing 8.7.

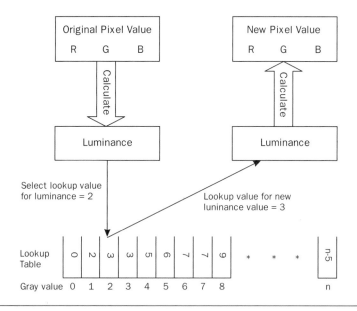

Figure 8.8 The Lookup Table

Listing 8.7 ContrastPlugIn, Part 1

```
// This is the main DLL file.
#include "stdafx.h"
#include "ContrastPlugIn.h"
using namespace Drawing;
using namespace ContrastPlugIn;

/// <summary>
/// Method that does the contrast calculation
/// based on the provided parameters.
/// This method is invoked by the application.
/// </summary>
/// <requirements>F:image_contrast_and_color</requirements>
void Contrast::ProcessImage(Bitmap& image,
             int param, int unused1, int unused2)
{
  // Image dimensions.
  unsigned int maxX = image.Width;
  unsigned int maxY = image.Height;
  // Pixel count initialized with 0.
  unsigned long totNumPixels = 0;
  // Number of possible color values.
  unsigned int maxPixValue = 0;
  // Stores color value of pixel.
  Color mycolor;
  // stores the new color values.
  int red, blue, green = 0;
  // Slider value normalized.
  const double step = ((double)param)/100.0;
  // Correction factor.
  double factor = (1.0 + step);

  int sum = 0;
  int pixVal = 0;
  double lutVal = 0;

  // Constant values for luminance calculation.
  const double rFactor = 0.299;
  const double gFactor = 0.587;
  const double bFactor = 0.114;
  // Only formats that have
```

```
// R, G, and B values stored as
// 8 bits per pixel are supported.
switch(image.PixelFormat)
{
case(Imaging::PixelFormat::Format24bppRgb):
case(Imaging::PixelFormat::Format32bppArgb):
case(Imaging::PixelFormat::Format32bppRgb):
case(Imaging::PixelFormat::Format32bppPArgb):
  maxPixValue = 255;
  break;
default:
  throw(new Exception("Error, Pixel format not supported for
          this operation!"));
  break;
}
```

Note that one of the problems with this algorithm is that it is sensitive to noise within the image.

Armed with this knowledge about histogram calculations, you'll find that the implementation of the contrast improvement functionality is relatively straightforward.

The Implementation of the Contrast Plugin

First, add two `using` statements to the `.cpp` file. In addition, add the necessary local variables that are needed for the contrast calculation.

The implementation presented in this section works correctly only when all three color values are stored as 8-bit values. To make sure that the image passed to the `ProcessImage` method is in the supported format, add a `switch` statement that checks this assumption. If the pixel format is supported, we set the maximum pixel value to 255; otherwise, we throw an exception that is caught by the application.

Next, declare the histogram as an array of unsigned integers with 255 entries (the maximum number of color values a pixel can have). Initialize all histogram values to 0. Then calculate the histogram by walking through all pixels in the image, calculate the corresponding grayscale value, and count the number of pixels having each grayscale value.

To extract a pixel's color information from an image, .NET provides a method on the `Bitmaps` class called `GetPixel(xPos, yPos)`. This method returns a value of type `color` that represents the color values of the pixel at the x position (xPos) and y position (yPos) of the image. Use that method to get the color information of the current pixel, and calculate the luminance of the current pixel. Add the pixel to the corresponding bucket of the histogram, and increase the total number of pixels counted so far by 1.

After the calculation of the histogram is finished, the lookup table is calculated. Create a lookup table using a for loop. Iterate through all the elements of the histogram. Implement the inner for loop, which accumulates the number of pixels having gray values less than the current one. Then calculate the lookup table entry for the current histogram entry by multiplying the sum by the number of gray values a pixel can take. Divide the result by the total number of pixels in the image, and reset the sum to 0 for the next iteration (see Listing 8.8).

Listing 8.8 ContrastPlugIn, Part 2

```
// Define the histogram and the lookup table
unsigned int* histogram = new unsigned int[maxPixValue];
unsigned int* lut = new unsigned int[maxPixValue];

// Initialize all values in the
// histogram to 0.
for( unsigned int q = 0; q <= maxPixValue; ++q)
{
  histogram[q] = 0;
}

// Walk through the whole image and
// calculate the histogram.
for(unsigned int i = 0; i < maxY; ++i)
{
  for(unsigned int j = 0; j < maxX; ++j)
  {
    // Get the color pixel value at the current position.
    Color mycolor = image.GetPixel(j,i);
    // Calculate the luminance value
    pixVal = (int)(((double)mycolor.R * rFactor) +
      ((double)mycolor.G * gFactor) +
      ((double)mycolor.B * bFactor));
    // Add the pixel to the histogram
    histogram[pixVal] += 1;
    // Count number of pixels in
```

```
      // the histogram.
      totNumPixels++;
    }
  }

  // Walk through all the values in the histogram
  for( unsigned int k = 0; k <= maxPixValue; ++k)
  {
    for( unsigned int l = 0; l < k; ++l)
    {
      // Add all pixels that were
      // accounted for already
      sum += histogram[l];
    }
    // Calculate the lookup table.
    // Accumulate all pixels with a
    // lower value * maximum value
    // divided by the total number of pixels in the
    // image, resulting in the new pixel value of the current
    // gray value.
    lut[k] = (int)(((double)sum*(double)maxPixValue)/
                    (double)totNumPixels);
    // reset the sum.
    sum = 0;
  }
```

With the lookup table in place, we can then process the image, as shown in Listing 8.9. Create a loop that walks through the entire image. Retrieve the color value for the current pixel, and calculate the luminance value for it. Look up the value for the current gray value by retrieving it from the lookup table. Then calculate each color component for the current pixel using a helper function called `calcNewValue`.

This helper function calculates the new color value, taking into account the contribution of the current color to the luminance factor. The result is then multiplied by `correctionFactor`, which represents the factor based on the track bar position in the GUI. Implement this helper function.

After the new color components of the current pixel have been calculated, set the color of the current pixel to the new color using `SetPixel` (xPos, yPos, Color::FromArgb(red, green, blue)). The overloaded method used to set the new color value is `Color::FromArgb`, which takes the three color values red, green, and blue as parameters. After the last pixel is calculated, the image is displayed on the screen.

Listing 8.9 ContrastPlugIn, Part 3

```
// Walk through the whole image
for(unsigned int i = 0; i < maxY; ++i)
{
  for(unsigned int j = 0; j < maxX; ++j)
  {
    // Get the current pixel value
    mycolor = image.GetPixel(j,i);
    // Calculate the resulting gray value
    pixVal = (unsigned int)(((double)mycolor.R * rFactor) +
              ((double)mycolor.G * gFactor) +
              ((double)mycolor.B * bFactor));
    // Get the lookup table value for the current pixel.
    lutVal = (double)lut[pixVal];

    // Calculate the new red, green, and blue value.
    red = calcNewValue(mycolor.R, rFactor, pixVal,
          factor, maxPixValue, lutVal);
    green = calcNewValue(mycolor.G, gFactor, pixVal,
          factor, maxPixValue, lutVal);
    blue = calcNewValue(mycolor.B, bFactor, pixVal,
          factor, maxPixValue, lutVal);
    // Set the pixel to the new RGB value
    image.SetPixel(j, i, Color::FromArgb(red, green, blue));
  }
}
}
unsigned int
Contrast::calcNewValue(unsigned int colorValue,
double colorFactor, unsigned int pixValue,
double correctionFactor, unsigned int maxPixValue,
                  double lookUpValue)
{
  // Calculate the new color value for the current pixel.
  // Take the source pixel color
  // distribution into account.
  if(pixValue < 1)
    pixValue = 1;
```

```
double result = (((double)colorValue*lookUpValue)/
        (double)pixValue) *correctionFactor;
// Check for overflow
result = ((result < maxPixValue) ? result : maxPixValue);
// Check for underflow
result = ((result < 0) ? 0 : result);

return (unsigned int)result;
}
```

It is obvious from this implementation that the image-processing calculation can take some time. If large images are loaded, the calculation will not be finished in interactive speed, and the user will have to wait for the result to be displayed on the screen. Certainly there are many opportunities to optimize this code. Some of the possible optimization improvements are shown in Chapter 10. But for now, we are happy to have the functionality in place.

In the next implementation step, we add an Apply button to the GUI to enable the user to apply the image processing over the entire image. In addition, we add a Reset button to restore the originally loaded image, in case the user wants to undo the changes.

The Apply and Reset Buttons

Drag two buttons from the Toolbox onto the Image Processing tab control, and rename them `ApplyProcessingButton` and `IPResetButton`. Double-click on the buttons to generate the click event handlers for both buttons. The `ApplyButton_Click` method calls the `applyImageProcessing` method and provides the loaded image as `tmpBitmap` to `PlugInInterface`.

Next, invalidate the control and update `thumbImage` to reflect the change in the Preview Image pane. The implementation is shown in Listing 8.10. The `IPResetButton_click` event handler simply calls the already implemented Reset button event handler and updates `thumbImage`.

Listing 8.10 The Apply and Reset Buttons

```
/// <summary>
/// Applies the current image-processing
/// operation to the currently loaded image.
```

```
/// </summary>
private void ApplyProcessingButton_Click(object sender,
System.EventArgs e)
{
  // Store a copy of the loaded image, on which the
  // image processing calculation is performed.
  plugInInterface.TmpBitmap = (Bitmap)PictureObject.LoadedImage;
  // Call the plugin via the interface
  plugInInterface.ApplyImageProcessing();
  // Invalidate the image displayed to show the changes.
  customScrollableControl.Invalidate();
  // Update the thumbnail image
  thumbImage = PictureObject.LoadedImage.GetThumbnailImage(
    picturePreView.Width,
    picturePreView.Height,null, IntPtr.Zero);
  // Let's see the result
  DisplayImage();
}
/// <summary>
/// Resets the image to the originally
/// loaded image.
/// </summary>
private void IPResetButton_Click(object sender,
            System.EventArgs e)
{
  this.ResetButton_Click(sender, e);
  // Create a new thumbImage and display it in the preview pane.
  thumbImage = PictureObject.LoadedImage.GetThumbnailImage(
      picturePreView.Width,
      picturePreView.Height,null, IntPtr.Zero);
  picturePreView.Image = (Image)thumbImage.Clone();
}
```

Now that we have implemented the infrastructure, the Apply button, and the Reset button, it is easy to add new plugin functionality to the application.

The general strategy for adding new functionality through dynamically loadable components (or plugins) is to add the GUI element and create an event handler for the user action on the GUI element. In the event handler, call the `applyImageProcessing` method and implement the plugin. In our plugin implementation, different .NET languages work together seamlessly. No special action had to be taken to use the C++ plugin within the C# code.

The Brightness Plugin Implementation Using J#

The next requirement to be implemented is the brightness correction plugin. To show that all .NET languages work as easily together as in the plugin just shown, we show the implementation of the brightness correction feature using J#. The first task is to create the GUI control and the event handler that will call the plugin.

Do It Yourself You have been assigned the task of implementing the `TrackBar` control according to the requirement specification. The implementation is very similar to the implementation of the contrast plugin described earlier in this chapter.

Compared with the contrast calculation, it's fairly trivial to implement the brightness correction. First, add to the solution a new class library project in the J# language, and call the new project `BrightnessPlugIn`. Then adjust the project settings to save the assemblies in the corresponding directory, as described for `ContrastPlugIn`.

Pass the `TrackBar` value as a parameter to the plugin interface instance. The brightness correction functionality adds the application-provided value to the luminance value of each pixel. We normalize the passed value by dividing it by the luminance, and then we multiply the resulting value with each color value to get the resulting color. After that, we check the new value for overflow. The implementation can be seen in Listing 8.11.

Listing 8.11 The Brightness Correction Plugin

```
package BrightnessPlugIn;

import System.*;
import System.Drawing.*;
import System.Drawing.Imaging.*;
import System.Math.*;

/**
 * Brightness Plugin
```

```
 * This class is dynamically loaded by the
 * application. Only the parameters for
 * sourceImage and offset are used.
 */
public class BrightnessPlugIn
{
  public BrightnessPlugIn()
  {
  }
  /**
   * This method is invoked by the
   * application to do the brightness correction.
   */
  public void ProcessImage(Bitmap sourceImage, int offset, int unused1,
int unused2) throws System.Exception
  {
    // Luminance factors.
    double rFactor = 0.299;
    double gFactor = 0.5874;
    double bFactor = 0.114;
    // Get image dimensions.
    int width = sourceImage.get_Width();
    int height = sourceImage.get_Height();
    // Stores the color value of a pixel.
    Color mycolor;
    int maxPixValue = 0;
    int pixFormat =
Bitmap.GetPixelFormatSize(sourceImage.get_PixelFormat());
    // Check whether the pixel storage is 8
    // bits per pixel.
    switch(pixFormat)
    {
      case 24:
      case 32:
        maxPixValue = 255;
        break;
      default:
        throw(new System.Exception("Error, Pixel format not
                supported for this operation!"));

    }
```

```
      double luminance;
      // Walk through the image, calculate the
      // new pixel values.
      for(int i = 0; i < height; ++i)
      {
        for(int j = 0; j < width; ++j)
        {
          mycolor = sourceImage.GetPixel(j,i);
          luminance = mycolor.get_R()*rFactor +
            mycolor.get_G()*gFactor + mycolor.get_B()*bFactor;
          // Make sure luminance is bigger than 1.
          // If the value were much smaller,
          // a division by 0 exception could occur.
          if(System.Math.Abs(luminance) < 1)
            luminance = 1;
          // Calculate the normalized offset factor.
          luminance = ((double)offset + luminance)/luminance;
          // Calculate the new color values.
          int redValue = calcNewValue(mycolor.get_R(),
              maxPixValue, luminance);
          int greenValue = calcNewValue(mycolor.get_G(),
              maxPixValue, luminance);
          int blueValue = calcNewValue(mycolor.get_B(),
              maxPixValue, luminance);
          // Set the new color values.
          sourceImage.SetPixel(j, i, Color.FromArgb(redValue,
              greenValue, blueValue));
        }
      }
    }
    /**
     * This method calculates the final
     * value and checks for overflow and
     * underflow.
     */
    private int calcNewValue(int oldValue, int maxPixValue,
      double correctionFactor)
    {
      // Calculate the resulting color value.
      int result = (int)(oldValue * correctionFactor);
      // Check for overflow.
      result = ((result < maxPixValue) ? result : maxPixValue);
```

```
    // Check for underflow.
    result = ((result < 0) ? 0 : result);
    return result;
  }
}
```

In addition, we add to the project a reference to `System.Drawing.dll`. Compared with the calculation of the contrast correction, the brightness correction is less computationally expensive. But still, it will take some time if the calculation is applied to a large image.

The Color Correction Plugin Using Visual Basic

The functionality of color correction takes the `TrackBar` value and adds it to the corresponding color component of each pixel within the image.

Do It Yourself Implement the three color `TrackBar` controls according to the requirement specification. The implementation is very similar to the implementation of the previously described controls.

You can implement the plugin in Visual Basic (as in the solution provided on the accompanying CD) or in any other .NET language.

Hint: Make sure that the plugin is saved in the `bin` and `bind` directories. Otherwise, the component will not be found by the application. Also, do not forget to add the `using` statements and the references to the assembly namespace that is needed for the plugin functionality.

The Red Eye Removal Tool

The last component to be implemented provides the functionality that attempts to correct the appearance of red eyes within pictures. This plugin is implemented using the C# programming language.

If the red eye tool is selected and the mouse is moved inside the image, then a red rectangle is shown at the current position of the mouse. The size of the rectangle to be drawn is 10 pixels in width and height. Then, if the user clicks the mouse, the area within the rectangle is saved and the plugin is called. The plugin walks through each pixel within the rectangle area and reduces the red value of each pixel to 80 percent of its original value.

The first step in implementing the `RedEye` tool is to create a button on the Image Processing tab control. Rename the button `redEyeButton`, change the text to `Remove Red Eye`, and create an event handler for the click event. To use the red eye tool, we add a new enumeration member called `RedEyeTool` to the graphics tool enumeration. To select the tool when the mouse button is clicked, set `toolSelected` to `RedEyeTool` in the `redEye Button_click` event handler. In addition, we add a new flag, `mouseIn Control`, to the `PhotoEditorForm` class; this flag indicates whether or not the mouse is within `customScrollableControl`. Therefore, we set `mouseInControl` to `true` whenever the `customScrollableControl` Mouse Enter event handler is called, and we set `mouseInControl` to `false` when the `MouseLeave` event occurs.

If the mouse is within the control and the red eye tool is selected, then a red rectangle is drawn at the position of the cursor. To accommodate this behavior, we add the drawing code for the red rectangle to the `custom ScrollableControl_MouseMove` event handler. Then, to update the position of the mouse, we set `Param1` to the current x position of the mouse and set `Param2` to the y value if the `MouseMove` event is raised and the red eye tool is selected. Then we draw the loaded image, invalidate the control, and draw the rectangle with the width and height equal to 10 pixels. The pen used to draw the rectangle is red.

If the mouse is not moved within the control, then we must draw the red eye rectangle if `customScrollableControl` is repainted. Therefore, we add the code that draws the rectangle at the current mouse position if the paint event handler of the custom scrollable control is called.

To make the tool work, the last application change we make is to change the `MouseDown` event handler of `customScrollableControl`. Therefore, we call the `applyImageProcessing` method with the area of the image contained within the red rectangle as parameter.

Do It Yourself   Implement the described red eye removal functionality.
    Hint: The sample source code provided on the CD shows a possible implementation.

The plugin is implemented using C#. In the Photo Editor solution, create a new C# project that is of type `Class Library`. Name the project `Red EyePlugIn`, and rename the created class and constructor `RedEyePlugIn`. Change the build properties of the project to output the compiled assemblies into the `bind` or `bin` directory, and define a name for the XML documentation file.

We implement the plugin itself by walking through the pixels within the rectangular area shown on the screen. For each pixel within that area, the red component is reduced to 80 percent of its original value. The implementation of this feature can be seen in Listing 8.12.

Listing 8.12 The Red Eye Correction Plugin

```
using System;
using System.Drawing;

namespace RedEyePlugIn
{
  /// <summary>
  /// RedEyePlugIn class is loaded
  /// at run time by the application.
  /// </summary>
  /// <requirements>F:image_special_effects</requirements>
  public class RedEyePlugIn
  {
    /// <summary>
    /// Constructor.
    /// </summary>
    public RedEyePlugIn()
    {
    }
    /// <summary>
    /// ProcessImage method. Invoked by the application.
    /// Red component is reduced to 80% to remove red eyes.
    /// </summary>
    public void ProcessImage(Bitmap sourceImage,
            int xVal, int yVal, int areaVal)
    {
      Color myColor;
      // Walk through the area of the displayed
      // rectangle within the image.
      for(int i = yVal; i < (yVal + areaVal); ++i)
      {
        for (int j = xVal; j < (xVal + areaVal); ++j)
        {
          // Get the current pixel
          myColor = sourceImage.GetPixel(j,i);
```

```
        // Set the red value to 80% of the original value
        // and keep the other values.
    sourceImage.SetPixel(j, i,
        Color.FromArgb((int)(myColor.R*0.8),
            (int)(myColor.G), (int)(myColor.B)));
        }
      }
    }
  }
}
```

To compile the project we also add a reference to `System.Drawing.dll`. The resulting application is shown in Figure 8.9.

With the `RedEyePlugIn` functionality implemented, all required features for this iteration are provided. The next step is to write some unit tests to make sure the functionality is working as described in the requirements.

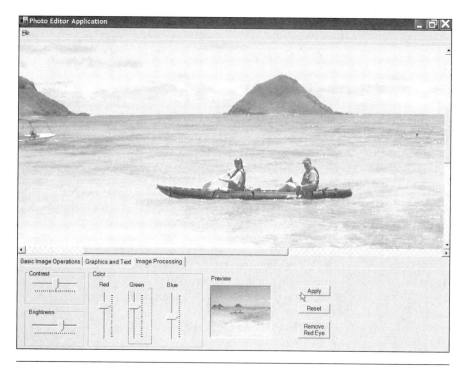

Figure 8.9 The New Application GUI

8.6 Unit Tests

T

The unit tests for the functionality implemented in this iteration must prove that the plugins that were developed can be loaded by an application at run time. In addition, the tests should show that the calculation is done correctly.

For image-processing algorithms such as the contrast functionality, it can be very difficult to prove exact correctness. For the unit tests in this chapter, the proof of correctness is to calculate some pixel values and then check them against the expected output. Ideally, the proof should validate that the calculation of all the pixels in the image is correct. In some cases, you can do this by applying a second algorithm that performs the same output by using a different algorithm.

Sometimes it is not possible to have a second algorithm to check the result against. In that case, it's very common to use a gold standard to verify the result of the images. The *gold standard* is a result that has been defined as correct by experts, and the actual output of the calculation is compared against it. After the standard is defined, the comparison can be made either automatically or manually. In addition, you can use techniques that rely on statistics, such as mean, standard variation, and average, to identify whether the features of the two images are the same or at least similar.

With this knowledge in mind, we implement the tests of the plugin functionality. The first test case we'll look at is the unit test for the contrast plugin.

8.6.1 The Contrast Plugin Unit Test

The strategy to test the contrast plugin is to create an image whose color values are all zero except for the center pixel. The center pixel will have different red, green, and blue values. This enables a simple calculation of the expected result value at the center position. Another advantage of taking only the center pixel is that it provides the ability to prove whether the calculated value was stored in the correct pixel location.

The implementation of the test is shown in Listing 8.13. First, we create an image with the dimensions 100×75 pixels. Then we create an instance of `PlugInInterface`. After that, we initialize all the image pixels to 0 as color values, except for the center pixel of the image. We set the center pixel color values to Red = 100, Green = 75, and Blue = 50. Now we call the `ApplyImageProcessing` method, making sure that before calling the method we set the requested plugin name and parameter values. After the calculation is applied, we check the center pixel and the pixel just left of it for correctness. We dispose of the created image, and the test is concluded.

Listing 8.13 The Contrast Plugin Unit Test Implementation

```
/// <summary>
/// Test for F:image_contrast_and_color.
/// Checks whether the contrast plugin
/// can be loaded at run time and whether the
/// calculation is correctly performed on the image.
/// </summary>
/// <test>F:image_contrast_and_color</test>
[Test] public void ContrastPlugInTest()
{
  const int width = 100;
  const int height = 75;

  Console.WriteLine("image_contrast");
  // Create a new bitmap.
  Bitmap testImage = new Bitmap(width, height);

  PlugInInterface loader = new PlugInInterface();
  // Set all pixels in the image to black (0),
  // except for the center pixel, which is set to
  // Red = 100, Green = 75, Blue = 50
  for(int i = 0; i < height; ++i)
  {
    for(int j = 0; j < width; ++j)
    {
      if( i == ((height/2)) && (j == (width/2)))
      {
        testImage.SetPixel(j, i, Color.FromArgb(100, 75, 50));
      }
      else
      {
        testImage.SetPixel(j, i, Color.FromArgb(0, 0, 0));
      }
    }
  }
  loader.TmpBitmap = testImage;
  loader.SliderName = "Contrast";
```

```
loader.Param1 = 1;
loader.Param2 = loader.Param3 = 0;
// Invoke the ProcessImage method from the
// contrast plugin.
loader.ApplyImageProcessing();
// Test the center pixel color value for correctness
Color pixColor = testImage.GetPixel(width/2, height/2);
Assertion.AssertEquals("Center Pixel Red Value",
  pixColor.R, 255);
Assertion.AssertEquals("Center Pixel Green Value",
  pixColor.G, 243);
Assertion.AssertEquals("Center Pixel Blue Value", pixColor.B, 162);

// Check whether position on pixel before the centerPixel is 0
// value color.
pixColor = testImage.GetPixel(width/2 -1, height/2);
Assertion.AssertEquals("Center Pixel Red Value",
  pixColor.R, 0);
Assertion.AssertEquals("Center Pixel Green Value",
  pixColor.G, 0);
Assertion.AssertEquals("Center Pixel Blue Value", pixColor.B, 0);
testImage.Dispose();
amIPassed = true;
}
```

Do It Yourself Implement other tests to prove the correctness of the calculation performed by the plugin.

Hint: Check an image with uniform pixel values and one with equally distributed color values. Also use various image sizes.

8.6.2 The Color Plugin Unit Test

Testing the color plugin is a straightforward task that includes creating an image with known color values, applying an offset on the color values, and then verifying that the result is correct.

The implementation is shown in Listing 8.14. Start by creating a new `PlugInInterface` object, and then create a new `Bitmap` image with the given width and height. Then set each pixel in the image to the values red = 110, green = 99, and blue = 76. Invoke the color plugin, and perform the calculation with the provided color correction values (red = 55, green = 8, blue = 100). After the calculation is finished, check each pixel to determine whether the color values correspond to the sum of the original plus the offset value. If everything is correct, then the test is passed.

Listing 8.14 The Color Plugin Unit Test Implementation

```
/// <summary>
/// Test for F:image_contrast_and_color.
/// Checks whether the color plugin
/// can be loaded at run time and whether the
/// calculation is correctly performed on the image.
/// </summary>
/// <test>F:image_contrast_and_color</test>
[Test] public void ColorPlugInTest()
{
  const int width = 125;
  const int height = 90;
  Color pixColor;
  PlugInInterface loader = new PlugInInterface();
  Console.WriteLine("image_contrast_and_color");
  // Create a new bitmap.
  Bitmap testImage = new Bitmap(width, height);
  // Set all pixels in the image to
  // Red = 110, Green = 99, Blue = 76)
  for(int i = 0; i < height; ++i)
  {
    for(int j = 0; j < width; ++j)
    {
      testImage.SetPixel(j, i, Color.FromArgb(110, 99, 76));
    }
  }
  // Invoke the ProcessImage method from the
  // color plugin.
  loader.TmpBitmap = testImage;
  loader.SliderName = "Color";
  loader.Param1 = 55;
  loader.Param2 = 8;
  loader.Param3 = 100;
  loader.ApplyImageProcessing();
  // Walk through the entire image
```

```
for(int i = 0; i < height; ++i)
{
  for(int j = 0; j < width; ++j)
  {
    // Check each pixel and color component
    // for correctness.
    pixColor = testImage.GetPixel(j, i);
    Assertion.AssertEquals("Pixel Red Value",
      pixColor.R, 165);
    Assertion.AssertEquals("Pixel Green Value",
      pixColor.G, 107);
    Assertion.AssertEquals("Pixel Blue Value", pixColor.B, 176);
  }
}
testImage.Dispose();
amIPassed = true;
}
```

Do It Yourself Implement other tests to prove the correctness of the calculation performed by the plugin.

Hint: Check an image with uniform pixel values and one with equally distributed color values. Also use various image sizes.

8.6.3 The Red Eye Plugin Unit Test

The strategy for testing the red eye plugin is similar to the previously shown test implementations. First, an image is created with known color values. Then the red eye plugin is loaded with the required parameters. Then the result is checked against the expected color values. Listing 8.15 shows the implementation of the unit test.

The implementation of this test is very similar to that of the previous ones. The main difference lies in the calculation of the expected output values. For the red eye tool, only a rectangular part of the image is taken into account in applying the red eye reduction. In the example shown, the area of interest for the red eye tool is between the coordinates x = 50, y = 45 and x = 59, y = 54. Within that area, the tool reduces the red values of the image to 80 percent of their original values.

Listing 8.15 The Red Eye Plugin Unit Test Implementation

```
/// <summary>
/// Test for F:image_special_effects.
/// Checks whether the red eye plugin
/// can be loaded at run time and whether the
/// calculation is correctly performed on the image.
/// </summary>
/// <test>F:image_special_effects</test>
[Test] public void RedEyePlugInTest()
{
  const int width = 75;
  const int height = 90;
  Color pixColor;
  PlugInInterface loader = new PlugInInterface();
  Console.WriteLine("image_contrast_and_color");
  // Create a new bitmap.
  Bitmap testImage = new Bitmap(width, height);
  // Set all pixels in the image to
  // Red = 100, Green = 198, Blue = 55
  for(int i = 0; i < height; ++i)
  {
    for(int j = 0; j < width; ++j)
    {
      testImage.SetPixel(j, i, Color.FromArgb(100, 198, 55));
    }
  }
  // Invoke the ProcessImage method from the
  // red eye plugin.
  loader.TmpBitmap = testImage;
  loader.SliderName = "RedEye";
  loader.Param1 = 50;
  loader.Param2 = 45;
  loader.Param3 = 10;
  loader.ApplyImageProcessing();
  // Walk through the entire image
  for(int i = 0; i < height; ++i)
  {
    for(int j = 0; j < width; ++j)
    {
      // Check each pixel and color component
      // for correctness.
      pixColor = testImage.GetPixel(j, i);
```

```
   if(((j  >= 50) && (j < 60)) && ((i  >= 45) && (i < 55)))
   {
     Assertion.AssertEquals("Pixel Red Value",
       pixColor.R, 80);
   }
   else
   {
     Assertion.AssertEquals("Pixel Red Value",
       pixColor.R, 100);
   }
   Assertion.AssertEquals("Pixel Green Value",
     pixColor.G, 198);
   Assertion.AssertEquals("Pixel Blue Value", pixColor.B, 55);
  }
 }

 testImage.Dispose();
 amIPassed = true;
}
```

Figure 8.10 shows the output of a test run using the NUnit GUI.

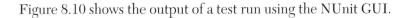

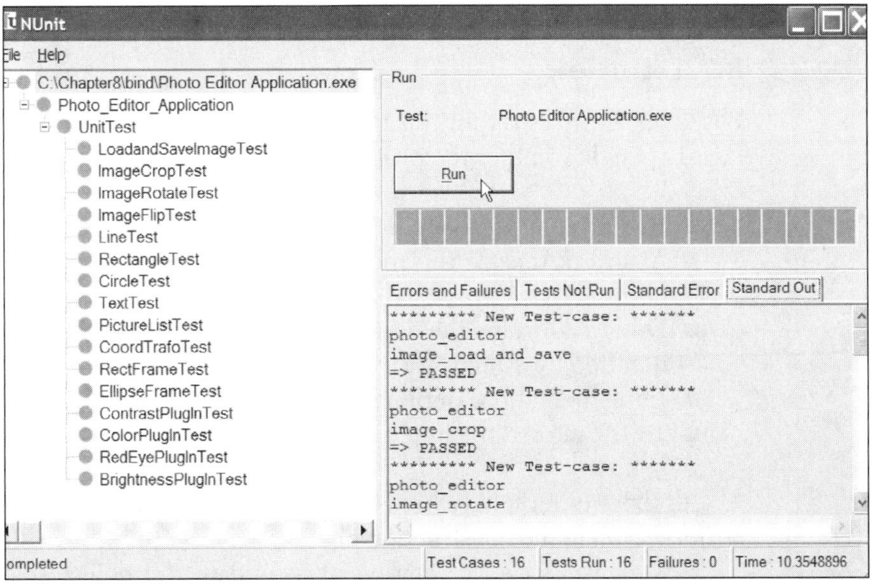

Figure 8.10 NUnit Output of Dynamically Loadable Component Test

---

Do It Yourself Implement other tests to prove the correctness of the calculation performed by the plugin.

In addition, implement some test cases for the brightness plugin. The strategy for testing the brightness functionality is very similar to that of the tests shown for the other plugins. Some tests for the brightness plugin are provided with the distributed source code on the book's CD.

Hint: Check an image with uniform pixel values and one with equally distributed color values. Also use various image sizes.

8.7 Conclusion

The objective for this chapter was to implement several image-processing functionalities that enable the user to alter the image on the pixel level. All required functionality that was scheduled for this iteration went through the core workflows: requirements, analysis, design, implementation, and test. The implementation was run, and initial unit testing was performed. In addition, we updated the project planning documents. The code documentation was generated, and the project is ready for the end of iteration review.

8.7.1 Review

Based on the goals set for this iteration, we review the following work artifacts to decide whether the project can proceed to the next iteration.

- Requirements: Refine the requirements and system scope.
- Analysis: Analyze the requirements by describing what the system does.
- Design: Develop the design of the functionality implemented in this iteration by using UML.
- Implementation: Implement the required functionality.
- Test: Unit-test the implemented features.

All these criteria have been fulfilled, so the project can move on to the next iteration in the construction phase.

Before we move on, however, we update the defect tracking sheet because one of the developers identified a scenario in which the application crashes. This defect is set to high priority and is scheduled to be fixed in the eighth iteration.

8.8 References for Further Reading

Reflection

Jeffrey Richter, *Applied Microsoft .NET Framework Programming* (Redmond, WA: Microsoft Press, 2002)

Simon Robinson et al., *Professional C#* (Birmingham, UK: Wrox Press, 2001)

```
http://msdn.microsoft.com/msdnmag/issues/02/08/NETReflection/
    default.aspx
```

```
http://www.c-sharpcorner.com/1/Reflection_in_net.asp
```

Image Processing

Nick Efford, *Digital Image Processing: A Practical Introduction Using Java* (Boston: Addison-Wesley, 2000)

James D. Foley et al., *Computer Graphics: Principles and Practice* (Reading, MA: Addison-Wesley, 1996)

Ihtisham Kabir, *High Performance Computer Imaging* (Greenwich, CT: Manning Publications Co., 1996)

CHAPTER 9

Accessing System Resources

 Unified Process:
Construction Phase and Seventh Iteration

This chapter discusses the seventh iteration of the project, in which we integrate unmanaged code into the photo editor application. Although .NET assemblies are usually easier to build, deploy, and maintain, there are valid reasons to invoke unmanaged code from a .NET application:

- It lets you use legacy components as building blocks for new applications.
- It improves execution speed of certain algorithms, a critical consideration.
- It gives you access to system resources or libraries that are not exposed through the .NET Framework.

This chapter demonstrates the latter case: the integration of a new feature based on OpenGL rendering functions.

This chapter continues the construction phase, and the goal is the successful implementation of the requirement F:image_3dtext and its unit test. Again, the go/no-go criterion is based on the unit test result.

9.1 Refining Requirements for 3D Text Display

R First let's refine the 3D text display requirement from Chapter 4 to better describe what exactly will be implemented. The initial requirement key, F:image_3dtext, is very general and does not yet address possible constraints, assumptions, or dependencies. For example, the 3D text function would not be practical if the user could not customize the appearance of the text by changing things like color, position, or font style. We need to decide which attributes will be customizable and which will simply be set to default values.

For the text, we plan to make the following attributes customizable by the user:

- A single line of text
- Position in the image where the text is placed
- Font color
- Font type (for example, Arial)
- Font style (for example, bold)
- Font size

In addition, the requirement that we need to fulfill says that users will be able to merge this text as a three-dimensional object into an existing image. Converting a two-dimensional line of text into a 3D object adds a variety of parameters:

- Depth of the 3D object: Standard text has only two dimensions: width and height. We need to select a depth, which adds the third dimension.
- Orientation or rotation of the 3D object: Looking straight at a 3D object does not show its depth and will not give a 3D impression. Only rotating the object will lead to nice effects.
- Lighting, material, and shading parameters: If those parameters are not set correctly, the entire surface of the rendered object (all its sides) might appear in the same color, thereby not allowing the user to recognize corners. It is necessary, for example, to set up a directional light to create shadows that enhance the shape of an object. Furthermore, material properties define an object's shininess or reflections that are visible on the object.

Our customer, the printing and embossing business, needs to be included in this refinement of requirement keys. There are a large number of options that we could implement but at the cost of impacting the schedule. Together with the customer, we create and agree on a new list of refined keys that does not require new planning and allocation of additional resources. Table 9.1 lists the refined requirement keys for implementing three-dimensional text.

Table 9.1 Refined Requirements for Three-Dimensional Text

Requirement	Type	Summary
F:image_3dtext	Functional	The photo editor shall allow the user to add three-dimensional text to an image.
F:image_3dtext_color	Functional	The user shall be able to select a color for 3D text.
F:image_3dtext_font	Functional	The user shall be able to select a font type (Arial, Helvetica, etc.) and style (bold, italic) for 3D text.
F:image_3dtext_rotate	Functional	The user shall be able to rotate the 3D text along x, y, and z axes.
C:image_3dtext_singleline	Constraint	3D text can be added only to a single line at a time.

9.2 Three-Dimensional Rendering Technologies

A⟩ Next, we analyze various technologies that can be used to render three-dimensional text in the photo editor application. We evaluate the strength and limitations of each technology before we decide on how to implement this requirement.

9.2.1 GDI+ and DirectX

Taking a closer look at GDI+, we realize that our requirements for three-dimensional text cannot be fulfilled using the graphics functionality provided by the .NET class library. All classes in GDI+ are restricted to two dimensions. This does not really surprise us because Microsoft offers a powerful 3D graphics library called DirectX (formerly Direct3D). Unfortunately, this library is targeted toward professional game developers. In addition to being dependent on the installation of a fairly large DirectX SDK package for development, it is rather difficult to learn and would not quite fit within the context of this book.

9.2.2 OpenGL

An easier-to-learn alternative to DirectX is OpenGL. It is also a powerful graphics library, providing—as DirectX does—access to the rendering capabilities of the video card installed in the user's computer. Because the OpenGL operations are performed by the video card itself and not in software, programs using OpenGL are also referred to as *hardware accelerated*. A true acceleration, of course, can be observed only if the algorithm is complex enough, and that is usually the case for rendering three-dimensional scenes. So it is arguable whether a two-dimensional photo-editing program should rely on special hardware to do certain operations or whether it would be better to implement them in software.

9.2.3 Software versus Hardware Rendering

Compared with the latest 3D games, rendering a line of text might seem to be a fairly simple task that could be implemented entirely in software without introducing any hardware dependencies. Unfortunately it is not simple. To achieve nice-looking results, you must be familiar with lighting models, shading, perspective projections, and so on. Even for a highly skilled person, implementing a software rendering algorithm from scratch is a time-consuming task. This is especially significant when we know that we can achieve a similar result with only a few lines of code using a 3D graphics library.

The easiest and fastest method to implement the 3D text feature appears to be OpenGL. Also, in recent years almost every PC sold comes with an OpenGL-compatible graphics card. As a result, we will not introduce any dependency on "special" hardware as long as we use no chip-dependent extensions. We add a constraint to the list of requirements stating the OpenGL graphics card dependency of the 3D text feature, as shown in Table 9.2.

Table 9.2 OpenGL Requirement for Three-Dimensional Text

Requirement	Type	Summary
`C:image_3dtext_opengl`	Constraint	Rendering three-dimensional text requires a graphics card compatible with OpenGL 1.2. No vendor-specific extension may be used.

9.3 Analyzing User Interface Needs

During the requirements analysis, we have identified a number of attributes that are user-customizable. Obviously, users must enter the text to be rendered in addition to selecting font, color, and orientation. The easiest way to collect all this information is through a Windows Form. This form can combine all inputs for the 3D text feature by providing controls for text, font, color, positions, and rotation. Figure 9.1 shows the desired layout for this form.

.NET provides access to Windows common dialogs for selecting a font and picking a color. These dialogs, shown in Figure 9.2, can be invoked by pressing the corresponding button on the 3D text form.

9.4 Using OpenGL.NET

We have already concluded that the OpenGL library will be used to implement the 3D text functionality. Now we must develop a design that allows the implementation of this feature within the photo editor application.

All .NET code is *managed*. This means that the .NET runtime has control over the code and can enforce things such as security rules or garbage collection. The OpenGL library, however, is not managed by the .NET runtime. It is therefore considered *unmanaged code* and requires special handling. To access unmanaged code from a .NET application, the code must be contained in a DLL.

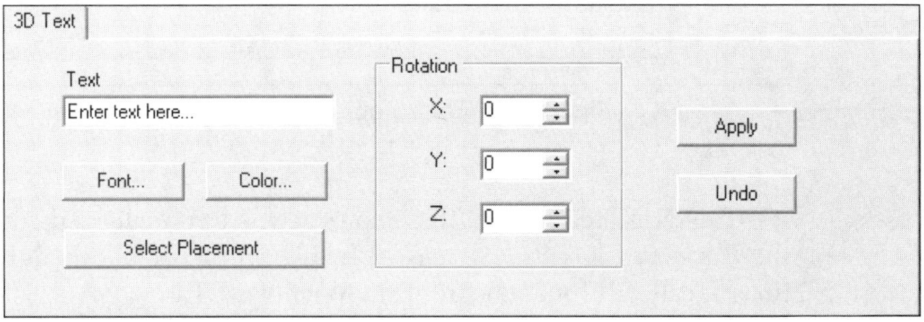

Figure 9.1 3D Text Form

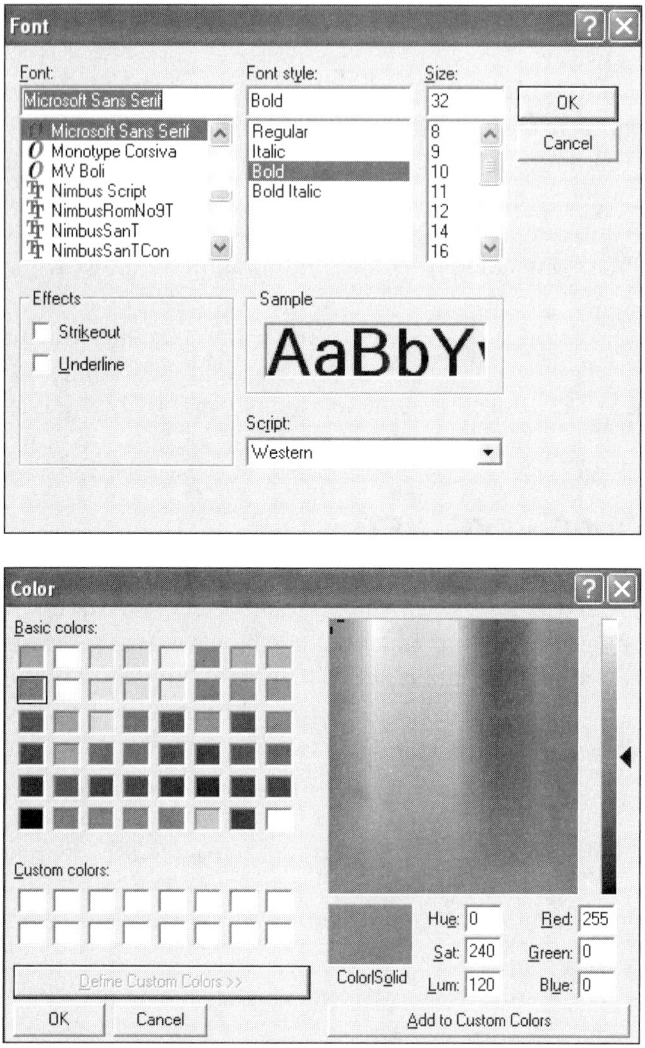

Figure 9.2 Font (Top) and Color Picker Forms

The .NET technology that allows access to unmanaged code is called the *Platform Invocation service* (PInvoke). PInvoke allows .NET applications to call API functions from any Windows DLL.

One approach to the integration of OpenGL rendering capabilities into the photo editor would be to declare all needed OpenGL API functions from `opengl32.dll` and `glu32.dll` within the .NET application. Another approach would be to build a new DLL that provides some high-level functions to render 3D text. Because all interfaces to unmanaged code in .NET, along with their parameters, must be declared manually, we decide to build a new DLL that provides only a few API functions that allow the photo editor to add 3D text to an image.

9.4.1 Rendering Three-Dimensional Text with OpenGL

We need very little knowledge about OpenGL to define the interfaces for the 3D Text DLL.

To render text using OpenGL, we create a window and a *rendering context* within that window. All OpenGL operations are rendered into the rendering context and are automatically displayed in the associated window.

For the photo editor application, however, offline rendering is desired. This means that we are not interested in displaying the text directly in a window but instead want to merge it into an existing `Bitmap` object that represents the loaded image. There are vendor-specific extensions (p-Buffer) for that purpose. However, the requirement `image_3dtext` prohibits the use of extensions, including p-Buffer, that are limited to a specific kind of graphics card.

Another way to achieve the same result is to create a window without making it visible on the screen. We can then read the content of the rendering context using the `glReadPixel` command.

Several libraries provide utility functions for drawing text in OpenGL, and some of them are even platform-independent. But because platform interoperability is not a requirement for the photo editor, the easiest and most straightforward approach should be taken. In our opinion this is to use the `wglUseFontOutlines` API function, which is supported on all Windows platforms. It directly converts a TrueType font into a set of OpenGL drawing commands. These commands are stored in lists, one for each letter. To draw text, you call those lists using the `glCallLists` API function.

The OpenGL library functions as a state machine. To modify the orientation or position of an object, you change the OpenGL state before drawing. For example, `glTranslate` modifies the translation of all objects drawn thereafter. In the same way, `glColor` changes the color in which those objects are rendered.

Having a basic understanding of OpenGL, we can now continue defining the interfaces for the 3D Text DLL as an extension to the photo editor application.

9.4.2 Three-Dimensional Text DLL Interfaces

Earlier in this chapter we decided that the 3D Text DLL will provide high-level API functions to render the text. Then we discovered that rendering text requires the creation of a window as well as conversion of a TrueType font into OpenGL commands. Both steps are rather time-consuming and should not be repeated every time the user adjusts the font color or the text position. Therefore, it makes sense to split these tasks into dedicated API functions. Table 9.3 lists the proposed API functions that we are planning to implement.

Before you define interfaces, it's a good practice to evaluate the usage of the proposed API functions in a sequence diagram for a typical use case. This helps you to understand the context in which the API functions are used. It also may help you discover wrong assumptions or may even lead to simplifications early on. The sequence diagram in Figure 9.3 shows how the API functions are invoked when the 3D text feature is used.

Table 9.3 Proposed 3D Text DLL API Functions

API Function Name	Parameters	Summary
CreateRC	Dimensions	Creates an OpenGL window and rendering context of the specified size
DeleteRC	None	Destroys a previously created window and rendering context
CreateOutlineFont	Font name, Font style	Converts the given TrueType font into OpenGL drawing commands
DeleteOutlineFont	None	Deletes a previously created OpenGL font
RenderText	Text, text size, color, rotation, image buffer	Renders text with the given attributes

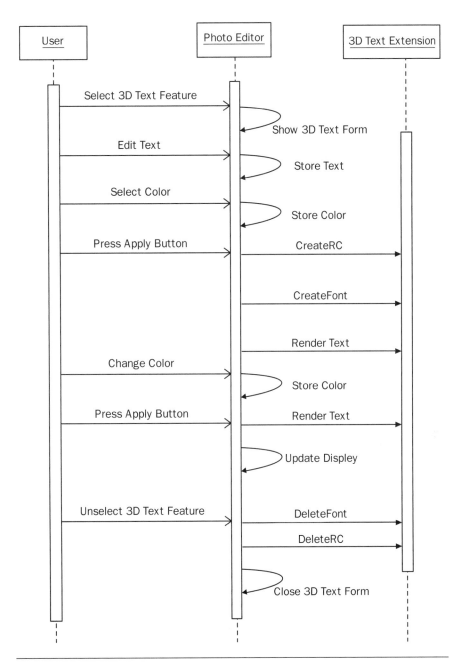

Figure 9.3 Sequence Diagram for 3D Text Feature

9.5 Adding 3D Text to the Photo Editor Application

The implementation consists of two parts. First, we implement and test the 3D Text DLL, using the graphics hardware for rendering. In the next step we add the user interface to the photo editor to complete the integration of the 3D text feature.

9.5.1 The 3D Text DLL Extension

Let's begin by creating a new project for the 3D text extension. Start Visual Studio, and open the Photo Editor solution. Then add a new project to the Photo Editor solution (right-click on it in Solution Explorer). Choose Visual C++ Projects, and then Win32 Project in the Win32 folder. Set the project name to 3DText and press OK. In the Win32 Application wizard, switch to the Application Settings window and set the application type to DLL before pressing Finish (see Figure 9.4).

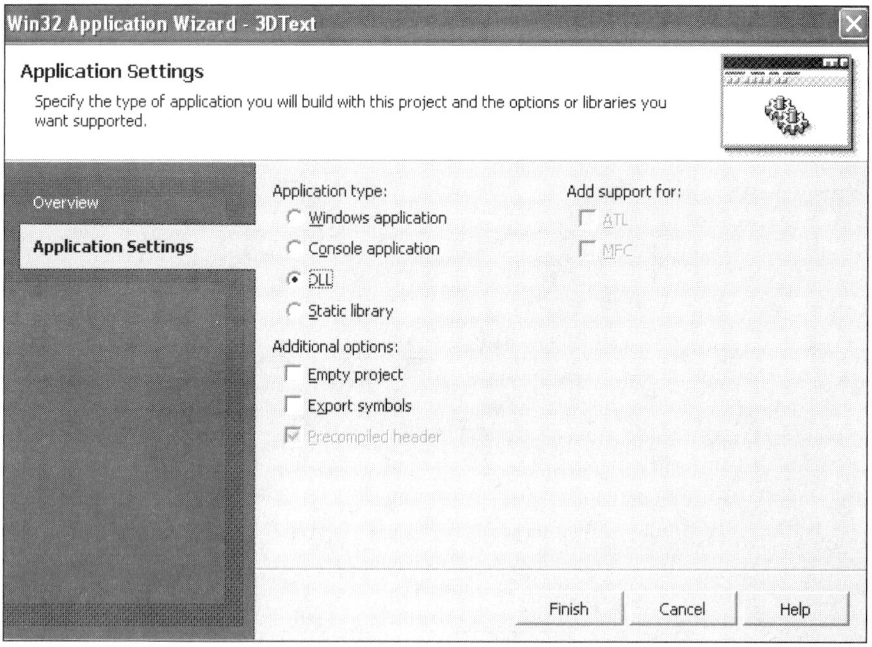

Figure 9.4 Win32 Application Wizard

The Application wizard creates a project. Using its context menu, make it the default startup project. Additionally, we change the configuration setting for Output Directory under the project properties to `bind` in debug configuration and `bin` in release configuration. As in all other projects, the build targets are now stored in a common `bin` (`bind`) folder.

The project contains the `3DText.cpp` file, to which we will add all code necessary for rendering three-dimensional text. Unlike typical C++ DLLs, there is no need to declare all exported functions in a separate header file because it cannot be used (included) from a .NET application. Later we discuss how interfaces to external DLLs can be declared within .NET applications.

OpenGL Window and Rendering Context

First, let's implement the basics. We start by creating an OpenGL window and rendering context, which are needed for any kind of OpenGL rendering. To access the OpenGL functions, add the `includes` shown in Listing 9.1 to the `stdafx.h` file.

Listing 9.1 stdafx.h: OpenGL includes

```
// stdafx.h : include file for standard system include files,
// or project-specific include files that are used frequently, but
// are changed infrequently
//

#pragma once

#define WIN32_LEAN_AND_MEAN      // Exclude rarely used stuff from
                                 // Windows headers
// Windows Header Files:
#include <windows.h>

// TODO: reference additional headers your program requires here
#include <gl\gl.h>   // OpenGL32
#include <gl\glu.h>  // Glu32
#include <gl\glaux.h>  // Glaux
```

We must also update the project configuration to reflect the dependencies on the OpenGL libraries. Open the 3D Text Property Pages window, and add the following libraries under Linker | Input | Additional Dependencies for all configurations (see Figure 9.5):

- `opengl32.lib`
- `glu32.lib`
- `glaux.lib`

Next, we implement the API function `CreateRC`. This function sets up an OpenGL rendering context in which we will render the text object. The initialization involves six steps:

1. Create a new (invisible) window: OpenGL needs a window handle in order to create a rendering context. Because we do not want to display the rendered result directly but instead want to copy it into the photo editor application, the window is not made visible and remains in the hidden state. Because there is no need for special handling of any window messages (such as mouse events), we

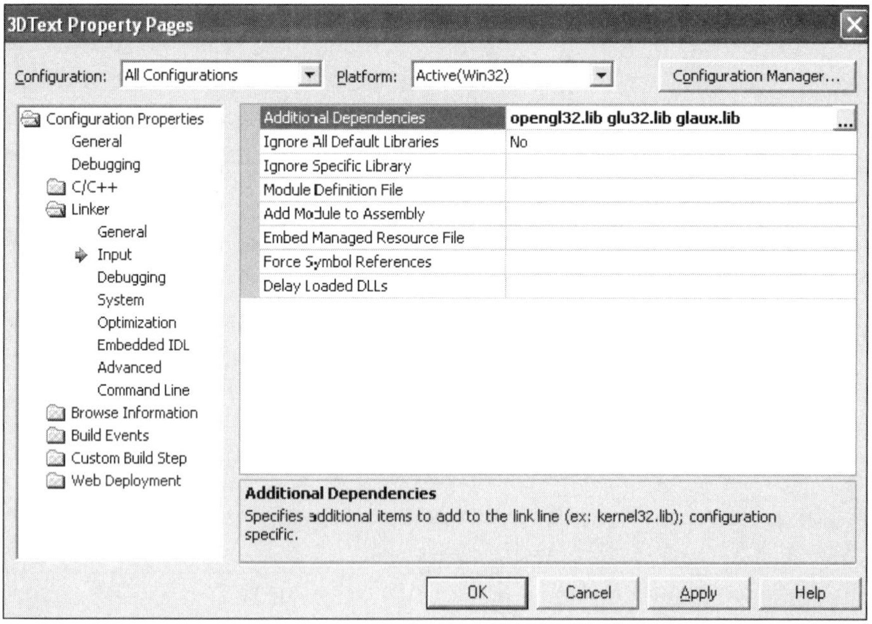

Figure 9.5 Adding OpenGL Libraries to Linker Dependencies

simply use the predefined system class for static windows. Furthermore, the window is created frameless so that its client area exactly matches the window size. In this way, the window will be exactly the same size as the rendering context, something that simplifies the later reading of the image buffer of the rendering context.

2. Check supported pixel formats: Some graphics cards may not support the required color depth or resolution. Therefore, we first query whether the installed graphics hardware supports the 24-bit RGB color format.

3. Set a suitable pixel format: After confirming that the 24-bit RGB color format is supported, we set the pixel format for the rendering context.

4. Create the rendering context: The rendering context is our interface to the graphics hardware. Before we can issue any OpenGL rendering calls, we must create and activate (make current) a rendering context.

5. Set up for 3D rendering: As discussed during the requirements analysis, there are many things to configure when we render 3D objects. After we create the rendering context, we can initially set those options that are static and not customizable by the user. When rendering with OpenGL, you can select an area within the rendering context where the rendering results are written. In our case, the viewport should match the size of the window. Also, the projection is set to perspective to achieve a better 3D impression. Finally, we define the camera or eye position within this method using the `gluLookAt` command. This command also lets us play a little trick to overcome a coordinate incompatibility between OpenGL and GDI+. Whereas in GDI+ the first image row at index zero refers to the top of an image, OpenGL assumes the opposite. However, by passing a negative up vector to `gluLookAt` we can compensate for this.

6. Store the dimensions of the rendering context: If we store the dimensions of the rendering context after it is initialized, there is no need to pass those arguments again when the text is later rendered.

The implementation of `DeleteRC` is far simpler; this function releases rendering and the device context and then destroys the window. Listing 9.2 shows the code for the both `CreateRC` and `DeleteRC`.

Listing 9.2 3DText.cpp: The CreateRC and DeleteRC Functions

```
// 3DText.cpp : Defines the entry point for the DLL application.
//

#include "stdafx.h"

static HWND hWnd;        // OpenGL Window Handle
static HDC hDC;          // Device Context (needed to create RC)
static HGLRC hRC;        // Rendering Context
static int imageDim[2];  // Dimensions of Offline Image Buffer
// Creates OpenGL window and rendering context of the specified size.
extern "C" BOOL PASCAL CreateRC(int width, int height)
{
  ////////////////////////////////
  // 1.) Create Window

  if ((width <= 0) || (height <= 0))
  {
    // invalid window size
    return FALSE;
  }

  // create window; do not need message handler, so use "Static" class
  hWnd = CreateWindowEx(0, "Static",
    "OpenGL Offline Rendering Context", WS_POPUP, 0, 0,
    width, height, NULL, NULL, GetModuleHandle(NULL), NULL);
  if (!hWnd)
  {
    // couldn't create a window
    return FALSE;
  }

  // get Windows device context
  hDC = GetDC(hWnd);
  if (!hDC)
  {
    // no device context
    return FALSE;
  }

  ////////////////////////////////
  // 2.) Check Supported Pixel Format
```

```
// set a default OpenGL pixel format descriptor, ask for 24-bit RGB
static PIXELFORMATDESCRIPTOR pfd =
{
  sizeof(PIXELFORMATDESCRIPTOR), 1,
  PFD_DRAW_TO_WINDOW | PFD_SUPPORT_OPENGL | PFD_DOUBLEBUFFER,
  PFD_TYPE_RGBA, 24,
  0, 0, 0, 0, 0, 0, 0, 0, 0, 0, 0, 0, 0, 16, 0, 0,
  PFD_MAIN_PLANE, 0, 0, 0, 0
};

// find a suitable pixel format
GLuint pixelFormat = ChoosePixelFormat(hDC,&pfd);
if (!pixelFormat)
{
      // desired format not supported
  return FALSE;
}

/////////////////////////////
// 3.) Set Pixel Format

// set pixel format
if(!SetPixelFormat(hDC, pixelFormat, &pfd))
{
  // error setting pixel format
  return FALSE;
}

/////////////////////////////
// 4.) Create Rendering Context

// create OpenGL rendering context
hRC = wglCreateContext(hDC);
if (!hRC)
{
  // error creating RC
  return FALSE;
}

// activate OpenGL RC
if(!wglMakeCurrent(hDC,hRC))
{
  // activation of RC failed
```

```
  return FALSE;
}


/////////////////////////////
// 5.) OpenGL Setup

// init viewport to window size
glViewport(0, 0, width, height);

// set perspective projection
glHint(GL_PERSPECTIVE_CORRECTION_HINT, GL_NICEST);
glMatrixMode(GL_PROJECTION);
glLoadIdentity();
gluPerspective(45.0f,(GLfloat)width/(GLfloat)height,0.1f, 100.0f);

// set eye position and viewing direction
glMatrixMode(GL_MODELVIEW);
glLoadIdentity();
gluLookAt(0, 0, -10, 0, 0, 0, 0, -1, 0);
// depth buffer setup
glClearDepth(1.0f);
glEnable(GL_DEPTH_TEST);
glDepthFunc(GL_LEQUAL);

// shading setup
glShadeModel(GL_SMOOTH);
glEnable(GL_LIGHT0);
glEnable(GL_LIGHTING);
glEnable(GL_COLOR_MATERIAL);

/////////////////////////////
// 6.) Store Dimensions of Image Buffer

imageDim[0] = width;
imageDim[1] = height;

return TRUE;
}

// deletes OpenGL window and rendering context
extern "C" void PASCAL DeleteRC()
{
```

```
if (hRC)
{
  // release and delete rendering context
  wglMakeCurrent(NULL, NULL);
  wglDeleteContext(hRC);
  hRC = NULL;
}

if (hDC)
{
  // release device context
  ReleaseDC(hWnd, hDC);
  hDC = NULL;
}

if (hWnd)
{
  // destroy window
  DestroyWindow(hWnd);
  hWnd = NULL;
}

imageDim[0] = 0;
imageDim[1] = 0;
}
```

OpenGL Font Creation

As mentioned earlier in this chapter, text output is not covered by the OpenGL standard. However, on Windows platforms there is a simple extension in place that lets you convert a TrueType font into an outline font that can be rendered by OpenGL. The conversion function stores each converted letter in a separate OpenGL list. Those lists can be invoked later in an arbitrary order, thereby allowing users to assemble words and sentences.

The CreateOutlineFont function must generate a set of OpenGL lists that store the outline font. Let's store the base of this list in static variables such as hWnd, hDC, and hRC. Furthermore, we must add a static array of type GLYPHMETRICSFLOAT that holds the information about the placement and size of each character. Using this array we can later compute the

exact center of a string and position it correctly. Listing 9.3 contains the
code for the `CreateOutlineFont` and `DeleteOutlineFont` functions.

Listing 9.3 3DText.cpp: The `CreateOutlineFont` and
`DeleteOutlineFont` Functions

```
static GLuint fontBase;                    // Base for Font CallLists
static GLYPHMETRICSFLOAT fontFormat[256];  // Descriptors of Font Format

// creates an OpenGL font
extern "C" BOOL PASCAL CreateOutlineFont(char *name, BOOL bold, BOOL italic)
{
  // activate OpenGL RC
  if(!wglMakeCurrent(hDC,hRC))
  {
    // activation of RC failed
    return FALSE;
  }

  // CallLists for 256 characters
  fontBase = glGenLists(256);

  HFONT font = CreateFont(-12, 0, 0, 0, bold ? FW_BOLD : FW_NORMAL,
    italic, 0, 0, ANSI_CHARSET,
    OUT_TT_PRECIS, CLIP_DEFAULT_PRECIS,
    ANTIALIASED_QUALITY, FF_DONTCARE | DEFAULT_PITCH, name);
  if (!font)
  {
    // error creating Windows font
    return FALSE;
  }

  HGDIOBJ oldObject = SelectObject(hDC, font);
  if (!oldObject)
  {
    // error selecting font
    return FALSE;
  }

  // convert to 3D outline font (20% depth)
  if (!wglUseFontOutlines(hDC, 0, 255, fontBase, 0.0f, 0.2f, WGL_FONT_
POLYGONS, fontFormat))
```

```
  {
    // creating font outlines failed
    return FALSE;
  }

  // unselecting font
  SelectObject(hDC, oldObject);

  return TRUE;
}

// delete an OpenGL font
extern "C" void PASCAL DeleteOutlineFont()
{
  glDeleteLists(fontBase, 256);
}
```

Rendering 3D Text

Now that we have in place all the utility functions for creating and deleting an OpenGL rendering context and outline font, we can implement the actual rendering function for three-dimensional text.

First, we set the current content of the offline buffer as OpenGL background so that the rendered text overlays the loaded digital picture. Because we used a negative up vector when initializing our OpenGL rendering in CreateRC, there is no need to flip the GDI+ image horizontally before copying it into the OpenGL rendering context. Next, the OpenGL state is modified so that the text line is centered and then rotated according to the passed parameters. After this, we render the text using the glCall List command. Then the rendering context is read back into the offline buffer provided by the calling application. Listing 9.4 shows the implementation of the RenderText function.

Listing 9.4 3DText.cpp: The RenderText Function

```
// renders 3D text
extern "C" BOOL PASCAL RenderText(char *text, int size, int color, int
rotX, int rotY, int rotZ, void *buffer)
{
  double scale = size / 16.;
```

```
// activate OpenGL RC
if(!wglMakeCurrent(hDC,hRC))
{
  // activation of RC failed
  return FALSE;
}

// set eye position and viewing direction
glLoadIdentity();
gluLookAt(0, 0, -10, 0, 0, 0, 0, -1, 0);

// set the current content of the external buffer as background
glDrawPixels(imageDim[0], imageDim[1], GL_RGB, GL_UNSIGNED_BYTE,
buffer);
glClear(GL_DEPTH_BUFFER_BIT);

// set text color
glColor3d((color & 0xff) / 255.0, ((color >> 8) & 0xff) / 255.0,
((color >> 16) & 0xff) / 255.0);

// compute the width and find the max. height of text
double width = 0;
double height = 0;
for (unsigned int i = 0; i < strlen(text); i++)
{
  width += fontFormat[text[i]].gmfCellIncX;
  height = max(height, fontFormat[text[i]].gmfBlackBoxY);
}

// scale font size
glScaled(scale, scale, scale);
glTranslated(-width / 2.0, -height / 2.0, 0.0);

// rotate, translate, and scale text according to parameters
glRotated(rotX, 1.0, 0.0, 0.0);
glRotated(rotY, 0.0, 1.0, 0.0);
glRotated(rotZ, 0.0, 0.0, 1.0);

// draw text
glPushAttrib(GL_LIST_BIT);
glListBase(fontBase);
glCallLists(strlen(text), GL_UNSIGNED_BYTE, text);
glPopAttrib();
```

```
// read rendered pixels back into the external buffer
glReadPixels(0, 0, imageDim[0], imageDim[1], GL_RGB, GL_UNSIGNED_
BYTE, buffer);

return TRUE;
}
```

Exporting API Functions

To make the functions available to other applications, the functions need to be marked so that they will be exported. You can do this in a separate module definition file. In Solution Explorer, add a new item to the source folder and choose Module Definition File. Name the file 3DText.def, and add the EXPORTS keyword. After EXPORTS list the API functions CreateRC, DeleteRC, CreateOutlineFont, DeleteOutlineFont, and RenderText. Then make sure that the file is set in the Linker Input section of the project properties (see Figure 9.6).

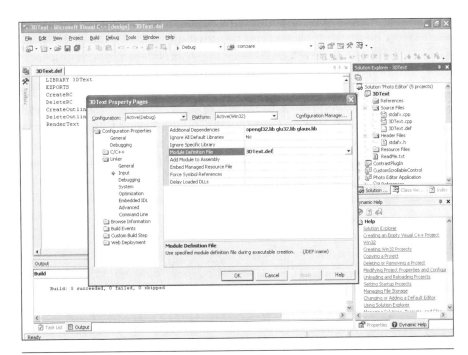

Figure 9.6 Setting a Module Definition File

9.5.2   Using PInvoke to Integrate the 3D Text DLL into .NET

A separate DLL is now available that provides rendering features for three-dimensional text. It's a good practice to write a wrapper class for these DLL functions that enables easy integration into the existing photo editor.

Writing a Wrapper Class

For the convenience of the application programmer and to reduce the likelihood of bugs and resource or memory leaks, we implement a wrapper class for the 3D Text DLL. The API functions provided by the DLL enforce a certain sequence, as shown earlier in the sequence diagram (Figure 9.3). A wrapper class can take the responsibility of ensuring the correct sequence as well as reduce the number of calls by caching certain information. As the OpenGL state machine, this wrapper class can manage its internal state and execute the necessary API functions when text is rendered.

Let's switch to the photo editor application project and add a new class called OGL3DText to it. First, we add the external DLL functions as private methods to the class, as shown in Listing 9.5. Because the function RenderText has a pointer argument, it must be declared unsafe. The .NET Framework enforces the rule that all code dealing directly with pointers must be declared unsafe because this code is often the source of malfunctions. A project containing unsafe code also must be compiled with the /unsafe option, which can be set via the project properties. To enable the use of pointers in this project, open the project properties window and set the Allow Unsafe Code Blocks option under Configuration Properties | Build to True.

Listing 9.5 OGL3DText.cs: External DLL Function Declaration

```
using System;
using System.Runtime.InteropServices;
using System.Drawing;
using System.Drawing.Imaging;

namespace Photo_Editor_Application
{
    /// <summary>
    /// Wrapper class for 3D Text DLL. All methods of this class are
    /// static because the 3D Text DLL does not support multiple
```

```
/// instances.
/// </summary>
public class OGL3DText
{
    private const string DLLNAME = "3DText.dll";

    // extern DLL function declaration
    [DllImport(DLLNAME)]
    private static extern bool CreateRC(int width, int height);
    [DllImport(DLLNAME)]
    private static extern void DeleteRC();
    [DllImport(DLLNAME, CharSet=CharSet.Ansi)]
    private static extern bool CreateOutlineFont(string name, bool
bold, bool italic);
    [DllImport(DLLNAME)]
    private static extern void DeleteOutlineFont();
    [DllImport(DLLNAME, CharSet=CharSet.Ansi)]
    private unsafe static extern void RenderText(string text, int size,
int color, int rotX, int rotY, int rotZ, void *buffer);

}
}
```

In the next step, we add set properties for all parameters that can be passed to the 3D Text DLL. Each set property changes flags that control whether the font or rendering context needs to be re-created due to a change in the font name, the font style, or the size of the rendering context. These flags are then checked in the render method, and the appropriate API functions of the 3D Text DLL are called. For cleanup purposes, it is desirable to have a method to delete the rendering context and the OpenGL outline font after the form for 3D text is closed and no further rendering takes place. Table 9.4 summarizes the class members, and Listing 9.6 shows their implementation.

Table 9.4 OGL3DText Class Members

Member	Type	Summary
Text	Property	Sets the text string to render.
Font	Property	Sets the font. Only font name, size, bold, and italic style properties are considered.

(continued)

Table 9.4 (*Cont.*)

Member	Type	Summary
Color	Property	Sets the text color.
Image	Property	Sets the image on which the text is rendered.
Placement	Property	Rectangle that defines an area within the background image where the text is rendered.
RotationX	Property	Sets the rotation along the x-axis.
RotationY	Property	Sets the rotation along the y-axis.
RotationZ	Property	Sets the rotation along the z-axis.
Render	Method	Method that renders 3D text using the properties of the class. It internally creates a rendering context and OpenGL outline font. The method returns a new bitmap with the rendered text.
Close	Method	Cleanup method that can be invoked to force the deletion of the rendering window and OpenGL outline font.

Listing 9.6 `OGL3DText.cs`: Class Member Implementation

```
. . .

/// <summary>
/// Indicates whether the OpenGL font needs to be re-created.
/// </summary>
private static bool fontChanged = true;
/// <summary>
/// Indicates whether the OpenGL rendering context needs to be re-
created.
/// This is the case if its size (not its position) changed.
/// </summary>
private static bool sizeChanged = true;

// private members for set properties
private static string text = "";
private static int fontSize = 24;
private static string fontName = "Arial";
private static bool fontBold = false;
private static bool fontItalic = false;
private static int fontColor = System.Drawing.Color.White.ToArgb();
```

```
private static System.Drawing.Bitmap image = null;
private static System.Drawing.Rectangle placement;
private static int rotX = 0;
private static int rotY = 0;
private static int rotZ = 0;

/// <summary>
/// Sets a text string to render.
/// </summary>
static public string Text
{
  set
  {
    text = value;
  }
}

/// <summary>
/// Sets the font. Only font name, size, bold, and italic style
/// properties are considered from the Font class.
/// </summary>
static public System.Drawing.Font Font
{
  set
  {
    // font size is changed via scaling
    // no need to re-create the font
    fontSize = System.Convert.ToInt32(value.Size);
    // all other attributes require us to re-create the font
    if (fontName != value.Name)
    {
      fontName = value.Name;
      fontChanged = true;
    }

    if (fontItalic != value.Italic)
    {
      fontItalic = value.Italic;
      fontChanged = true;
    }

    if (fontB\old != value.Bold)
    {
      fontBold = value.Bold;
```

```
        fontChanged = true;
      }
    }
}
/// <summary>
/// Sets the text color.
/// </summary>
static public System.Drawing.Color Color
{
  set
  {
    fontColor = value.ToArgb();
  }
}

/// <summary>
/// Sets the background image.
/// </summary>
static public System.Drawing.Bitmap Image
{
  set
  {
    image = value;
  }
}

/// <summary>
/// Defines a rectangle within the background image where the text
/// is rendered.
/// </summary>
static public System.Drawing.Rectangle Placement
{
  set
  {
    if (placement.Size != value.Size)
    {
      sizeChanged = true;
    }
    placement = value;
  }
}

/// <summary>
/// Sets the rotation along the x-axis.
```

```
/// </summary>
static public int RotationX
{
  set
  {
    rotX = value;
  }
}

/// <summary>
/// Sets the rotation along the y-axis.
/// </summary>
static public int RotationY
{
  set
  {
    rotY = value;
  }
}

/// <summary>
/// Sets the rotation along the z-axis.
/// </summary>
static public int RotationZ
{
  set
  {
    rotZ = value;
  }
}

/// <summary>
/// Renders three-dimensional text. Internally creates the rendering
/// context and font if necessary.
/// </summary>
///
/// <returns>The method returns a new bitmap with the rendered text.
</returns>
static public unsafe System.Drawing.Bitmap Render()
{
  // no background set
  if (image == null)
    return null;
```

```
// limit placement to boundaries of background image
if (placement.Right > image.Width)
{
  placement.X = image.Width - placement.Width;
}
if (placement.Bottom > image.Height)
{
  placement.Y = image.Height - placement.Height;
}
if ((placement.X < 0) | (placement.Y < 0) | (placement.Width <= 0) |
(placement.Height <= 0))
{
  return null;
}

// create new rendering context?
if (sizeChanged)
{
  DeleteRC();
  CreateRC(placement.Width, placement.Height);
}

// create new font?
if (fontChanged)
{
  DeleteOutlineFont();
  CreateOutlineFont(fontName, fontBold, fontItalic);
}

// clone region of interest (ROI) to get OpenGL rendering buffer
Bitmap roi = image.Clone(placement, PixelFormat.Format24bppRgb);

// lock memory and render 3D text into it
BitmapData renderData = roi.LockBits(new Rectangle(0, 0, roi.Width,
roi.Height), ImageLockMode.ReadWrite, PixelFormat.Format24bppRgb);
byte *renderBuffer = (byte*) renderData.Scan0.ToPointer();
RenderText(text, fontSize, fontColor, rotX, rotY, rotZ, renderBuffer);

// clone the background to get full size output buffer
Bitmap output = image.Clone(new Rectangle(0, 0, image.Width,
image.Height), PixelFormat.Format24bppRgb);

// get pointer to output buffer and copy ROI into it
```

```
  BitmapData targetData = output.LockBits(placement, ImageLockMode.Read
Write, PixelFormat.Format24bppRgb);
  byte *targetBuffer = (byte*) targetData.Scan0.ToPointer();

  // copy the rendered buffer (subregion) into the final image
  for (int y = 0; y < (roi.Height); y++)
  {
    // copy one line, each pixel 3 bytes (RGB)
    for (int x = 0; x < (3 * roi.Width); x++)
    {
      targetBuffer[targetData.Stride * y + x] = renderBuffer[render
Data.Stride * y + x];
    }
  }

  // unlock memory
  roi.UnlockBits(renderData);
  output.UnlockBits(targetData);
  // return a new Bitmap containing the final image
  return new Bitmap(output, new Size(output.Width, output.Height));
}

/// <summary>
/// Deletes font and rendering context. Must be called to destroy the
/// rendering context and OpenGL outline font after calling Render().
/// </summary>
static public void Close()
{
  DeleteOutlineFont();
  DeleteRC();
}
```

9.5.3 First 3D Text: A Unit Test

In contrast to previous iterations of the construction phase, we have implemented a set of classes in this chapter without doing any formal or informal testing. This has happened mainly because most of the implementation was done in unmanaged C++. We would have had to create a separate unmanaged C++ program to exercise and test this code earlier. However, our project goal is to add all unit tests to the NUnit framework for better test automation. Now that the .NET wrapper class has been implemented, it is easy to add a new test case to the NUnit framework.

It is often a challenge to evaluate the result of functionality as complex as rendering three-dimensional objects. This is especially true in real-life projects, where time and funding are usually limited. A common practice to test this kind of functionality is to conduct a manual review to validate the rendering output together with the test code. However, this approach interferes with our goal of developing a fully automated test suite at least for unit tests. Also, it requires that the author of the test code as well as an imaging expert be present each time the test is performed.

To overcome these obstacles at least to an extent, a good practice is to generate reference output, which is initially reviewed manually. After this reference output is reviewed, it can be stored in the depository and used for comparison in later test runs. In this way, we can perform the tests in a fully automated fashion as long as the reference output does not need to be modified. However, each change requires a new evaluation of the new rendering output and an update of the reference image in the depository. Using this approach, we add to the `UnitTest` class the utility method `CompareBitmaps`, which checks whether two given bitmaps are identical. Listing 9.7 shows the implementation of this method.

Listing 9.7 `UnitTest.cs`: The `CompareBitmaps` Method

```
/// <summary>
/// Compares two bitmaps.
/// </summary>
/// <param name="bitmap1">First bitmap.</param>
/// <param name="bitmap2">Second bitmap.</param>
/// <returns>True if the two bitmaps are identical, otherwise false.
</returns>
public bool CompareBitmaps(Bitmap bitmap1, Bitmap bitmap2)
{
  // compare image size
  if (bitmap1.Size != bitmap2.Size)
  {
    return false;
  }

  // compare all pixels
  for (int y = 0; y < bitmap1.Height; y++)
```

```
{
  for (int x = 0; x < bitmap1.Width; x++)
  {
    if (bitmap1.GetPixel(x, y) != bitmap2.GetPixel(x, y))
      return false;
  }
}


// size and all pixels are the same
return true;
}
```

Listing 9.8 shows the implementation of the unit test class for the 3D Text DLL and its wrapper class. This code renders three strings using the colors red, green, and blue and a different rotation axis for each string. In this way, it verifies that the color components (red, green and blue) are converted correctly and that the rotation matches the correct axis. The method CompareBitmaps is invoked at the end of the test to compare the rendering result with a stored reference image.

Listing 9.8 OGL3DTextUnitTest.cs: Unit Test for 3D Text

```
/// <summary>
/// Renders 3 strings in the different colors and orientation.
/// </summary>
/// <requirement>F:image_3dtext</requirement>
[Test]
public void OGL3DTextTest()
{
  Bitmap output = null;

  Bitmap input = new Bitmap(800, 600);
  // Set each pixel in image to gray.
  for (int Xcount = 0; Xcount < input.Width; Xcount++)
  {
    for (int Ycount = 0; Ycount < input.Height; Ycount++)
    {
      input.SetPixel(Xcount, Ycount, Color.DarkGray);
    }
  }
```

```
OGL3DText.Image = input;
OGL3DText.Color = Color.Red;
OGL3DText.Text = "OpenGL";
OGL3DText.Font = new Font("Arial Black", 40);
OGL3DText.Placement = new Rectangle(0, 0, 400, 400);
OGL3DText.RotationX = 30;
output = OGL3DText.Render();
Assertion.AssertNotNull("First string.", output);

OGL3DText.Image = output;
OGL3DText.Color = Color.LightBlue;
OGL3DText.Text = "and";
OGL3DText.Placement = new Rectangle(200, 0, 600, 600);
OGL3DText.RotationX = 0;
OGL3DText.RotationY = 60;
output = OGL3DText.Render();
Assertion.AssertNotNull("Second string.", output);

OGL3DText.Image = output;
OGL3DText.Color = Color.LightGreen;
OGL3DText.Text = ".NET";
OGL3DText.Placement = new Rectangle(400, 200, 400, 400);
OGL3DText.RotationY = 0;
OGL3DText.RotationZ = 30;
output = OGL3DText.Render();
Assertion.AssertNotNull("Third string.", output);

/*/ temporarily remove * on the left to create the reference output
if (output != null)
{
  output.Save("output.png", System.Drawing.Imaging.ImageFormat.Png);
}
// */
// load reference image and compare with the one just rendered
Bitmap reference = new Bitmap("output.png");
Assertion.AssertEquals("Compare with reference image", true, Compare
Bitmaps(output, reference));
}
```

The commented code in the test function stores the rendered image in a file; this image will become the reference output. Uncomment these lines the first time the test is executed, and manually validate the output. The image should match Figure 9.7, showing "OpenGL and .NET" in the col-

Figure 9.7 Reference Output for 3D Text Unit Test

ors red, blue, and green rotated along the x-, y-, and z-axes. After successful validation, you restore the comments to the code from which you earlier removed them, and you put the output file under version control (or at least write-protect it).

9.5.4 Implementing the User Interface

The integration into the photo editor application is not complete until we add the user interface for the 3D text feature. According to the user interface guidelines of the photo editor, we start by adding a new tabbed dialog to the main form. We follow these steps:

1. Open `PhotoEditor.cs` by double-clicking on it in Solution Explorer.
2. Add a new tab for 3D text via the properties window of the Tab control.
3. Open the TabPages Collection Editor via the Tab control properties, and change the name of the new tab to `3D Text`.

Table 9.5 `TextDialog` Controls

Name	Type	Summary
textBox	TextBox	Receives the text to render.
fontButton	Button	Button to invoke the font dialog.
fontDialog	FontDialog	Dialog that lets the user select a font and its style. The default font is defined in via the `Font` property.
colorButton	Button	Button to invoke the color dialog.
colorDialog	ColorDialog	Dialog that lets the user pick a text color. The default color is set via the `Color` property.
placementButton	Button	Button to enter text placement mode.
rotationX	NumericUpDown	Input for rotation along the x-axis.
rotationY	NumericUpDown	Input for rotation along the y-axis.
rotationZ	NumericUpDown	Input for rotation along the z-axis.
textApplyButton	Button	Applies the text to the image.
textUndoButton	Button	Undo button. Restores original image.

Now we add the form controls according to Figure 9.1. Table 9.5 summarizes the names and types of the controls that must be added.

It's simple to link the Font and Color buttons to the corresponding standard system dialogs. Add an event handler for the buttons by double-clicking them in the design view, and invoke the standard dialogs by calling the `ShowDialog()` member (see Listing 9.9).

Listing 9.9 `PhotoEditor.cs`: Font and Color Button Event Handler

```
/// <summary>
/// Invokes the font selection dialog for 3D text.
/// </summary>
/// <param name="sender"></param>
/// <param name="e"></param>
private void fontButton_Click(object sender, System.EventArgs e)
{
```

```
      fontDialog.ShowDialog();
}


/// <summary>
/// Invokes the color selection dialog for 3D text.
/// </summary>
/// <param name="sender"></param>
/// <param name="e"></param>
private void colorButton_Click(object sender, System.EventArgs e)
{
    colorDialog.ShowDialog();
}
```

The user interface is now implemented. What remains is to add event handlers for the following buttons:

- Apply: We set all text attributes in the OGL3DText helper class and then render the text onto the image. After the text is rendered, the display must be updated.
- Undo: Reverting to the previous image is already implemented in the Picture class. Here, we simply call the Reset() method.
- Placement: The photo editor already provides a tool to select a region of interest (ROI). This tool can be used to select the text placement as well. The handler for this method need only enter the region selection tool mode.

To update the image stored in the Picture class, we must first implement the set accessor for the LoadedImage property. Before replacing the current image, we clone it into the backUpImage field to fulfill the undo function (see Listing 9.10).

Listing 9.10 `Picture.cs`: The `LoadedImage` Property

```
/// <summary>
/// Accessor to get the currently loaded image.
/// </summary>
public Bitmap LoadedImage
{
    get
    {
```

```
      return loadedImage;
    }
    set
    {
      backUpImage = (Bitmap) loadedImage.Clone();
      loadedImage = value;
    }
  }
}
```

To add the event handler, again we just double-click on the buttons in the design view. Within the handler for the Apply button, we copy the attributes of the text into the OGL3DText helper class. We also check whether the region of interest is initialized, and we use this information to place the text. If the region object has not been created, the placement rectangle defaults to the entire image. After we set all attributes, we replace the loaded image in the photo editor with the image containing the rendered text. Listing 9.11 shows the event handler for the Apply, Undo, and Placement buttons.

Listing 9.11   PhotoEditor.cs: Event Handler for Apply, Undo, and Placement Buttons

```
/// <summary>
/// Event handler that renders 3D text into the image.
/// </summary>
/// <param name="sender"></param>
/// <param name="e"></param>
private void textApplyButton_Click(object sender, System.EventArgs e)
{
  // Apply was pressed, copy all attributes to OGL3DText
  OGL3DText.Image = this.PictureObject.LoadedImage;
  OGL3DText.Color = colorDialog.Color;
  OGL3DText.Text = this.textBox.Text;
  OGL3DText.Font = fontDialog.Font;

  if (regionComponent != null)
  {
    // use selected region
    OGL3DText.Placement = new Rectangle(
      regionComponent.StartPoint.X,
      regionComponent.StartPoint.Y,
```

```
      regionComponent.EndPoint.X - regionComponent.StartPoint.X,
      regionComponent.EndPoint.Y - regionComponent.StartPoint.Y);
  }
  else
  {
    // full image
    OGL3DText.Placement = new Rectangle(
      0, 0,
      this.PictureObject.LoadedImage.Width,
      this.PictureObject.LoadedImage.Height);
  }
  OGL3DText.RotationX = System.Convert.ToInt32(rotationX.Value);
  OGL3DText.RotationY = System.Convert.ToInt32(rotationY.Value);
  OGL3DText.RotationZ = System.Convert.ToInt32(rotationZ.Value);

  // render text and replace LoadedImage
  this.PictureObject.LoadedImage = OGL3DText.Render();

  // now update display
  this.DisplayImage();
}


/// <summary>
/// Event handler for 3D text Undo button.
/// </summary>
/// <param name="sender"></param>
/// <param name="e"></param>
private void textUndoButton_Click(object sender, System.EventArgs e)
{
  // revert to previous image and update display
  this.PictureObject.Reset();
  this.DisplayImage();
}


/// <summary>
/// Enters the 3D text placement mode.
/// </summary>
/// <param name="sender"></param>
/// <param name="e"></param>
private void placementButton_Click(object sender, System.EventArgs e)
{
  if(toolSelected == toolSelection.None)
```

```
  {
    toolSelected = toolSelection.ROITool;
  }
}
```

Implementing the event handler is the final step in integrating three-dimensional text rendering into the photo editor application. Figure 9.8 shows the finished result.

Figure 9.8 Finished Integration of 3D Text Feature

9.6 Conclusion: Don't Reinvent the Wheel

This chapter introduces .NET's platform invocation service, a powerful technology that enables the integration of native, unmanaged, and even hardware accelerated code into .NET applications.

PInvoke may play a key role in the acceptance of .NET as a new development platform in many companies because it allows the reuse of software components, even those that were not developed for the .NET Framework. Today, when the "better, faster, cheaper" principle is imposed on nearly every project, it is a necessity to build new versions of an application by using components of the older version. Furthermore, you can't avoid sharing components across multiple applications to cut down development time and maintenance costs. For example, Adobe uses a dialog manager component that offers common user interfaces that can be found in many of Adobe's products, including Photoshop, Illustrator, and Framemaker.

Nevertheless, there are some pitfalls to watch out for before you reuse or design reusable software components:

- New applications can profit from the robustness of existing components and will be deployed with fewer bugs. However, the opposite effect can occur if the reused code has not been well tested. In that case, all applications using this code will have inferior stability.
- Despite the advantages that code reuse can bring, it can also lead to mental blocks when you design a new system. By trying to reuse legacy code, you may also unintentionally adopt previous analyses and designs, perhaps overlooking a simpler solution.
- When you are developing reusable software building blocks, you must pay greater attention, and that leads to increased initial development time and cost. You must consider these costs in the project planning when such a component is built for the first time.
- Trying to think "strategically" and designing a software component to be ready for future extensions as well as reusability in other applications may lead to unnecessarily complex, overengineered designs. Adding too many layers for abstraction, separation, or interfaces may open the door to new bugs in these layers. Always remember that there are also other good practices—for example, keeping things simple.

9.7 References for Further Reading

OpenGL

Dave Astle, Kevin Hawkins, and Andre LaMothe, *OpenGL Game Programming* (Boston: Premier Press, 2002)

Dave Shreiner and the OpenGL Architecture Review Board, *The OpenGL Reference Manual* (also known as the blue book; accompanies the *Programming Guide*) (Reading, MA: Addison-Wesley, 1999)

Mason Woo, Jackie Neider, Tom Davis, Dave Shreiner, and OpenGL Architecture Review Board, *OpenGL Programming Guide* (also called the red book) (Reading, MA: Addison-Wesley, 1999)

`http://nehe.gamedev.net/`

CHAPTER 10

Performance Optimization, Multithreading, and Profiling

 Unified Process:
Construction Phase and Eighth Iteration

In the eighth iteration of the construction phase, we optimize the application's performance for certain use cases. This chapter will conclude the development of the photo editor application. In the next iteration (Chapter 11), we will begin the Online Photo Shop development.

  The overall task for this iteration is to improve the performance of the photo editor application and to improve interactivity. In addition, we will show you how to profile the photo editor application in order to identify possible bottlenecks and analyze performance. Based on the profiling results, we will refactor the photo editor application and optimize the implementation to achieve better performance.

10.1 Requirements for Performance Optimization

R Only one requirement key is implemented in this iteration (see Table 10.1). Performance improvements can become quite complex, and despite ever-faster computers, performance issues can be observed in almost all types of programs. For example, in image-processing or database applications, in which a lot of data is accessed or processed, performance usually is a big constraint. So far, the implementation of the photo editor application has not been designed for performance but for convenience and fast development.

363

Table 10.1 Refined Requirement Description

Requirement	Type	Summary
P:editor_optimizations	Performance	The application shall be profiled to uncover possible bottlenecks. On the basis of the profiling results, we will decide upon improvements that are implemented in this iteration. The overall goal of this development cycle is to provide better interactivity and to improve the performance of the image-processing algorithms.

Usually it is a good practice not to consider performance constraints when you first implement a feature. This does not mean that you don't consider performance but rather that you implement the functionalities without spending too much time on performance. When you have developed a working product, you then analyze the whole system to identify any bottlenecks. This practice makes perfect sense because it is very difficult to predict the performance of various subsystems that work together at implementation time. In many cases, guesswork by developers or management turns out to be wrong anyway, in which case you have spent valuable time in improving the performance at the wrong spot.

The first step in making performance improvements is to identify the bottlenecks of the system. To do that, it is advisable to use a profiling tool. Even though people are often tempted to guess what the bottlenecks in a system are, just as often they are wrong. Using a profiling tool is therefore highly recommended and saves the embarrassment of fixing bottlenecks that are not actually the major performance problems at all.

10.2 Analysis of the Editor Optimization Requirement

 Performance improvement is an iterative process that is typically broken down into four phases.

- Collecting performance data (profiling)
- Analyzing the collected data (possibly prototyping)

- Implementing the improvements
- Testing the implementation

Typically, you collect performance data with the help of a profiling tool. If no tool is available, you can collect data about the time spent in methods and functions of interest by using the performance counter or the internal timer provided by .NET. But be careful. Inserting timing measures can itself change the timing of the application. For example, if the data is written to a file while the program is running, the result might be not be correct because of the time consumed by the slow I/O calls.

Performance analysis is usually done via a top-down approach. First we look at the system level, then at the application level, and last at micro-architecture level. The top-down approach enables us to eliminate bottle-necks or inefficiencies in the analysis that might mask underlying problems in the lower layers.

We use a profiling tool for our initial performance analysis of the photo editor application. We use the tool to collect information about the system's overall performance (including all layers). After the initial performance analysis is finished, we develop a test program that enables us to prototype and to evaluate various optimization possibilities.

We highly recommend the use of profiling tools for the initial system analysis. Profiling tools enable developers to identify bottlenecks in systems very quickly. As with all development, the 80/20 rule is applicable to system optimization: You will spend 20 percent of the total time implementing 80 percent of the improvements. Therefore, it is advisable to look into the "big" improvement possibilities first before getting bogged down in details of minor improvements.

10.2.1 Profiling the Photo Editor Application

As mentioned before, profiling is the task of collecting performance data of a software system. In the example shown here, we use the Quantify tool from Rational to uncover bottlenecks and to analyze the performance of the application.

The first step is to record overall reports of common use cases in which performance problems are experienced. The use case we use to record the data is the contrast calculation that is applied to an image:

A user changes the contrast using the `Contrast` control and applies the result to the entire image using the `Apply` button.

This scenario is run with an instrumented version of the application that is run from within the profiler application. (*Instrumented* means that the profiler does the magic of recording and timing all method calls.) Figure 10.1 shows the collected data for this use case. The figure shows the collection of all the method calls that were made, including the number of calls to the method and some additional timing measures.

To identify problem areas, we sort the list by the time spent in each method (shown in the Method Time column). The first column shows the name of the method that was executed; the second column lists how often it was called, and the third column shows the accumulated time that was spent in the method. The column M+D Time shows the time spent in the described method and all its descendants.

The profiling result shows that the most time is spent in the method GetPixel() of the Bitmap class. This is not surprising because the method, in the case of the contrast calculation, is called twice for each pixel in the

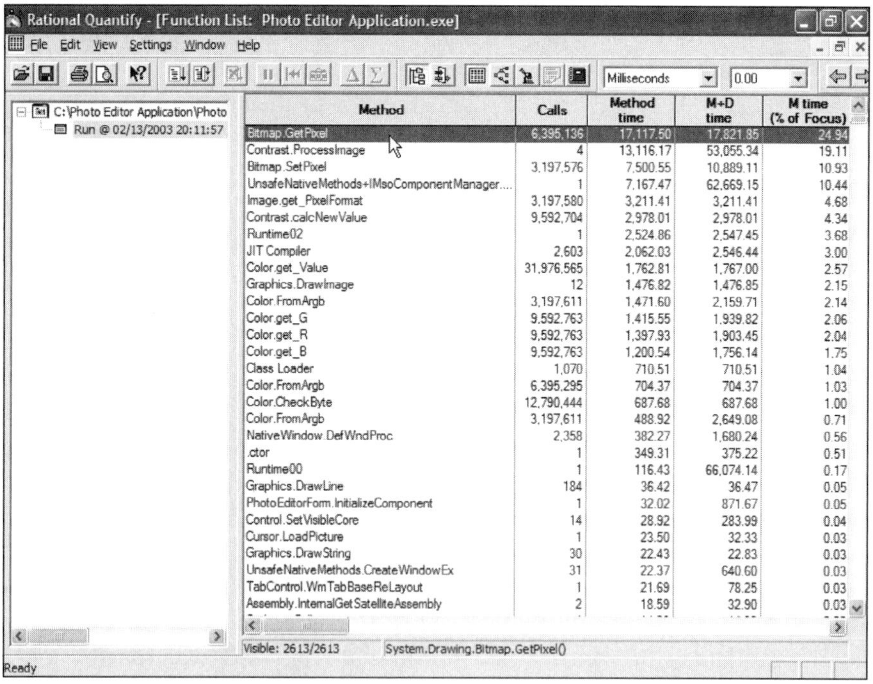

Figure 10.1 Profiling Result for the Photo Editor Application

image. (In addition, this method is called twice for each calculation of the intermediate result shown in the preview pane.)

We can drill down the list of methods to inspect the profiling data for any method in different views. Figure 10.2 shows the `Contrast` plugin's `ProcessImage` method.

This pie chart view shows a method and all the calls to other methods. In the example, the `ProcessImage` method calls the `GetPixel` and `Set Pixel` methods of GDI+. The calls to get and set the pixel take by far the most time and are good candidates for optimization.

10.2.2 Optimization Possibilities and Prototyping

Based on the profiling results, it seems feasible to change the implementation of the plugin to use pointer arithmetic to get and set the pixel values of the image instead of using the GDI+-provided `get` and `set` methods.

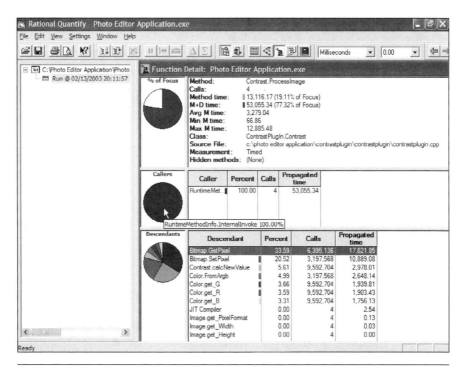

Figure 10.2 Profiling the Invoked `ProcessImage` Method

With this performance optimization, we want to improve the application's overall performance, and in addition we would like to optimize the GUI response time. This means that the application GUI should not block when a lengthy calculation is being applied on an image. Instead, the GUI should still respond to the user, with the restriction that no new calculation on the image can be started before the current calculation is finished. In other words, all image calculations are handled sequentially, but other GUI operations (such as switching tab controls) can be performed.

10.3 Design of the Optimizations

The overall design of the application does not change very much from the design shown in Chapter 9. But we must take into account a few considerations before implementing the optimization features. These considerations deal with the implementation of the increased user responsiveness of the GUI. Before we start making design decisions, let's look at some background information about performance optimizations.

10.3.1 Performance Optimization Options

There are several possibilities for improving the overall performance of an application. These opportunities for performance optimizations can be divided into six categories:

- Optimize utilization
- Improve efficiency
- Reduce latency
- Increase concurrency
- Improve throughput
- Eliminate bottlenecks

To optimize the photo editor application, we try to address as many of the six categories as possible. To optimize utilization, we make sure that the compiler uses optimizations that generate efficient code. To improve efficiency, we will use the data we collected using the profiling tool. We have identified a hot spot of inefficient execution resulting from the use of the Get- and SetPixel methods of GDI+.

Another aspect we keep in mind is to reduce *latency*, or slow GUI response, within the application. In addition, we will try to increase the concurrency of the application. Unfortunately, we cannot improve throughput very much because that is usually done by using multiple processors. But we have no influence over the hardware users are running, and it would not be acceptable to restrict the application to run only on dual-processor machines. Last but not least, we will try to eliminate bottlenecks as we improve the application's performance.

Now that we know what we are intending to improve, we need to have some knowledge of how these improvements can be implemented.

10.3.2 Multithreading and Symmetric Multiprocessing

When talking about performance optimizations, we often mention multithreading and symmetric multiprocessing (SMP). It is no different in the case of the photo editor application.

Symmetric multiprocessing refers to the hardware of a system. If a system has more than one microprocessor available, then we talk about SMP. Each CPU executes a distinct set of program threads. The operating system is responsible for scheduling the tasks for each processor. SMP improves the throughput of a system.

Multithreading is a software construct that allows for parallel execution of software. Each thread has its own call stack and CPU state, but threads share memory with the process they are bound to. Multithreading programming is used to improve concurrency, reduce latency, and improve throughput.

10.3.3 Design of the Multithreaded GUI

When we talk about multithreading, a question often arises: Why not use multiple processes? The answer is that we can create a thread with very little overhead. In addition, it is convenient for the programmer that all threads created within one process share the same memory. This makes data sharing very easy (sometimes too easy, as when we must synchronize data access in order for the application to perform its task correctly).

To decide on the design of the photo editor application, let's first look at the goals of this iteration and the techniques we can use to implement them:

- Reduce latency: If a lengthy calculation is started, the GUI will be able to react to user input if the GUI code and the calculation code are running in separate threads.
- Improve concurrency: With multithreading we can improve concurrency. We can shorten the execution time of lengthy operations such as image processing.

- Improve throughput: By improving throughput with multithreading, we can also shorten execution time. Throughput is improved by enabling multiple threads to use processors in parallel. If one of the threads is waiting for data to become available, another thread can be executed on the CPU and thus shorten execution time and improve user responsiveness.
- Eliminate bottlenecks and improve efficiency: By profiling, we identify bottlenecks. Based on the performance data, we then eliminate the bottlenecks with the goal to improve the performance of the system.

For the first three points on our list, multithreading seems to be a viable option for the photo editor application. Therefore, we analyze the use of multithreading in more detail in the following sections.

A common strategy to improve a GUI's user responsiveness is to implement multiple threads that can execute independently. A *thread* is an entity that can execute by itself within the process it is bound to. Usually an application uses one thread, which is started automatically by the system at program startup. The developer can create additional threads in a program that run in parallel.

If a computer with multiple processors is used, then two threads can run in parallel. If a single-processor machine is used, then the operating system uses a technique called *preemptive multitasking*, which makes multiple threads look as if they are running in parallel, even though they are sharing one processor. It is entirely up to the operating system to schedule time for each thread to execute. In addition, Intel recently released new processors that allow for *hyperthreading*: the ability to execute two threads in parallel on a single processor.

The action of the operating system in switching between the executions of different threads is also known as *context switching*. Windows uses a round-robin algorithm to schedule time for each of the created threads. The developer has no influence on when exactly the context switches occur. Therefore, it is the task of the developer to synchronize the access of data that is used by two or more concurrent threads. This process, known as *thread synchronization,* is done by using methods for data locking, such as mutual exclusion. In the simplest case, data is locked by the action of the thread requesting a lock to the data. Another thread requesting the same lock must wait until the first thread releases the lock. This implies that if a lock is not released by a thread, the system might hang. Therefore, it is important to be very careful when working with multiple threads and locking mechanisms.

In addition to increased user responsiveness, an implementation using multiple threads can result in improved performance and throughput. If computers with multiple processors or Intel processors with hyperthreading support are used, threads will execute in parallel, and that shortens the execution time. Multithreaded applications achieve improved throughput because if one thread is waiting for a lengthy operation (such as a file read from disk) to finish, another thread can use the processor's idle time for execution.

Multithreading should be used with caution because of potential problems such as race conditions and deadlocks. Both of these are very unpleasant and should be avoided by careful design and implementation.

Race conditions result in corrupted data and unexpected behavior. Because race conditions depend highly on the context switches of the system, they are observed in many kinds of strange behavior of the system.

Deadlocks are easier to detect because the application simply appears to hang. In many cases deadlocks are also dependent on race conditions whose behaviors are, as mentioned before, not predictable.

Race Conditions

Let's look closely at what constitutes a *race condition*. Imagine that thread A is applying the contrast operation to image 1. In the meantime, a second thread, thread B, applies the color correction function to the same image, image 1. In this case the image is being read and written by two threads at the same time. It is up to the operating system to distribute time to each thread. For the developer, this means that there is no way to find out which operation is applied first to a pixel. In some cases, the order of operations does not matter, but in many cases it is essential to the output.

The problem can be solved by synchronizing access to the resource (in this case, the image) that is used to perform the requested operation. This synchronization is also called *locking*. Locking enables programmers to restrict access to a resource to a single thread at a time. In our example, the loaded image needs to be locked while it is altered by thread A. If thread B tries to acquire the lock, it will fail because the image is locked. When thread A finishes its calculation, it releases the lock, and thread B can acquire the lock and perform its operation on the image. Whenever two threads are trying to write to the same data or whenever one thread is writing data that another thread is reading, a lock should be used to ensure that the result of the applied operation is as expected (situations in which two threads are reading the same data are obviously OK as long as the data is not altered). If a lock for an object is acquired by a thread, a second thread that tries to acquire the same lock must wait until the first thread releases it.

This type of serialization is very important when you deal with threads, but it can cause the application to hang if a deadlock is caused by a failure to release the lock when appropriate. Usually, locks should be acquired just before the start of the operation for which the lock is needed and should be released as soon as the data is no longer being used or altered.

Deadlocks

A *deadlock* is a situation in which two or more threads try to work on the same data at the same time and for that reason block each other from proceeding. Deadlocks can happen under many possible scenarios. Imagine three threads called thread A, thread B, and thread C. Thread A holds a lock on object A, thread B holds a lock on object B, and thread C holds a lock on object C. Now thread A tries to acquire a lock on object B, which is held by thread B. Thread B waits for a lock on object C, and thread C is trying to get a lock on object A. In this case, none of the threads can proceed because each thread needs an object that is locked by another thread. Figure 10.3 shows this deadlock scenario.

To recover from this situation, the threads must release the locks of all the objects they are working on and try again in different time spans.

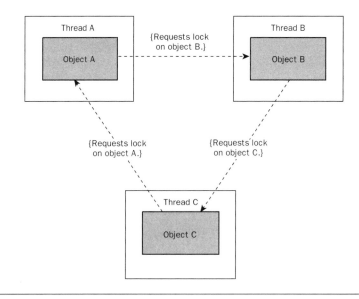

Figure 10.3 Deadlock Example

The best way to recover from deadlocks is to avoid them. For example, the threads could acquire all the locks they need in the same order. This would mean that thread C should acquire the lock first on object A and then on object C. In this way, if object A is locked by thread A, thread C would have to wait until object A was released. At the same time, thread A would have to wait for thread B to release object B, something that eventually will happen because thread B can now acquire the lock to object C, do the necessary work, and release the locks for objects B and C, thereby enabling thread A to do its work, and so on. The described scenario can be seen in Figure 10.4.

Design of the Multithreading Feature

The strategy for the photo editor application is to provide a single *mutex* (mutual exclusion) object, which enables the developer to protect data against corruption by another thread during a calculation. The threads are created using the .NET Framework–provided thread pool capabilities. The calculation of the image-processing operations is done on a copy of the image data; after the thread finishes, the resulting image is shown on the screen.

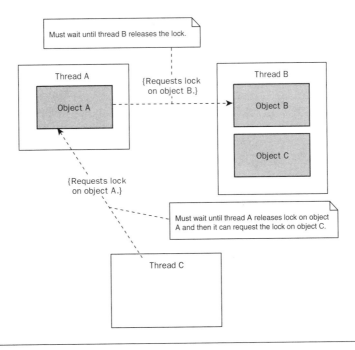

Figure 10.4 Avoiding a Deadlock

In the design review for this chapter, we discover that the class diagram provided in the sixth iteration was not complete. Therefore, we add a defect on the documentation of the defect tracking sheet (provided in the doc directory of the sample solution of this chapter on the accompanying CD), and we update the class diagram to fix this document issue. The class diagram of the photo editor is changed slightly to put the ApplyImage Processing method and the necessary properties into a new class called PlugInInterface. This interface does the locking of the data and invokes the plugin at run time. In addition, the ApplyImageProcessing method of the PlugInInterface class serves as the entry point of the thread created to do the image processing. The updated class diagram is shown in Figure 10.5.

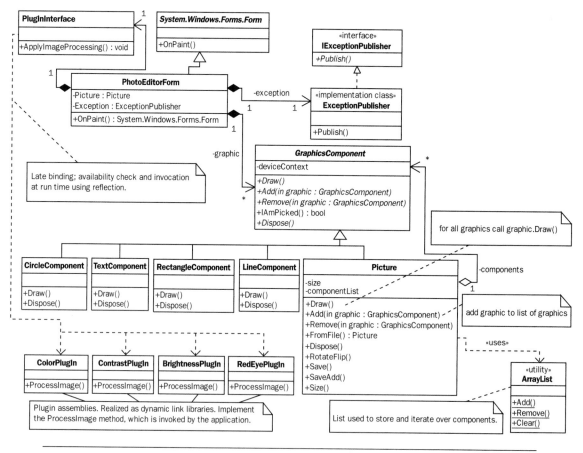

Figure 10.5 Class Diagram with PlugInInterface

For the multithreaded application, it is a good practice to provide a state chart for the typical lock scenario. This will clarify the states of the multithreaded system in the critical scenario.

State Chart of the Lock Scenario

The critical scenario for the image-processing operations of the photo editor occurs if two threads are trying to use the same image data for read or write access at the same time. The state chart in Figure 10.6 shows the handling of such scenarios.

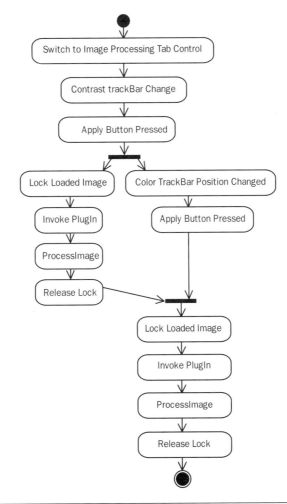

Figure 10.6 State Chart of the Critical Lock Scenario

The state chart shows that a second execution of a plugin component must wait until the first thread has finished the image processing and has released the lock. After the lock has been released, the second thread can acquire the lock and start the calculation.

After the design changes for the optimization functionality are reviewed and released, the project team is ready to move on to the implementation workflow.

10.4 Project Management Issues

The customer has approached the project management with a request to finish the project earlier than originally planned. The customer is willing to put some additional money into the project, which can be used to add more developers. The hope of the customer is that with more money, we can add more people to the project and thereby complete it earlier.

The customer's assumption might be valid if the project were at the very beginning. But the project is already three-fourths completed, so adding more people might not let us finish earlier. Not only would the new people have to learn about the project and the domain, but also they would take time away from the current developers to get up to speed. Thus, adding more people at this point would most likely result in the project's being released even later than originally planned. The flaw in the customer's assumption can be compared to the idea that if one woman can have a baby in nine months, then nine women could have a baby in one month.

For this reason we turn down the request of the customer at this point in the project. Instead, the project team suggests other scenarios in which the project can be delivered earlier than scheduled.

10.4.1 Relation of Project Scope, Cost, Quality, and Time

Classic project management defines three variables (cost, schedule, and project scope) that are dependent on each other. For any two of the variables, the third one is given and cannot be chosen. In software development, sometimes we define one additional variable: the quality of the product. The following list shows the four project management variables for software development.

- Scope: The scope of a project is defined by the deliverable features.
- Schedule: The schedule is defined by time needed to complete the project.
- Quality: The quality of the project is defined by the amount of testing, code reviews, and other quality assurance activities performed.
- Cost: The cost of the project is equivalent to the expenses the project has. This includes the cost of the people working on the project.

Figure 10.7 shows the classic project management variables and the four variables of software development project management.

For any three given variables in software development, the fourth variable is already set. This means, for example, for a given scope, schedule, and quality, the cost is not variable but is given through the other three variables. This means that the customer can set at most three of the four variables, and the project team delivers the other variable based on the three chosen by the customer.

In addition, note that the cost factor can be adjusted only within limits. As mentioned before, adding people (which would be a cost) at the end of a project will not result in the expected earlier release of the project. On the other hand, if we want to finish the project earlier than scheduled, we could decrease the scope or lower the quality. Both actions would decrease the time we need to finish the product.

10.4.2 Early Delivery Possibilities

With the knowledge of the four variables, we can now prepare some proposals for resolving the customer request for early delivery of the project.

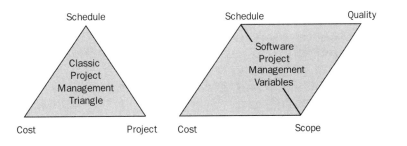

Figure 10.7 Project Management Variables

Reduced Quality (Resolution Proposal 1)

The project can be delivered with less quality. This means that the transition phase will be cut short, and testing will not be as extensive as planned.

Reduced Scope (Resolution Proposal 2)

Some features will be cut. The application will be delivered with fewer features than originally planned, but the transition phase and testing of the implemented features will be done as planned.

Release as Planned (Resolution Proposal 3)

This is the preferred option. The project will be delivered as planned. All the features will be implemented, and testing will be done as planned. The advantage of this proposal is that all basic features will be available (remember that we have already delayed implementation of certain advanced features to a future release, as noted on the defect tracking sheet), and the application will be delivered with sound quality because testing will be done extensively in the transition phase.

After review of the resolution proposals, the customer agrees that the best solution is to deliver the product as planned. It would not make sense to deliver an insufficiently tested application to the users and would incur the risk of our customer losing business because of avoidable defects in the software. Also, the customer agrees that all features that were planned for in the first release are basic features that must be provided. Therefore, the project is to be delivered as planned, with the features as planned.

10.4.3 Other Actions

The posted project plan shows that the project is still in accordance with the plan. No problems are reported that would make new planning necessary.

In the final phase of the development, stand-up meetings are introduced. These short meetings are held every other morning for the remainder of the project. During the stand-up meeting, all participants are standing and everyone gives an update on the status of current work. This type of meeting is supposed to last no longer than 12 minutes, and the purpose is to increase communication of status and problems within the project team. The identified problems usually are not solved in the stand-up meeting, in which case we schedule follow-up meetings with only the relevant project team members.

Stand-up meetings are conducted to get an update from the team members every other day (without taking too much of everybody's productive time), to increase communication among team members, increase visibility to all parties involved, and to have some coffee.

10.5 Multithreading and Optimization Implementation

This section describes the implementation of the optimization and multithreading feature. First we discuss the optimization of the contrast plugin, and then we move on to show how the multithreading feature is implemented to improve GUI responsiveness.

10.5.1 Prototyping Solutions for Performance Optimization

To prototype various optimizations and to try out various implementations, we create a Windows Forms application. We add a new Visual Studio C++ project of type `Windows Forms Application (.NET)` to the `Photo Editor` solution. Give the new project the name `Performance Tests`, and create the project.

We do not change the output path for the assemblies of this project because the application is not part of the deliverables, and the application is not dependent on the photo editor application at all. The goal of this prototype application is to implement and time possible optimizations. Based on the results of the prototype implementations, we will choose a concrete optimization and then implement it in the photo editor application. The performance test GUI that we want to develop is shown in Figure 10.8. Change the form of the created application to match the GUI shown in Figure 10.8.

Table 10.2 shows the elements that are used in the Performance Test GUI.

After we have defined the GUI, we implement the button click event handler, which is used to start and run the performance test. While the test is executing, the progress bars shown on the GUI are updated to reflect the

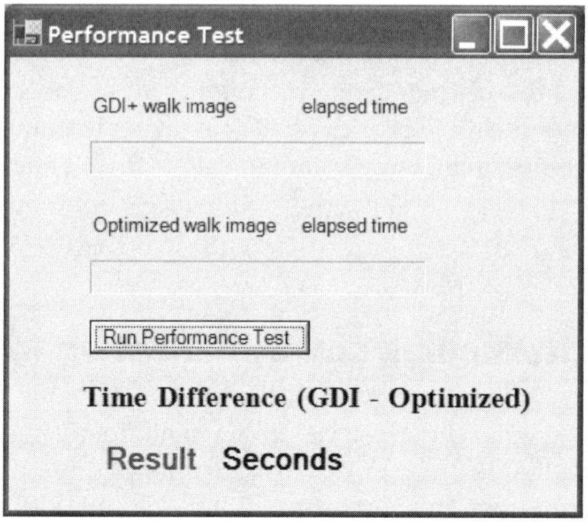

Figure 10.8 Performance Test GUI

progress of the calculation. In addition, the text "elapsed time" is replaced with the actual execution time of the corresponding execution. The Result value then shows the difference in execution time between using the GDI+-provided pixel get/set methods and the optimized pixel accessor method.

The calculation assumes that the optimized method executes faster. Therefore, the result is calculated by subtracting the optimized execution time from the GDI+ execution time.

Table 10.2 Performance Test GUI Elements

Element	Value/Text
Label	Label1/GDI+ walk image
Label	Label2/Optimized walk image
Label	Label3/Result
Label	Label4/Time difference (GDI – Optimized):
Label	Label5/Seconds
Label	Label6/elapsed time
Label	Label7/elapsed time
ProgressBar	progressBar1
ProgressBar	progressBar2
Button	Button1/Run Performance Test

Do It Yourself Implement a test to show the performance difference in accessing pixel information between using pointer arithmetic and using the GDI+ `get` and `set` pixel methods. Use the Performance Test GUI to display the results.

Listing 10.1 shows a sample solution. An interesting detail is that the progress bar is not updated after each pixel calculation but rather after a whole line is calculated. This avoids flickering of the progress bar in case too many updates are called.

Listing 10.1 Performance Tests

```
/// <summary>
/// At button click some tests are done and timed.
/// The result is displayed in the window and gives
/// the time difference between optimized and unoptimized
/// calculation. The calculation is based on the
/// difference = GDI+ - Optimized
/// Assuming the optimized version runs faster
/// so the value is positive.
/// </summary>
private: System::Void button1_Click(System::Object *  sender, System::
EventArgs *  e)
  {
  // Load the image to access it with GDI+
  Bitmap* myImage =
    new Bitmap(Image::FromFile("..\\..\\..\\..\\bin\\Hawaii.jpg"));
  // create region, the size of the image
  System::Drawing::Rectangle imageSize;
  imageSize.X = 0;
  imageSize.Y = 0;
  imageSize.Width = myImage->Width;
  imageSize.Height = myImage->Height;
  // Copy the image
  Bitmap __gc* myClone = myImage->Clone(
    imageSize,
    Imaging::PixelFormat::Format24bppRgb);
  // Lock the image for read write access with pointer
  // arithmetic.
  Imaging::BitmapData* imageData = myClone->LockBits(
    imageSize,
```

```
    Imaging::ImageLockMode::ReadWrite,
    Imaging::PixelFormat::Format24bppRgb);
 // Get the pointer to first element
 char* imagePtr = (char*) imageData->Scan0.ToPointer();
const int zero = 0;
// initialize progress bar to 0
progressBar1->set_Value(zero);
progressBar2->set_Value(zero);
// two clock values to
// measure execution time
clock_t start, finish;
double  duration, duration2;
Color  pixColor;
int numPixels = myImage->Height*myImage->Width;

/* Start time measure. */
start = clock();
// Do GDI+ calculation.
for(int i = 0; i < myImage->Height; ++i)
  {
    for(int j = 0; j < myImage->Width; ++j)
    {
      // Just get and set the pixels
      pixColor = myImage->GetPixel(j, i);
      myImage->SetPixel(j, i, pixColor);
    }
    progressBar1->set_Value((i*j*100)/numPixels);
  }
// Stop the time
finish = clock();
// Get the elapsed time
duration = (double)(finish - start) / CLOCKS_PER_SEC;
// Display duration of execution
label6->set_Text(duration.ToString());
// Start the time
start = clock();
// Walk over image using pointers.
for( int i = 0; i < myImage->Height; ++i)
  {
    for(int j = 0; j < (myImage->Width*3) ; j += 3)
    {
      // Set RGB values, each of
      // which is one char long
```

```
            imagePtr[imageData->Stride*i + j]= (unsigned char)100;
            imagePtr[imageData->Stride*i + j + 1]=
                (unsigned char)150;
            imagePtr[imageData->Stride*i + j + 2]=
                (unsigned char)200;
        }
        // Update progress bar
        progressBar2->set_Value((i*100)/myImage->Height);
            }
    // Stop the clock.
    finish = clock();
    // Calculate elapsed time.
    duration2 = (double)(finish - start) / CLOCKS_PER_SEC;
    // Display time needed for execution
    label7->set_Text(duration2.ToString());
    // Calculate difference between execution times.
    double diff = duration - duration2;
    // free allocated memory.
    myImage->Dispose();
    //Unlock data
    myClone->UnlockBits(imageData);
    // display time difference between executions
    label3->set_Text(diff.ToString());
}
```

Before you can compile the new project, you must add an `include` statement for `#include <time.h>` in the `PerformaceTests.h` header file right after the `#pragma` definition. You can execute the project from within the solution by right-clicking on the `PerformanceTests` project and selecting Debug | Start New Instance (or Step into New Instance). Make sure to run the test in release mode.

The execution of the test application confirms our suspicion that accessing pixel data using pointer arithmetic is much faster than using the accessor methods provided by GDI+. Figure 10.9 shows a sample output of a release-mode compiled `PerformanceTests` run.

The result of the test is very encouraging. The performance gain that we achieved by accessing pixels through pointer arithmetic is tremendous. With this knowledge, the next step is to change the implementation of the contrast plugin to use the optimized pixel access method shown in the performance test.

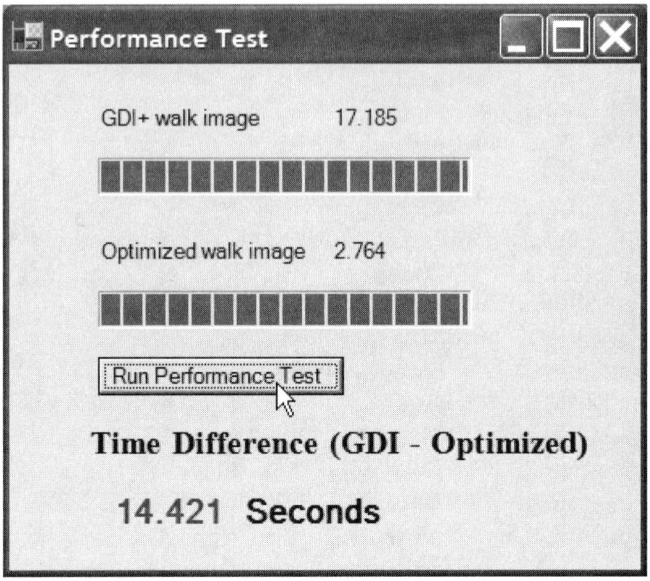

Figure 10.9 Performance Test Result

Because the performance gain was achieved so easily, you may wonder why we used a profiler. The answer is that, in general, a profiler is very useful in identifying bottlenecks, whereas for prototype testing it is more efficient to use a small test program that can easily be changed and sometimes can be added to the validation test suite as a test program.

10.5.2 Implementing the Contrast Plugin Using Pointer Arithmetic for Pixel Access

Based on the prototype, we now implement the contrast plugin. The task of the implementation is to walk through the entire image using pointer arithmetic rather than the set and get methods provided by GDI+. The implementation shown in this example is based on the implementation of the existing contrast plugin. The alternative would be to start a new project, in which case we would have two projects that build a plugin with the same name. We would have to make sure that the optimized plugin was not overwritten by a build of the original plugin, and so on. By changing the implementation of the existing contrast component, we avoid this extra work. If we want to build the old component, then we will just build the plugin with the sample solution of Chapter 8 or 9.

To start the implementation, open the `ContrastPlugIn.cpp` file. Add the following line to the beginning of the file:

```
using namespace Imaging;
```

Then, after the image width and height are set to the maximum x and y values, we create a rectangle the size of the image with the origin in `x = 0` and `y = 0`. Next, we define a pointer to an `unsigned char` with the name `imagePtr`. Then we create a pointer to `BitmapData`, which we name `image Data`.

Before we can get a pointer to the source image data, we lock the data by calling `sourceImage->LockBits`. The parameters passed are the rectangle (with the size of the image that we created before), `ImageLock Mode::ReadWrite` to indicate that we want to read and write to the image data, and the pixel format of the image that we want a pointer to. Now we can get the pointer to the image data by calling `imageData->Scan0.To Pointer()`. This part of the implementation is shown in Listing 10.2.

Listing 10.2 Optimized Contrast Plugin

```
void Contrast::ProcessImage(Bitmap& image,
            int param, int unused1, int unused2)
{
  // Image dimensions.
  unsigned int maxX = image.Width;
  unsigned int maxY = image.Height;
  // Rectangle the size of the image
  Rectangle imageRect;
  imageRect.X = 0;
  imageRect.Y = 0;
  imageRect.Width = maxX;
  imageRect.Height = maxY;
  Rectangle rect(0, 0, maxX, maxY);
  // 8-bit pointer to image data
  unsigned char* imagePtr;

  //image data
  BitmapData* imageData;
```

```
// Lock the image data before asking for a pointer;
imageData = image.LockBits(
  rect,
  ImageLockMode::ReadWrite,
  PixelFormat::Format24bppRgb);
// Scan0.ToPointer returns a pointer to the image data
// as void*, which is cast to 8 bpp or unsigned char *.
imagePtr = (unsigned char*)imageData->Scan0.ToPointer();

// Pixel count initialized with 0.
unsigned long totNumPixels = 0;
```

The next change that we implement has to do with walking through the image to calculate the histogram. Within the nested `for` loop, we delete the following line:

```
Color myColor = image.GetPixel(j, i);
```

In its place we use a mechanism that gets the pointer values via pointer arithmetic. When using pointer arithmetic we must extract each color component from the image separately. In addition, we change the loop so that we can get all three color values of each pixel by multiplying the pixels in x direction by 3 (that is because we have three color components per pixel, so we have three times as many color values as number of pixels in a row). Then we exchange the line that gets a single color value of the current pixel with the lines shown in Listing 10.3.

Listing 10.3 Extracting the Color Values of the Image Pixels

```
// Walk through the whole image
// and calculate histogram.
for(unsigned int i = 0; i < maxY; ++i)
{
  for(unsigned int j = 0; j < maxX*3; j += 3)
  {
    // Calculate the luminance value
    red = imagePtr[imageData->Stride * i + j];
    green = imagePtr[imageData->Stride * i + j + 1];
    blue = imagePtr[imageData->Stride * i + j + 2];
    // Calculate luminance value of current pixel
```

```
    pixVal = (int)(((double)(red) * rFactor) +
      ((double)(green) * gFactor) +
      ((double)(blue) * bFactor));
    // Add the pixel to the histogram
    histogram[pixVal] += 1;
    // Count number of pixels in
    // the histogram.
    totNumPixels++;
  }
}
```

The current position of the pointer for the red color component is calculated by multiplying the number of pixels in each row (which is also called *stride*) by the current position in the y direction plus the current position in the x direction (plus 1 for the green color component, plus 2 for the blue color component). The calculation of the lookup table stays as it is.

The next change takes place in the nested `for` loop where we calculate the new pixel value based on pointer operations. We extract the three color components from each pixel as shown before. The calculation of the new red and green value must change accordingly. These changes are shown in Listing 10.4. After the calculation of the image is finished and before the method is exited, we unlock the bitmap.

Listing 10.4 Calculation of the New Pixel Value Using Pointers

```
// Walk through the whole image
// and calculate the new value of each pixel.
for(unsigned int i = 0; i < maxY; ++i)
{
  // Three values for each pixel (RGB).
  for(unsigned int j = 0; j < maxX*3; j += 3)
  {
    red = imagePtr[imageData->Stride * i + j];
    green = imagePtr[imageData->Stride * i + j + 1 ];
    blue = imagePtr[imageData->Stride * i + j + 2];
    // Calculate luminance value of current pixel.
    pixVal = (int)(((double)red * rFactor) +
      ((double)green * gFactor) +
      ((double)blue * bFactor));
    // Get the lookup table value for the current pixel.
    lutVal = (double)lut[pixVal];
```

```
    // Calculate the new red, green, and blue values.
    imagePtr[imageData->Stride * i + j ] =
      calcNewValue(red, rFactor, pixVal, factor,
      maxPixValue, lutVal);
    imagePtr[imageData->Stride * i + j + 1] =
      calcNewValue(green, gFactor, pixVal, factor,
      maxPixValue, lutVal);
    imagePtr[imageData->Stride * i + j + 2] =
      calcNewValue(blue, bFactor, pixVal, factor, maxPixValue,
      lutVal);
  }
}
// Unlock the image in order
// to copy the new data into the bitmap.
image.UnlockBits(imageData);

}
```

Do It Yourself Think of alternative methods to calculate the image-processing operations more efficiently. Use the profiling tool to identify the bottlenecks, and extend the prototype application to test various implementations before putting them into the application.

After the implementation of the optimized plugin is finished, run the application in the profiler. The contrast calculation should show a considerable performance improvement. If the improvement does not meet the requirements for speed-up, then further optimizations must be made.

Figure 10.10 shows that the implemented optimizations resulted in a considerable performance gain. This performance improvement is better than expected, and no further improvements are made at this time.

10.5.3 Multithreading Implementation to Increase GUI Responsiveness

Additional threads that are created by the developer to perform a certain task are often referred to as *worker threads*. The .NET Framework defines the namespace System.Threading, which provides classes and interfaces to support multithreaded programming.

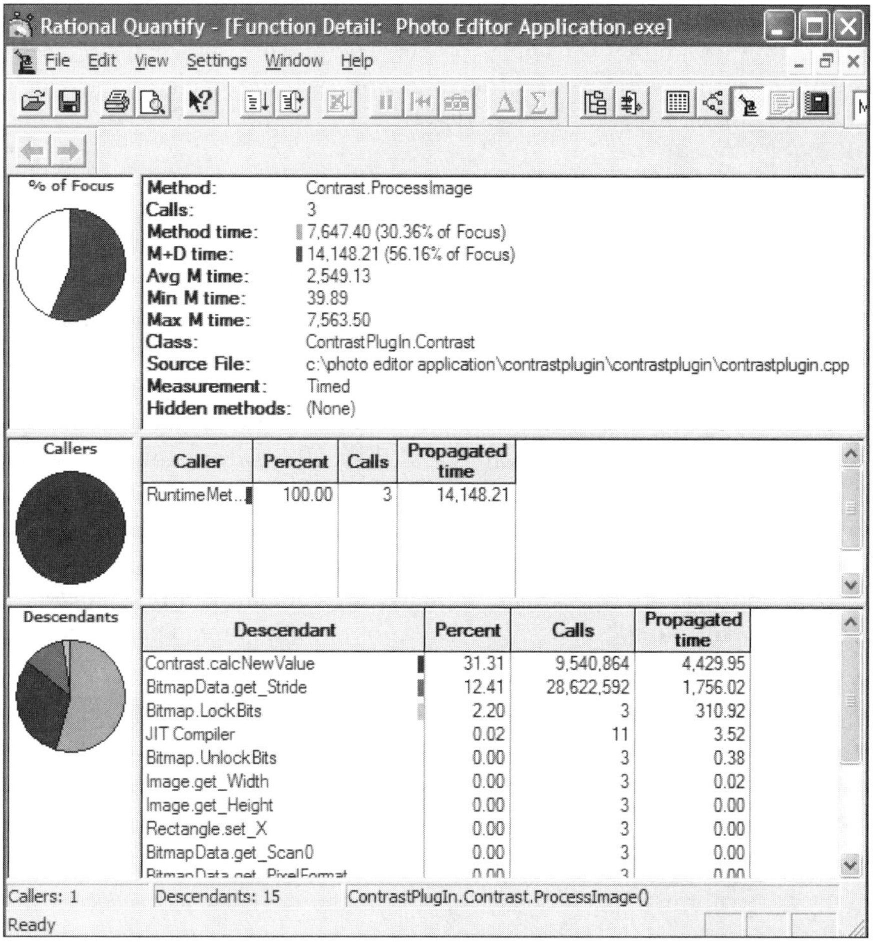

Figure 10.10 Profiling Result of the Optimized Plugin

There are two basic techniques for working with threads. The first one is to use worker threads that are created on-the-fly, and the second one is to use the thread pool classes of the .NET Framework. Before we implement multithreading, let's look at the differences between the two approaches.

You define a worker thread by creating a new instance of `Thread ()`. Merely creating the thread does not make it do anything. To start a thread, you call the `Thread.Start()` method. The details of its entry point are provided as a parameter. The entry point details are actually the details of a method that is used as the entry point when a thread is started. The .NET Framework defines the following delegate declaration, which is used to provide the method used as the entry point:

```
public delegate void ThreadStart()
```

A *thread pool* is a .NET Framework-managed collection of worker threads. This collection of threads enables a more efficient use of threads by letting the developer post work items to the thread pool. The command to add a work item to the list is `ThreadPool.QueueUserWorkItem(...)`. This call takes a method or delegate as a parameter that is used as the entry point for the thread. The work item is then scheduled to be executed by the next thread that becomes available. After a work item is posted, you cannot delete the item.

The thread pool is allocated the first time an instance of the thread pool is created. By default, the maximum number of threads is limited to 25 threads per processor, although this default can be changed if necessary. The example shown in this section uses the thread pool functionality for the optimized implementation of the photo editor.

For more detail on threading and synchronization possibilities, please consult the MSDN documentation provided with .NET.

10.5.4 Using Thread Pools and Locks

The thread that will do the calculation of the image-processing operation will run in parallel to the application, so we use a delegate to call the application at the time the `ApplyImageProcessing` method finishes. When the application is called, we update the display and some properties. The delegate is declared in the `PhotoEditor.cs` file as the first statement after the namespace `Photo_Editor_Application` is defined:

```
/// <summary>
/// Declaration of event used to indicate the completion of
/// an image calculation. Signature uses .NET provided
/// delegate definition.
/// </summary>
public delegate void EventHandler(object sender,
  EventArgs args);
```

We use a `Mutex` in the `PlugInInterface` to ensure that only one image-processing calculation is run at a time. Therefore, we declare a `private` property of type `Mutex` and name it `lockImageProcessing` in the `PlugIn Interface` class. In addition, we define a `public` `get` accessor to get a reference to the `Mutex` from the photo editor application. Then we add the following line and create a new instance of a `Mutex` in the constructor of `PlugInInterface`:

```
using System.Threading;
```

Using a Mutex for Synchronization

In the photo editor application, we use a `Mutex` to ensure that only one thread accesses the image data at a time for writing. Therefore, before we start the actual calculation, a `Mutex` must be acquired by the thread. If the `Mutex` has already been acquired by another thread, then the current thread must wait until the first thread releases the `Mutex`. The `Mutex` class defines the method `WaitOne` to accommodate this common scenario. The `WaitOne` method acquires the `Mutex` if it is not in use; otherwise, the method waits for the `Mutex` to be released and then acquires it. To prevent the application from hanging, we can provide an optional parameter that defines a maximum time to wait before the acquisition is considered failed and an exception is thrown.

After the `Mutex` is acquired, the calculation can be performed. At the end of the calculation the `Mutex` is released so that other threads can work on the new image data. If the lock is not released, the application might hang forever (at least if no timeout was specified in the `WaitOne` method).

Mutex and Delegate Implementation

There are a few changes that we have to make in `PlugInInterface` to make this work. First, we add the following line to the constructor:

```
lockImageProcessing = new Mutex();
```

Then we add the following line to lock the image as soon as we enter the `ApplyImageProcessing` method:

```
lockImageProcessing.WaitOne();
```

Then we release the lock as soon as the `Invoke` method returns:

```
lockImageProcessing.ReleaseMutex();
```

After that, we specify the event handler delegate and invoke the registered event handler methods. The implementation for that is shown in Listing 10.5.

Listing 10.5 Delegate Implementation

```
/// <summary>
/// Specification of the event handler delegate.
/// </summary>
public event EventHandler Notify;
/// <summary>
/// Invokes all registered event handler methods.
/// </summary>
protected virtual void OnNotify(EventArgs e)
{
  Notify(this, e);
}
```

Our next task is to hook the application up to post a work item that is then executed in parallel. To use the `ApplyImageProcessing` method as entry point for the posted work package, we change its definition to

```
public void ApplyImageProcessing(Object stat)
```

ThreadPool Implementation and Application Adaptation

In the `PhotoEditorForm` class we add a new property of type `Mutex` that we call `lockImage`. This property will hold a reference to the `Mutex` created by the `PlugInInterface` class and is used to check whether another thread is already using the image data for another image-processing calculation.

After that, we define an event handler method. The event handler is called `ThreadFinished`, and its signature is the same as the default delegate definition, which takes a sender `object` and `EventArgs` as parameters. In the constructor of `PhotoEditorForm` we assign the `lockImage` mutex to a reference to `lockImageProcessing`, which is one of the properties we added to the `PlugInInterface` class. After that, we register the event handler method `ThreadFinished` so that it is called as a delegate when the calculation in the `ApplyImageProcessing` method is finished. We also define a Boolean flag, `fromApply`, which will be `true` if the call came from the `ApplyImageProcessing` method.

The implementation of this part is shown in Listing 10.6.

Listing 10.6 Application Adaptation

```
using System;
using System.Drawing;
using System.Collections;
using System.Windows.Forms;
using Microsoft.ApplicationBlocks.ExceptionManagement;
using System.Threading;

namespace Photo_Editor_Application
{
  /// <summary>
  /// Declaration of event used to indicate the completion of
  /// an image calculation. Signature uses .NET provided
  /// delegate definition.
  /// </summary>
  public delegate void EventHandler(object sender,
                    EventArgs args);
            *
            *
            *

    /// <summary>
    /// Constructor of the application class.
    /// PhotoEditorForm provides the GUI for the photo
    /// editor project.
    /// </summary>
    public PhotoEditorForm()
    {
          *
          *
          *

      plugInInterface = new PlugInInterface();
      lockImage = plugInInterface.LockImageProcessing;
      plugInInterface.Notify +=
        new EventHandler(this.ThreadFinished);
      picturePreView.Image = thumbImage;
      // Calls helper method to draw the image
      DisplayImage();
```

```
   }
   /// <summary>
   /// This method is called when a worker
   /// thread is finished with
   /// the calculation. If Apply was the reason for execution
   /// then update the loaded image and the thumbnail.
   /// </summary>
   /// <param name="sender">Object that sent the event.</param>
   /// <param name="e">The event arguments. Not used</param>
   /// <requirements>F:editor_optimization</requirements>
   public void ThreadFinished(object sender, EventArgs e)
   {
     if(fromApply)
     {
       //PictureObject.LoadedImage.Dispose();
       PictureObject.LoadedImage =
         (Bitmap)plugInInterface.TmpBitmap.Clone();
       thumbImage =
         plugInInterface.TmpBitmap.GetThumbnailImage(
           picturePreView.Width, picturePreView.Height,null,
           IntPtr.Zero);
       // picturePreView.Image = (Image)thumbImage.Clone();
       fromApply = false;
       DisplayImage();
     }
   }
   /// <summary>
   /// Flag used to indicate whether Apply button
   /// was reason for calculation of new image.
   /// </summary>
   private bool fromApply = false;
   /// <summary>
   /// Holds a reference to the plugInInterface Mutex.
   /// </summary>
   private Mutex lockImage;
```

According to the requirements, we use multiple threads to enable interactivity of the application even when an image-processing calculation is executed. This means that if a new thumbnail calculation is done, no improvement is necessary.

This leads us to implement another `applyImageProcessing` method, which is called by the `trackBar` event handlers to set up `PlugInInterface` for calculation of the thumbnail. Therefore, we add a `private applyImage Processing` method to the `PhotoEditorForm` class. This method is called from all the `trackBar` event handlers. Within the method, a copy of the thumbnail is stored in `plugInInterface.tempImage` for calculation. Then we check whether the `Mutex` was acquired by another thread, and, if it was, the method waits until it can acquire the `Mutex`.

Note: A `Mutex` can be acquired multiple times by the same thread without locking. For each acquisition of a `Mutex`, a corresponding release must be called so that other threads are not locked out.

The next step is to call `ApplyImageProcessing` of `plugInInterface` to execute the actual calculation. The parameter `null` must be provided but is not used. After the calculation is done, the lock is released. This is possible because the image processing is executed sequentially (that is, in the same thread) if the execution was done on a thumbnail image. Now we update the preview image. A sample implementation is shown in Listing 10.7.

Listing 10.7 The `private applyImageProcessing` Method

```
/// <summary>
/// This method is called when a new thumbnail is
/// calculated for previewing a transformation.
/// </summary>
private void applyImageProcessing()
{
  // Copy the current thumbnail to the tmpBitmap,
  // which is used as the image on which the
  // image-processing calculation is performed.
  plugInInterface.TmpBitmap = (Bitmap)thumbImage.Clone();
  // Wait until Mutex is released and acquire it.
  lockImage.WaitOne();
  // Call the PlugInInterface method to do the magic.
  plugInInterface.ApplyImageProcessing(null);
  // Release the acquired lock
  lockImage.ReleaseMutex();
  // Set the preview image to a copy of the calculated tmpImage.
  picturePreView.Image = (Image)plugInInterface.TmpBitmap.Clone();
}
```

The next task is to actually implement the `ApplyProcessingButton_Click` event handler. When the image-processing functionality is applied to the entire image, a new work item is posted to a new thread, which will do the calculation and call the application when the processing is finished. Therefore, we copy the loaded image first and set `tmpBitmap` of `plugIn Interface` to contain the created copy. This avoids access violations in case `customScrollableControl` tries to repaint the loaded image and the image is locked because a calculation is being performed.

Next, we send the work item to the queue to be processed by a thread in the thread pool. Then the flag indicating that the calculation was done on the entire image is set to `true`. The implementation of this functionality can be seen in Listing 10.8.

Listing 10.8 Using the Thread Pool

```
/// <summary>
/// Applies the current image-processing
/// operation to the currently loaded image
/// using the thread pool functionality.
/// </summary>
private void ApplyProcessingButton_Click(object sender,
    System.EventArgs e)
{
  try
  {
    // Store a copy of the loaded image on which the
    // image-processing calculation is performed.
    plugInInterface.TmpBitmap =
      (Bitmap)PictureObject.LoadedImage.Clone();
// Use a thread pool and add a work item to the list of items
    // that need to be calculated.
    ThreadPool.QueueUserWorkItem(
      new WaitCallback(plugInInterface.ApplyImageProcessing));
    // Set flag to indicate that this calculation was done
    // on the entire image.
    fromApply = true;
  }
  catch(Exception exception)
  {
    ExceptionManager.Publish(exception);
  }
}
```

The implementation is almost complete except for the callback method that is called when a thread finishes the calculation to let the application know that the data can be used. Therefore, we implement the method `ThreadFinished`.

In the new method we first check whether the preceding calculation was done on the entire image. If it was, then we set the loaded image to the newly calculated image, create a new thumbnail, and store it in the `thumb Image` property. Then we reset the flag that shows whether the calculation was done on the entire image to `false`. We do this before the `Display Image()` method is called to propagate the changes. Listing 10.9 shows the implementation of the `ThreadFinished` method.

Listing 10.9 The `ThreadFinished` Method

```
/// <summary>
/// This method is called when a worker thread is finished with
/// the calculation. If Apply was the reason for execution,
/// then update the loaded image and the thumbnail.
/// </summary>
/// <param name="sender">Object that sent the event.</param>
/// <param name="e">The event arguments. Not used</param>
/// <requirements>F:editor_optimization</requirements>
public void ThreadFinished(object sender, EventArgs e)
{
  // If calculation was done on entire image...
  if(fromApply)
  {
    // ...get a copy of the bitmap calculated and store it as
    // the loaded image in order to display it.
    PictureObject.LoadedImage =
      (Bitmap)plugInInterface.TmpBitmap.Clone();
    // Set the thumbnail image to the newly calculated image.
    thumbImage = plugInInterface.TmpBitmap.GetThumbnailImage(
      picturePreView.Width, picturePreView.Height,null,
        IntPtr.Zero);
    // Reset the flag.
    fromApply = false;
    // Show the world the new image.
    DisplayImage();
  }
}
```

For this change to work, we must add the following line in the `Apply ImageProcessing` method just before the method returns:

```
OnNotify(new EventArgs());
```

Without this line, the event handler will not be called and the `Apply` button will not work.

The complete solution is provided as sample solutions on the accompanying CD. To test the implementation, load a large image into the photo editor application, and apply an image-processing calculation to the entire image. Then try to switch to another tab control to see whether the application is still responding to user inputs. If it is, then the goal of this iteration has been achieved. Figure 10.11 shows a snapshot of the application.

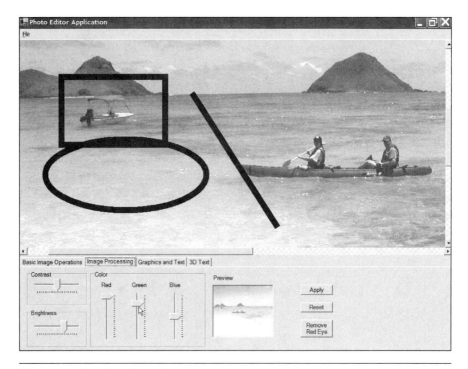

Figure 10.11 The Photo Editor Application

Do It Yourself The defect with the ID 00006 (found in Chapter 8) is still open. It is your task to find a fix for this problem. A sample solution is provided in the source code on the CD (search for "Defect0006").

Suspicion: Check out the spin control. Make sure that the problem does not exist in a test application with only a spin control on the form. See sample solution for the test application and the solution.

10.6 Unit Tests

In this iteration we did not change the behavior of the application. In fact, the application should behave exactly like the application developed in Chapter 9. The only difference is the optimized implementation of the algorithms and the improved GUI responsiveness. Neither feature should change the characteristics of the application. For that reason, no new test is added. Instead, the existing tests are rerun to make sure that the application did not change its behavior.

Do It Yourself In testing new defects (Defect0008 and Defect0009) were found and added to the Defect tracking sheet. It is your task to debug and test the problems. Add more test cases to the unit tests. Is there a way to test the GUI responsiveness and performance?

10.7 Conclusion

The objective of this chapter was to implement optimizations to the existing system. All required functionality that was scheduled for this iteration went through the core workflows: requirements, analysis, design, implementation, and test. The implementation was run, and initial unit testing was performed. In addition, the project planning documents were updated. The code documentation was generated. Therefore, the project is ready for the end of iteration review.

10.7.1 Review

Based on the goals set for this iteration, the following work artifacts are reviewed to decide whether the project can proceed to the next iteration.

- Requirements: Refine the requirements and system scope.
- Analysis: Analyze the requirements by describing what the system does.
- Design: Develop the design of the functionality implemented in this iteration by using UML.
- Implementation: Implement the required functionality.
- Test: Unit-test the implemented features.

All these criteria have been fulfilled, so the project can move on to the next iteration in the construction phase, when we will start the development of Online Photo Shop.

10.8 References for Further Reading

Profiling Tools

www.automatedqa.com

www.borland.com

www.rational.com

Performance Analysis

http://cedar.intel.com/media/training/perf_meth/tutorial/
   index.htm

http://developer.intel.com/design/pentium4/manuals/

http://www.intel.com/intelpress/sum_soc.htm

Multithreading

Jim Beveridge and Robert Wiener, *Multithreading Applications in Win32* (Reading, MA: Addison-Wesley, 1997)

Doug Lea, *Concurrent Programming in Java* (Boston: Addison-Wesley, 2000)

http://cedar.intel.com/media/training/hyper_threading_intro/
   tutorial/index.htm

http://www.c-sharpcorner.com/2/mt_beginner1.asp

CHAPTER 11

Building the Web Application with ASP.NET

 Unified Process:
Construction Phase and Ninth Iteration

This chapter starts the ninth iteration, which continues the construction phase. The goal is to complete the design, implementation, and unit test of the majority of Web-based requirement keys. In this chapter we implement the framework for the online presence of the printing and embossing business.

11.1 Online Store Requirements

The overall product vision, along with the initial set of requirements, was defined during the inception phase of the Unified Process in Chapter 4. The preceding iteration concluded the development of the photo editor application, which allows customers to do simple image postprocessing using their personal computers. The construction phase now continues with the development of the Web site for the business, which allows online customers to order products customized with their personal images.

The initial project plan created in Chapter 4 anticipated the following requirements to be addressed in the ninth iteration of the project:

- `F:order_products`
- `F:product_browse`
- `F:product_options`
- `F:product_customize`
- `F:product_shopping_cart`

- `F:order_checkout`
- `F:checkout_shipping`
- `C:checkout_shipping_cont`
- `F:checkout_payment`
- `C:checkout_payment_method`

However, further analysis of typical use cases of the product also led to a change request for the Online Photo Shop Web site, and this change requires adjustments to the original project plan. Analyzing the typical use cases has shown that online customers will return to the Web site and place new orders for products such as prints, cups, or T-shirts as long as they are satisfied with the service. To ease the ordering process for returning customers, it has been decided to store the shipping and payment information for each new customer. When a customer returns, he or she can simply update the stored information if necessary. Of course, this information needs to remain confidential between the business and the online customer and therefore must be placed in a secure area of the Web site. Furthermore, each online customer will be required to log in to the order section of the Web site with an identifier and password. See Table 11.1 for the definition of the new requirement key.

In the initial project plan we tried to group requirement keys by technical areas. This led to (for example) all Web-Form-related requirement keys being placed in the ninth iteration. This kind of grouping usually makes it easier to assign developer resources and to minimize dependencies between iterations and thereby to enable developers to work in parallel. But adding the login page and security aspects of the entire checkout area to this iteration would be overload it and would introduce a higher risk to the entire project. On the other hand, there seems to be a buffer in the tenth iteration; the plan was to use this buffer to address summarizing an order and securing payment information. Furthermore, security aspects now overlap with the newly added login requirement. We therefore rearrange

Table 11.1 Customer Login Requirement

Requirement	Type	Summary
`F:customer_login`	Functional	Returning customers shall be able to use their previous shipping and payment information by providing their e-mail identifier and a password.

Table 11.2 Refined Iterations 9 and 10

Phase	Iteration	Type: Requirement Key

Construction phase	Iteration 9	`F:order_products`
		`F:product_browse`
		`F:product_options`
		`F:product_customize`
		`F:product_shopping_cart`

	Iteration 10	`F:customer_login`
		`F:order_checkout`
		`F:checkout_shipping`
		`C:checkout_shipping_cont`
		`F:checkout_payment`
		`C:checkout_payment_method`
		`R:checkout_payment_secure`
		`F:checkout_summarize`

all checkout- and security-related requirement keys to fall in the tenth iteration. Table 11.2 shows the updated project plan.

The focus for the ninth iteration, which is described in this chapter, is now limited to the following:

- Managing an XML product catalog: We need to design a generic format for products and product attributes such as pricing and shipping cost. We will implement utility classes that provide access to this catalog.
- Implementing an online product browser: Maintaining static Web pages is a very time-consuming and risky task. Manual updates can lead to incorrect or outdated product descriptions or, even worse, outdated pricing. For this reason a Web browser interface for the XML product catalog needs to be implemented.
- Customizing products with uploaded images: The main idea behind the business's online store is the capability of customers to order customized products. An interface needs to be developed that allows users to upload an image for each ordered item.
- Shopping cart: Customers must be able to place items in a personal shopping cart while browsing the product catalog. After items have been placed into the shopping cart, the customer can proceed to the checkout procedure.

Table 11.3 Requirements of Iteration 9

Requirement	Type	Summary
F:order_products	Functional	Ordering products via an Internet site shall be provided. A product catalog is provided as an XML document.
F:products_browse	Functional	Customers shall be able to browse through the products catalog, which is provided in form of formatted HTML documents.
F:product_options	Functional	Customers shall be able to choose between options offered for a particular product.
F:product_customize	Functional	Customers shall be able to customize a product with personal digital pictures.
F:product_shopping_cart	Functional	Customers shall be able to add products to a shopping cart while browsing through the product catalog.
C:online_shop_codebehind	Constraint	Web forms shall be created using the Visual Studio Web Form wizard and follow separation of code and design (code behind).
C:online_shop_ stateservice	Constraint	To allow for future scalability, the ASP State service shall be used to implement session management.

Table 11.3 summarizes all requirement keys for the online store that are addressed in this chapter. As per project definition, for all iterations of the construction phase we must complete design, implementation, and unit tests for all requirement keys to fulfill the go/no-go criterion for this iteration.

11.2 Analyzing Interfaces and Activities

 In this section we analyze and define interfaces between the online shop software and the printing and embossing business on one side and the online customers on the other. The following interfaces are to be defined:

■ A product catalog format that allows the business to describe and update all offered products
■ Online store activities that can be performed by the online customers
■ Web forms that display or collect necessary information.

11.2.1 The XML Product Catalog

The product catalog represents the interface of the printing and embossing business to the Web application. It is the primary base for generating the Web pages to be browsed by the online customers. From our experience most projects are best approached in a top-down fashion. You first define the interfaces and then move downward to the top-level class design and then down to the utility classes and so on. For that reason we define our system's interfaces with the two actors—the business and the online customer (see Figure 4.1: Use Case Diagram for Online Photo Shop)—before we proceed with the design workflow.

The business offers products that are customizable with personal digital images. Prints in various formats form the most important product group. But other items, such as cups, mouse pads, and framed pictures, also must be addressed. To accommodate this we use a list of products, where each product contains a list of options. For each product we define an identifier, a name, a summary, and an image that will be shown on generated HTML pages. Listing 11.1 shows a product catalog example.

Listing 11.1 `products.xml`: Product Catalog Example

```
<?xml version="1.0" encoding="utf-8" ?>
<doc>
  <products>
    <product id="print" name="Prints">
      <summary>Order prints and enlargements from your favorite digital
pictures. You can choose from three different sizes up to 8x10 inches!
Our prints are always done on high-quality Kodak photo paper and
processed within two business days.</summary>
      <image>img/prints.jpg</image>
      <option id="4x6" name="Small (4x6 inches)" price="0.59">
        <summary>Small prints 4x6 inches.</summary>
        <size>5x7</size>
      </option>
```

```
      <option id="5x7" name="Regular (5x7 inches)" price="0.99">
        <summary>Medium-size prints 5x7 inches.</summary>
        <size>6x8</size>
      </option>
      <option id="8.5x11" name="Poster (8x10 inches)" price="3.99">
        <summary>Poster size prints (8x10 inches).</summary>
        <size>9x12</size>
      </option>
      <option id="wallet" name="Wallet (4 per sheet)" price="0.99">
        <summary>Wallet size prints (4 per sheet).</summary>
        <size>9x12</size>
      </option>
     </product>
   <product id="cup" name="Cups">
     <summary>Order cups customized with your personal pictures or
graphics. Create one for each member of your family! A cup with a
personal message or picture is also a great gift.</summary>
      <image>img/cups.jpg</image>
      <option id="mug" name="Coffee/Tea Mug" price="13.99">
        <summary>White</summary>
        <size>6x6x6</size>
        <weight>0.5</weight>
      </option>
      <option id="latte" name="Set of Two 'Cafe Latte' Cups" price="24.99">
        <summary>Black</summary>
        <size>6x6x6</size>
        <weight>0.5</weight>
      </option>
    </product>
  </products>
</doc>
```

To compute the shipping cost for each order, the product options contain not only the price but also information about the size and weight. One of the advantages of using an XML file to describe the products is that we can add more information later if it becomes necessary.

11.2.2 Online Store Activities

The online customer interacts through the Web pages with Online Photo Shop. The initial architecture description in Chapter 4 mentions a shopping cart form and a checkout form. Although designing HTML documents that describe and advertise products is not a requirement, we still need to implement a dynamic Web page that lets the online customer browse through all products. Furthermore, we have decided that access to the checkout area requires the customer to log in so that any previous payment and shipping information can be displayed.

The basic workflow of how the customer interacts with the Web forms of the online store is simple. Initially the customer will be directed to the browser page, where all products are advertised. Users can add items to the shopping cart and customize the items with a digital image while browsing. This site also contains a link to the shopping cart to let users review all items placed in it. After reviewing the shopping cart, the customer can continue shopping and return to the product browser, or proceed to checkout. During checkout, users must go through an identification or login step to enter the secure area where previous shipping and payment information is shown. Figure 11.1 visualizes the states of the online shop in a UML activity diagram.

In a UML activity diagram, each state represents a condition during which a form waits for input or performs an action. Arrows show transitions from one state to another. A *guarded* transition is assigned a condition under which the transition takes place. In the example in Figure 11.1, two guarded transitions are connected to the decision element under the Show Shopping Cart state. These transitions represent the two link buttons in the Web form, which redirect the customer either back to the browser form or forward to the checkout form. The black circles on the top and the bottom represent the initial and the final states of this diagram, in our case entering the Web site and completing the order.

11.2.3 Web Forms

Before starting the design workflow of this iteration, we define the basic structure of the important Web forms. The purpose is mainly to capture information and data that is processed and displayed on these forms, not to design the layout or look and feel.

The first Web form we analyze is the browser form, where we will display information from the product catalog. The customer must also be able to select between available product options and upload a personal image to customize the item. Figure 11.2 shows a sketch of the browser form using prints as an example product.

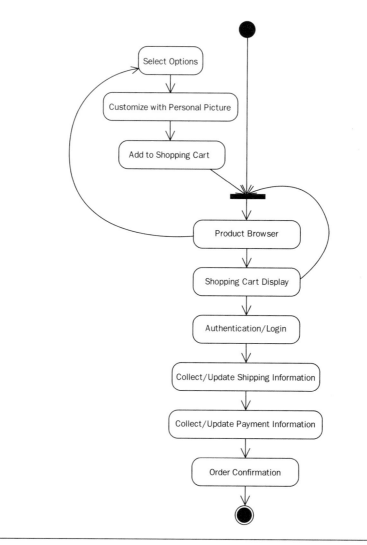

Figure 11.1   Activity Diagram for Online Photo Shop

At any point while browsing through products, the customer must be able to check and view the items already placed in the shopping cart. For this purpose we add a navigation bar at the top of the form. Using the shopping cart link on the right, the customer can display all items placed in the shopping cart. Figure 11.3 shows a sketch of this form. Here, too, we add a navigation bar that allows the customer to continue shopping or proceed to checkout.

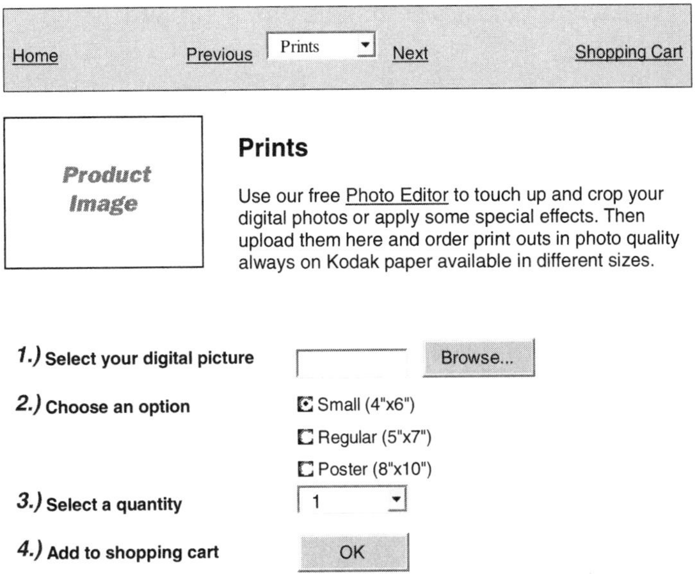

Figure 11.2 Sketch of Catalog Browser Form

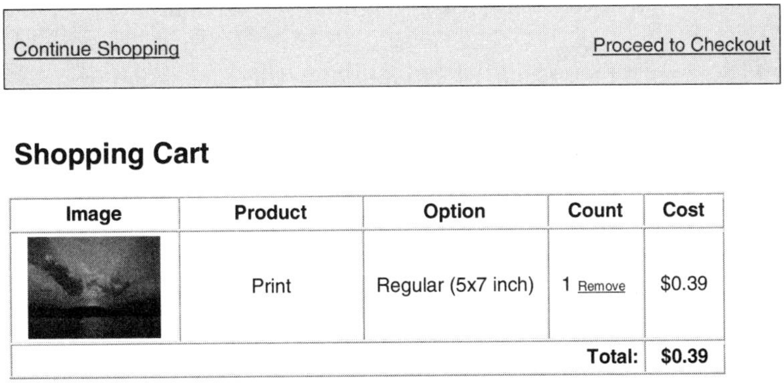

Figure 11.3 Shopping Cart Form

Hand-drawn sketches are perfectly fine for determining which information is presented in which form. Alternatively, design tools such as Frontpage or even Word (which was used here) are useful for creating possible layouts. Just avoid getting lost in details or graphics that are not important to the logic of the application. Designs usually change quite frequently, and it is almost certain that a completely different layout will be applied to all pages before the product is released. For the same reason, it is highly recommended that you use code behind technology, rather than interweave the code with the HTML, during the implementation. For the development of Online Photo Shop, the use of code behind is even mandated by an architectural requirement.

11.3 Breakdown of the Code Modules

Now that we have analyzed the activities and interfaces of the online shop, we can start breaking the functionality into modules. Some functions will be needed across many forms, and it is useful to encapsulate those functions into utility classes. For example, parsing the XML product catalog will be necessary for almost every activity:

- Product browser: Retrieves the product description, image, and available options
- Shopping cart: Gets the pricing of the items in the shopping cart
- Checkout: Computes the total of the order, including shipping cost based on the total weight or size of all items

In this section we break down the functional items into modules and develop a class diagram for Online Photo Shop. Figure 11.4 shows the class diagram of the Web application part of Online Photo Shop.

11.3.1 The Product Parser

Because parsing the XML product catalog is needed across almost every aspect of the online store, we create a utility class with simple high-level API functions that return the list of all products, the list of options for a given product, and the complete set of information stored in the XML file with each product or option item.

11.3.2 The Shopping Cart

Another area that stretches across multiple forms is the shopping cart. The .NET Framework provides containers and lists from which the shopping cart can be inherited. Because each item in this online store is customizable by personal images, we must create a unique identifier for each item in the

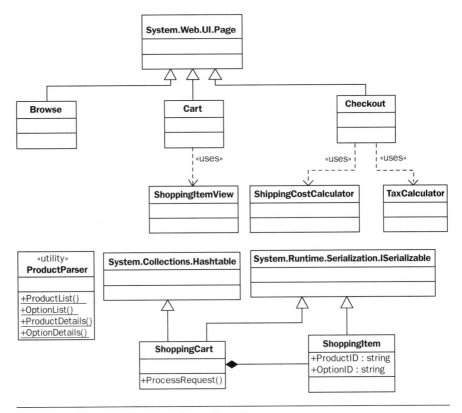

Figure 11.4 Class Diagram for Online Shop

shopping cart. This unique identifier lets us associate each ordered item with its own digital image. We will create a class that encapsulates all information stored with an ordered item, including the following:

- Product code
- Selected option
- Quantity
- Name of the uploaded image on the server
- Path of the uploaded image on the client

Storing the image location on the client lets us later display the images quickly and easily in the shopping cart. We could downsize the uploaded images to a thumbnail size and send them back for display, but we have a better plan. We directly specify the path of the image on the client, along with the desired display size, in the shopping cart form, and have Internet Explorer take care of the downsizing.

Because we must use unique identifiers for each shopping cart item, it makes sense to inherit the shopping cart from a hash table collection, which offers fast access to all the elements using the unique identifier. According to the requirement `C:online_shop_stateservice`, the information stored in the shopping cart must also be serializable so that we can transfer it to the ASP.NET State server. To fulfill this requirement, both the class implementing the shopping cart and the class representing a shopping item must inherit from `ISerializable` and must implement the serialization methods.

Furthermore, we encapsulate functionality that deals with the display of the shopping cart items in a dedicated class (`ShoppingItemView`). This class formats a shopping cart item for display in a data list. For example, this class translates product and option codes of a shopping cart item into a name and a description.

11.3.3 Web Forms

The Web forms that must be implemented in this iteration are the product browser and the shopping cart view. We create both forms using Visual Studio.NET. These forms inherit from the .NET Framework class `System.Web.UI.Page` and use code behind technology to separate program logic from HTML design.

11.3.4 Calculators

Following the revised project plan described at the beginning of this chapter, we have decided to address the checkout process in the next iteration. However, while we are breaking the functionalities into modules we can already see that it's a good idea to encapsulate all the algorithms that we use to compute the tax and shipping cost. Tax and shipping cost may vary regionally and may change over time. It is therefore a good idea to split these functional items into separate classes for easier maintenance.

11.4 Implementation of Online Photo Shop

All required interfaces and modules for this iteration have been defined, and we can now begin the implementation of our online shop.

11.4.1 Creating a New Web Application

For the Web application of Online Photo Shop, we create a new project. The developer workstation can also serve as a Web server for the Online Photo Shop project. All that is required is a local installation of Microsoft Internet Information Server (IIS). To run the Web server on a different machine, for `localhost` you must substitute the server's machine name or IP address throughout the remainder of this chapter.

After setting up IIS, start Microsoft Visual Studio.NET and choose New Project. Create a new C# ASP.NET Web application and set the location to `http://localhost/OnlinePhotoShop`. A new project will be created by the application wizard.

Next, we delete the unneeded default form `Webform1.aspx` from the project. Then we configure the version control for the source files. For this, open the Visual Studio Options via the Tools menu and use Visual Source Safe settings under the Source Control folder for the General and the SCC Provider settings (see Figure 11.5).

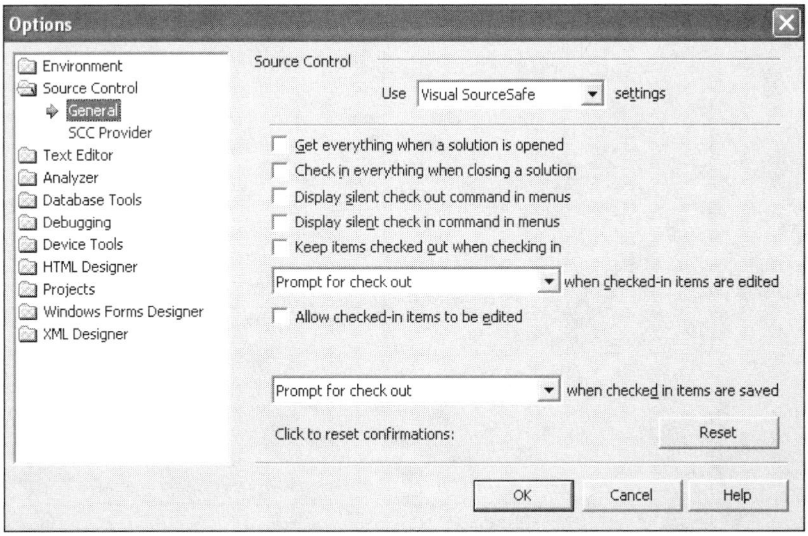

Figure 11.5 Source Control Settings for Visual Studio.NET

Next, we configure source control for the virtual directory that has been created. Open the Internet Services Manager console, which can be found in Control Panel under Administrative Tools. In Internet Services Manager, choose the virtual directory of `OnlinePhotoShop` in Default Web Site, and open the Properties window (see Figure 11.6). Click on the Server Extensions tab, and choose Visual Source Safe in the Version Control field. Now close and reopen the project on the developer machine to make sure that source control has been set up correctly.

Team Development This book assumes that only one developer works on the project at a time, a practice referred to as *isolated team development*. In many real-life projects, however, this isolation is not feasible because multiple developers must work on the same project or even the same source files simultaneously (non-isolated). A variety of options exist for setting up your development environment for team work. "Team Devel-

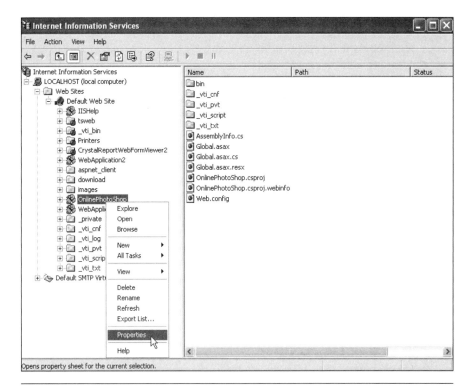

Figure 11.6 Internet Services Manager

opment with Visual Studio .NET and Visual Source Safe" is a comprehensive document explaining those options and their advantages and disadvantages as well as good practices. It can be downloaded from the Internet using the following link: `http://microsoft.com/downloads/release.asp?ReleaseID=35981`

11.4.2 Parsing the XML Product Catalog

Let's first add the product catalog sample file `products.xml` from Listing 11.1 to the `OnlinePhotoShop` project. Just add a new XML file to the solution and fill it with the products shown in Listing 11.1.

Reading the Product List

Next, we define a new class for the `ProductParser` utility. This class provides the application with a set of helper methods that parse the XML product catalog for various products and options. Add a member variable `mFilename` of type `string` to the class, and set it within the constructor as shown in Listing 11.2. This member stores the file name of the product catalog throughout the lifetime of this class.

Listing 11.2 `ProductParser.cs`: The `ProductParser` Class Declaration

```
using System;
using System.Collections;   // Hashtable, SortedList
using System.Xml;           // XmlTextParser

namespace OnlinePhotoShop
{
  /// <summary>
  /// Utility class providing helper methods to parse an XML
  /// product catalog file.
  /// </summary>
  /// <requirement>F:order_products</requirement>
  /// <requirement>F:products_options</requirement>
  public class ProductParser
  {
    /// <summary>
    /// Private member that stores the path of the XML product
    /// catalog file.
    /// </summary>
    private string mFilename;
```

```
/// <summary>
/// Constructor.
/// </summary>
/// <param name="filename">Path of XML product catalog
/// file.</param>
public ProductParser(string filename)
{
  mFilename = filename;
}
}
}
```

Now we add a method to parse the file for a list of all products. But before adding this method to the class, we must choose or define a return type. Because the list of products will be used as a data source for drop-down lists or similar controls, it is desirable to store each product identifier together with its description in a list. The .NET Framework provides the collections `Hashtable` and `SortedList`, in which all entries consist of a Key field and a Value field. The `Hashtable` class provides faster access to the elements, whereas `SortedList`, as the name implies, sorts the items in alphabetical order. We can use both classes to group product code and product name in each entry and return such a collection after all products have been parsed. Because we would like to bind the returned list directly to Web page controls, we use the `SortedList` class for the product and option list and use the `Hashtable` class for querying details on the products and options.

The .NET Framework class `XmlTextReader` provides a fast implementation of parsing XML documents. To find all products in the file, we must read all nodes and check the elements for the product tag. If a product tag has been found, the attribute's ID and name are added to the returned list. To avoid parsing additional tags within the same product, we call `Read InnerXml()` and the parser advances to the next product tag. Listing 11.3 shows the implementation for a product list query.

Listing 11.3 `ProductParser.cs`: The `ProductList()` Method

```
/// <summary>
/// Queries all products from a product catalog.
/// </summary>
/// <returns>SortedList where product identifiers are stored in
```

```
/// the Key field, and product names in the Value field.</returns>
public SortedList ProductList()
{
  SortedList table = new SortedList();
  XmlTextReader parser = new XmlTextReader(mFilename);

  // read all nodes
  while(parser.Read())
  {
    if (parser.NodeType == XmlNodeType.Element)
    {
      if (parser.Name == "product")
      {
        // found a product tag, add new item to list
        table.Add(parser.GetAttribute("id"),
          parser.GetAttribute("name"));

        // read the "inside" of the product tag
        // to advance to next product
        parser.ReadInnerXml();
      }
    }
  }

  return table;
}
```

Checking Progress through Informal Testing

To monitor our progress with the implementation and check whether the newly added parser method works, we add the Web form `Browse.aspx` to the project. From the Toolbox, drag and drop a `DropDownList` Web form control to the design view, and set the property (ID) to `Product`. The control must be initialized in the `Page_Load` method. To add code to this method, you must open the code behind file. Right-click on `Browse.aspx` in Solution Explorer, and select View Code to open `Browse.aspx.cs`. Locate the `Page_Load` method, and add the code to get the product list using the `ProductParser` class and associate it with the `Product` control.

Listing 11.4 shows how to associate the product list from the product parser with a `DropDownList` control. `DataValueField` selects which properties from the list entries represent the values that are set via the control and eventually transmitted back to the server. In our implementation we use the product identifiers stored in `Key` for this field. On the other hand, `TextValueField` defines the property of the list item that is displayed on the screen. We associate `Value` with this field, which contains the product name.

Listing 11.4 `Browse.aspx.cs`: The `PageLoad()` Method

```
private void Page_Load(object sender, System.EventArgs e)
{
  // Put user code to initialize the page here
  if (!Page.IsPostBack)
  {
    // Initialize the product parser
    ProductParser catalog = new
      ProductParser(Server.MapPath("products.xml"));

    // Get the product list and set it in the Product control
    SortedList products = catalog.ProductList();
    Product.DataValueField = "Key";
    Product.DataTextField = "Value";
    Product.DataSource = products;
    Product.DataBind();
    Product.SelectedIndex = 0;
  }
}
```

To better understand this, let's start the application and look at the HTML client code generated by IIS for the product list. Running the application requires setting the initial Web page via the project properties. Open the properties via the Project menu, and choose Configuration Properties, Debugging, where you enter `Browse.aspx` in the Start Page setting. Now the application can be started with the F5 function key.

You will see a Web page with a drop-down list showing Prints and Cups. Let's take a look at the HTML code by selecting the menu View Source in Internet Explorer. Near the end of the code you will find the HTML tags for `select` and `option`, which represent the drop-down list.

```
<select name="Product" id="Product" style="Z-INDEX: 101; LEFT: 416px;
POSITION: absolute; TOP: 24px">
```

```
<option selected="selected" value="print">Prints</option>
<option value="cup">Cups</option>
</select>
```

You can see that the `id` attribute of the product tag in the XML file has been placed in the `value` field of the `option` tags, but it is not visible to the user. The `value` field, however, contains the name attribute and is displayed on the screen. This example shows that we differentiate between the identifiers and the text displayed to the user.

Finding Product Options

We now extend the `ProductParser` class by an additional method to parse for each product's option list. The code in Listing 11.5 shows how to generate a list of options for a given product. As with the list of products, each node must be checked for the product key. If the product's identifier does not match the one passed as an argument to this method, all the inner content of this tag is skipped. We also skip all option tags of any product that does not match the passed argument. Therefore, any encountered option tag must belong to the wanted product and can be added to the table that is returned to the caller. For any encountered option tag the attributes `id`, `name`, and `price` are read and merged into the `value` field.

Listing 11.5 `ProductParser.cs`: The `OptionList()` Method

```
/// <summary>
/// Queries all options of a given product from a product
/// catalog.
/// </summary>
/// <param name="product">Product identifier whose available
/// options will be returned.</param>
/// <returns> SortedList of product options. Each entry's Key
/// field refers to the option identifier, and the Value field
/// refers to the option name plus price.</returns>
public SortedList OptionList(string product)
{
  SortedList table = new SortedList();
  XmlTextReader parser = new XmlTextReader(mFilename);

  // read all nodes
  while(parser.Read())
```

```
    {
      if (parser.NodeType == XmlNodeType.Element)
      {
        switch(parser.Name)
        {
          case "product":
          if (parser.GetAttribute("id") != product)
          {
            // different product,
            // "eat" up all its content
            parser.ReadInnerXml();
          } break;
          case "option":
          {
            // option found, add to list
            double price =
              Convert.ToDouble(parser.GetAttribute("price"));
            table.Add(parser.GetAttribute("id"),
                parser.GetAttribute("name") + " - "
                + price.ToString("C"));
          } break;
        }
      }
    }

    return table;
}
```

Extracting the Product Details

Next, we add a method to parse for all information stored in the XML product catalog for a single product. In our product catalog example in Listing 11.1, each product has only two subtags (summary and image), but it would be better to implement the method in a more generic way so that we can add new tags to the product catalog as needed. To address this issue, all encountered tags within a product tag (except for the option fields) are added to a Hashtable object, which is then returned by this method. The tag names are used as keys to identify the values. Listing 11.6 shows the implementation of the ProductDetails() method.

Listing 11.6 `ProductParser.cs:` The `ProductDetails()` Method

```
/// <summary>
/// Queries all properties of a given product from a product
/// catalog excluding the product options. To query the product
/// options, use OptionList().
/// </summary>
/// <param name="product">Product identifier whose properties
/// will be returned.</param>
/// <returns>Hashtable of properties. The keys in the hash table
/// refer to the tag names, and the values refer to the text stored
/// within the tag. The returned hash table also contains the
/// product name attribute.</returns>
public Hashtable ProductDetails(string product)
{
  XmlTextReader parser = new XmlTextReader(mFilename);
  Hashtable table = new Hashtable();
  string field = "";

  // read all nodes
  while(parser.Read())
  {
    switch (parser.NodeType)
    {
      case XmlNodeType.Element:
      {
        switch(parser.Name)
        {
          case "product":
          {
            // if not the wanted product read the inner xml
            // otherwise add product name to table
            if (parser.GetAttribute("id") != product)
              parser.ReadInnerXml();
            else
              table["name"] = parser.GetAttribute("name");
          }break;
          case "option":
          {
            // not interested in option tag
            parser.ReadInnerXml(); break;
```

```
      }
      default:
      {
        // store name of current tag
        field = parser.Name; break;
      }
    }
  } break;
  case XmlNodeType.Text:
  {
    // store the content using the tag name
    // as key in the hash table
    table[field] = parser.ReadString();
  } break;
    }
  }

  return table;
}
```

We need a similar implementation for a given product option, a task we leave to you.

Do It Yourself As with `ProductDetails()`, we need a method to parse the details of a given option. This task has been assigned to you. The method takes two string parameters (`product` and `option`), which define the product and the product option identifier to parse for. In addition to adding all subelements of the option, we must add the attributes `id`, `name`, and `price` to the `Hashtable` object.

Adding Unit Tests

At this point the implementation of the `ProductParser` class is complete, and some informal "testing" has been done. It is a good practice to add the unit tests before continuing with the implementation of the next class. This practice actually reduces integration time in most cases because malfunctions are discovered early on. From our experience the greatest dangers come from not doing unit testing early, instead trying things on-the-fly during application development. The latter approach gives the developer the wrong impression that things are working correctly although there are hidden bugs. These problems usually impact many more people in their later work and cause increased cost as well as significant schedule delays.

We have been involved in many large projects and have seen many software malfunctions even in simple utility classes implemented by senior software engineers. In one project, an insufficiently tested and late-tested utility class to read configuration values from a text file led to several weeks' delay in the release schedule of a large project involving several dozen people. The class had been implemented by the technical leader of the project, and therefore no one suspected it of having any errors. But very late during the system tests, many problems occurred when the team incorporated this class with other components and tested various application configurations. A project must minimize the risk of such situations.

As we did with the photo editor, we continue using the NUnit framework for our unit testing by following these steps:

1. Add a new class `UnitTest`: This class will encapsulate all unit test methods for the Online Photo Shop application.
2. Add a reference to `nunit.framework.dll`: Add a reference to `OnlinePhotoShop` project in Solution Explorer.
3. Use the `NUnit.Framework` namespace: Add a state to use `NUnit.Framework` to the `UnitTest.cs` file. For simplicity, we also add the namespaces needed for the test code at this point: `System.IO`, `System.Runtime.Serialization.Formatters.Binary`, `System.Collections`, `System.Xml`, and `System.Configuration`.
4. Set the `[TestFixture]` attribute: The `[TestFixture]` attribute must be set for the `UnitTest` class in the file `UnitTest.cs`.

To validate the correctness of the implementation, we need to know about the data in the XML product catalog. One way is to manually create a product catalog only for testing containing some known values. Another way is to programmatically create a synthetic product catalog file in which each element or attribute has a unique value. The latter choice has the advantage that later it would be easy to add stress or performance tests that could test against thousands of products and product options. Even though there is no such requirement for Online Photo Shop, we use the approach of a generated product catalog over the manually created one.

Listing 11.7 shows an XML product catalog file defining two products. In this file every element or attribute value is composed of the element's or attribute's name plus a sequence number for each product and option.

A test can now very easily validate the content of the file by comparing element values against their names.

Listing 11.7 Generated Product Catalog Example

```xml
<?xml version="1.0" encoding="utf-8" ?>
<doc>
  <products>
    <product id="product_id1" name="product_name1">
      <summary>product_summary1</summary>
      <image>product_image1</image>
      <option id="option_id11" name="option_name11" price="1.1">
        <summary>option_summary11</summary>
      </option>
      <option id="option_id12" name="option_name12" price="1.2">
        <summary>option_summary12</summary>
      </option>
    </product>
    <product id="product_id2" name="product_name2">
      <summary>product_summary2</summary>
      <image>product_image2</image>
      <option id="option_id21" name="option_name21" price="2.1">
        <summary>option_summary21</summary>
      </option>
      <option id="option_id22" name="option_name22" price="2.2">
        <summary>option_summary22</summary>
      </option>
    </product>
  </products>
</doc>
```

In Listing 11.8 the method `CreateProductCatalog` shows how this synthetic product catalog file can be created programmatically.

Again, the importance of unit testing can be underlined by an error in the `XmlTextReader` class of .NET Framework 1.1 when you use the `ReadInnerXML` method to parse XML text files that do not use any indentation. A minimal level of unit testing should always be done even for classes provided by external frameworks or toolkits, including the .NET Framework itself. In a fairly short time, Microsoft has developed one of the largest class libraries ever built, and it would be a miracle if the problem that we found here were the last one.

Listing 11.8 UnitTest.cs: The CreateProductCatalog() Method

```
/// <summary>
/// Creates a temporary XML product catalog with a given set of
products and options.
/// </summary>
/// <param name="products">Number of product entries in the
catalog.</param>
/// <param name="options">Number of options for each product.</param>
/// <returns>File path of the generated XML product catalog.</returns>
string CreateProductCatalog(int products, int options)
{
  // Get path for a temporary file
  string file = System.IO.Path.GetTempFileName();

  // create a temp XML file
  XmlTextWriter writer =
    new XmlTextWriter(File.CreateText(file));
  // Bug in .NET Framework, ReadInnerXML works only indented
  writer.Formatting = System.Xml.Formatting.Indented;

  writer.WriteStartDocument();
  writer.WriteStartElement("doc");
  writer.WriteStartElement("products");

  for (int p = 1; p <= products; p++)
  {
    writer.WriteStartElement("product");
    writer.WriteAttributeString(
      "id", "product_id" + p.ToString());
    writer.WriteAttributeString(
      "name", "product_name" + p.ToString());

    writer.WriteElementString(
      "summary", "product_summary" + p.ToString());
    writer.WriteElementString(
      "image", "product_image" + p.ToString());

    for (int o = 1; o <= options; o++)
    {
      writer.WriteStartElement("option");
      writer.WriteAttributeString(
        "id", "option_id" + p.ToString() + o.ToString());
```

```
    writer.WriteAttributeString(
      "name", "option_name" + p.ToString() + o.ToString());
    writer.WriteAttributeString(
      "price", p.ToString() + "." + o.ToString());
    writer.WriteElementString("summary",
      "option_summary" + p.ToString() + o.ToString());
    writer.WriteElementString("weight",
      "0." + p.ToString() + o.ToString());
    writer.WriteEndElement();  // option
  }

  writer.WriteEndElement();  // product
 }
 writer.WriteEndElement();  // products
 writer.WriteEndElement();  // doc
 writer.WriteEndDocument();
 writer.Close();

 return file;
}
```

Writing a test to validate the `ProductList` and `OptionList` methods of the `ProductParser` class is now very simple. Listing 11.9 shows a method that tests both lists. First, we create a temporary product catalog with 10 products, each product having five options. Then each item in the product list is checked for correctness. The product name must simply match the identifier used for the lookup. To validate the functionality of the `Option List` method, we pick one product and retrieve its options. The validation of the option list is similar to that of the product list.

Listing 11.9 `UnitTest.cs`: The `ProductParserListsTest()` Method

```
/// <summary>
/// Test the ProductList and OptionList methods of ProductParser.
/// </summary>
/// <requirement>F:order_products</requirement>
/// <requirement>F:products_options</requirement>
[Test]
public void ProductParserListsTest()
{
  string tmpFile = this.CreateProductCatalog(10, 5);
```

```
ProductParser parser = new ProductParser(tmpFile);

// check product list
SortedList p = parser.ProductList();
Assertion.AssertEquals(p.Count, 10);
for (int i = 0; i < p.Count; i++)
{
  Assertion.AssertEquals(
    p["product_id" + (i + 1).ToString()],
    "product_name" + (i + 1).ToString());
}

// check one option list, pick one from the center
SortedList o = parser.OptionList("product_id3");
Assertion.AssertEquals(o.Count, 5);
for (int i = 0; i < o.Count; i++)
{
  Assertion.AssertEquals(
    o["option_id3" + (i + 1).ToString()],
    "option_name3" + (i + 1).ToString() + " - "
      + (3 + (i + 1) / 10.0f).ToString("C"));
}

File.Delete(tmpFile);
}
```

When running the test using the NUnit GUI, we are surprised by a failed test. Looking closer, we can see that an error occurs when a file is deleted (see Figure 11.7).

Let's assume that the access rights to the temporary file allow its deletion; perhaps the cause of this error is that the file is still in use. Although the .NET runtime frees all unreferenced objects after garbage collection kicks in, the time when objects will be destroyed is not determined. Because we do not close the file handle before any of the parsing methods returns to the caller, the `XmlTextParser` object goes out of scope with an open file handle. So only after the garbage collection picks up and destroys this object can the file finally be closed. Because the parsing methods are used very frequently in the Online Photo Shop application, this would lead to increasing consumption of file handles in a system. To avoid problems that can be caused by this, we add `parser.Close()` before returning

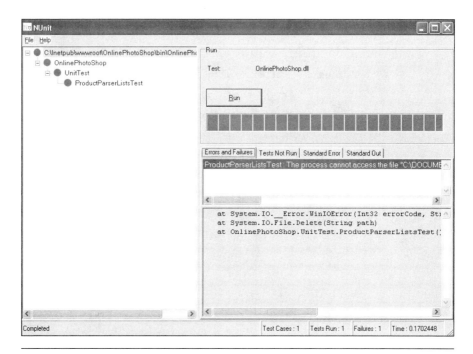

Figure 11.7 Failed Unit Test

from the parsing methods `ProductList`, `OptionList`, `ProductDetails`, and `OptionDetails`. Compiling the assembly and rerunning the test now results in a passed test.

Next, we add the method `ProductParseDetails` to test the `Product Details` and `OptionDetails` methods. As with the preceding test, the implementation is straightforward. We create a temporary product catalog and validate some parsed elements against the synthetic data stored in the catalog. Listing 11.10 shows the test code.

Listing 11.10 `UnitTest.cs`: The `ProductParserDetailsTest()` Method

```
/// <summary>
/// Test the ProductDetails and OptionDetails methods of ProductParser.
/// </summary>
/// <requirement>F:order_products</requirement>
/// <requirement>F:products_options</requirement>
```

```
[Test]
public void ProductParserDetailsTest()
{
  string tmpFile = this.CreateProductCatalog(20, 3);

  ProductParser parser = new ProductParser(tmpFile);

  // check product details of the 20th entry
  Hashtable p = parser.ProductDetails("product_id20");
  Assertion.AssertEquals((string) p["name"], "product_name20");
  Assertion.AssertEquals(
    (string) p["summary"], "product_summary20");
  Assertion.AssertEquals(
    (string) p["image"], "product_image20");

  // check some option details (3rd product, 2nd option)
  Hashtable o = parser.OptionDetails(
    "product_id3", "option_id32");
  Assertion.AssertEquals((string) o["name"], "option_name32");
  Assertion.AssertEquals(
    (string) o["summary"], "option_summary32");
  Assertion.AssertEquals(
    (string) o["price"], (3.2f).ToString());

  File.Delete(tmpFile);
}
```

11.4.3 The Online Shop Portal

Having implemented a product catalog parser, we can now extend the `Browse.aspx` Web form to allow cycling through all products and displaying the available options for each product. We start by defining the basic layout of the page according to Figure 11.2. Open the `Browse.aspx` design window, and switch from `GridLayout` to `FlowLayout` in the Documents Properties field. Then add three borderless tables (header, product, and order section) to format the sections using multiple columns. Figure 11.8 shows the table layout for `Browse.aspx`.

After adding the tables, place the previously added Product dropdown list in the center column of the header section. Changing the product selection invalidates all the information currently displayed, so we set this

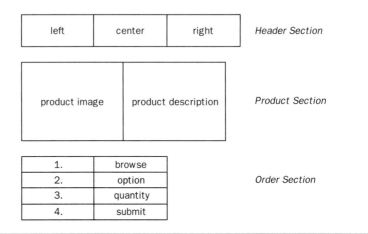

Figure 11.8 Table Layout for `Browse.aspx`

control's `AutoPostBack` property to `True`. In this way, a change in the product selection will trigger an automatic response to the Web server.

Before adding new code to the page, let's complete the design of the form by adding all controls:

- Header: Drag and drop two `Button` controls next to the Product drop-down list. Set the `ID` and `Text` properties for the left button to `Previous`, and for the right button to `Next`. Then add a `Hyperlink` control to the right column, and change the `Text` property to `Shopping Cart` and the `NavigateUrl` to `Cart.aspx`, which will be implemented later in this chapter.
- Product: Add two `Label` controls to the product description column of the product section. Set the label `ID` properties to `Product Heading` and `ProductSummary`. Also add an `Image` control to the product image column, and change its `ID` property to `ProductImage`.
- Order: Add a `File Browser` control for the image to the form. Drag and drop a `File` field from the HTML section in the Toolbox into the browse column. Right-click on the control and select Run As Server Control. Then change the `id` property of this control to `Image`. Now place a `RadioButtonList` into the option column, and set the `ID` to `Option`. The quantity column is filled with a `DropDown List` control, whose `ID` property is set to `Quantity`. To finish the

order section, place a `Button` control in the submit column. Change the `ID` property of the button to `AddButton`, and the `Text` property to `Add`. Also add another label for user feedback below the button. Set the `ID` to `Feedback`, and clear the `Text` property so that nothing is displayed by default.

Figure 11.9 shows the completed design of the `Browse.aspx` form.

Because we want to upload binary data, we also need to manually check the HTML code generated by the form designed in Visual Studio. You can switch to the HTML view using the context menu of the design window. First, we make sure that the `<form>` tag spans the entire page (from `<body>` to `</body>`). This is most likely not the case, and you must manually move the form closing tag `</form>` right before the `</body>` tag. Next, add the `encType` attribute to the form tag, and set its value to `"multipart/form-data"`. This allows transmission of binary files (in our case, images) to the server (see Listing 11.11).

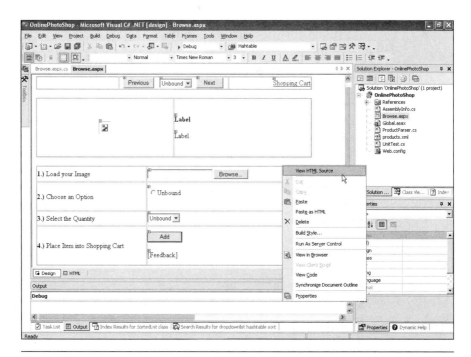

Figure 11.9 `Browse.aspx` Design

Listing 11.11 Browse.aspx: Modifying the <form> Tag

```
<%@ Page language="c#" Codebehind="Browse.aspx.cs"
AutoEventWireup="false" Inherits="OnlinePhotoShop.Browse" %>
<!DOCTYPE HTML PUBLIC "-//W3C//DTD HTML 4.0 Transitional//EN" >
<HTML>
  <HEAD>
    <title>Browse</title>
  </HEAD>
  <body>
    <form id="Form1" method="post" runat="server"
                      enctype="multipart/form-data">
      <P>

      . . .

    </form>
  </body>
</HTML>
}
```

The design of the form is complete, and it's time to add the logic behind it. Open the code for the form by right-clicking on Browse.aspx in Solution Explorer and selecting View Code. We first implement the utility method shown in Listing 11.12 for the Browse form class, which updates all controls depending on the currently selected product.

Listing 11.12 Browse.aspx.cs: The UpdateProduct() Method

```
/// <summary>
/// Updates the ProductHeading, ProductSummary, ProductImage, and
Option controls depending on the currently selected product in the
Product control.
/// </summary>
private void UpdateProduct()
{
  ProductParser catalog = new
    ProductParser(Server.MapPath("products.xml"));

  // set the available options for this product
  Option.DataValueField = "Value";
  Option.DataTextField = "Text";
```

```
Option.DataSource =
  catalog.OptionList(Product.SelectedValue);
Option.DataBind();
Option.SelectedIndex = 0;

// get the product details
System.Collections.Hashtable details =
  catalog.ProductDetails(Product.SelectedValue);

// update controls in product section
if (details["name"] != null)
   ProductHeading.Text = (string) details["name"];

 if (details["summary"] != null)
    ProductSummary.Text = (string) details["summary"];

 if (details["image"] != null)
    ProductImage.ImageUrl = (string) details["image"];
}
```

The `UpdateProduct` method uses the helper class `ProductParser` (implemented earlier in this chapter) to retrieve the product options and details from the XML catalog. This method must be invoked from the `Page_Load` method to properly initialize all controls. Also, the `Quantity` control must be associated with a data source containing numbers. This list is also generated in the `Page_Load` method. Listing 11.13 shows the updated code.

Listing 11.13 `Browse.aspx.cs`: Updated `Page_Load()` Method

```
private void Page_Load(object sender, System.EventArgs e)
{
  // Put user code to initialize the page here
  if (!Page.IsPostBack)
  {
    // Initialize the product parser
    ProductParser catalog = new
      ProductParser(Server.MapPath("products.xml"));

    // Get the product list and set it in the Product control
    Hashtable products = catalog.ProductList();
```

```
    Product.DataValueField = "Key";
    Product.DataTextField = "Value";
    Product.DataSource = products;
    Product.DataBind();
    Product.SelectedIndex = 0;

    // Fill Quantity with a list of numbers
    ArrayList numbers = new ArrayList();
    for (int i = 1; i <= 20; i++)
    {
      numbers.Add(i.ToString());
    }
    Quantity.DataSource = numbers;
    Quantity.DataBind();
    Quantity.SelectedIndex = 0;

    // Update all other controls
    this.UpdateProduct();
  }
}
```

Now that we have properly initialized the form, it is time to give it a first try in the Web browser. To launch the form from Visual Studio, you must set it as the start page of the project. Select Debugging in the Configuration Properties section of the project properties, and set the Start Page field to `Browse.aspx`. Now the form can be launched in Internet Explorer from Visual Studio by selecting Debug and Start or by pressing F5. The default product should be cups, giving two options to choose from.

If you are wondering about the error icon in the image, this is caused by the missing image file that has been specified in the XML product catalog. To solve this problem, create an `img` folder under the `OnlinePhotoShop` project, and copy two images for the cups and prints product categories there.

Although the page looks nearly complete, we have not yet implemented the navigation logic. To do so, go back to the design view and double-click on the `Product` drop-down list control. Visual Studio generates a message handler for the event of a changed selection in the drop-down list. All you need to do is to call the `UpdateProduct` method to update the option list and product description fields.

Next, double-click on the buttons in the header section. This will create event handlers for the event of those buttons being pressed or clicked. Fill the handlers with code that increments or decrements the selected index of the `Product` control. There, we also need to consider the boundary conditions of being at the start or end of the product list. After the implementation of the event handlers shown in Listing 11.14, we can navigate through the product catalog using the drop-down list as well as the Next and Previous buttons.

Listing 11.14 `Browse.aspx.cs`: Event Handlers

```
/// <summary>
/// Called when a new product is selected in the Product control.
Updates the product description and optionlist by calling
UpdateProduct().
/// </summary>
/// <param name="sender">Sending object.</param>
/// <param name="e">Event arguments.</param>
private void Product_SelectedIndexChanged(object sender,
System.EventArgs e)
{
  this.UpdateProduct();
}


/// <summary>
/// Called when the Next button is pressed. Selects the next product in
the list and updates the product description and optionlist by calling
UpdateProduct().
/// </summary>
/// <param name="sender">Sending object.</param>
/// <param name="e">Event arguments.</param>
private void Next_Click(object sender, System.EventArgs e)
{
  if ((Product.SelectedIndex + 1) < Product.Items.Count)
  {
    Product.SelectedIndex++;
  }
  else
  {
    Product.SelectedIndex = 0;
```

```
  }
  this.UpdateProduct();
}

/// <summary>
/// Called when the Previous button is pressed. Selects the previous
product in the list and updates the product description and optionlist
by calling UpdateProduct().
/// </summary>
/// <param name="sender">Sending object.</param>
/// <param name="e">Event arguments.</param>
private void Previous_Click(object sender, System.EventArgs e)
{
  if (Product.SelectedIndex > 0)
  {
    Product.SelectedIndex--;
  }
  else
  {
    Product.SelectedIndex = Product.Items.Count - 1;
  }
  this.UpdateProduct();
}
```

This completes the implementation of the requirement keys F:products_browse and F:product_options. The keys left to implement in this iteration are F:product_shopping_cart and F:product_customize. Figure 11.10 shows the form rendered by Internet Explorer.

11.4.4 The Shopping Cart

To start the implementation of the shopping cart functionality, we design a class that describes a single order item. This class is very simple and mainly provides data encapsulation by using get accessors. The properties to be implemented are as follows:

- Product: Product identifier of the item
- Option: Identifier of the option selected for this item
- Quantity: Quantity of items ordered

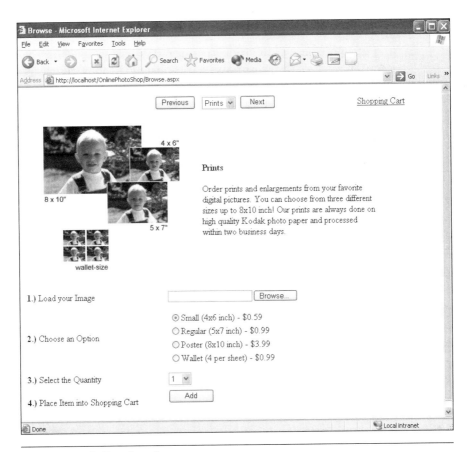

Figure 11.10 Rendered `Browse.apsx`

- `ClientPath`: Path for image file on the client computer
- `ServerPath`: Path of the uploaded image

Add a new class `ShoppingItem` to the project, and add members and `get` accessors for those properties.

Do It Yourself Add `private` member variables and `get` accessors for `Product`, `Option`, `Quantity`, `ClientPath`, and `ServerPath` to the `ShoppingItem` class. Also provide a constructor that initializes all members.

Serialization for the ASP.NET State Server

Because of the architectural requirement `c:online_shop_stateservice` (see Chapter 4), this class must be serializable to allow the usage of the ASP Session State service. To make a class serializable, it must be inherited from `ISerializable` and must implement the serialization function as well as a deserialization constructor (see Listing 11.15). Furthermore, the class must have the `Serializable` attribute set, and the permission flags for `GetObject Data` must allow the `SerializationFormatter`.

To switch the application to use the session state service from ASP.NET, we must change the `Web.config` file. Locate the `sessionState` tag in the configuration section, and change the value of the `mode` attribute from `InProc` to `StateServer`. To run the application now, we must first start the service called `"ASP.NET State Service"`. You do so by running the following command:

```
net start "ASP.NET State Service"
```

Listing 11.15 `ShoppingItem.cs`: Serialization

```
using System;
using System.Runtime.Serialization;
using System.Security.Permissions;

namespace OnlinePhotoShop
{
/// <summary>
/// Class that contains all information to describe one item in the
shopping cart (product id, option id, quantity, and image locations).
/// </summary>
[Serializable()]
public class ShoppingItem : ISerializable
{
  #region ISerializable Members

  /// <summary>
  /// The serialization function.
  /// </summary>
  /// <param name="info">The object to be populated with serialization
information.</param>
  /// <param name="context">The destination context of the
serialization.</param>
```

```
[SecurityPermissionAttribute(SecurityAction.Demand,Serialization
Formatter=true)]
  public void GetObjectData(SerializationInfo info, StreamingContext
context)
{
   info.AddValue("Product", mProduct);
   info.AddValue("Option", mOption);
   info.AddValue("Quantity", mQuantity);
   info.AddValue("ClientPath", mClientPath);
   info.AddValue("ServerPath", mServerPath);
}


/// <summary>
/// The deserialization constructor.
/// </summary>
/// <param name="info">The object populated with serialization
information.</param>
/// <param name="context">The source context of the serialization.
</param>
  public ShoppingItem(SerializationInfo info, StreamingContext context)
  {
    mProduct = (string) info.GetValue("Product",
                        typeof(string));
    mOption = (string) info.GetValue("Option",
                        typeof(string));
    mQuantity = (int) info.GetValue("Quantity",
                        typeof(int));
    mClientPath = (string) info.GetValue("ClientPath",
                        typeof(string));
    mServerPath = (string) info.GetValue("ServerPath",
                        typeof(string));
  }
  #endregion


  ...
```

The ShoppingCart Class

The next step is to implement the ShoppingCart class. This is a collection class to which elements of type ShoppingItem can be added. To uniquely identify items placed in the shopping cart, we inherit the class from Hashtable. An integer value is used as a key that will be incremented for each newly added item. Add a new class `ShoppingCart` inherited from `Hashtable` to the project, and define the following two members:

- `mNextKey (int)`: A private enumerator for unique numbers. This enumerator is incremented every time a new item is added to the list.
- `mID (string)`: A private storage for a unique identifier string (`SessionID`). This string is used to generate server-side file names for uploaded images.

In the constructor of this class, you must initialize the two members. Instead of putting in new logic to generate unique identifiers for each shopping cart object, we make this a required parameter for the constructor. In this way, the Web form instantiating the object can pass the `SessionID` of the current HTTP request, which is ensured to be unique by design.

As with the `ShoppingItem` class, the `ShoppingCart` class must be inherited from `ISerializable`. Add this parent class and the `Serializable` attribute to the class definition. Then implement the serialization function and deserialization constructor to serialize the two added member variables. Both methods must call the base class so that the items stored in the collection are also serialized. Listing 11.16 shows the implementation of the `ShoppingCart` class to this point.

Listing 11.16 `ShoppingCart.cs`

```
using System;
using System.Collections;
using System.Runtime.Serialization;
using System.Security.Permissions;
using System.Configuration;

namespace OnlinePhotoShop
{
/// <summary>
/// Class that stores a number of shopping items associated with a
unique key. This class and the items stored in it are serializable and
allow the class to be stored within a Session object even when using
ASP Session State service.
/// </summary>
[Serializable()]
```

```
public class ShoppingCart : Hashtable, ISerializable
{
  /// <summary>
  /// Private enumerator for unique numbers. This enumerator is
incremented every time a new item is added to the list.
  /// </summary>
  private int mNextKey;
  /// <summary>
  /// Private storage for unique identifier string (SessionID). This
string is used to generate server-side file names for uploaded images.
  /// </summary>
  private string mID;

  #region ISerializable Members

  /// <summary>
  /// The serialization function.
  /// </summary>
  /// <param name="info">The object to be populated with serialization
information.</param>
  /// <param name="context">The destination context of the
serialization.</param>

[SecurityPermissionAttribute(SecurityAction.Demand,SerializationFormatt
er=true)]
  override public void GetObjectData(SerializationInfo info,
StreamingContext context)
  {
    base.GetObjectData(info, context);
    info.AddValue("NextKey", mNextKey);
    info.AddValue("ID", mID);
  }

  /// <summary>
  /// The deserialization constructor.
  /// </summary>
  /// <param name="info">The object populated with serialization
information.</param>
  /// <param name="context">The source context of the
serialization.</param>
  public ShoppingCart(SerializationInfo info, StreamingContext context)
    : base(info, context)
```

```
  {
    mNextKey = (int) info.GetValue("NextKey", typeof(int));
    mID = (string) info.GetValue("ID", typeof(string));
  }


  #endregion
  /// <summary>
  /// Constructor.
  /// </summary>
  /// <param name="id">SessionID of current HTTP request.</param>
  public ShoppingCart(string id)
  {
    mNextKey = 0;
    mID = id;
  }
 }
}
```

Now we implement `AddItem`, a method to add new items to the shopping cart. This method takes a number of input parameters posted by the Web form. It then generates a unique file name from the `mID` and `mKey` members to store the image file on the server. After the image is saved, a new `ShoppingItem` is stored in the hash table. The code for this method is shown in Listing 11.17.

Listing 11.17 `ShoppingCart.cs`: The `AddItem()` Method

```
/// <summary>
/// <summary>
/// Adds a new item to the shopping cart.
/// </summary>
/// <param name="product">Product identifier.</param>
/// <param name="option">Selected product options.</param>
/// <param name="image">Image file to customize the item with.</param>
/// <param name="quantity">Quantity of the ordered item.</param>
public void AddItem(string product, string option, System.Web.
HttpPostedFile image, int quantity)
{
  if (image != null)
  {
    // pick a new key
    int key = mNextKey++;
```

```
    // save the image to the upload directory
    string extension = image.FileName.Substring(image.FileName.
LastIndexOf("."));
    string store = ConfigurationSettings.AppSettings["ImageStore"];
    string path = store + "\\" + mID + "_" + key.ToString() +
extension;
    image.SaveAs(path);

    // add the item to the order list
    this[key] = new ShoppingItem(
                    product,
                    option,
                    quantity,
                    image.FileName,
                    path);
  }
}
```

Configuring the Web Application

The ShoppingCart class needs a storage directory for the uploaded images. Instead of hard-coding the path into the code, we read it from the application configuration settings. To add this setting to the OnlinePhotoShop configuration file, open the Web.config file of the project and add the following section following the system.web section:

```
<appSettings>
    <add key="ImageStore" value="C:\OnlinePhotoShopData\uploads" />
</appSettings>
```

The value attribute of the ImageStore key must be set to the image storage location on the server. A network path also can be specified if the images are stored on a dedicated file server. Just make sure that a correct path is entered that specifies an existing directory.

Shopping Cart Unit Tests

Now it is time to add new unit tests for ShoppingItem and ShoppingCart. Both classes are serializable to allow the usage of ASP.NET's session state service. To test the serialization of any class, we add a SerializationTest method to the UnitTest class that serializes a given class in a binary file and then deserializes a class from the same file. This class is then returned to the caller.

The other two methods (`ShoppingItemTest` and `ShoppingCartTest`) in Listing 11.18 are the test methods for the `ShoppingItem` and `Shopping Cart` classes. There, an instance of the class is created with known properties. Then another instance of the class is created using the `Serialization Test` method, and we validate that all properties of both instances match.

Listing 11.18 `UnitTest.cs`: The `ShoppingItem` and `ShoppingCart` Unit Tests

```
/// <summary>
/// Helper function that serializes an object into a stream and returns
/// the deserialized object from the same stream.
/// </summary>
/// <param name="obj">Object for serialization.</param>
/// <returns>Deserialized object.</returns>
Object SerializationTest(Object obj)
{
  // Opens a file and serializes the object into it
  // in binary format
  string tmpFile = System.IO.Path.GetTempFileName();
  Stream stream = File.Open(tmpFile, FileMode.Create);
  BinaryFormatter bformatter = new BinaryFormatter();
  bformatter.Serialize(stream, obj);
  stream.Close();

  //Opens file and deserializes the object from it
  stream = File.Open(tmpFile, FileMode.Open);
  bformatter = new BinaryFormatter();
  Object deserialized = bformatter.Deserialize(stream);
  stream.Close();

  return deserialized;
}


/// <summary>
/// Tests the ShoppingItem class.
/// </summary>
/// <requirement>F:product_shopping_cart</requirement>
[Test]
```

```
public void ShoppingItemTest()
{
  // test constructor
  ShoppingItem item = new ShoppingItem("product", "option", 123,
"clientPath", "serverPath");
  Assertion.AssertEquals(item.Product, "product");
  Assertion.AssertEquals(item.Option, "option");
  Assertion.AssertEquals(item.Quantity, 123);
  Assertion.AssertEquals(item.ClientPath, "clientPath");
  Assertion.AssertEquals(item.ServerPath, "serverPath");

  // test (de)serialization
  ShoppingItem item2 = (ShoppingItem) this.SerializationTest(item);
  Assertion.AssertEquals(item2.Product, "product");
  Assertion.AssertEquals(item2.Option, "option");
  Assertion.AssertEquals(item2.Quantity, 123);
  Assertion.AssertEquals(item2.ClientPath, "clientPath");
  Assertion.AssertEquals(item2.ServerPath, "serverPath");
}

/// <summary>
/// Tests the ShoppingCart class.
/// </summary>
/// <requirement>F:product_shopping_cart</requirement>
[Test]
public void ShoppingCartTest()
{
  // test constructor

  ShoppingItem item = new ShoppingItem("product", "option", 123,
  "clientPath", "serverPath");

  ShoppingCart cart = new ShoppingCart("id");

  // AddItem requires an HttpPostedFile
  // if null, nothing should happen
  cart.AddItem("product", "option", null, 123);
  Assertion.AssertEquals(cart.Count, 0);

  // Add two keys to test serialization
  cart.Add("key1", new ShoppingItem("product1", "option1", 1,
  "clientPath1", "serverPath1"));
  cart.Add("key2", new ShoppingItem("product2", "option2", 2,
  "clientPath2", "serverPath2"));
```

```
ShoppingCart cart2 = (ShoppingCart) this.SerializationTest(cart);
Assertion.AssertEquals(cart2.Count, 2);
 // Check one property (already tested in ShoppingItemTest)
Assertion.AssertEquals(((ShoppingItem)cart2["key1"]).Product,
"product1");
 Assertion.AssertEquals(((ShoppingItem)cart2["key2"]).Product,
"product2");
}
```

Integration of the Shopping Cart into the Product Browser

After adding the unit test, we integrate the shopping cart into the Web form
`Browse.aspx`. By double-clicking on the Add button in the design view, we
add to the `Browse` class a new event handler for pressing this button.
Within this handler the shopping cart needs to be retrieved from the current session, and if no shopping cart is yet stored a new one must be created. Then a new item will be added to that cart, and the feedback label
updated. Listing 11.19 shows the code for the event handler.

Listing 11.19 `Browse.aspx.cs`: The Add Button Event Handler

```
/// <summary>
/// Called when Add button is pressed. Adds a new item of the currently
selected product, option, and quantity to the shopping cart.
/// </summary>
/// <param name="sender">Sending object.</param>
/// <param name="e">Event arguments.</param>
private void AddButton_Click(object sender, System.EventArgs e)
{
  // Report error if no image is selected
  if (Image.PostedFile.ContentLength == 0)
  {
    Feedback.Text = "Before adding an item to the shopping cart you
must select an image.";
    Feedback.ForeColor = System.Drawing.Color.Red;
  }
  else
  {
    try
    {
      // retrieve shopping cart information from session object
```

```
ShoppingCart cart =
  (ShoppingCart) Session["ShoppingCart"];
if (cart == null)
{
  // no cart in this session yet, create one
  cart = new ShoppingCart(Session.SessionID);
  Session["ShoppingCart"] = cart;
}

// add the order
cart.AddItem(
  Product.SelectedValue,
  Option.SelectedValue,
  Image.PostedFile,
  Quantity.SelectedIndex + 1);

Feedback.Text = Quantity.SelectedValue + " item(s) added to your
shopping cart.";
  Feedback.ForeColor = System.Drawing.Color.Black;
}
catch
{
  Feedback.Text = "The item could not be added to the shopping
cart. Please try again another time.";
  Feedback.ForeColor = System.Drawing.Color.Red;
}
  }
}
```

Now, when the page is launched in the Web server, navigating through the product catalog should work as well as adding an item from it to the shopping cart. Each time a product is added, the feedback label is updated with the selected quantity of this item. What is left to do is to create a new form to display all the items in the shopping cart.

Shopping Cart Web Page

Add a new Web form, Cart.aspx, to the project. As with Browser.aspx, switch to FlowLayout and design the form according to Figure 11.3 using tables. Add two Hyperlinks controls to the header that navigate back to Browse.aspx or to the Checkout.aspx form, which is implemented in the next iteration. For the table of shopping cart items, add only the header and the footer of the empty table. The items will be generated using the shopping cart object stored in the current session. The only control that needs to be added to this table is a label next to the Total column displaying the total cost of the order. Add a `Label` control and set the `ID` property to `Total`.

To complete the page design, switch to the HTML view and place a `Repeater` control between the header and the footer of the shopping cart table, as shown in Listing 11.20.

Listing 11.20 `Cart.aspx`: The Repeater Control

```
<asp:Repeater id="Table" runat="server">
  <ItemTemplate>
    <tr>
      <td align="center">
        <img src=
        '<%# DataBinder.Eval(Container.DataItem, "Image") %>'
        border="0" width="100">
      </td>
      <td align="center">
        <%# DataBinder.Eval(Container.DataItem, "Product") %>
      </td>
      <td align="center">
        <%# DataBinder.Eval(Container.DataItem, "Option") %>
      </td>
      <td align="center">
        <%# DataBinder.Eval(Container.DataItem, "Quantity") %>
        <asp:LinkButton CommandArgument=
          '<%# DataBinder.Eval(Container.DataItem, "Key") %>'
          runat="server" Font-Size="X-Small" Font-Italic="False">
          Remove
        </asp:LinkButton>
      </td>
      <td align="right">
        <%# DataBinder.Eval(Container.DataItem, "Price") %>
      </td>
    </tr>
  </ItemTemplate>
</asp:Repeater>
```

Using the tags in the style `<%# DataBinder.Eval(Container.Data Item, "Property") %>` you can insert property values from the bound data source into the table. The class `ShoppingItemView` provides those properties needed to display the shopping cart.

Immediately following the quantity value we add a `LinkButton` control that allows the customer to remove an item from the cart. Because this button is inserted for each row in the table, an argument must be specified to identify the item. Therefore, `ShoppingItemView` must also provide the hash table key of the item.

Figure 11.11 shows the completed design of the `Cart.aspx` form.

Next, we implement the `ShoppingItemView` class needed to generate the table. This class has properties named after the table columns: `Image`, `Product`, `Option`, `Quantity`, and `Price`. It must also provide an accessor to the hash table key that is used in the shopping cart. Using this key, we can easily remove an item from the cart if the customer wants to do this. Furthermore, we add an accessor to the unformatted price of the item so that the total for the entire shopping cart can be calculated easily. Because the

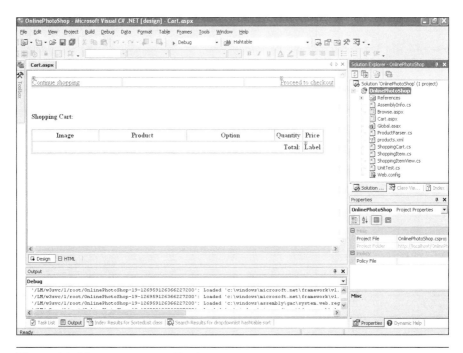

Figure 11.11 `Cart.aspx`: Design

constructor of the class will format a given item for display, we need to pass the product catalog file so that description and attributes can be queried from there via the ProductParser utility class. Also, we pass the hash table key because the key is not known to instances of ShoppingItem itself. Listing 11.21 shows the code for the ShoppingItemView class.

Listing 11.21 ShoppingItemView.cs

```
/// <summary>
/// Formatted version of ShoppingItem for displaying it in the shopping
cart table.
/// </summary>
/// <requirement>F:product_shopping_cart</requirement>
public class ShoppingItemView
{
  /// <summary>
  /// Private member to store the hash table key of the item.
  /// </summary>
  int mKey;
  /// <summary>
  /// Private member to store the product name.
  /// </summary>
  string mProduct;
  /// <summary>
  /// Private member to store the option name.
  /// </summary>
  string mOption;
  /// <summary>
  /// Private member to store the quantity of the ordered item.
  /// </summary>
  int mQuantity;
  /// <summary>
  /// Private member to store the image path.
  /// </summary>
  string mImage;
  /// <summary>
  /// Private member to store the price of the ordered items.
  /// </summary>
  double mPrice;

  /// <summary>
  /// Constructor.
```

```
/// </summary>
/// <param name="file">Path of the product catalog file.</param>
/// <param name="key">Shopping cart hash table key of the
item.</param>
/// <param name="item">Shopping item that will be formatted for
output.</param>
public ShoppingItemView(string file, int key, ShoppingItem item)
{
  mKey = key;
  mImage = item.ClientPath;
  mQuantity = item.Quantity;

  // get the product name
  ProductParser parser = new ProductParser(file);
  mProduct =
    (string) parser.ProductDetails(item.Product)["name"];

  // get the option name and item price
  System.Collections.Hashtable details =
    parser.OptionDetails(item.Product, item.Option);
  mOption = (string) details["name"];
  double price =
    System.Convert.ToDouble((string) details["price"]);
  mPrice = (price * item.Quantity);
}

/// <summary>
/// Key in shopping cart hash table.
/// </summary>
public string Key
{
  get
  {
    return mKey.ToString();
  }
}

/// <summary>
/// Product name.
/// </summary>
public string Product
{
```

```csharp
    get
    {
      return mProduct;
    }
}

/// <summary>
/// Option name.
/// </summary>
public string Option
{
  get
  {
    return mOption;
  }
}

/// <summary>
/// Quantity.
/// </summary>
public int Quantity
{
  get
  {
    return mQuantity;
  }
}

/// <summary>
/// Path of image file.
/// </summary>
public string Image
{
  get
  {
    return mImage;
  }
}

/// <summary>
/// Formatted price for this item.
/// </summary>
```

```
public string Price
{
  get
  {
    return mPrice.ToString("C");
  }
}

/// <summary>
/// Unformatted price for this item.
/// </summary>
public double Subtotal
{
  get
  {
    return mPrice;
  }
}
}
```

Before completing the integration into a Web form, we add another small unit test for the ShoppingItemView class. Using the synthetic product catalog, again it is easy to validate whether the ShoppingItemView class has replaced a product and option identifier with the correct product and option name. Listing 11.22 shows the code for the ShoppingItemView unit test.

Listing 11.22 UnitTest.cs: The ShoppingItemViewTest() Method

```
/// <summary>
/// Tests the ShoppingItemView class.
/// </summary>
/// <requirement>F:product_shopping_cart</requirement>
[Test]
public void ShoppingItemViewTest()
{
  string tmpFile = this.CreateProductCatalog(2, 2);

  // create a shopping item to format for viewing
  ShoppingItem item = new ShoppingItem("product_id1", "option_id12",
  10, "clientPath", "serverPath");
```

```
// create the formatted view class
ShoppingItemView view = new ShoppingItemView(tmpFile, 555, item);

Assertion.AssertEquals(view.Key, "555");
Assertion.AssertEquals(view.Product, "product_name1");
Assertion.AssertEquals(view.Option, "option_name12");
Assertion.AssertEquals(view.Quantity, 10);
Assertion.AssertEquals(view.Subtotal, 12);   // 1.20 * 10
Assertion.AssertEquals(view.Price, 12.ToString("C"));
Assertion.AssertEquals(view.Image, "clientPath");

File.Delete(tmpFile);
}
```

The final task in this iteration is to add the initialization and the button event handler code of the `Repeater` control to the code behind `Cart.aspx`. The data binding for the `Repeater` control needs to be updated on page initialization as well as after an item has been removed. Therefore, we add a new method, `UpdateCart`, that generates a formatted list of shopping cart items and updates the total amount of the order. Listing 11.23 shows the implementation of this method.

Listing 11.23 `Cart.aspx.cs`: The `UpdateCart()` Method

```
/// <summary>
/// Generates a list of formatted shopping cart items and binds
/// them to the repeater control.
/// </summary>
public void UpdateCart()
{
  // retrieve shopping cart information from session object
  ShoppingCart cart = (ShoppingCart) Session["ShoppingCart"];
  if (cart == null)
  {
    cart = new ShoppingCart(Session.SessionID);
    Session["ShoppingCart"] = cart;
  }

  // copy shopping cart items into a formatted list
  ArrayList list = new ArrayList();
```

```
IDictionaryEnumerator i = cart.GetEnumerator();

double total = 0;
while(i.MoveNext())
{
  ShoppingItemView item = new ShoppingItemView(
    Server.MapPath("products.xml"),
    (int) i.Key,
    (ShoppingItem) i.Value);

  list.Add(item);
  total += item.Subtotal;
}

// bind the formatted list to the table
Table.DataSource = list;
Table.DataBind();

// update total cost label
Total.Text = total.ToString("C");
}
```

To properly initialize the table, the `UpdateCart` method must be invoked within the `Page_Load` method of this class if the page is not being posted back.

Because we defined the header and footer of the shopping cart table outside the `Repeater` control, it is not visible in the design view. Therefore, we must manually add a command handler for the Remove button placed inside the `Repeater` control. Do this by opening the region Web Form Designer-generated code and adding the following line to the `Initialize Component` method:

```
this.Table.ItemCommand += new System.Web.UI.WebControls.RepeaterCommand
EventHandler(this.Table_ItemCommand);
```

Next, the message handler method needs to be added to the class. Listing 11.24 shows the code that gets the hash table key from the command argument and deletes the item along with the image file associated with it.

Listing 11.24 `Cart.aspx.cs`: The Button Event Handler

```
/// <summary>
/// Command handler for buttons pressed within the table (remove).
/// </summary>
/// <param name="source">Source object.</param>
/// <param name="e">Event argument.</param>
private void Table_ItemCommand(object source,
System.Web.UI.WebControls.RepeaterCommandEventArgs e)
{
  // remove from cart
  string cmd = (string) e.CommandArgument;
  int key = System.Convert.ToInt32(cmd);
  ShoppingCart cart = (ShoppingCart) Session["ShoppingCart"];

  if (cart != null)
  {
    System.IO.File.Delete(
      ((ShoppingItem) cart[key]).ServerPath);
    cart.Remove(key);
    this.UpdateCart();
  }
}
```

11.5 Conclusion

The implementation of all four requirement keys is now complete. After adding products to the shopping cart in the product browser form, we can click on the Shopping Cart link at the top of the page, which links to `Cart.aspx`. There, the items are read from the session object and displayed as shown in Figure 11.12.

In this chapter programming of unit tests has been exercised to a great extent. In doing so, we have achieved a significant improvement:

- Minor problems and bugs have been addressed immediately after initial implementation. If you have worked through this chapter and have not simply proceeded with the sample solutions, you will have encountered failed test cases a number of times (just as we did).

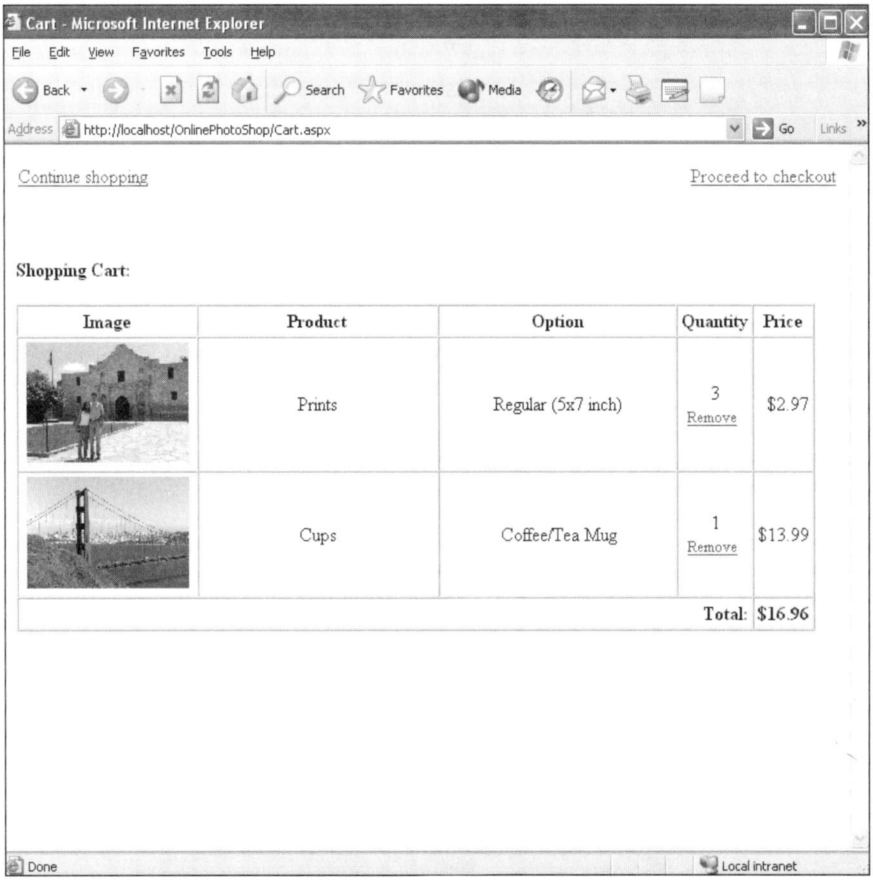

Figure 11.12 Shopping Cart Form

- We have detected resource leaks in the product parser that could have caused system instability due to a lack of system handles. After typical memory leaks were eliminated by the introduction of automatic memory management in the .NET runtime, unreleased resources may become the new challenge to programmers. As we have seen, without strict testing these leaks remain widely undetected but can cause major instabilities for the entire system.
- We have detected a bug in the `XmlTextReader` class, which is part of the .NET Framework. This is a particularly unexpected problem because XML support is often mentioned as an important feature of

the .NET Framework. The fact that a product has a huge installed base may give you the wrong feeling about its quality. To give another example, in our past projects we have come across bugs in basic clipping functions in the OpenGL driver for graphic boards that have sold millions of units. Nobody is perfect!

After fixing a few bugs and implementing a workaround for the problem found in the .NET Framework, our code has passed all unit tests, and the go/no-go criteria for this iteration have been fulfilled. Early testing is a major factor in product robustness. Furthermore, we have shown that even for Web-based applications, fully automated unit tests are feasible.

In the next iteration, the construction phase of this project will be completed with the implementation of a secure checkout procedure for Online Photo Shop.

11.6 Reference for Further Reading

ASP and XML

Jeffrey P. McManus, *C# Developer's Guide to ASP.NET, XML, and ADO.NET* (Boston: Addison-Wesley, 2002)

CHAPTER 12

Security and Database Access

 Unified Process:
Construction Phase and Tenth Iteration

In Chapter 11 we implemented the foundation for Online Photo Shop using ASP.NET technology. We created a Web site where online customers can browse the product catalog and place items in a shopping cart. This iteration, which is the last iteration in the project's construction phase, will complete the implementation of the Web site by adding the checkout procedure. We use ADO.NET technology to store and retrieve each customer's personal profile to or from a database. Furthermore, security plays a role as we design and implement the form that collects the payment and shipping information. As defined in the project planning, the successful run of the unit tests for the functionality implemented in this iteration is required to proceed to the transition phase.

12.1 Secure Checkout

R In the ninth iteration, we had to adjust the project plan to take into account a new requirement that led to a slight redesign of the online store. So instead of dealing only with secure payment, we now must also implement all the forms for the checkout procedure. Now that the shopping cart functionality is in place, the overall goal for this iteration is the completion of customer orders, which involves a number of tasks:

- Creating a customer database: Each customer's personal profile needs to be stored so that returning customers do not have to reenter all their information.

- Authentication of online customers: Shipping and payment information may be displayed only after a customer is authenticated by a secret password.
- Entering or updating shipping and payment information: New users must enter their shipping and payment information to complete the order. Returning customers should be able to update this information when they place a new order.
- Shipping and tax computation: After the shipping information is entered, we need to compute local sales tax and shipping cost.
- Order summary for order processing: After the order has been completed it must be summarized for order processing.

Table 12.1 shows the requirement keys that will be addressed during this tenth iteration.

Table 12.1 Requirements of Iteration 10

Requirement	Type	Summary
F:customer_login	Functional	Returning customers shall be able to use their previous shipping and payment information by providing e-mail and a password.
F:order_checkout	Functional	At any point while browsing through the product catalog, customers shall be able to proceed to checkout and finalize the order.
F:checkout_shipping	Functional	During checkout, shipping information needs to be collected.
C:checkout_shipping_cont	Constraint	Shipping is possible to U.S. customers only.
F:checkout_payment	Functional	During checkout, payment information needs to be collected.
C:checkout_payment_method	Constraint	Payment is possible by credit or debit card only. A separate billing address shall *not* be collected (must match shipping address).
F:checkout_summarize	Functional	For each completed order, the entire order information shall be transferred to order processing.
C:online_shop_codebehind	Constraint	Web forms shall be created using the Visual Studio Web Form wizard and follow separation of code and design (code behind).

12.2 Integrating Externally Supplied Software

⟨ A ⟩ Many canned solutions are available for online stores. It is hardly necessary to reinvent the wheel and design everything, ranging from the customer database to scalable Web farms, from scratch. Many times it is far more efficient to integrate externally supplied components or even complete solutions and customize them to the business's needs. However, our selection of third-party software should not be based on what we find first or is free on the Internet but instead should follow a process that ensures that we choose the software that best fits the application's needs.

However, to make this chapter more readable and more fun to follow along with, we have greatly simplified many issues related to the online store, and we choose external software based exclusively on the fact that it is freely available to all readers. However, in this section we summarize steps that should be followed when you build applications using third-party software.

We must verify that the third-party software meets the demands of our project and is efficient in terms of technology and cost. We must also ensure that any functionality used in the end product works correctly. Typically, we make this verification by using a *validation plan*.

12.2.1 Validation of Externally Supplied Software Products

There are several reasons you might consider using third-party software in your product. For example, in Online Photo Shop we need a database for storing and recalling customer data. It would be an enormous task to write a database system. The option of writing our own database is not reasonable for the following reasons. First, we do not have the expertise in database system development, nor do we have the resources to develop such a system. Second, many commercial database systems are available that have been proven to work in various projects.

Thus, it is obviously cost-effective to evaluate, validate, and use an off-the-shelf database. Before using a third-party product, however, we need to make sure that it solves our problem and works as described, and that we have an integration plan. Therefore, we use a validation plan that includes steps described in the following sections.

Technology and Cost Analysis

In the first step, we define our requirements for the third-party product. Based on these requirements, we gather information about the commercially available tools. This is technical information—such as features, limitations, references from companies using the software, and the learning curve that is involved—but also includes the cost of the software. Based on the collected information, we evaluate the technology against the requirements we have defined. The evaluation often includes prototyping of various scenarios to learn more about the features, usage, and limitations of the product.

Another point that needs to be considered is the cost-effectiveness of the product we are evaluating. For example, later in this chapter we describe our use of an Excel-based database instead of a full-blown database system such as Structured Query Language (SQL) Server. This decision was based on the fact that we did not want readers to go through the process of installing and setting up a full-blown database system. In addition, there was certainly the cost factor. Using Excel avoided the cost of a license for a database system such as Microsoft SQL Server.

The decision process should be visible to all team members. The developers should be able to voice concerns about using the technologies in question. At the end of the analysis process, a decision about using a third-party product is made.

Note that in many cases it will be necessary to allow time and budget to train the developers on the third-party product before you start verifying and integrating it.

Validation of External Software Packages

After the decision is made to use a specific third-party product, we need to validate its functionality. This is usually done via *acceptance tests,* whose goal is to prove that the product works as specified for its intended use.

From our experience, the tests should not include the integration of the third-party product. Rather, they should test only the third-party software, for several reasons. First, we want to validate only the functionality of the third-party product, not the integration into our product. Second, developing the tests separately will allow the developers to learn about the use of the third-party product without having to deal with implementation issues at the same time. Third, these tests will be run on future upgrades of the third-party product to ensure that the behavior does not change.

After the third-party product has been validated, the next step is to start integrating it into our software.

Integration of a Third-Party Product

The integration of the acquired software follows the same process steps we have used in developing our software. The requirements definition and analysis have been done, so the next step is to define the design that specifies the integration of the third-party software into our software.

A good practice is to use an interface layer to separate the third-party implementation from the implementation of the end product. By using an interface layer, we ensure better maintainability. For example, if we later want to use another third-party product or if the third-party product changes its interfaces, we can simply adapt the interface layer without changing the rest of the implementation.

We base the implementation on the defined design. The final step is to write the unit, integration, and system tests for the newly implemented functionality that uses the third-party product.

12.3 E-mail, Password, Credit Card: Creating a Customer Profile

The goal for this iteration is to complete the online ordering process by implementing the code to collect the necessary customer information. Also, we want to store this information in a database for later use. But before we start the implementation, we need to know exactly what information will be collected and which forms we will use.

12.3.1 User Interfaces

After online customers have put items into their shopping cart, they can proceed to the checkout procedure. This area of Online Photo Shop will require a login step to identify the customer. We need this identification to make sure that we do not display someone's payment information to any third party. Also, new customers can use the login page to register themselves using their e-mail address and a password. Figure 12.1 shows the sketch of the login page.

After a customer is logged in, the shipping and payment information is collected for new customers, or verified for returning customers. This can actually be done on the same page. For returning customers, however, by default the fields will be set to the information used for the most recent order. Figure 12.2 shows the layout of the checkout form.

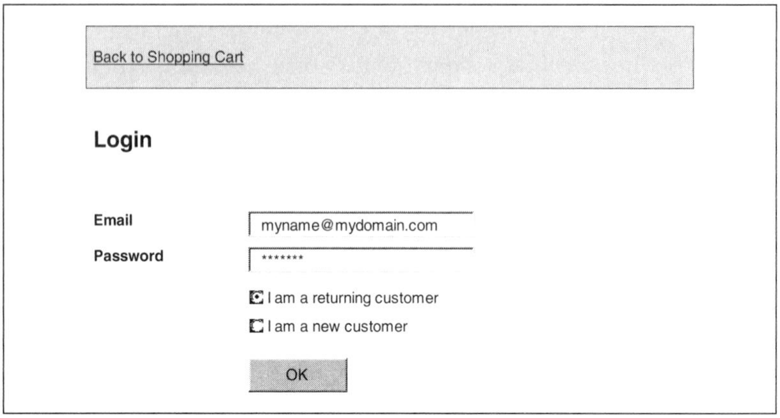

Figure 12.1 Login Form

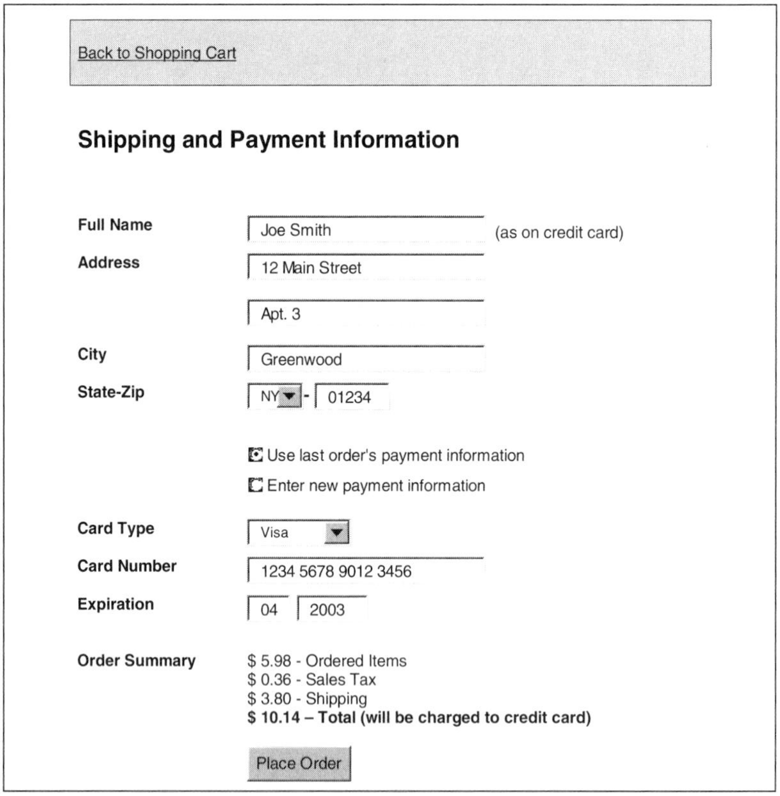

Figure 12.2 Checkout Form

12.3.2 Database Records

The data fields shown in Figures 12.1 and 12.2 also help to define the customer profile that will be stored in the customer database. Table 12.2 summarizes all fields and their types.

12.3.3 Tax and Shipping

Before an order can be completed, we need to compute the total cost, including shipping and sales tax if applicable. The business is a New Jersey-based company, so sales tax applies only to customers with NJ residences. The sales tax in New Jersey is 6%.

Only one shipping method is offered at this time. The cost of shipping consists of a fixed base amount of $1.25 plus $3.00 per pound.

12.3.4 Finalizing an Order

The requirement key `F:checkout_summarize` requires the Online Photo Shop application to make the information for each completed order available to order processing. We decide to use structured text files in XML format to make this information accessible to other applications. This XML

Table 12.2 Customer Profile

Field	Type	Summary
Email	Char[50]	Customer's e-mail address. The e-mail address is also used to identify the customer.
Password	Char[50]	Secret password used to authenticate the customer.
Name	Char[50]	Customer's full name.
Address1	Char[50]	First line of address.
Address2	Char[50]	Second line of address (optional).
City	Char[50]	U.S. city.
State	Char[2]	U.S. state (abbreviation).
Zip	Integer	Five-digit U.S. ZIP code.
CCType	Char[10]	Credit card type (Visa, MasterCard, etc.).
CCNumber	Char[16]	Credit card number (16 digits).
CCExpMonth	Integer	Credit card's expiration month.
CCExpYear	Integer	Credit card's expiration year.

file will contain the complete customer record, including shipping address and payment entered at the time of the order. Furthermore, the total amount of the order will be provided along with the amounts for shipping and sales tax. Next, all items ordered will be stored along with the file name of the uploaded digital picture for customizations. Such a file is shown in Listing 12.1.

Listing 12.1 Example of Completed Order in XML

```xml
<?xml version="1.0" encoding="utf-8" ?>
<doc>
<customer>
 <Email>joe.smith@mail.com</Email>
 <Name>Joe Smith</Name>
 <Address1>100 Main St.</Address1>
 <Address2>Apt. 12</Address2>
 <City>New Town</City>
 <State>NJ</State>
 <Zip>08150</Zip>
 <CCType>Visa</CCType>
 <CCNumber>1234-5678-9087-6543</CCNumber>
 <CCExpMonth>05</CCExpMonth>
 <CCExpYear>2007</CCExpYear>
 <Charged Order="$31.97" Tax="$1.92" Shipping="$4.25" Total="$38.14" />
</customer>
<order>
 <item product="cup" option="mug" quantity="2"
image="C:\OnlinePhotoShopData\uploads\image1.jpg" />
 <item product="print" option="8.5x11" quantity="1"
image="C:\OnlinePhotoShopData\uploads\image0.jpg" />
 </order>
</doc>
```

The directory in which to store completed orders will be defined in the `Web.config` file of Online Photo Shop. We will address this parameter, among others, later in this chapter.

12.4 Secure Web Applications

⟩D⟩ The design of Online Photo Shop was developed to a great extent in Chapter 11. What remains is to implement a secure design for the checkout process, where sensitive information is collected. Security presents three main aspects: authentication, authorization, and encryption.

12.4.1 Authentication

For Online Photo Shop, we must store each customer's profile to speed checkout and avoid recurring typing mistakes. However, before displaying any kind of previously collected payment or shipping information, we must determine who the customer is, a process known as *authentication*. The identity of a customer is usually authenticated by a login process, in which the customer is asked to enter a unique identifier together with a secret password (also referred to as *credentials*). This information is then compared against storage or a database, and the customer is authenticated if the information entered matches the information stored.

The requirement key F:customer_login defines the identifier as the customer's e-mail address. This not only is convenient for the customer but also simplifies the implementation. The application does not need to worry about the uniqueness of identifiers chosen by the customers. Instead, it can handle duplicate e-mail addresses as invalid inputs.

ASP.NET supports three very different mechanisms for authentication. Windows Authentication is an authentication service provided by Microsoft's Internet Information Services, in which IIS filters all requests and checks the user permissions even before ASP.NET is invoked to render a page. However, this mechanism can authenticate users only against Windows 2000 domain credential stores. Therefore, Windows Authentication can be recommended only for corporate intranets or similar applications. It also gives us no control over the user interface in which the credentials are entered. It therefore does not allow a custom design of a login form such as the one shown in Figure 12.1.

ASP.NET also provides an infrastructure called Forms Authentication. This product overcomes the limitations of Windows Authentication, but it requires the developer to design a login page and write code for registering new users and validating credentials of existing users. When a request for a page is made, ASP.NET automatically checks for an authentication *ticket*. If this ticket is not present, the request is redirected to the specified login page. The code behind the login page must then verify the user credentials, generate a new authentication ticket, and redirect the request back to the initially requested page. Because ASP.NET stores the authentication information in cookies, this method requires the user to enable cookies.

The third authentication method is called Passport. Here, Microsoft provides a centralized Internet authentication service, thereby eliminating the need for online shoppers to create a unique identifier and a password for each online store where they shop. Furthermore, users do not have to reenter their shipping and payment information because this information is also kept centralized. Without a doubt, Passport overcomes some inconveniences for online shoppers. However, a centralized service offering personal information such as home addresses, phone numbers, and credit card numbers becomes a likely target for hackers. Similarly, many people have legitimate concerns about their privacy when their authentication at all online stores is done through one company. On the other hand, people might feel more comfortable storing a personal profile at a service provided by a company that has a lot of expertise in the field of Internet security, rather than entering this information repeatedly at online stores that might not have the latest security patches installed or do not care very much about privacy.

After evaluating the advantages and limitations of all three mechanisms, we decide to implement the checkout process based on Forms Authentication. Open the project's `Web.config` file, change the authentication mode to `Forms`, and set the URL for the login page to `Login.aspx`:

```
<authentication mode="Forms">
    <forms loginUrl="Login.aspx" />
</authentication>
```

12.4.2 Authorization

After a user has been authenticated, *authorization* controls access to certain areas or files. In Online Photo Shop, any anonymous Internet user can browse the catalog and place items in the shopping cart. However, to proceed to the checkout, all customers must identify themselves in order to retrieve personal information stored during previous visits. Therefore, access to the checkout area is restricted to registered customers only; in other words, only registered customers are authorized to enter the checkout area.

To define a new area where different authorization attributes apply, we add a new folder to the project and name it `checkout`. To this folder we will later add the checkout and order confirmation forms. After creating the folder, open the `Web.config` file and add a new section to the configuration:

```
<?xml version="1.0" encoding="utf-8" ?>
<configuration>

  ...

 <!- restricted access to checkout folder ->
 <location path="checkout">
   <system.web>
     <authorization>
       <allow roles="Customer" />
       <deny users="*" />
     </authorization>
   </system.web>
 </location>

</configuration>
```

This section dictates that access to all pages under the `checkout` folder is restricted to authenticated users whose role is `Customer`. All others will be denied access to this folder.

12.4.3 Encryption

When a Web application exchanges data between the client and the Web server over the Internet, the data potentially could be hijacked by unauthorized parties. Remember that the Internet is a network of connected computers that can be operated by anyone—someone from a company or organization, from a university, or from the government, including computer hobbyists or even criminals. You have no influence on how and via which nodes data packets are routed, and at any point someone could scan the packets for sensitive information such as credit card numbers.

Data is exchanged as-is using Transmission Control Protocol/Internet Protocol (TCP/IP) and is accessible to any computer through which it is routed. But you can make the data unreadable for others by *encrypting* it. Secure Socket Layer (SSL) does exactly that. All data transferred between the client and the server is encrypted using a secret key. The longer the key, the harder it is for an outsider to crack the encryption.

SSL runs between TCP/IP and higher-level protocols such as Hypertext Transport Protocol (HTTP). TCP/IP is used by SSL on behalf of the higher-level protocol, but it also allows two computers on the Internet to authenticate each other and establish an encrypted connection. Authentication is important to users if they are sending their credit card information to a server and want to check the server's identity. SSL uses standard public key cryptography techniques to validate a server's certificate and public ID. For this, the client checks a number of conditions:

- Has the certificate been issued by a *certificate authority* (CA) that is on the client's list of trusted CAs?
- Is today's date within the validity period of the certificate?
- Does the domain name specified in the certificate match the actual server's domain name?
- Does the issuing CA's public key validate the issuer's digital signature?

Only when all these questions can be answered yes is the server authenticated. After the authentication, an encrypted connection is established, and it requires the encryption of all sent information on the sender's side and *decryption* (translation of the encrypted data back into the original) by the receiver, thus making it unreadable by any third party in between. In addition, all data is secured using a mechanism for detecting whether the data has been tampered with during transmission.

The secure connection is established in a number of steps. First, the client creates a *pre-master secret* and encrypts it using the server's public key. After the server receives the pre-master secret, both client and server independently perform a series of steps to create a common *master secret*, starting with the same pre-master secret. This master secret is then used to generate symmetric session keys that are used to encrypt and decrypt information exchanged during an SSL session.

To be considered a secure application, Online Photo Shop must encrypt the customer authentication before storing it in a cookie. Furthermore, all forms under the checkout directory must be transferred between the Web server and the client using SSL to fulfill the requirement `R:checkout_payment_secure`. Using SSL requires no extra implementation but only a configuration effort. Because a cost is associated with obtaining secure server certificates, we will not focus on SSL configuration in this chapter. Instead, in the references section you will find references on obtaining a server certificate and setting up a secure connection via SSL.

12.5 Database Access with ADO.NET

ADO.NET is an interface library that provides access to various kinds of data providers, such as SQL, OLE DB, and ODBC. Although each data provider has its own set of classes, they are conceptually the same. The main classes are as follows:

- `Connection`: Used to establish a connection to a database; this connection is necessary to execute a command or read data. To connect to an SQL database, you use the `SqlConnection` class; an `Odbc Connection` class is used to connect to an ODBC data provider.
- `Command`: Executes a database command such as `SELECT`, `INSERT`, or `UPDATE`. Requires a database connection.
- `DataReader`: Exposes the data resulting from the execution of a `SELECT` command.

Although the classes that establish a database connection and execute commands are specific to the type of the data source, the database commands themselves are all based on SQL and are mostly compatible between the various kinds of data sources. The commands needed for this project are `SELECT`, `INSERT`, and `UPDATE`.

To promote cost efficiency, we store the customer information in a Microsoft Excel sheet, which is specified in the application's configuration file. The ODBC service has an Excel driver that can be used to store the customer records in an XLS file. However, we will encapsulate all database dependencies in an additional layer to allow the replacement of the data provider later based on growth of the business.

Figure 12.3 shows the class diagram for the data access layer. `DataTable` is a simple .NET Framework class for caching the content of a database table, in our case the customer table. `CustomerDB` is an abstract class providing higher-level API functions specific to the kind of operations performed by Online Photo Shop—namely, validating login credentials and creating a new user account. `CustomerDB` also defines an abstract method to create a new `DbDataAdapter` instance. This method must be implemented by inherited classes because it is specific to the data source type. For now, `SqlCustomerDB` will not be implemented. It is shown only to visualize how this possible future change can be addressed.

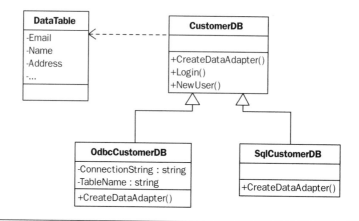

Figure 12.3 Class Diagram for Database Access Utilities

12.6 Putting It All Together

We can now start implementing the checkout process for the online store, which involves creating a database template, a utility class that wraps database access, and finally the login and checkout forms.

12.6.1 Creating the Data Source

Let's begin the implementation by creating a new spreadsheet and entering the fields from Table 12.2 into the first row. Before saving the file as `database.xls` to a location on the Web server's hard drive, rename the first sheet Customers (see Figure 12.4).

Office Suite If you don't have access to Microsoft Excel, you can download the free office suite OpenOffice at `http://www.openoffice.org` (also on the CD that accompanies this book). With the included Calc program you can create spreadsheets and save them in Excel format.

Next, we add the spreadsheet to the ODBC data sources using the ODBC Data Source Administrator (accessible via Control Panel | Administrative Tools). Choose the System DNS tab, and press the Add button. Then choose Microsoft Excel Driver and complete the ODBC Microsoft Excel Setup dialog (see Figure 12.5):

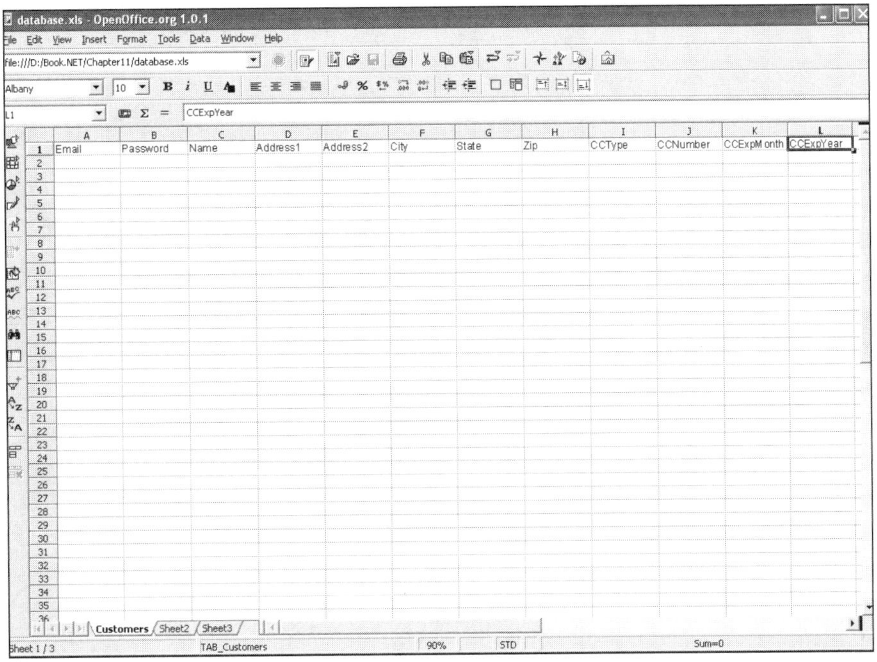

Figure 12.4 Creating the Customer Table

- Data Source Name: `OnlinePhotoShopDB`
- Description: `Database for Online Photo Shop Project.`
- Workbook: Point to the file shown in Figure 12.4.
- Read Only: Make sure this check box is unchecked in the Select Workbook dialog.

Next, we change the security attributes of the file folder where the database is stored to allow Internet guests to modify the database. By default, only read access is granted, and adding any new users in our Online Photo Shop application would result in a rather misleading error message: "Operation must use an updateable query."

To change the folder access permissions, open Windows Explorer. If your computer is not registered in a domain, first click on Menu Tools | Folder Options and choose the View tab. Then uncheck the advanced setting Use Simple File Sharing. Otherwise, the Security tab in the file properties dialog is always hidden. Next, select the folder in Windows Explorer

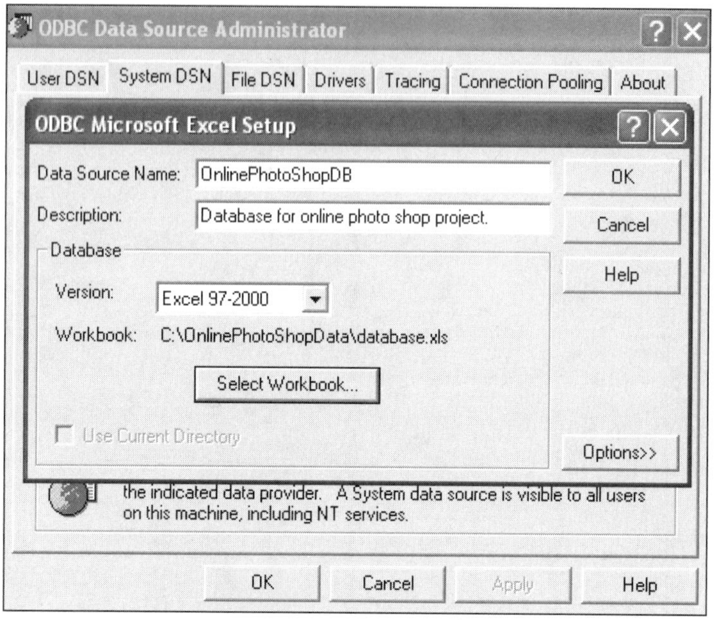

Figure 12.5 Adding an ODBC Data Source

where the database is stored, and open its properties dialog. In the Security tab, add the Internet guest accounts (LOCALHOST\IUSR_LOCALHOST and LOCALHOST\IUSR_COMPTERNAME) with full control permissions to the users.

12.6.2 The Data Access Layer

In the design workflow earlier in this chapter, it was decided to implement a layer on top of the database access to allow the replacement of the Excel sheet by a different data source.

The CustomerDB Class

We begin with the implementation of the abstract class CustomerDB. In addition to defining the abstract method CreateDataAdapter it implements the public methods Login and NewUser. The Login method provides the application with an API function to verify the login credentials entered by the customer. It returns true if a record matching the e-mail address and password was found. NewUser first verifies that the e-mail address does

not already exist in the customer database, and if no matching record was
found it inserts a new row in the customer table. Listing 12.2 shows the
implementation of the `CustomerDB` class.

Listing 12.2 `CustomerDB.cs`: Abstract Customer Database
Representation

```
using System;
using System.Data;
using System.Data.Common;

namespace OnlinePhotoShop
{
  /// <summary>
  /// Abstract class providing API functions to access the customer
  /// database.
  /// </summary>
  public abstract class CustomerDB
  {
    abstract public DbDataAdapter CreateDataAdapter(string
selectCondition);

    /// <summary>
    /// Authenticates a customer.
    /// </summary>
    /// <param name="email">Customer's e-mail address.</param>
    /// <param name="password">Secret password used for
    /// authentication.</param>
    /// <returns>Returns true if the authentication was
    /// successful.</returns>
    public bool Login(string email, string password)
    {
      // find matching record
      // (e.g., WHERE Email='user@mail.com' AND Password= 'secret' )
      DbDataAdapter dataAdapter = this.CreateDataAdapter(
        " WHERE Email = '" + email +
        "' AND Password = '" + password + "'");

      // query customer DB
      DataTable customer = new DataTable();
      dataAdapter.Fill(customer);
```

```
  if (customer.Rows.Count == 1)
  {
    // query successful
    return true;
  }

  // e-mail or password is incorrect
  return false;
}

/// <summary>
/// Adds a new customer to the database.
/// </summary>
/// <param name="email">Customer's e-mail address.</param>
/// <param name="password">Secret password used for
/// authentication.</param>
/// <returns>Returns true if the customer was added to the
/// database.</returns>
public bool NewUser(string email, string password)
{
  // see whether the e-mail already exists
  DbDataAdapter dataAdapter = this.CreateDataAdapter(
    " WHERE Email = '" + email + "'");

  // query customer DB
  DataTable customer = new DataTable();
  dataAdapter.Fill(customer);

  if (customer.Rows.Count != 0)
  {
    // account already created
    return false;
  }

  // insert new user into database
  string [] newCustomer = new string[2];
  newCustomer[0] = email;
  newCustomer[1] = password;
  customer.Rows.Add(newCustomer);

  // commit changes to database
  dataAdapter.Update(customer);
```

```
        return true;
      }
    }
}
```

The *OdbcCustomerDB* Class

To access our database in the form of an Excel sheet, we need an ODBC-specific implementation for the `execute` method. For this purpose we add a new class, `OdbcCustomerDB`, which overrides the abstract method `Create DataAdapter` inherited from `CustomerDB`. This method must create a new `OdbcDataAdapter` object and set the commands for selecting, inserting, and updating a customer in the table. The connection string and database table name are accessed via class properties. For the Online Photo Shop application, the connection string is `"DSN=OnlinePhotoShopDB"` and the table name is `"[Customers$]"`, referring to the first sheet in the Excel file. But instead of coding those numbers in the source code, we add them to the `Web.config` file in the `<appSettings>` section:

```
<appSettings>
    <add key="ImageStore" value="C:\OnlinePhotoShopData\uploads" />
    <add key="DBConnection" value="DSN=OnlinePhotoShopDB" />
    <add key="CustomerTable" value="[Customers$]" />
 </appSettings>
```

The `get` accessors for `ConnectionString` and `TableName` can now simply return the configuration setting. Listing 12.3 shows the implementation of this class.

Listing 12.3 `OdbcCustomerDB.cs`: ODBC-Specific Database Access

```
using System;
using System.Data;
using System.Data.Common;
using System.Data.Odbc;
using System.Configuration;

namespace OnlinePhotoShop
{
  /// <summary>
```

```
/// From CustomerDB-inherited class that creates data adapter
/// for ODBC data sources.
/// </summary>
public class OdbcCustomerDB : CustomerDB
{
  /// <summary>
  /// Returns the database connection string read from the
  /// application setting DBConnection.
  /// </summary>
  protected string ConnectionString
  {
    get
    {
      return ConfigurationSettings.AppSettings["DBConnection"];
    }
  }

  /// <summary>
  /// Returns the table where the customer records are stored
  /// read from the application setting CustomerTable.
  /// </summary>
  protected string TableName
  {
    get
    {
      return ConfigurationSettings.AppSettings["CustomerTable"];
    }
  }

  /// <summary>
  /// Creates a new data adapter for the customer database.
  /// </summary>
  /// <param name="selectCondition">Condition attached to the
  /// SELECT command.</param>
  /// <returns>DbDataAdapter to customer database.</returns>
  public override DbDataAdapter CreateDataAdapter(string
selectCondition)
  {
    OdbcConnection conn = new OdbcConnection(ConnectionString);
    OdbcDataAdapter dataAdapter = new OdbcDataAdapter();

    // Select Command
    OdbcCommand cmdSelect = new OdbcCommand();
```

```
    dataAdapter.SelectCommand = cmdSelect;
    cmdSelect.CommandText = "SELECT * FROM " + this.TableName + " " +
selectCondition;
    cmdSelect.CommandType = CommandType.Text;
    cmdSelect.Connection = conn;

    //Update Command
    OdbcCommand cmdUpdate = new OdbcCommand();
    dataAdapter.UpdateCommand = cmdUpdate;
    cmdUpdate.CommandText = "UPDATE [Customers$] SET " +
      "Name = ?,Address1 = ?,Address2 = ?,City = ?, " +
      "State = ?,Zip = ?,CCType = ?,CCNumber = ?," +
      "CCExpMonth = ?,CCExpYear = ? " +
      "WHERE Email = ?";
    cmdUpdate.CommandType = CommandType.Text;
    cmdUpdate.Connection = conn;
    cmdUpdate.Parameters.Add(new OdbcParameter("Name", OdbcType.
VarChar, 50, "Name"));
    cmdUpdate.Parameters.Add(new OdbcParameter("Address1", OdbcType.
VarChar, 50, "Address1"));
    cmdUpdate.Parameters.Add(new OdbcParameter("Address2", OdbcType.
VarChar, 50, "Address2"));
    cmdUpdate.Parameters.Add(new OdbcParameter("City", OdbcType.
VarChar, 50, "City"));
    cmdUpdate.Parameters.Add(new OdbcParameter("State", OdbcType.
VarChar, 2, "State"));
    cmdUpdate.Parameters.Add(new OdbcParameter("Zip", OdbcType.Int,
5, "Zip"));
    cmdUpdate.Parameters.Add(new OdbcParameter("CCType", OdbcType.
VarChar, 10, "CCType"));
    cmdUpdate.Parameters.Add(new OdbcParameter("CCNumber", OdbcType.
VarChar, 16, "CCNumber"));
    cmdUpdate.Parameters.Add(new OdbcParameter("CCExpMonth",
OdbcType.Int, 2, "CCExpMonth"));
    cmdUpdate.Parameters.Add(new OdbcParameter("CCExpYear", OdbcType.
Int, 4, "CCExpYear"));
    cmdUpdate.Parameters.Add(new OdbcParameter("Email", OdbcType.
VarChar, 50, "Email"));

    //Insert Command
    OdbcCommand cmdInsert = new OdbcCommand();
    dataAdapter.InsertCommand = cmdInsert;
```

```
      cmdInsert.CommandText = "INSERT INTO [Customers$] (Email,
Password) VALUES (?,?)";
      cmdInsert.CommandType = CommandType.Text;
      cmdInsert.Connection = conn;
      cmdInsert.Parameters.Add(new OdbcParameter("Email",OdbcType.
VarChar,50,"Email"));
      cmdInsert.Parameters.Add(new OdbcParameter("Password",OdbcType.
VarChar,50,"Password"));

      return dataAdapter;
    }
  }
}
```

Testing Database Access

The implementation of the utility classes for database access is not complete until we add a unit test. As usual, we do this before continuing with the integration into the Web pages. In Chapter 11, we added the class `UnitTest`, which contains all unit test cases for Online Photo Shop. Now we add another test case, `OdbcCustomerDBTest`, to this class.

In a real-life scenario we would use a dedicated data source just for testing. But to keep things simple we will use a dedicated customer account for testing. The test procedure is defined as follows:

1. Create a dedicated test login if it does not yet exist.
2. Set all fields for this customer to known values.
3. Commit the changes to the database.
4. Create a new `DataTable` using the same test account.
5. Check whether all fields of the test account have been set to the values assigned previously.

Listing 12.4 shows the implementation of these steps to test database access.

Listing 12.4 `UnitTest.cs`: Tester for `OdbcCustomerDB` Class

```
  . . .

using System.Data;
using System.Data.Common;
```

```
 ...

/// <summary>
/// Tests the OdbcCustomerDB class.
/// </summary>
/// <requirement>F:customer_login</requirement>
[Test]
public void OdbcCustomerDBTest()
{
  OdbcCustomerDB db = new OdbcCustomerDB();

  // create account to test with
  db.NewUser("tester@unit.test", ".netACompleteDevelopmentCycle2003");

  // log in
  Assertion.Assert(db.Login("tester@unit.test", ".netAComplete
DevelopmentCycle2003"));

  // log in using wrong password
  Assertion.Assert(!db.Login("tester@unit.test", "wrongPassword"));

  // create new record
  DbDataAdapter dataAdapter = db.CreateDataAdapter(" WHERE Email =
'tester@unit.test'");

  DataTable customer = new DataTable();
  dataAdapter.Fill(customer);

  customer.Rows[0]["Name"] = "Name";
  customer.Rows[0]["Address1"] = "Address1";
  customer.Rows[0]["Address2"] = "Address2";
  customer.Rows[0]["City"] = "City";
  customer.Rows[0]["State"] = "ST";
  customer.Rows[0]["Zip"] = "12345";
  customer.Rows[0]["CCType"] = "CCType";
  customer.Rows[0]["CCNumber"] = "CCNumber";
  customer.Rows[0]["CCExpMonth"] = "12";
  customer.Rows[0]["CCExpYear"] = "2003";

  // update and read to record2
  dataAdapter.Update(customer);
  DataTable customer2 = new DataTable();
  dataAdapter.Fill(customer2);
```

```
// check whether identical
Assertion.AssertEquals(customer2.Rows[0]["Name"], "Name");
Assertion.AssertEquals(customer2.Rows[0]["Address1"], "Address1");
Assertion.AssertEquals(customer2.Rows[0]["Address2"], "Address2");
Assertion.AssertEquals(customer2.Rows[0]["City"], "City");
Assertion.AssertEquals(customer2.Rows[0]["State"], "ST");
Assertion.AssertEquals(customer2.Rows[0]["Zip"], "12345");
Assertion.AssertEquals(customer2.Rows[0]["CCType"], "CCType");
Assertion.AssertEquals(customer2.Rows[0]["CCNumber"], "CCNumber");
Assertion.AssertEquals(customer2.Rows[0]["CCExpMonth"], "12");
Assertion.AssertEquals(customer2.Rows[0]["CCExpYear"], "2003");
}
```

When executing the test case given in Listing 12.4 from the NUnit test runner application, an error is reported in opening the database. At first this seems to be surprising; when the test is called directly from code of the Online Photo Shop project itself, everything works fine. So it must be a configuration problem. Indeed, the `Web.config` file is used only when the application runs within IIS. We need to create a separate configuration file for the test runner. To do this, we create an XML file named `OnlinePhoto Shop.dll.config` in the folder where `OnlinePhotoShop.dll` is located (`...\wwwroot\OnlinePhotoShop\bin`) and add to it the configuration settings for the connection string and table name:

```
<?xml version="1.0" encoding="utf-8" ?>
<configuration>
  <appSettings>
   <add key="DBConnection" value="DSN=OnlinePhotoShopDB" />
   <add key="CustomerTable" value="[Customers$]" />
  </appSettings>
</configuration>
```

Executing the test now should result in a failure-free run.

12.6.3 The Database Singleton

Now it is time to put the implemented and tested classes for the database access to work. Because we inherit a data-source-specific class from an abstract base class, the interfaces cannot just be declared static. Instead, an instantiation of a data-source-specific class such as `OdbcCustomerDB` is necessary to access the database. However, to minimize code changes when switching data sources later in the project, we should avoid instantiating classes of type `OdbcCustomerDB` or `SqlCustomerDB` directly wherever the database is accessed. Instead, we can use the Class Factory and Singleton design patterns to instantiate only a single object of, for example, `Odbc CustomerDB` per application, which returns a new data adapter object inherited from the data-provider-independent class `DbDataAdapter`. When the data provider needs to be changed, we simply replace the instantiation of this singleton.

Open the file `Global.asax.cs` and add the following lines to the `Application_Start` handler:

```
// add class through which the customer database is accessed
Application.Add("CustomerDB", new OdbcCustomerDB());
```

An instance derived from `CustomerDB` is now accessible throughout the entire application via the global setting `"CustomerDB"`, and if the data source changes, only one code line needs to be touched. You could go even further and store a configuration item that specifies which class to instantiate for the customer database.

12.6.4 The Login Page

During the design workflow of this iteration, we added a section to the `Web.config` file that defines the authorization for all pages located in the `checkout` folder. There, a link to `Login.aspx` is given, and we implement that functionality next.

Add a new form, `Login.aspx`, to the project. As with `Browse.aspx` and `Cart.aspx`, we first switch the page layout to FlowLayout in the property window of the form. Then drag and drop the needed elements according to Figure 12.1 and the property tables given next.

Properties of Hyperlink1

NavigateUrl	Cart.aspx
Text	Back to Shopping Cart

Properties of TextBox1

NavigateUrl	Cart.aspx
(ID)	Email

Properties of RequiredFieldValidator1

ControlToValidate	Email
ErrorMessage	Please enter your email.

Properties of TextBox2

TextMode	Password
(ID)	Password

Properties of RequiredFieldValidator2

ControlToValidate	Password
ErrorMessage	Please enter a password.

Properties of RadioButton1

Text	I am a returning customer.
Checked	True
GroupName	CustomerGroup
(ID)	ReturningCustomerButton

Properties of RadioButton2

Text	I am a new customer.
Checked	False
GroupName	CustomerGroup
(ID)	NewCustomerButton

Properties of Label1

Text	Invalid email or password!
Visible	False
ForeColor	Red
(ID)	ErrorLabel

Properties of Button1

Text	Login
(ID)	LoginButton

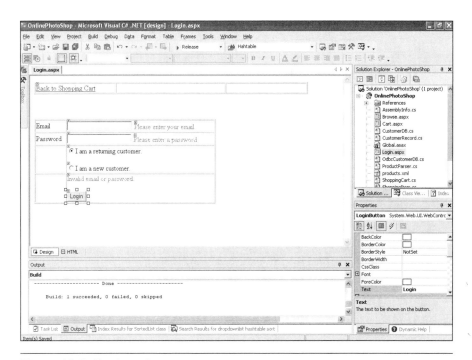

Figure 12.6 Design of `Login.aspx`

The required field validators as well as the `Error` label are used to inform the customer if login credentials have not been entered or are invalid. Figure 12.6 shows the design view of the login page.

For the Login button, an event handler is needed that validates the given credentials. The handler can easily be added by double-clicking the button. If the customer has been authenticated (either by validating the password or by adding a new user to the customer database), we issue a Forms Authentication ticket. For security reasons (see section 12.4) this ticket must be encrypted because it is stored in a cookie, which is transferred to the client. The cookie is recognized by IIS and allows the user to access pages that require authorization for a given time. Listing 12.5 shows the implementation of the Login button event handler. Before this code can be compiled, the namespace `System.Web.Security` must be added to the form at the beginning of the code file.

Listing 12.5 Login.aspx.cs: Code Behind the Login Page

```
using System;
using System.Web;
using System.Web.SessionState;
using System.Web.UI;
using System.Web.UI.WebControls;
using System.Web.UI.HtmlControls;
using System.Web.Security;

namespace OnlinePhotoShop
{
  /// <summary>
  /// Summary description for Login.
  /// </summary>
  public class Login : System.Web.UI.Page
  {
    protected System.Web.UI.WebControls.HyperLink HyperLink1;
    protected System.Web.UI.WebControls.TextBox Email;
    protected System.Web.UI.WebControls.TextBox Password;
    protected System.Web.UI.WebControls.RequiredFieldValidator Required
FieldValidator1;
    protected System.Web.UI.WebControls.RadioButton Returning
CustomerButton;
    protected System.Web.UI.WebControls.RadioButton NewCustomerButton;
    protected System.Web.UI.WebControls.Button LoginButton;
    protected System.Web.UI.WebControls.Label ErrorLabel;
    protected System.Web.UI.WebControls.RequiredFieldValidator Required
FieldValidator2;

    private void Page_Load(object sender, System.EventArgs e)
    {
      // Put user code to initialize the page here
    }

    #region Web Form Designer generated code
    override protected void OnInit(EventArgs e)
    {
      //
      // CODEGEN: This call is required by the ASP.NET Web Form
Designer.
      //
      InitializeComponent();
```

```csharp
    base.OnInit(e);
}


/// <summary>
/// Required method for Designer support - do not modify
/// the contents of this method with the code editor.
/// </summary>
private void InitializeComponent()
{
    this.LoginButton.Click += new System.EventHandler(this.LoginButton_
Click);
    this.Load += new System.EventHandler(this.Page_Load);

}
#endregion
private void LoginButton_Click(object sender, System.EventArgs e)
{
    bool issueTicket = false;
    CustomerDB db = (CustomerDB) Application.Get("CustomerDB");

    if (ReturningCustomerButton.Checked)
    {
        // verify login credentials
        issueTicket = db.Login(Email.Text, Password.Text);
    }
    else
    {
        // new customer
        issueTicket = db.NewUser(Email.Text, Password.Text);
    }

    if (issueTicket)
    {
        // issue new authentication ticket
        FormsAuthenticationTicket ticket =
new FormsAuthenticationTicket(1,
            Email.Text,
            System.DateTime.Now,
            System.DateTime.Now.AddMinutes(20),
            false,
            "Customer",
            FormsAuthentication.FormsCookiePath);
```

```
        // encrypt the ticket
        string encTicket = FormsAuthentication.Encrypt(ticket);

        // create the cookie
        Response.Cookies.Add(new HttpCookie(FormsAuthentication.
FormsCookieName, encTicket));

        // redirect back to original URL
        Response.Redirect(FormsAuthentication.GetRedirectUrl(Email.
Text, false));
      }
      else
      {
        ErrorLabel.Visible = true;
      }
    }
  }
}
```

As set in the `Web.config` file section, all users having the role of a customer are authorized to access files in the `checkout` folder. For Online Photo Shop this is the only role currently used, but in the future other roles (such as administrator) or different levels of memberships might be added. Because no roles are yet stored in the database, it has been hard-coded to `Customer` in the event handler shown in Listing 12.5. We pass the roles to the user data argument in the form's authorization ticket so that this information also gets encrypted and cannot be modified by a client. Next, we change the `Application_AuthenticateRequest` method in the `Global.asax.cs` file to change the current user from anonymous to one that has the customer role (see Listing 12.6).

Listing 12.6 `Global.asax.cs: Application_AuthenticateRequest`

```
using System.Web.Security;
using System.Security.Principal;

  . . .

protected void Application_AuthenticateRequest(Object sender,
EventArgs e)
{
```

```
if (Request.IsAuthenticated)
{
   // if authenticated, change the current user from anonymous
   FormsIdentity user = (FormsIdentity) User.Identity;
   FormsAuthenticationTicket auth = user.Ticket;
   // assume all user roles are passed via comma-separated list in
UserData
   HttpContext.Current.User = new GenericPrincipal(user, auth.
UserData.Split(','));
  }
}
```

12.6.5 The Checkout Form

The core functionality of this chapter will be visible through the checkout form, which summarizes the order and collects shipping as well as payment information. Add a new Web form `Checkout.aspx` to the project's `checkout` folder. You need to place the form into this folder so that it is located in an area with restricted access. Now set the page layout to FlowLayout and start the design of the form as shown in Figure 12.2. Table 12.3 summarizes the ID names and control types to be used in the design of this form.

Table 12.3 Controls in `Checkout.aspx`

ID Name	Control Type
HyperLink1	HyperLink (set NavigateUrl to ../Cart.aspx)
Email	Label
Name	TextBox
Address1	TextBox
Address2	TextBox
State	DropDownList
Zip	TextBox
LastPayment	RadioButton (use Payment in GroupName)
NewPayment	RadioButton (use Payment in GroupName)
CCType	DropDownList
CCNumber	TextBox
CCExpMonth	TextBox
CCExpYear	TextBox
Order	Label

(continued)

Table 12.3 (*Cont.*)

ID Name	Control Type
Tax	Label
Shipping	Label
Total	Label (highlight)
Button	Button

The `State DropDownList` control must be set to automatic post-back so that sales tax and shipping can be immediately updated whenever the customer selects a different state. Figure 12.7 shows the completed design of the checkout form.

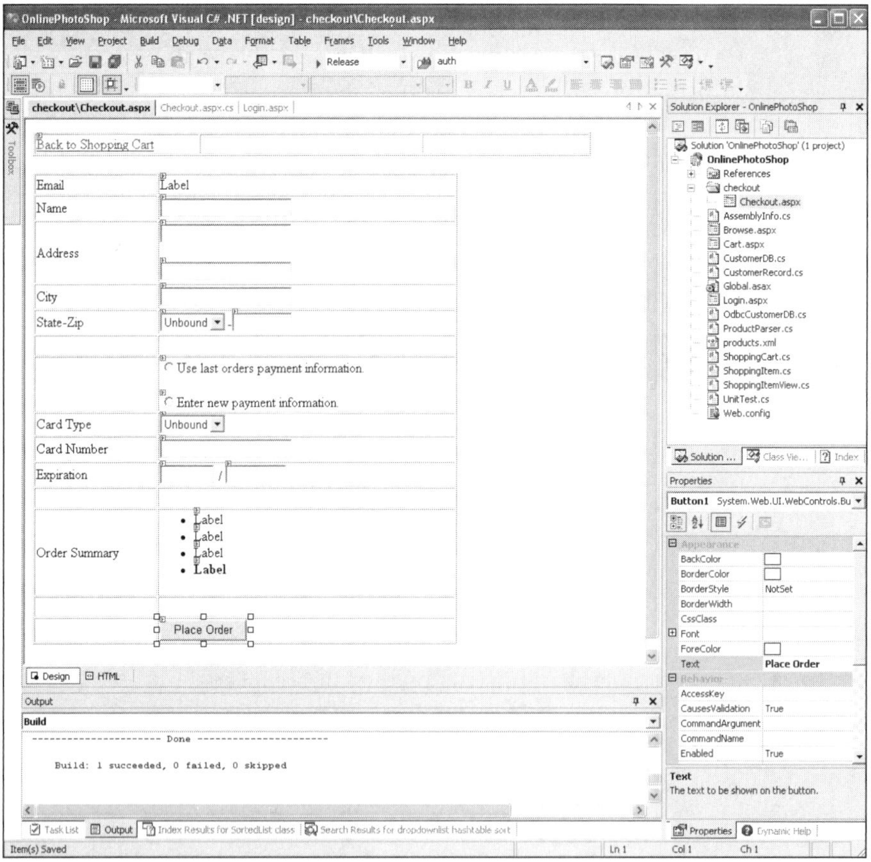

Figure 12.7 Design of `Checkout.aspx`

Tax and Shipping Cost

During the design workflow of the preceding iteration (Chapter 11), we developed a class diagram that requests a dedicated class for computing tax and shipping for a given order. Let's first add a new class, `TaxCalculator`, that computes the sales tax on an order. Because the business is based in New Jersey, the sales tax of 6% is collected from New Jersey customers only (see Listing 12.7).

Listing 12.7 `TaxCalculator.cs`

```
using System;

namespace OnlinePhotoShop.checkout
{
  /// <summary>
  /// Computes the sales tax for a given order and state.
  /// </summary>
  public class TaxCalculator
  {
    static public double Compute(double total, string state)
    {
      switch (state)
      {
        case "NJ":  return total * 0.06;
      }

      return 0;
    }
  }
}
```

During the analysis workflow earlier in this chapter, we established the need for only one shipping method based on a fixed amount of $1.25 plus $3.00 per pound. The implementation for this is fairly trivial and is shown in Listing 12.8.

Listing 12.8 `ShippingCostCalculator.cs`

```
using System;

namespace OnlinePhotoShop.checkout
{
```

```
/// <summary>
/// Computes the shipping cost for a given weight.
/// </summary>
public class ShippingCostCalculator
{
  static public double Compute(int method, double weight, string
  state)
  {
    // right now ground shipping only, $1.25 + $3 per pound
    // (all states same)
    return (1.25 + (weight * 3));
  }
}
}
```

Computing the Order Total

Computing the total cost as well as the total weight of an order is a useful addition to the existing ShoppingCart class. This information is needed to compute the shipping and applicable sales tax. Listing 12.9 shows the implementation for the two new methods added to the ShoppingCart class.

Listing 12.9 ShoppingCart.cs: The GetTotalOrder() and GetTotalWeight() Methods

```
/// <summary>
/// Computes the total of all items in the shopping cart.
/// </summary>
/// <param name="productCatalog">Product catalog file.</param>
/// <returns>Total cost of all items in the shopping cart.</returns>
public double GetTotalOrder(string productCatalog)
{
  double total = 0;
  ProductParser parser = new ProductParser(productCatalog);

  IDictionaryEnumerator i = this.GetEnumerator();
  while(i.MoveNext())
  {
    ShoppingItem item = (ShoppingItem) i.Value;

    // get the product details
    System.Collections.Hashtable details = parser.OptionDetails(item.
Product, item.Option);
```

```
    // add to total
    double price = System.Convert.ToDouble((string) details["price"]);
    total += (price * item.Quantity);
  }

  return total;
}

/// <summary>
/// Computes the total weight of all items in the shopping cart.
/// </summary>
/// <param name="productCatalog">Product catalog file.</param>
/// <returns>Total weight of all items in the shopping cart.</returns>
public double GetTotalWeight(string productCatalog)
{
  double total = 0;
  ProductParser parser = new ProductParser(productCatalog);

  IDictionaryEnumerator i = this.GetEnumerator();
  while(i.MoveNext())
  {
    ShoppingItem item = (ShoppingItem) i.Value;

    // get the product details
    System.Collections.Hashtable details = parser.OptionDetails(item.
    Product, item.Option);

    // add to total
    double weight = System.Convert.ToDouble((string) details
["weight"]);
    total += (weight * item.Quantity);
  }

  return total;
}
```

Do It Yourself The methods we have added to the `ShoppingCart` class for computing the total cost and weight of all items placed in a shopping cart require new test cases on the unit test level. It is your responsibility to develop a new test case that verifies the extended `ShoppingCart` class. The test case will be added to the `UnitTest` class of the project.

Finalizing the Order

All groundwork for the checkout process is now finished, and we complete the implementation by adding the code behind the form, which must address four tasks:

- Summarize the order: The total cost of all items in the shopping cart, shipping fees, and sales tax must be computed, and the appropriate labels on the form updated. This task is fairly trivial. We use the new methods of ShoppingCart to compute total cost and weight of an order and pass those values to the ShippingCostCalculator and TaxCalculator classes.
- Initialize all input fields: When the page is loaded, all input fields must be initialized with the profile stored in the customer database. The initialization of the input fields should be added to the existing method Page_Load(). We use the global CustomerDB object to query a customer record from the database.
- Update customer record: After the user has finished entering or updating the shipping and payment information, we must update the customer profile in the database. This can be added to the event handler of the order button, and again the global CustomerDB object can be used for the database transactions.
- Store order: The completed order, including shipping and payment information, must be finalized and stored in XML format to a dedicated directory. This is best done through a new method that saves the customer record as well as the items in the shopping cart in an XML file using the XmlTextWriter class provided by the .NET Framework.

Listing 12.10 shows the complete implementation for the code behind the checkout form.

Listing 12.10 Checkout.aspx.cs: Finalizing Orders

```
using System;
using System;
using System.Collections;
using System.Data;
using System.Data.Common;
```

```
using System.Web;
using System.Web.SessionState;
using System.Web.UI;
using System.Web.UI.WebControls;
using System.Web.UI.HtmlControls;
using System.Web.Security;
using System.Configuration;
using System.Xml;
using System.IO;

namespace OnlinePhotoShop.checkout
{
  /// <summary>
  /// Checkout form collecting shipping and payment information.
  /// </summary>
  /// <requirement>F:order_checkout</requirement>
  /// <requirement>F:checkout_shipping</requirement>
  /// <requirement>C:checkout_shipping_cont</requirement>
  /// <requirement>F:checkout_payment</requirement>
  /// <requirement>F:checkout_payment_method</requirement>
  /// <requirement>F:checkout_summarize</requirement>
  public class Checkout : System.Web.UI.Page
  {
    protected System.Web.UI.WebControls.HyperLink HyperLink1;
    protected System.Web.UI.WebControls.Label Email;
    protected System.Web.UI.WebControls.TextBox Name;
    protected System.Web.UI.WebControls.TextBox Address1;
    protected System.Web.UI.WebControls.TextBox Address2;
    protected System.Web.UI.WebControls.TextBox City;
    protected System.Web.UI.WebControls.DropDownList State;
    protected System.Web.UI.WebControls.TextBox Zip;
    protected System.Web.UI.WebControls.RadioButton LastPayment;
    protected System.Web.UI.WebControls.RadioButton NewPayment;
    protected System.Web.UI.WebControls.DropDownList CCType;
    protected System.Web.UI.WebControls.TextBox CCNumber;
    protected System.Web.UI.WebControls.TextBox CCExpMonth;
    protected System.Web.UI.WebControls.TextBox CCExpYear;
    protected System.Web.UI.WebControls.Label Order;
    protected System.Web.UI.WebControls.Label Tax;
    protected System.Web.UI.WebControls.Label Shipping;
    protected System.Web.UI.WebControls.Button Button;
    protected System.Web.UI.WebControls.Label Total;
```

```csharp
private void Page_Load(object sender, System.EventArgs e)
{
  if (!this.IsPostBack)
  {
    // get user id (e-mail) and retrieve customer record
    FormsIdentity user = (FormsIdentity) User.Identity;
    FormsAuthenticationTicket auth = user.Ticket;
    CustomerDB db = (CustomerDB) Application.Get("CustomerDB");
    DbDataAdapter dataAdapter = db.CreateDataAdapter(" WHERE Email =
'" + auth.Name + "'");

    DataTable customer = new DataTable();
    dataAdapter.Fill(customer);

    // set fields with values loaded from database
    Email.Text = (string) customer.Rows[0]["Email"];
    Name.Text = (string) customer.Rows[0]["Name"];
    Address1.Text = (string) customer.Rows[0]["Address1"];
    Address2.Text = (string) customer.Rows[0]["Address2"];
    City.Text = (string) customer.Rows[0]["City"];

    // create list of states
    ArrayList states = new ArrayList();
    states.Add("AZ");
    states.Add("NJ");
    states.Add("NY");
    states.Add("TX");
    State.DataSource = states;
    State.DataBind();

    // select state from database
    for (int i = 0; i < states.Count; i++)
      if (((string)states[i]) == (string) customer.Rows[0]["State"])
        State.SelectedIndex = i;

    Zip.Text = (string) customer.Rows[0]["Zip"];

    // create credit card types and select last used one
    ArrayList cctypes = new ArrayList();
    cctypes.Add("Visa");
    cctypes.Add("Master");
    CCType.DataSource = cctypes;
    CCType.DataBind();
```

```
      if ((string) customer.Rows[0]["CCType"] == "Master")
        CCType.SelectedIndex = 1;
      else
        CCType.SelectedIndex = 0;

      CCNumber.Text = (string) customer.Rows[0]["CCNumber"];
      CCExpMonth.Text = (string) customer.Rows[0]["CCExpMonth"];
      CCExpYear.Text = (string) customer.Rows[0]["CCExpYear"];

      if (CCNumber.Text.Length == 0)
        NewPayment.Checked = true;
      else
        LastPayment.Checked = true;

      // update the order summary
      this.UpdateSummary();
    }

    // do not cache this page
    Response.Expires = -1;
  }


  /// <summary>
  /// Computes order total, tax, and shipping and updates labels on
Web page.
  /// </summary>
  public void UpdateSummary()
  {
    // retrieve shopping cart information from session object
    ShoppingCart cart = (ShoppingCart) Session["ShoppingCart"];
    if (cart == null)
    {
      cart = new ShoppingCart(Session.SessionID);
      Session["ShoppingCart"] = cart;
    }

    if (cart.Count == 0)
    {
      Response.Redirect(@"..\Empty.aspx");
    }

    // update order label
    double total = cart.GetTotalOrder(Server.MapPath(@"..\products.xml"));
Order.Text = total.ToString("C");
```

```csharp
    // compute tax
    double tax = TaxCalculator.Compute(total, State.SelectedValue);
    Tax.Text = tax.ToString("C");

    // compute shipping
    double weight = cart.GetTotalWeight(Server.MapPath(@"..\products.
xml"));
    double shipping = ShippingCostCalculator.Compute(0, weight,
State.SelectedValue);
    Shipping.Text = shipping.ToString("C");

    // update total
    total += shipping + tax;
    Total.Text = total.ToString("C");
}


/// <summary>
/// Called when the state changes. Updates the order summary.
/// </summary>
/// <param name="sender"></param>
/// <param name="e"></param>
private void State_SelectedIndexChanged(object sender, System.
EventArgs e)
{
    // Update summary. Shipping or tax might change.
    this.UpdateSummary();
}


/// <summary>
/// Creates a new order based on the items in the shopping cart and
the given customer record.
/// After the order is saved the items in the shopping cart are
removed.
/// </summary>
/// <param name="customer">Customer record.</param>
private void SaveOrder(DataTable customer)
{
    ShoppingCart cart = (ShoppingCart) Session["ShoppingCart"];
    if (cart != null)
    {
        // Get path for a temporary file
        string file = (string) ConfigurationSettings.AppSettings
["OrderStore"] + "\\order_" + Session.SessionID.ToString() + ".xml";
```

```
        // create a temp XML file
        XmlTextWriter writer = new XmlTextWriter(File.CreateText(file));
        writer.Formatting = Formatting.Indented;
        writer.WriteStartDocument();
        writer.WriteStartElement("doc");

        writer.WriteStartElement("customer");

        writer.WriteElementString("Email", (string)
customer.Rows[0]["Email"]);
        writer.WriteElementString("Name", (string)
customer.Rows[0]["Name"]);
        writer.WriteElementString("Address1", (string)
customer.Rows[0]["Address1"]);
        writer.WriteElementString("Address2", (string)
customer.Rows[0]["Address2"]);
        writer.WriteElementString("City", (string)
customer.Rows[0]["City"]);
        writer.WriteElementString("State", (string)
customer.Rows[0]["State"]);
        writer.WriteElementString("Zip", (string)
customer.Rows[0]["Zip"]);
        writer.WriteElementString("CCType", (string)
customer.Rows[0]["CCType"]);
        writer.WriteElementString("CCNumber", (string)
customer.Rows[0]["CCNumber"]);
        writer.WriteElementString("CCExpMonth", (string)
customer.Rows[0]["CCExpMonth"]);
        writer.WriteElementString("CCExpYear", (string)
customer.Rows[0]["CCExpYear"]);

        writer.WriteStartElement("Charged");
        writer.WriteAttributeString("Order", Order.Text);
        writer.WriteAttributeString("Tax", Tax.Text);
        writer.WriteAttributeString("Shipping", Shipping.Text);
        writer.WriteAttributeString("Total", Total.Text);
        writer.WriteEndElement();  // charged
        writer.WriteEndElement();  // customer

        writer.WriteStartElement("order");

        IDictionaryEnumerator i = cart.GetEnumerator();
        while(i.MoveNext())
```

```
        {
          ShoppingItem item = (ShoppingItem) i.Value;
          writer.WriteStartElement("item");
          writer.WriteAttributeString("product", item.Product);
          writer.WriteAttributeString("option", item.Option);
          writer.WriteAttributeString("quantity", item.Quantity.
ToString());
          writer.WriteAttributeString("image", item.ServerPath);
          writer.WriteEndElement();  // item
        }
        writer.WriteEndElement();  // order

        writer.WriteEndElement();  // doc
        writer.WriteEndDocument();
        writer.Close();

        // delete all shopping cart items
        cart.Clear();
      }
    }

    #region Web Form Designer generated code
    override protected void OnInit(EventArgs e)
    {
      //
      // CODEGEN: This call is required by the ASP.NET Web Form Designer.
      //
      InitializeComponent();
      base.OnInit(e);
    }

    /// <summary>
    /// Required method for Designer support - do not modify
    /// the contents of this method with the code editor.
    /// </summary>
    private void InitializeComponent()
    {
      this.Button.Click += new System.EventHandler(this.Button_Click);
      this.Load += new System.EventHandler(this.Page_Load);

    }
    #endregion
```

```csharp
/// <summary>
/// Called when the place order button is pressed. Updates the
customer record and
/// saves the order.
/// </summary>
/// <param name="sender"></param>
/// <param name="e"></param>
private void Button_Click(object sender, System.EventArgs e)
{
  // get user id (e-mail) and retrieve customer record
  FormsIdentity user = (FormsIdentity) User.Identity;
  FormsAuthenticationTicket auth = user.Ticket;
  CustomerDB db = (CustomerDB) Application.Get("CustomerDB");
  DbDataAdapter dataAdapter = db.CreateDataAdapter(" WHERE Email =
'" + auth.Name + "'");

  DataTable customer = new DataTable();
  dataAdapter.Fill(customer);

  // update fields
  customer.Rows[0]["Name"] = Name.Text;
  customer.Rows[0]["Address1"] = Address1.Text;
  customer.Rows[0]["Address2"] = Address2.Text;
  customer.Rows[0]["City"] = City.Text;
  customer.Rows[0]["State"] = State.SelectedValue;
  customer.Rows[0]["Zip"] = Zip.Text;

  // update payment if necessary
  if (NewPayment.Checked)
  {
    customer.Rows[0]["CCType"] = CCType.SelectedValue;
    customer.Rows[0]["CCNumber"] = CCNumber.Text;
    customer.Rows[0]["CCExpMonth"] = CCExpMonth.Text;
    customer.Rows[0]["CCExpYear"] = CCExpYear.Text;
  }

  // store back into database
  dataAdapter.Update(customer);

  // now save the order
  this.SaveOrder(customer);
```

```
        // say thank you
        Response.Redirect("Completed.aspx");
    }
  }
}
```

As you can see from the code in Listing 12.10, the method `Update` `Summary()` redirects the request to the page `Empty.aspx` if the shopping cart does not contain any items. This page must be added to the project and should display an error message and provide a link that takes the customer back to the product browser. If a customer clicks on checkout with an empty shopping cart, it usually is not a case of disturbed customers but disabled cookies in Internet Explorer. Providing more information and help for the customer on how to enable cookies is definitely a good idea, too.

The other redirection added to the code takes place after the order has been saved and the shopping cart has been emptied. This page can provide some feedback that the order has been received. It could also display contact information for the customer service department and instructions on how to track an order if this service is provided. Add a form `Completed.aspx` to the project under the `checkout` directory, which is called for every completed order.

Finally, we add the new configuration parameter for the directory where the completed orders are stored. Open the `Web.config` file, and add the directory to the `appSettings` section:

```
<appSettings>
  <add key="ImageStore" value="C:\OnlinePhotoShopData\uploads" />
  <add key="OrderStore" value="C:\OnlinePhotoShopData\orders" />
  <add key="DBConnection" value="DSN=OnlinePhotoShopDB" />
  <add key="CustomerTable" value="[Customers$]" />
</appSettings>
```

Of course, this directory must also be created before we test the application.

12.7 No Longer under Construction

Finally, all major requirements for the Online Photo Shop application are in place, and we can place our first order. Figure 12.8 visualizes the sequence of a complete order cycle.

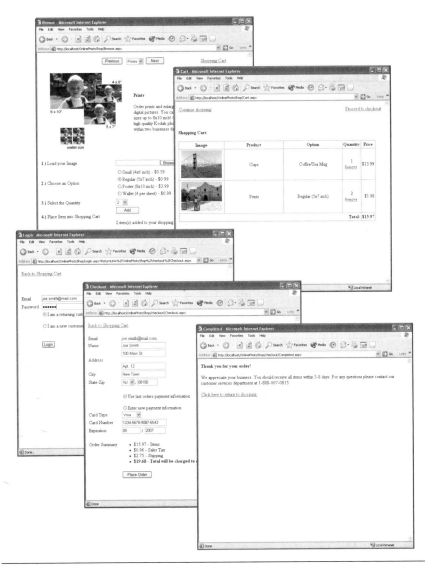

Figure 12.8 Order Cycle with the Online Photo Shop

Finished!? Not quite. The implementation of all major requirements concludes the construction phase of the project and leads to the transition phase, when the product is rolled out. The release of the product, however, involves a few more steps: formal testing of all implemented features in the form of integration and system tests, tracing of requirement keys to code, and of course deployment. All these steps are addressed in the next iteration, which is described in Chapter 13.

12.8 References for Further Reading

ADO

Bob Beauchemin, *Essential ADO.NET* (Boston: Addison-Wesley, 2002)

Jeffrey P. McManus and Jackie Goldstein, *Database Access with Visual Basic .NET* (Boston: Addison-Wesley, 2003)

Rebecca M. Riordan, *Microsoft ADO.NET Step by Step* (Redmond, WA: Microsoft Press, 2002)

SSL

http://wp.netscape.com/security/techbriefs/ssl.html

http://www.verisign.com

SQL

http://www.w3schools.com/sql

Office Suite

http://www.openoffice.org

CHAPTER 13

Product Release

Unified Process:
Transition Phase and Eleventh Iteration

We have now completed the design and implementation of all required functionality, and we shift our focus from construction to the release of the product. This is known as the transition phase of the Unified Process, the final iteration of the project.

We concentrate here on software deployment, integration test, and requirements tracing. For the five core workflows, we plan to achieve the following goals:

- Requirements: Usually this workflow is not applicable to the transition phase. However, we postponed to this iteration the definition of requirements for deployment of the software. Therefore, we must determine, in collaboration with the business customer, which is the best way of distributing the developed software.
- Analysis: In this phase, this workflow is applicable only to software deployment and problems that have been found during integration testing. If we detect malfunctions of the software that lead to changes in the design or implementation, we must analyze the impact of these defects on the remaining components (this is also known as *impact analysis*). If the impact introduces a high risk to the overall release of the software, we must determine, together with the customer, whether the problem must be fixed or whether we can document it in the release notes and fix it in a later version or service pack.
- Design: No major changes to the design should be made in the transition phase. We change the design only to address problems found during testing. An impact analysis must be created for all changes.
- Implementation: Implementations necessary for the software deployment are done during this phase. Furthermore, smaller bug fixes may be addressed.

■ Test: Unit tests have been written and performed to fulfill the criteria to continue with the next iteration within the construction phase. In this phase, all unit tests will be rerun and additional integration tests will be created. Before the software can be released, the deployment procedure also must be tested to make sure the customer is able to install and use the software. Furthermore, we trace all requirement keys to implementation, unit test, and integration test to ensure that no requirements have been forgotten.

The acceptance criteria to conclude the transition phase include the successful run of all unit and integration tests. All problems found during these tests either must be corrected or, with customer approval, must be listed in the release notes. Furthermore, all requirement keys must be traceable to the implementation and to at least one unit or integration test where applicable.

13.1 Deployment

As described in Chapter 4, the photo editor portion of Online Photo Shop is meant to be a downloadable tool offered to online customers to prepare their photos before ordering prints. For a proper release of the product to the business, we must offer a solution to deploy the software to its customers. Also, we must address deployment of the online software running on the Web server.

After talking to the business representative, we add the requirements listed in Table 13.1 to the project. Both requirements are added to the plan of the eleventh iteration of the project. The schedule has been adjusted to allow for two additional days of development time.

13.1.1 Options for Distributing .NET Applications

Microsoft bundles an installation wizard in Visual Studio.NET that makes it easy to create setup programs. The setup program can be configured to install applications directly from the Web without a separate download or uncompressing step. Therefore, we can deploy the photo editor application using this wizard.

Table 13.1 Deployment Requirements

Requirement	Type	Summary
F:photo_editor_deployment	Functional	An online installer for the photo editor shall be provided, which can be linked to any Web page. No manual setup steps involving copying or uncompressing shall be required.
F:onlinephotoshop_deployment	Functional	The software for Online Photo Shop shall be provided on a CD along with installation instructions for system and Web administrators.

Deployment of the Online Photo Shop application is also fairly simple. All application files are located in the IIS folder `OnlinePhotoShop` and can simply be copied to the target machine. Installation notes will guide the administrator in setting up the ODBC data source, folders that receive uploaded images, and orders as well as starting up the ASP.NET State service.

13.1.2 Creating a Setup Program

Let's begin by creating the photo editor installer. Start Developer Studio.NET, and create a new project. Select the Setup Wizard template under Setup and Deployment Projects, and name the project `Photo Editor` (see Figure 13.1).

On the second page of the wizard, choose Create a Setup for a Windows Application. Then on the next page, add the following files from Chapter 10's `bin` folder to the Additional Files to Include list:

- `Photo Editor Application.exe`
- `3DText.dll`
- `BrightnessPlugIn.dll`
- `ColorPlugIn.dll`
- `RedEyePlugIn.dll`
- `Hawaii.jpg`

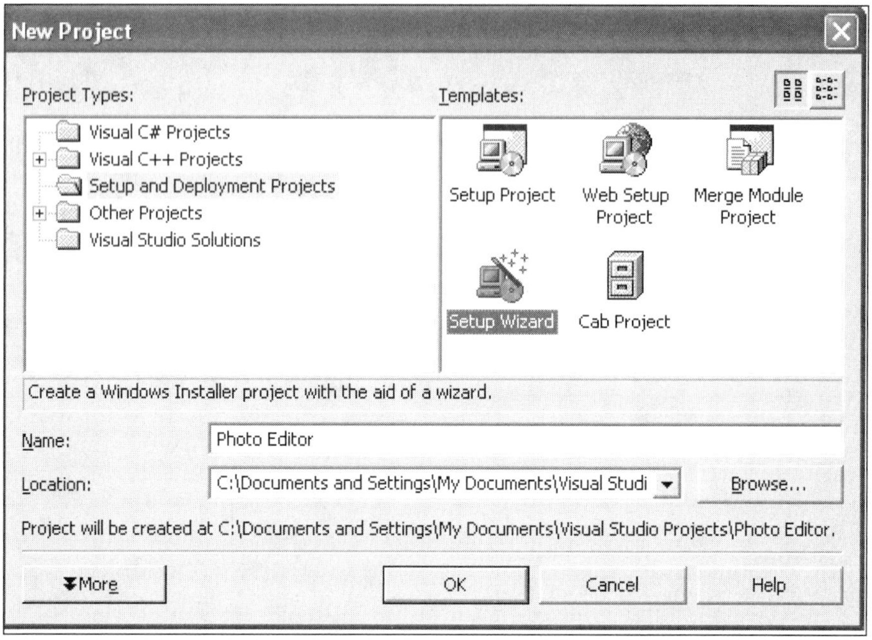

Figure 13.1 Setup Project Wizard

After you finish the wizard dialog, a project for the setup program is created. This project requires only a few modifications to match our requirement that it be installable directly from a Web page.

Open the project properties, and change the Bootstrapper setting from Windows Installer Bootstrapper to Web Bootstrapper. A *bootstrapper* is a very small Windows executable that will launch an installation, but it does not contain the installable program itself. The Web location where the installable packages are stored must be given in the next dialog (see Figure 13.2). Because the program will be installed via Internet download, it also makes sense to change the Compression setting to Optimized for Size.

In the File System view, create a shortcut to the photo editor application and add it to the user's Program menu. In this way, users will be able to start the application directly from their Start | Programs menu. Also, reduce the path for the application folder to `[ProgramFilesFolder]\ [ProductName]` because the photo editor is the only application that is

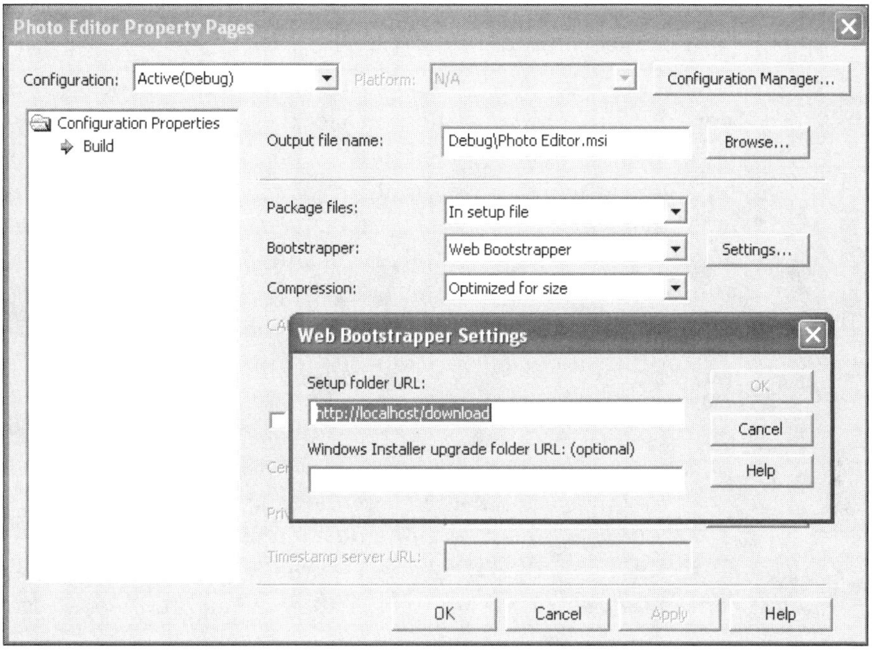

Figure 13.2 Project Settings for the Setup Program

distributed to end customers. In addition, set the `AlwaysCreate` property of the user's Program menu to `True`.

You can try the newly created setup routine by building the project and copying the generated files into a download directory, which must be created in the `wwwroot` folder of IIS. Now the installation should start when you launch the Web address `http://localhost/download/setup.exe`.

13.1.3 Deploying Web Applications

As mentioned earlier, deploying .NET Web applications is fairly simple. This has not always been the case. Even though old ASP Web applications could simply be copied from one system to another, almost all of those applications somewhat depended on configuration settings read from the system registry. Furthermore, all external components (COM) where required to be globally registered. If you had multiple applications running that depended on a COM object, this object could not be updated for only one application. Matters usually became even worse when an application had to be installed on a Web farm.

.NET applications, however, do not require object registration; they keep the configuration settings in a local XML configuration file (see Chapters 11 and 12) that is located in the Web applications folder. So if you copy the entire folder to a different server, the configuration is automatically duplicated without the need to run any registration scripts. Also, all assemblies used by Online Photo Shop are also located in this folder, and there is no need to register them. So by copying the `OnlinePhotoShop` folder we deploy the application's Web pages, assemblies, and configuration.

For the proper operation of the Online Photo Shop Web application, however, further setup steps are required:

- Configuring the directory as an IIS application: A new virtual directory must be created. This allows application-specific configuration settings such as the authentication mode.
- Setting up the ODBC data source: The customer database, an Excel spreadsheet for now, needs to be copied to the system and configured as a systemwide ODBC data source.
- ASP.NET State service: Online Photo Shop relies on the ASP.NET State service for session management. This service must be configured to automatically start up when the application runs.
- Finalizing the configuration: The directories that hold image uploads and orders need to be created and configured in the local configuration file. Also, the name of the customer database must be set.

When we negotiated the new requirements for deployment with the customer, it was agreed that no automated setup needs to be created for the installation of the Web server software. Therefore, we need only summarize those setup steps in an installation notes document.

We will package the following on an installation CD: the zipped folder of the Online Photo Shop Web application, a download folder containing the photo editor setup program and installation package, an empty customer database, and the installation notes.

13.1.4 Online Photo Shop Installation Notes

This procedure describes the setup and configuration of the Online Photo Shop application on a Web server.

Prerequisites

The following software needs to be installed on the target computer:

- Microsoft Windows XP Professional Edition, SP1
- Microsoft Internet Information Server (IIS) 6.0
- Microsoft .NET Framework 1.1

Installation

Figure 13.3 shows the installation procedure.

Figure 13.3 Installation Procedure for the Online Photo Shop Application

Step	Action	Result
1	Unzip the file `OnlinePhotoShop`.`zip` located on the installation media to the `wwwroot` folder (e.g., `C:\Inetpub\wwwroot`).	In `wwwroot` a new subfolder, `OnlinePhotoShop`, is created.
2	Create a dedicated directory on the target computer where the customer database is stored (e.g. `C:\OnlinePhotoShopData`).	
3	Copy the file `database.xls` from the installation media to a dedicated directory on the target computer.	Database file is located on target computer (e.g., `C:\OnlinePhotoShop Data\database.xsl`).
4	Change the security permissions of the dedicated folder to allow full control to the Internet guest accounts. The Internet guest accounts name is machine-specific because it also contains the computer's name.	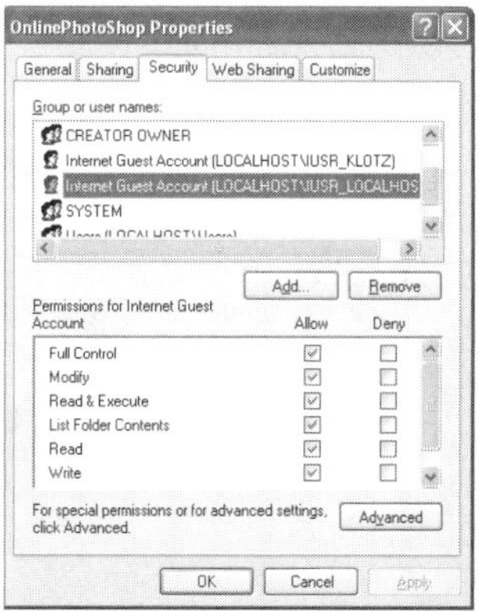

(continued)

Figure 13.3 (*Cont.*)

Step	Action	Result
5	In the dedicated directory, create a subfolder for uploaded images and completed orders.	Two new subfolders are created (e.g., `C:\OnlinePhotoShopData\uploads` and `C:\OnlinePhotoShopData\orders`).
6	Open the `WebConfig.XML` file of the OnlinePhotoShop Web application, and adjust the settings for `ImageStore` and `OrderStore` in the `appSettings` section.	For the application to receive image uploads and completed orders, the keys for `ImageStore` and `OrderStore` must point to the folders created.
7	Add the spreadsheet to the ODBC data sources using the ODBC Data Source Administrator (accessible via Control Panel | Administrative Tools). Choose the System DSN tab and press the Add button. Then choose Microsoft Excel Driver and complete the following dialog: ■ Data Source Name: `OnlinePhotoShopDB` ■ Description: Database for Online Photo Shop Project. ■ Select Workbook: Point to `database.xls`. ■ Read Only: Make sure this check box is unchecked.	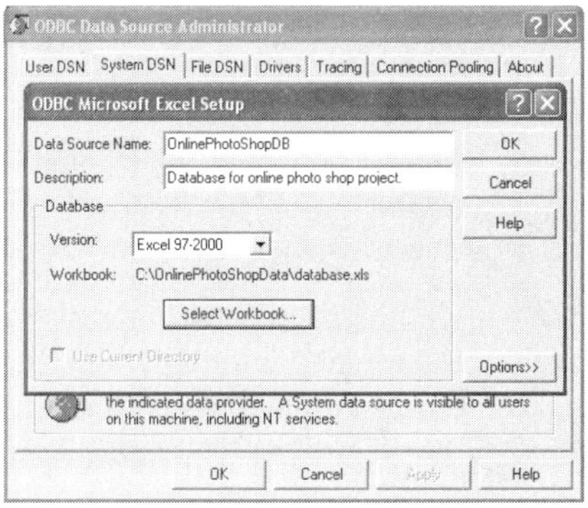
8	Open the Internet Information Services management console, and create a new virtual directory named `shop` that points to the previously unzipped `OnlinePhotoShop` application folder. The execute permissions should be set to ASP scripts only.	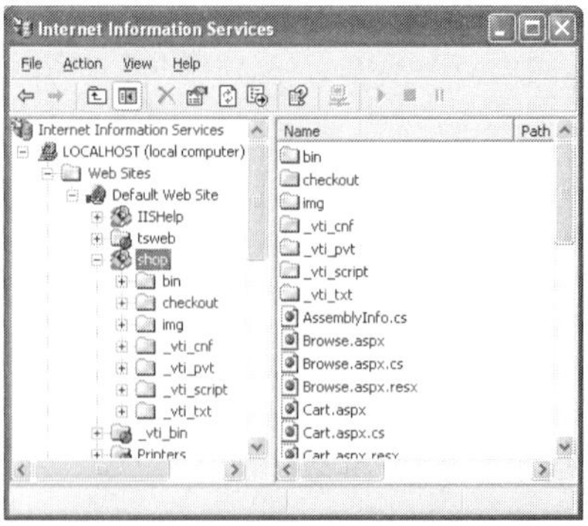

Figure 13.3 (*Cont.*)

Step	Action	Result
9	Open the Services Management console (accessible via Control Panel), and change the startup type of the ASP.NET State service to Automatic.	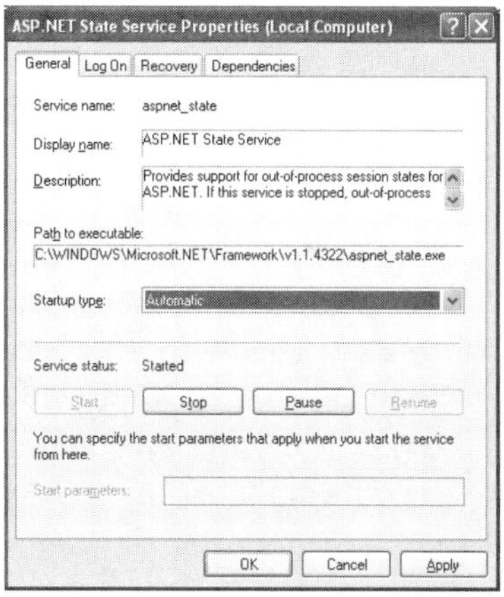
10	Make the downloadable photo editor application available by copying the download folder from the installation media to the wwwroot folder (e.g., C:\Inetpub\wwwroot).	New subfolder download is created containing Setup.exe and Photo Editor.msi.

Do It Yourself We have created a setup program for the photo editor and have written the installation notes for Online Photo Shop. Creating an installation package on a CD has been assigned to you as the last step to fulfill the two requirements for deployment.

13.2 Integration Test

Creating and executing integration tests is the main focus during a project's transition phase. Whereas the unit test should cover the entire implemented functionality on the class level, we use integration tests to test the interactions between classes. Classes can be seen as the building blocks of an application. Now the application as a whole will be tested.

13.2.1 Test Automation

Unit tests are performed throughout project development to ensure that code changes do not break already implemented functionality. In contrast, integration tests are usually executed during the transition phase only. The initial need for test automation is therefore not as urgent as it is for the unit tests. However, most software projects are intended to run over time, producing service packs, updates, and new versions with extended functionality. Therefore, it's a good idea to keep test automation in mind for the integration tests.

Automating integration tests is far more difficult than automating unit tests because all tests require some sort of user interaction. It would go beyond the scope of this book to try to implement automated integration tests. For more information, see the references section for links to available products that address test automation involving user interfaces.

13.2.2 Creating a Test Book

Tests that cannot be programmed because they require user interaction are usually defined in a document called a *test book*. To describe the test cases it's a good practice to use a tabular format. The header should contain a test identifier as well as the requirement keys that are being tested. The main table for each test consists of four columns:

- Step Number: A sequence number that helps the tester to execute the tests in the correct order. This number also helps us to identify the location where a problem has been found.
- Description: A detailed description of the current test step (for example, "Enter value 123 into field xxx").
- Expected: A detailed description of the expected test result or output. For an imaging application, this can be a reference image.
- Result: Column where the tester can check whether a test step has been executed successfully and has led to the expected result or output.

In Chapter 4 we discussed the advantages of a structured text document (XML, TeX) over a formatted document (Microsoft Word), and it was decided to capture the project's requirements in an XML document. To improve readability on screen and in the printed document, we developed a separate XSL formatting file. A similar argument can be made when you're creating test books. Here, too, a structured document allows for better tracing and automation.

Listing 13.1 shows the template that we use for the XML test book. One test book can describe multiple *test fixtures,* each consisting of multiple test cases that combine a number of test steps. Each test case must be identified by a unique name and can contain a summary field as well as several requirement keys. Test steps have only two fields: the test description and a field for the expected result.

Listing 13.1 `TestBookTemplate.xml`: Test Book Document Example

```
<?xml:stylesheet type="text/xsl" href="TestBook.xsl" ?>
<?xml version="1.0" ?>
<doc>
  <testfixture name="Title (e.g., Photo Editor Integration Tests)">
    <test name="Test Case 1">
      <summary>Test case 1 summary</summary>
      <requirement>Requirement key</requirement>
      <step>
        <description>Description for first test step.</description>
        <expected>Expected result after first test step.</expected>
      </step>
      <!-- insert other test steps here ... -->
    </test>
  <!-- insert other test cases here ... -->
 </testfixture>
</doc>
```

If the template in Listing 13.1 looks confusing, you might wonder whether it wouldn't be much easier to create the test books using text processing software such as MS Word. Indeed, for very small projects this might be an easier solution, especially if the team has no expertise in XML and XSL. However, in past projects we have observed that many document review findings relate to formatting errors, and significant effort is spent on correcting them in every version. This effort should be minimized or even eliminated and instead be spent on improving test cases.

As we did for the requirement specification, we will develop a formatting file that is used for displaying the book on screen or printing it. As shown in Figure 13.4, it's good to use a spreadsheet-like layout. From our experience this layout is best suited for executing the tests.

Test Case 1 Description of the test case - Requirement key 1 - Requirement key 2			
Step	**Description**	**Expected**	**Result**
1	Description for step 1	Expected result after step 1	Passed /Failed

Test Case 2 Description of the test case - Requirement key 3			
Step	**Description**	**Expected**	**Result**
1	Description for step 1	Expected result after step 1	Passed /Failed
2	Description for step 2	Expected result after step 2	Passed /Failed
3	Description for step 3	Expected result after step 3	Passed /Failed

Figure 13.4 Test Book Layout

Enforcing a simple step-by-step template on all test cases might seem a bit restrictive at first, but keep in mind that the tests are usually executed by people who have not been involved in the development of the software. Also, it is highly desirable to have the descriptions so clear and simple that there is no room for interpretation. Ideally, any person who does not have any background knowledge of the project should be able to execute the tests and evaluate the results. We therefore recommend keeping the test procedures as simple as possible.

Generating the XSL formatting file for the test books is similar to generating the requirement specification formatting file. However, it is not realistic to try to remove all formatting capabilities from the test books. Picture the description for filling in all inputs in a dialog without using any lists, line breaks, and so on. Also, the expected output column for the photo editor tests might contain images and screenshots. It is therefore necessary to allow users to use formatting styles such as bulleted lists or to add images to both the description and the expected field in the XML document. Those formatting instructions can be inserted as HTML tags and can be copied directly to the output while applying the XSL file using the `<xsl:copy-of>` command. Listing 13.2 shows the XSL formatting file for the test book template created earlier.

Listing 13.2 `TestBook.xsl`: Test Book Formatting File

```
<?xml version="1.0" encoding="UTF-8" ?>
<!--
      TestBook.XSL: Formatting file for test books.

  -->
<xsl:stylesheet version="1.1" xmlns:xsl="http://www.w3.org/1999/
XSL/Transform">
<xsl:template match="/">
<html>
<body>
<!--
    For each testfixture:
    - print headline
    - create new table
  -->
<xsl:for-each select="/doc/testfixture">
  <a>
    <xsl:attribute name="name">
      <xsl:value-of select="@name" />
    </xsl:attribute>
    <h1><xsl:value-of select="@name" /></h1>
  </a>
  <table border="1" cellpadding="4" cellspacing="0">

  <!--
    For each test case:
    - new test case header (incl. name, summary, and requirement keys)
    - new table header (step, description, expected, result)
    -->
  <xsl:for-each select="test">
    <tr><td colspan="4">
      <b><xsl:value-of select="@name"/></b>
```

```
<br><xsl:value-of select="summary" /></br>
<font size="-1">
<xsl:for-each select="requirement">
  <li><xsl:value-of select="current()" /></li>
</xsl:for-each>
</font>
</td></tr>
<tr bgcolor="#d0d0d0">
  <td><b>Step</b></td>
  <td><b>Description</b></td>
  <td><b>Expected</b></td>
  <td><b>Result</b></td>
</tr>
<!--
    For each test step:
    - output step number
    - copy description field
    - copy expected field
    - create result radio button
    -->
<xsl:for-each select="step">
  <tr>
    <td align="center" bgcolor="#d0d0d0">
      <b><xsl:number value="position()" /></b>
    </td>
    <td valign="top"><xsl:copy-of select="description" /></td>
    <td valign="top"><xsl:copy-of select="expected" /></td>
    <td valign="bottom">
      <input type="radio" value="passed">
        <xsl:attribute name="name">
        <xsl:value-of select="concat(parent::*/@name, '_',
position())" />
        </xsl:attribute>
        Passed
      </input>
      <input type="radio" value="failed">
        <xsl:attribute name="name">
        <xsl:value-of select="concat(parent::*/@name, '_',
position())" />

        </xsl:attribute>
        Failed
      </input>
```

```
        </td>
      </tr>
    </xsl:for-each>
    <tr>
    <td colspan="4" height="20" /></tr>
  </xsl:for-each>
  </table>
</xsl:for-each>

</body>
</html>
</xsl:template>
</xsl:stylesheet>
```

Instead of just putting a text line in each row of the Result column, we add HTML radio button controls. We implement functioning radio buttons by also setting the attributes for the name field based on the test case and the step number. This means that in each row the tester can switch the result between passed and failed before printing the test book. Of course this does not make very much sense, but this functionality is the foundation for recording and publishing the results of automated tests.

The test book can be made available via the project's intranet site, and the test results can be recorded and published as the tester executes them. This is of great use in large projects consisting of many components that may be developed at multiple sites. Because the requirements are included in the tests, the keys can be traced to the implementation and from there to the author of the code for immediate notification. As you can see, there are many possibilities for automation if structured text files are used for capturing requirements and tests and if XML headers are added to the code. However, for small projects like the photo editor and Online Photo Shop, the effort of implementing this kind of automation is not justified.

Now let's switch to the content of the test book. As defined by the go/no-go criteria for this phase, all requirement keys must be covered by an integration test. It is therefore a good idea to create a list of all requirement keys from the requirement specification document, grouping them into logical units. Theoretically it would be best to have a single test case for each requirement key. In this way, if one test case fails the functionality addressed by this particular requirement, the key can easily be localized. However, testing of most functionality requires a number of setup steps, and it makes sense to group certain requirements into one test case if they share common prerequisites. In this way, we reduce the execution time of the test book.

Figure 13.5 shows the description of the test cases for Online Photo Shop rendered in Internet Explorer. HTML formatting tags have been used to enhance the readability of the test steps and expected results. Also, reference images are linked within the document using `hyperlink` and `image` elements:

```
<a href="testimg/shoppingcart.bmp" target="_new">
  <img width="200" src="testimg/shoppingcart.bmp" />
</a>
```

Do It Yourself You have been assigned the task of creating the integration test specification for the photo editor. Reference images can be used to define the expected output.

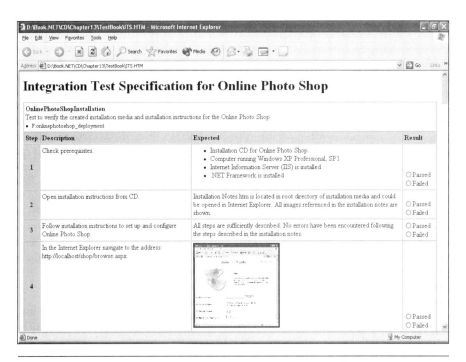

Figure 13.5 ITS.XML: Integration Test Specification for Online Photo Shop

13.3 Requirements Tracing

In larger projects with many requirements, tracing of requirement keys is a necessity to ensure the completion of all deliverables. But even for smaller projects, the number of requirement keys increases throughout the life cycle, and it becomes too complex to bear everything in mind.

Requirements tracing ensures that all defined keys have been considered in the core workflows of the Unified Process. For readability, the book does not show the requirements everywhere they have been analyzed or the design is discussed, but we can trace all keys to code, unit, and integration tests.

First, we create XSL formatting files to extract the requirement keys from the following XML document types:

- The requirement specification
- Code documentation (implementation and unit tests)
- The integration test specification

To ease the comparison of the extracted keys, it is best to output them as plain text lines. Listing 13.3 shows the XSL file to extract all keys from the requirement specification.

Listing 13.3 `KeysInRS.xsl`: Formatting File to Extract Keys from RS Documents

```
<?xml version="1.0" encoding="UTF-8" ?>
<!--
XSL file that extracts all requirement keys from an XML requirement
specification.
  -->
<xsl:stylesheet version="1.0"
xmlns:xsl="http://www.w3.org/1999/XSL/Transform">
<xsl:output method="text" />
<xsl:template match="/">
<xsl:for-each select="/doc/requirements/requirement">
  <xsl:value-of select="@name" />
  <xsl:text />
</xsl:for-each>
</xsl:template>
</xsl:stylesheet>
```

To extract the requirement keys from the implementation, we use the code documentation file generated with Visual Studio. The `requirement` tag is listed under a member (either class or method). Because the unit tests are also added to the same solution, we check whether the member name includes `Test`. If it does not include `Test` in its name, the key belongs to the actual implementation of functionality; otherwise, it is a method that implements a unit test.

Listing 13.4 shows the XSL formatting file to extract keys that belong to the actual implementation. To extract keys belonging to test code, we remove the `not()` keyword from the test attribute.

Listing 13.4 `KeysInCode.xsl`: Formatting File to Extract Keys from Implementation

```
<?xml version="1.0" encoding="UTF-8" ?>
<!--
XSL file that parses a code documentation XML file and outputs all
implemented requirement keys not in test code.
  -->
<xsl:stylesheet version="1.0"
xmlns:xsl="http://www.w3.org/1999/XSL/Transform">
<xsl:output method="text" />
<xsl:template match="/">
<xsl:for-each select="/doc/members/member">
  <xsl:if test="not(contains(@name, 'Test'))">
  <xsl:for-each select="requirement">
    <xsl:value-of select="current()" />
    <xsl:text />
  </xsl:for-each>
  </xsl:if>
</xsl:for-each>
</xsl:template>
</xsl:stylesheet>
```

So far, we have hard-coded links to the formatting stylesheet in the XML file itself. This is rather inconvenient because we need to apply different stylesheets to the same document. Also, it would be nice to extract the keys from a command line program so that we can put all necessary steps into a command batch file instead of executing them manually.

For this purpose, we create a small tool that takes two arguments: an XML document file and an XSL formatting file. The formatted result of applying the stylesheet to the XML document is output to the standard console. Listing 13.5 shows the code for a command line tool that can be used to apply a stylesheet to an XML document.

Listing 13.5 `FormatXML.cs`: Tool for Formatting an XML Document

```
using System;
using System.IO;
using System.Xml;
using System.Xml.XPath;
using System.Xml.Xsl;

namespace FormatXML
{
  /// <summary>
  /// Tool that formats an XML document using an XSL stylesheet.
  /// </summary>
  class Class1
  {
    /// <summary>
    /// The main entry point for the application.
    /// </summary>
    [STAThread]
    static void Main(string[] args)
    {
      if (args.Length != 2)
      {
        Console.Error.WriteLine("Missing or invalid arguments!");
        return;
      }

      try
      {
        XslTransform xslt = new XslTransform();
        xslt.Load(args[1]);
        XPathDocument xpathdocument = new
          XPathDocument(args[0]);
        XmlTextWriter writer = new XmlTextWriter(Console.Out);
        writer.Formatting=Formatting.Indented;
```

```
      xslt.Transform(xpathdocument, null, writer, null);
    }
    catch
    {
      Console.Error.WriteLine("Error reading input file!");
    }
  }
  }
}
```

After compiling this tool, we copy it to a location listed in the system's `Path` environment variable. Next, remove the hard links to the formatting stylesheets from the `RS.XML` and `ITS.XML` documents. To format the requirement specification to an HTML document named `RS.htm`, type this command:

```
FormatXML RS.XML RS.XSL > RS.HTM
```

The following command will list all requirement keys defined in the requirement specification:

```
FormatXML RS.XML KeysInRs.XSL
```

Using XSL stylesheets and the formatting tool, we can now easily trace requirements in the various core workflows. Table 13.2 lists the tracing results.

For each key, all core workflows should be traceable. We must analyze missing workflows to determine whether they were skipped to implement certain functionality or to test for them. In most cases it will turn out that the functionality was implemented, but it was skipped to add the key at the proper location. Other keys, such as architectural requirements, are not really traceable to an implementation and should be evaluated during code reviews.

We have traced almost all the requirement keys of the project throughout the different workflows of the photo editor application as well as Online Photo Shop. There are only a few keys missing, and they refer to general constraints or limitations of the software and do not address functionality that needs to be implemented. Such keys (for example, the coding conventions document) are therefore not traceable to code or test but should be considered during the architectural design or process definitions.

Table 13.2 Tracing Results

Requirement Key	Code	Unit Test	Integration Test
F:order_products	yes	yes	yes
F:products_browse	yes	yes	yes
F:product_options	yes	yes	yes
F:product_customize	yes	yes	yes
F:product_shopping_cart	yes	yes	yes
F:order_checkout	yes	yes	yes
F:customer_login	yes	yes	yes
F:checkout_shipping	yes	yes	yes
C:checkout_shipping_cont	yes	yes	yes
F:checkout_payment	yes	yes	yes
R:checkout_payment_secure	yes	yes	yes
C:checkout_payment_method	yes	yes	yes
F:checkout_summarize	yes	yes	yes
F:order_confirmation	yes	no	no
F:photo_editor	yes	no	yes
F:error_handling	yes	no	yes
F:image_crop	yes	yes	yes
F:image_brightness	yes	yes	yes
F:image_contrast_and_color	yes	yes	no
F:image_graphics_annotations	yes	yes	yes
F:image_graphics_special_effects	yes	yes	no
F:image_3dtext	yes	yes	yes
F:image_3dtext_color	yes	yes	yes
F:image_3dtext_font	yes	yes	yes
F:image_3dtext_rotate	yes	yes	yes
C:image_3dtext_singleline	yes	yes	yes
C:image_3dtext_opengl	yes	no	no
F:image_text_annotations	yes	yes	yes
F:image_rotate	yes	yes	yes
F:image_flip	yes	yes	yes
F:image_special_effects	yes	yes	yes
P:editor_optimizations	no	no	no
F:editor_system_test	no	no	yes
F:image_format	yes	no	yes
C:online_shop_codebehind	no	no	yes
C:online_shop_stateservice	no	yes	yes
C:imageprocessing_library	no	no	yes
C:platform_os	no	no	yes
F:photo_editor_deployment	no	no	yes

13.4 Software Maintenance

Both the photo editor application and Online Photo Shop have been successfully tested and are ready for deployment. We now must choose a process and strategy for software maintenance, which begins as soon as the product is released to the customer for the first time. According to the IEEE standard (1219) software maintenance is defined as follows:

> Modification of a software product after delivery to correct faults, to improve performance or other attributes, or adapt the product to a modified environment.

13.4.1 Change Request Management

Throughout the project, we have used a defect tracking process to capture bugs and possible improvements that could not be addressed in the initial release of the software. We used a simple spreadsheet to record and track this information. However, for larger projects a number of commercial and freeware software packages are available for this purpose. Real-life projects can quickly accumulate from several dozen to a few hundred bug reports per release cycle, and it can be challenging to manage those without using specialized tools.

Tools to manage change requests (for example, bugs, improvements, or new features) can simplify a number of frequently repeated tasks:

- Progress tracking: All electronically filed reports can easily be sorted and filtered using various criteria such as release version or current status. Using this filtering, it is easy to see which problems are scheduled but not yet solved during a particular maintenance release. This form of progress tracking can also be used to validate internal milestones such as feature or code freezes.
- Prioritizing and scheduling: Most tracking tools allow you to configure multiple release versions so that change requests can be deferred to future versions. Also, assigning priorities helps in scheduling the change requests, a benefit that is particularly useful in larger projects. Other information, such as the number of bugs reported in previous versions, can help in planning future releases. If in prior versions an average of 10 bugs per 100 lines has been the

reality, it is safe to assume that this release will drop to 1 defect. The necessary buffers should therefore be allocated in the project plan.

- Resource allocation: Good tools allow you to assign resources for investigating, implementing, or validating a change request. The developer or tester who is assigned to investigate, analyze, or implement a change is automatically notified via e-mail. Also, it is possible to get an overview of how many change requests are assigned to a person. Some tools even provide fields where you can enter the estimated effort for correction after an investigation, information that helps in selecting a developer for the implementation.

- Process enforcement: Change request management software often lets you customize the workflow in which the change requests are processed. This allows your organizational processes to be enforced. You could, for example, require that each implemented change request be forwarded to a tester for validation and that a tester attach an electronic copy of the test record before the request can be closed.

- Process improvement: Many tools can automatically collect additional information, such as timestamps, project phases, or iterations of state changes (for example, when a bug was reported, analyzed, implemented, or tested). Using this information you can create statistics that help you identify areas for improvement. For example, it is usually simple to compute the average bug closing time, how many bugs have been filed after code freeze, how many bugs have been found by the test team versus external customers, and many more.

13.4.2 Maintenance Strategies

The cost of software maintenance is commonly estimated to be 60 percent to 80 percent of the total budget for software development. It is therefore crucial to choose good practices and optimize maintenance processes and procedures in order to stay competitive. There are four main maintenance strategies you can follow:

- Fixed staff and variable schedule: This strategy is followed by most organizations that have a fixed group of maintenance engineers, who analyze, implement, and unit-test change requests from a backlog queue one by one. The management then declares feature freeze depending on the mission's needs. The integration test phase following the feature freeze will determine the release date.

- Fixed schedule and variable staff: In this model the product release date is established between customer and supplier based first on the mission's needs. Then the priority changes are agreed upon in a so-called Version Content Notice (VCN) or Statement of Work (SOW). The necessary resources are allocated to the release, and work is started on the changes. Often the resources also come from a fixed group of maintenance engineers (as in the fixed staff/variable schedule model), but here they are assigned to particular software releases as needed. Content and staffing also might be renegotiated throughout the project. When a final project agreement is achieved between customer and supplier, unit and integration testing is completed and the new version is released. The fixed schedule/variable staff strategy is often used for projects that develop libraries or low-level components that become building blocks for higher-level applications.

- Variable schedule and variable staff: Organizations that do not have a fixed software maintenance staff usually follow the variable schedule/variable staff model. After the content of a release is determined, schedule and cost are negotiated with contractors, who work on the change requests. While the contractors design, implement, and test the changes, multiple reviews throughout these phases ensure the quality of the release.

- Fixed staff and fixed schedule: From our experience the fixed staff/fixed schedule model is not very commonly used. It is applied in projects or organizations that have clearly defined need dates but for whom the addition of resources is not feasible. For example, working on the project might require highly specialized skills that are not offered by any contractors and cannot be acquired simply by training.

Each of the maintenance strategies has strengths and weaknesses in various areas, including performance, quality, efficiency, and costs. From our experience there is no gold standard for a software maintenance process, and all software processes need to be tailored to project needs and environments. However, the large percentage of the total software budget spent on maintenance makes it important to optimize this process to stay competitive in today's software business.

Because our team is very small, it is not feasible to allocate a fixed maintenance group for the photo editor application and Online Photo Shop project. Furthermore, contracts with our customer, the printing and embossing business, are very specific about release dates of the software. We therefore choose a fixed schedule/variable staff maintenance strategy, which allows us to allocate developers within the organization to a particular release as needed.

13.5 Wrap-Up

Equally important in completing a project is to learn from its successes and failures. As a good practice we recommend a wrap-up session with the entire team after each software release. This gives us an opportunity for celebration as well as brainstorming about best practices, newly used tools, and ways to improve processes, communication, or customer relationships.

The project has concluded, and we now want to take a closer look at some of the practices we applied throughout the book, analyzing what worked well and where we see room for improvement.

13.5.1 Project Planning

Throughout almost all chapters in this book, we had to perform the project planning task to adjust to events and new circumstances. Revising a project plan is a necessity for most software projects and does not mean that the initial plan was simply bad. Far worse is to keep working with an outdated project plan and not to communicate with the customer throughout the project.

Within this project we had a very good experience with planning the entire project in dedicated phases and relatively small iterations. All iterations had clearly defined go/no-go criteria, a practice that allowed us to identify and address project and schedule risk at any given time. The Unified Process worked pretty well for this project, and we will continue following this process for similar projects.

13.5.2 Requirements Refinement and Customer Feedback

In most projects, requirements change or are added throughout the life cycle. For the Unified Process, which is an iterative and requirements-driven approach, refining requirements in all iterations is part of the process itself. Refined or even newly added requirements are not a synonym for feature creep, but instead allow us to identify new risks and adjust the project plan and schedule if necessary. Involving the customer throughout these iterations provides valuable feedback on features and priorities.

13.5.3 Prototyping

Prototypes can provide valuable input for design decisions that deal with technically challenging aspects, and prototypes can even be used to evaluate new technologies, as exercised in Chapter 3. Specifically, throw-away prototyping, where code developed during prototyping is not intended to be used in the product, seems to be a good way of separating out single aspects and trying to solve them one by one instead of "prototyping" the product up front. The clearly defined goals also help us to stay focused on the issue under investigation.

Despite its name, throw-away prototype code and the results of the investigation are not necessarily destroyed. Instead, they should be archived and referenced in design documents or used for training purposes. For example, the SmartNotes application from Chapter 3 can be incorporated into our in-house .NET overview training as a hands-on session.

13.5.4 Use of Unified Modeling Language and Design Patterns

We often used UML diagrams for visualization, a practice that helped in the abstraction and analysis of problems. The advantage of using the standardized notation of UML is that it is widely acknowledged as the industry standard and therefore is understood by many managers, developers, and testers in the field. This is particularly important when external contractors are added to a project.

The UML standard covers a variety of notations and diagrams for different purposes that have been used within this project:

- Use case diagrams (requirements analysis)
- Class diagrams (design)
- Sequence diagram (design)
- Activity diagram (functional analysis and design)

Furthermore, a large number of design patterns documented in UML can be seamlessly integrated into the project.

13.5.5 Documentation

Proper documentation of software's requirements, function, design, and code greatly improves quality and maintainability. In this project we created all software documentation in the form of XML documents or embedded XML comments in source code, together with XSL stylesheets for formatting purposes. The structure enforced by XML greatly simplified the tracing of all requirements through the workflows. Visual Studio supports the creation of complete source documentation in a single XML document, including our custom fields, such as `<requirement>`. Tracing requirement keys to source code was therefore extremely simplified and required only that we apply a very short XSL formatting file. Also, Visual Studio's integrated support for embedded code comments made it easy to create complete hyperlinked source documentation in HTML format.

However, we also observed a couple of drawbacks. First, writing large documents such as the requirements specification in a simple text editor is not to everyone's taste. Unless you are familiar with enhanced and feature-rich editors, you can easily lose the overview while working on these plain text files. Furthermore, the previously encountered formatting errors in the documents created in Word have now been replaced by typing errors due to the missing spell-checker. We therefore need to analyze which tool can combine the advantages of both approaches. To do so, we should find out which text processing software allows export to structured XML documents or at least offers third-party tools to accomplish this. Another direction could be to investigate which text editors offer the integration of features such as spell-checking or highlighting to make the editing process easier.

Second, despite the pretty looks of the generated HTML source code documentation, there are many links to pages that contain very little useful information. Often, the majority of added functionality is based on the .NET Framework class library, which is not linked to the generated HTML documentation. The few comments from newly added methods are spread loosely throughout the documentation and usually do not give the reader a good understanding of what is implemented and how.

We can try to increase the usefulness of the generated HTML documentation by changing our processes. For example, we could make reviewing the generated documentation part of all code reviews, reviewing the generated HTML documentation before reviewing the actual implementation. The reviewers should then be able to understand the concepts of the implementation before looking at the code itself.

13.5.6 Automated Testing

A lot of effort has been spent throughout the entire project on implementing unit tests. Potential design issues, bugs, and even problems in third-party software can be identified early on. We have not experienced any major problems during the integration of the components and did not find any bugs during our integration/system testing. This result can be credited to the strict process that required unit tests for each iteration in the construction phase and was directly bound to the go/no-go criteria for these iterations. Using fully automated tests based on the NUnit framework allowed us to rerun all tests very frequently and thereby discover potential side effects. Even during the development of the Web application, the unit testing became a substantial factor in quality improvement.

In later projects we will definitely continue developing unit tests in the NUnit framework. The command line version of this framework should be used to introduce nightly test runs. This can be combined with a nightly build, ensuring that code changes do not break already implemented functionality.

The table format used in the integration/system test specification has proven to be good choice. Any tester in our organization was able to execute tests, and the format did not leave any room for interpretation. In future releases we want to start automating the collection and evaluation of test results by further refining the generated HTML test specification so that the test results are collected directly from the selected radio buttons. For this purpose the test specifications will be accessible through the intranet server to authenticated testers, who can then enter the test results online via a tablet PC.

13.5.7 Error Handling through Exceptions

Using exceptions to propagate fatal errors (instead of using function return status) greatly increased our productivity. Using the exception publisher, additional information about the error (including the source code location) was immediately available. When we used function return status instead of exceptions, the only information a tester had was that something had failed. It was then up to a developer to "dig in" and debug step-by-step through hundreds of lines of code until the area where the error occurred was reached.

13.5.8 Designing for Extensibility

Most software projects start small. However, in many cases numerous new features are added over time, often exceeding the original number of lines of code by a magnitude. It is therefore desirable to design a product for extensibility early on.

This may seem obvious now, but from our experience it is often neglected in the beginning stage of a project. Separating software not only logically but also physically (for example, into dynamically loaded plugins) can speed build time as well as help us reuse those modules in other projects. Modules that have not changed during a specific software release can be taken from an archive and do not necessarily need to be built from scratch or retested. In the photo editor application, all special effects and image filter operations are encapsulated into a dynamically loadable plugin, reducing build and testing effort in future releases and also allowing us to deploy bug fixes or performance improvements tailored to only one specific operation.

13.5.9 Code Reuse

Building software is a time-consuming, resource-intensive, and therefore very expensive process. To stay competitive, it is a good practice to write reusable software components. This must be considered when you plan a project because the development of reusable software initially demands greater efforts in design, documentation, and test.

.NET's Platform Invocation service (PInvoke) also allows the seamless integration of unmanaged legacy code such as COM objects. Although programmers tend to have reservations about using someone else's creation, there is no need to reinvent the wheel if an old COM object that has been stabilized and optimized over time still fulfills the requirements of a given task. PInvoke is an important feature that allows us to turn applications over to the .NET technology slowly without introducing major risks due to a rewrite of the existing code.

13.6 References for Further Reading

Test Automation

http://nunit.org

http://www.io.com/~wazmo/papers/seven_steps.html

http://www.rational.com/products/teamtest

http://www.segue.com/html/s_solutions/silk/s_silk_product.htm

http://www-svca.mercuryinteractive.com/products/winrunner

Bug Tracking Tools

http://savannah.gnu.org/projects/gnatsweb

http://www.gnu.org/software/gnats/

http://www.rational.com/products/clearquest/

http://www.techexcel.com/Products/DevTrack/DTOverview.html

Index

A

Abstract classes, 124, 199–207
Acceptance criteria, 506
Acceptance tests, 462
Accessors, 153
    for custom controls, 157
Activator.CreateInstance, 287, 289
Active Solution Configuration list box, 140
Actors, 74
Adaptive development model, 44–Add/Remove
        Toolbox Items, 160–163
Add Windows Form, 64
ADO.NET, 16
    database access with, 471–472
*After the Gold Rush: Creating a True Profession
        of Software Engineering* (McConnell), 24
Aggregation, 126, 127
Agile software development, 25–26
Aliasing, 196, 197
Alpha component, 195, 249–250. *See also* color
nderson, Rick, 10
Antialiasing, 196, 197
App.config file, 145
App.ico file, 132
Applications
    client, 57
    creating Visual Studio.NET, 132–137
    deploying, 12–13, 507
    instrumented, 366
    smart client, 16–17
    Web, 17–18, 413–456, 509–513
ApplyImageProcessing, 285, 290
    multithreading and, 374

    mutex and delegate implementation and,
        391–392
applyImageProcessing method, 305–306
Architectural baseline, 115
Architecture
    requirements, defining, 110–111
    in Scrum model, 42
    in V development model, 32
*Architecture-Centric Software Project Manage-
        ment: A Practical Guide* (Paulish), 23
ARGB values, 249–251. *See also* color
ArrayList class management, 205–207
ASP (Active Server Pages), 17–18
ASP.NET, 16
    authentication in, 466–467
    Session State service, 438–439
    SQL Server, 109–110
    state management in, 109–110
    State service, 109
    Web applications with, 17–18, 401–458
Assemblies
    in ASP.NET, 17
    binding, 11–12
    building, 140
    in CLR, 3–5
    definition of, 3–4
    loading at run time, 283–287, 286–287
    name definition for, 145
    package diagrams of, 277–278
    private/isolated, 10–11
    searching for types and methods in, 282–312
    shared, 11–12
    versioning and, 10–12

Also from Addison-Wesley

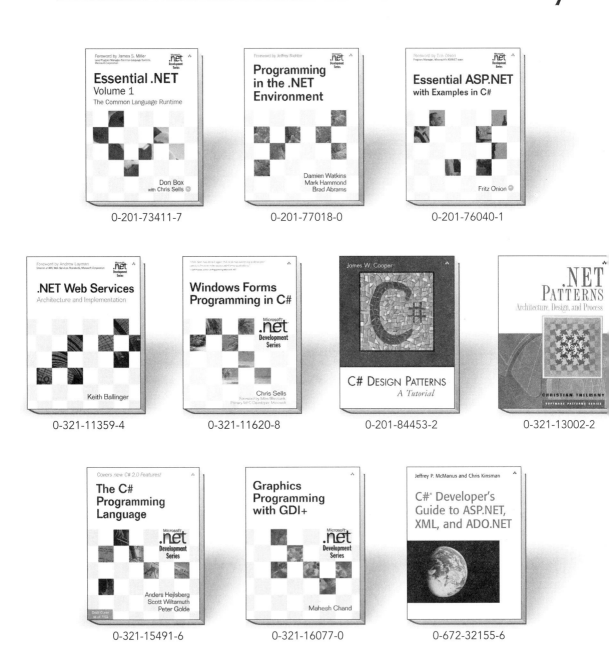

Essential .NET Volume 1 — The Common Language Runtime — Don Box with Chris Sells
0-201-73411-7

Programming in the .NET Environment — Damien Watkins, Mark Hammond, Brad Abrams
0-201-77018-0

Essential ASP.NET with Examples in C# — Fritz Onion
0-201-76040-1

.NET Web Services — Architecture and Implementation — Keith Ballinger
0-321-11359-4

Windows Forms Programming in C# — Chris Sells
0-321-11620-8

C# DESIGN PATTERNS — A Tutorial — James W. Cooper
0-201-84453-2

.NET PATTERNS — Architecture, Design, and Process — CHRISTIAN THILMANY
0-321-13002-2

The C# Programming Language — Anders Hejlsberg, Scott Wiltamuth, Peter Golde
0-321-15491-6

Graphics Programming with GDI+ — Mahesh Chand
0-321-16077-0

C#® Developer's Guide to ASP.NET, XML, and ADO.NET — Jeffrey P. McManus and Chris Kinsman
0-672-32155-6

For information about these titles, including sample chapters, go to **www.awprofessional.com.**

inform IT

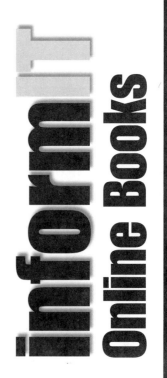

CD-ROM Warranty

Addison-Wesley warrants the enclosed CD-ROM to be free of defects in materials and faulty workmanship under normal use for a period of ninety days after purchase. If a defect is discovered in the CD-ROM during this warranty period, a replacement CD-ROM can be obtained at no charge by sending the defective CD-ROM, postage prepaid, with proof of purchase to:

Editorial Department
Addison-Wesley Professional
Pearson Technology Group
75 Arlington Street, Suite 300
Boston, MA 02116
Email: AWPro@awl.com

Addison-Wesley makes no warranty or representation, either expressed or implied, with respect to this software, its quality, performance, merchantability, or fitness for a particular purpose. In no event will Addison-Wesley, its distributors, or dealers be liable for direct, indirect, special, incidental, or consequential damages arising out of the use or inability to use the software. The exclusion of implied warranties is not permitted in some states. Therefore, the above exclusion may not apply to you. This warranty provides you with specific legal rights. There may be other rights that you may have that vary from state to state. The contents of this CD-ROM are intended for personal use only.

More information and updates are available at:
http://www.awprofessional.com/0321168828